Metaverse and Immersive Technologies

Scrivener Publishing
100 Cummings Center, Suite 541J
Beverly, MA 01915-6106

Industry 5.0 Transformation Applications

Series Editor: Dr. S. Balamurugan and Dr. Sheng-Lung Peng

Scope: The increase in technological advancements in the areas of artificial intelligence (AI), machine learning (ML) and data analytics has led to the next industrial revolution, "Industry 5.0". The transformation to Industry 5.0 collaborates human intelligence with machines to customize efficient solutions. This book series aims to cover various subjects under promising application areas of Industry 5.0 such as smart manufacturing, green ecology, digital medicine, supply chain management, smart textiles, intelligent traffic, innovation ecosystem, cloud manufacturing, digital marketing, real-time productivity optimization, augmented reality and virtual reality, smart energy consumption, predictive maintenance, smart additive manufacturing, hyper customization and cyber physical cognitive systems. The book series will also cover titles supporting technologies for promoting potential applications of Industry 5.0, such as collaborative robots (Cobots), edge computing, Internet of Everything, big data analytics, digital twins, 6G and beyond, blockchain, quantum computing and hyper intelligent networks.

Publishers at Scrivener
Martin Scrivener (martin@scrivenerpublishing.com)
Phillip Carmical (pcarmical@scrivenerpublishing.com)

Metaverse and Immersive Technologies

An Introduction to Industrial, Business and Social Applications

Edited by

**Chandrashekhar A, Shaik Himam Saheb,
Sandeep Kumar Panda**
ICFAI Foundation for Higher Education, Hyderabad, Telangana, India

S. Balamurugan
*Albert Einstein Engineering and Research Labs
Coimbatore, Tamilnadu, India*

and

Sheng-Lung Peng
*Department of Creative Technologies and Product Design
National Taipei University of Business, Taiwan*

Scrivener
Publishing

WILEY

This edition first published 2023 by John Wiley & Sons, Inc., 111 River Street, Hoboken, NJ 07030, USA and Scrivener Publishing LLC, 100 Cummings Center, Suite 541J, Beverly, MA 01915, USA
© 2023 Scrivener Publishing LLC
For more information about Scrivener publications please visit www.scrivenerpublishing.com.

Wiley Global Headquarters
111 River Street, Hoboken, NJ 07030, USA

For details of our global editorial offices, customer services, and more information about Wiley products visit us at www.wiley.com.

Limit of Liability/Disclaimer of Warranty
While the publisher and authors have used their best efforts in preparing this work, they make no representations or warranties with respect to the accuracy or completeness of the contents of this work and specifically disclaim all warranties, including without limitation any implied warranties of merchantability or fitness for a particular purpose. No warranty may be created or extended by sales representatives, written sales materials, or promotional statements for this work. The fact that an organization, website, or product is referred to in this work as a citation and/or potential source of further information does not mean that the publisher and authors endorse the information or services the organization, website, or product may provide or recommendations it may make. This work is sold with the understanding that the publisher is not engaged in rendering professional services. The advice and strategies contained herein may not be suitable for your situation. You should consult with a specialist where appropriate. Neither the publisher nor authors shall be liable for any loss of profit or any other commercial damages, including but not limited to special, incidental, consequential, or other damages. Further, readers should be aware that websites listed in this work may have changed or disappeared between when this work was written and when it is read.

Library of Congress Cataloging-in-Publication Data

ISBN 978-1-394-17454-6

Cover image: Pixabay.Com
Cover design by Russell Richardson

Set in size of 11pt and Minion Pro by Manila Typesetting Company, Makati, Philippines

Printed in the USA

10 9 8 7 6 5 4 3 2 1

Dedication

Dedicated to my sisters Susmita, Sujata, Bhaina and Sukanta; nephew Surya Datta; wife Itishree (Leena); my son Jay Jagdish (Omm); and Late father Jaya Gopal Panda, and Late mother Pranati Panda.

Sandeep Kumar Panda

Contents

Preface

The 1990s brought the proliferation of the internet throughout the world. Researchers developed various computer-mediated virtual environments including social networks, video conferencing, virtual 3D worlds, augmented reality applications, and Non-Fungible Token games. The term 'metaverse' has been coined to encompass the digital transformation in every aspect of our physical lives. At the core of the metaverse is the vision of an immersive internet as a gigantic, unified, persistent, and shared realm. While metaverse may seem futuristic, it is catalyzed by emerging technologies, such as extended reality, human-computer interaction, artificial intelligence, blockchain, computer vision, IoT and robotics, edge and cloud computing, and future mobile networks. In terms of applications, the metaverse ecosystem allows human users to live and play within a self-sustaining, persistent, and shared realm. The metaverse is a virtual and visual world that combines physical and digital experiences. At present, the development and implementation of the metaverse is in the nascent stage and lacks a framework for visual construction and scrutiny. Therefore, this book offers a 360-degree exploration of the metaverse, with a focus on avatars, content creation, virtual economy, social acceptability, security, privacy, trust, and accountability.

This book provides a thorough explanation of how the technology behind metaverse and other virtual reality is changing the world. The primary objective is to present the revolutionary innovation of the 21st Century—the metaverse—and exhibit its wide range of applications in different domains. Although blockchain and VR/AR were the first popularly known applications of the metaverse, several other applications also exist. While some still believe the metaverse is overhyped, in reality, it is transforming almost every industry—healthcare, 3D, 4D, industry, game industry, business management, artificial intelligence, and IoT, just to name a few.

This technological breakthrough not only paved the way for virtual reality, but provides useful solutions for other areas of technology. The unique nature of the technology, which is a single, shared, immersive, persistent, 3D virtual space where humans experience life in ways not possible in the physical world, makes it suitable for all real-world applications. The technology has great potential to transform business, and companies are already in the race for different product offerings.

The book is organized to cover all aspects of the metaverse, including its fundamentals, features, working principles, and application in different sectors.

Chapter 1 presents an in-depth analysis of the technologies used in the metaverse and provides a solid foundation from which to further study this fascinating field. Specifically, the chapter presents the fundamental characteristics of a novel-distributed metaverse architecture in terms of ternary-world interactions. The benefits and drawbacks of the metaverse are explored, along with the current pressing problems faced by metaverse systems and their most cutting-edge solutions. Finally, the chapter proposes new avenues for the study of metaverse system developments.

Chapter 2 investigates the expected utilization of blockchain innovation in the metaverse, explicitly in the spaces of AR, VR, and MR. The specialized parts that utilize blockchain in these virtual conditions are examined, including how it tends to be leveraged to get client data and works with exchanges inside the virtual world. Also analyzed are the difficulties and amazing possibilities that come from coordinating blockchain innovation in the metaverse, like issues of versatility, interoperability, and reception. Also discussed is the potential for future development and the latest headway in the combination of blockchain innovation with the metaverse, as well as likely roads for additional examination in this field.

Chapter 3 provides basic information about blockchain, its consensus algorithms, its usage and problems in the metaverse, how it can used for solving metaverse issues, and future directions.

Chapter 4 describes how the metaverse relies upon blockchain technology and its components, such as data acquisition, data interoperability, data storage, privacy, and security.

Chapter 5 provides a clear understanding about the usage of the metaverse in healthcare industries and day to day healthcare applications. The metaverse is important in many healthcare innovations, for example the ophthalmology spectacle frame selection is easier in online applications because the lenskart uses metaverse technologies.

Chapter 6 discusses many topics related to the metaverse, including its characteristics and immersive reality, the functions of VR, AR, and MR, why extended reality serves as its foundation, how to access it now, open issues, the creation of apps, obstacles, and its advantages over 2D learning settings. Finally, the chapter suggests a future research agenda that will be helpful to academics, industry experts, and decision-makers alike.

Chapter 7 explains how VRMAW is a one-of-a-kind, cutting-edge welding solution that promotes digital technology for teaching inexperienced welders. It outlines how to use metal arc welding while also being cost-effective, environmentally friendly, and clean.

Chapter 8 thoroughly explores the potential of creating 3D parametric computer-aided models using the AR technique.

Chapter 9 introduces a metaverse-based platform that was designed with the online education ecosystem in mind. This platform shows that online teaching and educational activities can be performed within the immersive metaverse, as well as holistic educational activities like learning, communication, and empathy.

Chapter 10 pertains to eye diseases, Keratoconus, and the use of corneal topography to inspect for various defects in the eye.

Chapter 11 addresses the latest findings of a study on the possible uses of the metaverse in the industrial sector, and the significance of applying it to the industrial supply chain.

Chapter 12 clearly describes various applications of augmented reality in multiple domains, including gaming, construction, tourism, and many more.

Chapter 13 expresses the importance of virtual reality (VR) in various manufacturing industries. VR is a powerful invention and interactive technology that significantly impacts our lives. Often known as immersive multimedia, VR replicates a physical presence for the audience in both the real and virtual worlds.

Chapter 14 explores the exciting world of mixed reality (MR). MR combines elements of both virtual and augmented reality to create a truly immersive and interactive experience. The chapter discusses the technologies used in MR, its current applications in multiple industries (e.g., entertainment and education), and its potential for future developments in fields such as healthcare and manufacturing.

Chapter 15 provides basic information about the technical aspects of artificial intelligence (AI), its role and importance in the metaverse, and suggested research directions.

Chapter 16 gives basic information about IoT, its relationship and importance to the metaverse, and the contribution of IoT in the creation of the metaverse. The chapter looks at IoT applications, the advantages and challenges of an IoT-based metaverse, and possible research directions.

Topics presented in each chapter are unique to this book and are based on the unpublished work of its esteemed contributors. The editors attempted to cover all the new trends and experiments in regards to the metaverse. This book should serve as a reference for a larger audience, such as system architects, practitioners, developers, and researchers.

Our thanks go to Wiley and Scrivener Publishing for their continuous support and guidance in the production of this volume.

Chandrashekhar A
*Department of Mechatronics, Faculty of Science and Technology (IcfaiTech),
ICFAI Foundation for Higher Education (IFHE), Deemed to be University,
Hyderabad, Telangana, India*

Acknowledgment

The preparation of this edited book was like a journey that we had undertaken for several months. We wish to express our heartfelt gratitude to Director Prof. (Dr.) K. L. Narayana, Faculty of Science and Technology (IcfaiTech), ICFAI Foundation for Higher Education, Hyderabad, Telangana, India, ICFAI Society, our families, friends, colleagues, and well-wishers for their constant support throughout this journey. We express our gratitude to all the chapter contributors, who allowed us to quote their remarks and work in this book. We would like to acknowledge the hard work of the authors and their cooperation during the revisions of their chapters. We would also like to acknowledge the valuable comments of the reviewers which have enabled us to select these chapters out of the so many chapters we received and improve the quality of the chapters. We wish to acknowledge and appreciate the Wiley-Scrivener team especially Martin Scrivener for their continuous support throughout the entire process of publication. Our gratitude is extended to the readers, who gave us their trust, and we hope this work guides and inspires them.

Metaverse: A Study on Immersive Technologies

Dileep Kumar Murala[1] and Sandeep Kumar Panda[2]*

[1]Computer Science and Engineering, Faculty of Science and Technology, ICFAI Foundation for Higher Education, Hyderabad, Telangana, India
[2]Data Science and Artificial Intelligence, Faculty of Science and Technology, ICFAI Foundation for Higher Education, Hyderabad, Telangana, India

Abstract

The Metaverse is a concept that is currently being developed for the future generation of the Internet. It aims to provide an autonomous, completely immersive, and spatiotemporal virtual community where people can work, play, and interact. Recent advancements in cutting-edge technology such as augmented reality, Artificial Intelligence, and blockchain are making the once-fantastical metaverse seem more like a plausible reality. This paper presents an in-depth analysis of the technologies utilized in the Metaverse, providing a solid foundation from which to further study this fascinating field. To be more specific, we look into the fundamental characteristics of a novel distributed metaverse architecture in terms of ternary-world interactions. The benefits and drawbacks of the metaverse are then explored, along with the current pressing problems that metaverse systems face and the most cutting-edge solutions to those problems. Finally, we propose new avenues for metaverse system development study.

Keywords: Augmented reality, artificial intelligence, blockchain, metaverse

*Corresponding author: skpanda00007@gmail.com

Chandrashekhar A, Shaik Himam Saheb, Sandeep Kumar Panda, S. Balamurugan and Sheng-Lung Peng (eds.) *Metaverse and Immersive Technologies: An Introduction to Industrial, Business and Social Applications*, (1–42) © 2023 Scrivener Publishing LLC

1.1 Introduction

1.1.1 The Emergence of the Metaverse

The term "metaverse," which was first used by author Neal Stephenson in his science fiction novel Snow Crash, was first published in 1992 [1]. "Meta" comes from the Greek for "beyond," and "verse" means "universal." The novel depicted the metaverse as a virtual counterpart to the real world or a dystopian version of the internet. Shared term "metaverse" is also used to describe virtual worlds where users can enter as digital avatars and conduct business or social interactions with other users. The metaverse is intended to be an alternative to the World Wide Web that is more immersive. There have been several expansions of the Metaverse. In the late 1970s, text-based interactive games like MUD (Multi-User Dungeon) were released, depicting a multiplayer virtual environment with role-playing, interactive narrative, and online conversation. At the time, the term "Metaverse" didn't exist. These games might be considered the forerunners of the Metaverse. Commercial virtual worlds like Second Life were created during the post-millennial era, which marked the start of the second phase. After that, a fully virtualized 3D environment was approved, such as OpenSimulator, which is normally compatible with Second Life [2].

The metaverse is an ever-present, cooperative online environment where users can participate in interactive narratives. It combines several technologies, including Mixed Reality (MR), Virtual Reality (VR), Extended Reality (XR), Augmented Reality (AR), the Internet of Things (IoT), Artificial Intelligence (AI), Non-Fungible Tokens (NFTs), and Information and Communications Technology (ICT) infrastructure. The Metaverse is currently being developed by IT firms as the successor to the mobile Internet. The Metaverse will eventually surpass the Internet in terms of transforming new service ecosystems in all spheres of human endeavor, including healthcare, education, entertainment, e-commerce, and smart industries. The excitement surrounding the Metaverse is primarily driven by two factors. First off, the COVID pandemic has caused a paradigm shift in how people currently engage in work, entertainment, and socializing. As more individuals get used to doing these physical activities in virtual reality, the Metaverse will become necessary. Second, the Metaverse is becoming a more real prospect thanks to newly developed technical enablers [3, 32].

1.1.2 Core Attributes of a Metaverse

The basic characteristics of the Metaverse include:

Synchronous and live: The Metaverse will be a living experience for every-one, just like "real life," with pre-scheduled and self-contained events.

Persistent: It simply keeps going without ever pausing, restarting, or stopping.

Available individually and concurrently: Everyone can join the Metaverse and participate in an event, venue, or activity with their agency. In a well-functioning economy, people and corporations should be able to cre-ate, own, invest in, sell, and be reimbursed for many acts that create value. These actions include creating, selling, and being remunerated for goods and services.

An experience: All aspects of the user's environment, including online and offline spaces, closed and open systems, and public and private networks, should be considered [33, 71].

A wide range of contributors: There should be a wide variety of content and activities, with many different people (some of whom work independently, others for for-profit enterprises) involved [4].

Offer unprecedented interoperability: There needs to be seamless shar-ing of information, digital assets, content, and other elements throughout the various platforms; for instance, a car built for Rocket League (or even Porsche's website) may be adapted for use in Roblox. The way things work in the digital world of today is comparable to the way a shopping mall operates, with each establishment having its own money, ID cards, propri-etary units of measurement for items such as shoes or calories, and sepa-rate dress requirements, among other things [5, 72].

1.1.3   Key Features of Metaverse

Infrastructure: Answers to the question "What are the key characteris-tics of the metaverse?" would emphasize infrastructure. In the context of the metaverse, infrastructure refers primarily to the technological infra-structure supporting the metaverse. In addition to utilizing high-tech components such as GPUs, the infrastructure consists of communica-tion technologies such as Wi-Fi, cloud computing, and 5G. The contin-ued expansion of the metaverse is one of its defining features. Therefore, the metaverse architecture must offer ultra-low latency, tremendously fast speeds, and expanded capacity [34, 35]. A robust infrastructure serves as the basis for smooth, value-based experiences for all metaverse users. Recent endeavors make the emphasis on infrastructure as a crucial entrance among metaverse elements abundantly clear. The ICT Ministry of South Korea laid the groundwork for an alliance between seventeen distinct enterprises and eight distinct industry organizations. To promote the growth of the metaverse ecosystem, the industry alliance offers crucial opportunities for enhancing the metaverse's infrastructure [6, 73].

Human Interface Technologies: When discussing infrastructure as one of the primary metaverse characteristics, it is natural to resort to human interface technologies. For joining the metaverse, users can utilize technology such as VR headsets, haptics, AR glasses, and many more. The human interface technologies aid in transferring users to the metaverse's endless immersive places. However, advances are being made to human interface technology for the metaverse. Smartphones, laptops, tablets, and personal computers can also function as metaverse access points when equipped with the necessary features [7, 74].

Digital Avatars: Avatars are a key feature among the significant characteristics of the metaverse. Digital avatars are one of the core components of the metaverse's design. Users can develop digital avatars for unconventionally expressing their thoughts and feelings in the metaverse. You can use the metaverse features to create personalized digital avatars, allowing you to create a digital version of your favorite superhero. Intriguingly, the ability to create and modify digital avatars in the metaverse also provides new opportunities for gamification. Consequently, digital avatars build the foundation for an engaging and immersive experience within the metaverse. Imagine 4.66 billion internet users creating digital avatars, exploring the metaverse, exchanging knowledge, and engaging with other avatars. Isn't this a truly revolutionary experience?

Decentralization: Decentralization would be the second most prominent response to the question, "What are the key characteristics of the

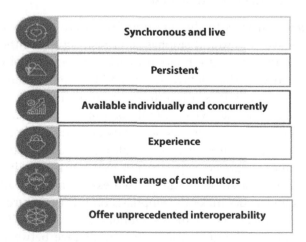

Figure 1.1 Core attributes of a metaverse.

metaverse?" The metaverse is envisioned as an open, shared reality in which users can travel fluidly between platforms. Users of the Metaverse might generate their own virtual experiences and assets with monetary worth and sell them without the need for centralized authorities [37]. This is where decentralization, a prominent aspect of the metaverse, would be found. Some of the most important technologies promoting the democratization of the metaverse are blockchain, edge computing, and AI [8]. Users can obtain complete control and ownership over their assets and experiences in the metaverse through decentralization. Consequently, the decentralized character of the metaverse plays a significant role in deciding the freedom of users. Therefore, the decentralization aspect differentiates the metaverse from the current Internet [36].

Experiences: The metaverse is essentially an open, featureless virtual environment devoid of experiences. The most significant highlight of the metaverse's essential aspects is that the experiences facilitate the transfer of multiple physical events under a virtual roof. Most importantly, the metaverse promises to link together all physical and digital experiences. For instance, students and professionals could remotely collaborate in shared learning and working areas. In the metaverse, it is possible to create more interactive user experiences by combining disparate events under a single context. Teachers can take kids on a field trip without actually traveling to the location [9].

Security: There is no reason to forsake metaverse security precautions, though. One of the most significant difficulties that organizations all around the world face today is ensuring their networks are secure. Therefore, security problems also offer negative issues for the metaverse. To address such problems, the metaverse provides ecosystem-wide ethical and privacy rules as security measures. Although the metaverse is still under development, the importance of security as one of its defining characteristics cannot be emphasized. The metaverse requires improved user protection measures and user IDs. It is reasonable to emphasize the relevance of ethical behavior given the number of companies working on the creation of the metaverse [10].

Persistence: You would also remark on another notable element of the metaverse in the form of persistence. A popular misconception about the metaverse is that it is a virtual reality universe. You must don your VR headsets to access the metaverse's virtual universe. However, what happens when the headset is removed? Does the universe within the metaverse end there? No. The metaverse continues to function even when you are unplugged. Imagine playing an online multiplayer game in which the other players continue to play even when you are not present. VR experiences are exclusive to the company or brand that offers the experience. In contrast, the metaverse is an infinite, open realm that never sleeps, exactly like the physical universe. Therefore, persistence stands out as one of the most significant features of the metaverse, as it is always accessible [11].

Production Economy: In terms of value, the creator economy has precedence over all other aspects of the metaverse. How will the metaverse provide users with value? Games, in general, are certainly entertaining to try out for a while. However, this does not justify the purchase of pricey devices to engage in the metaverse.

What About Work and Education?

You could still access Zoom meetings on your mobile device and interact in virtual workplaces using your laptops and desktop computers. The creator economy provides metaverse users with access to design tools for the creation of digital products and experiences that they may own and trade on markets. Therefore, the creator economy is one of the most noticeable metaverse characteristics demonstrating its future significance [12, 38, 39]. Figure 1.1 shows the core attributes of a metaverse.

1.1.4 Layers of Metaverse

Jon Radoff is an entrepreneur, author, and game designer who has written extensively about "Building the Metaverse." The seven layers of his conceptual framework explain the metaverse market's value chain. Infrastructure is the foundation layer, so without a suitable framework, subsequent advancements are not possible [12]. As a result, technical operations are

Figure 1.2 Seven layers of metaverse.

situated smack dab in the middle of the metaverse's various layers. Figure 1.2 explain the seven layer of the Metaverse. The stages involved in the framework are gaining experience, making discoveries, establishing a creator economy, conducting spatial computing, decentralizing power, and interacting with humans.

Layer 1: Experience

The majority of firms and individuals are now focusing on this layer. In digitally-driven environments, users interact with content such as gaming, retail, NFTs, e-sports, and theatre. The metaverse is not only a three-dimensional depiction of reality. It will be the pinnacle of the virtualization of physical space, goods, and distance. When physical space dematerializes, the limitations that are imposed physically will be lifted. As a result, the metaverse will provide everyone with an abundance of experiences they cannot currently enjoy. Multiple Interactive Live Events (MILEs) hosted on platforms such as Decentraland and Roblox exemplify how the metaverse will make these events available to anyone. Live entertainment-inspired events, such as music concerts and immersive theatre, which have already been featured in Fortnite, Roblox, and Rec Room will become more prevalent in video games. Social entertainment will supplement e-sports and internet groups. According to Jon Radoff, customers are increasingly becoming content providers [12]. Not only in the obsolete sense of "user-generated content," but also as events and social interactions."

Layer 2: Exploration

The discovery layer is concerned with the pulls and pushes that expose new experiences to humans. "Pull" refers to an incoming system in which users actively seek information and experiences, whereas "push" is more outgoing and consists of procedures that alert users of upcoming metaverse encounters [13, 40]. In truth, the discovery layer is the most profitable for businesses. Among the inbound and outbound discovery methods are:

Inbound: Marketing strategies include user-generated content, search engines, real-time presence, app stores, and earned media.

Outbound: social media, paid media, and earned media.

Outbound: Display advertising, email, and social media, as well as notifications

Community: Generated content is a significantly more cost-effective method of discovering new things than traditional marketing. As content becomes easier to exchange, barter, and share across an increasing number of metaverse contexts, it becomes a marketing asset. Content markets will replace application marketplaces as a discovery mechanism.

Real-time presence is a crucial facilitator of incoming discovery. The discovery of metaverse experiences will not rely solely on content, but also on knowledge of what other metaverse enthusiasts are doing right now. In the end, interpersonal interactions through shared experiences are what the metaverse is all about. When a person joins Steam, Battle.net, Spotify, Xbox, or PlayStation, they may be able to view the games their friends are playing. These gaming systems have skillfully utilized real-time presence to boost in-game engagement [41].

The metaverse can digitize social institutions and develop a decentralized identity ecosystem, moving authority from a few monolithic entities to social groupings to facilitate the frictionless flow of knowledge and experiences. Display advertising, alerts, emails, and social media are the most effective outbound channels for discovery. Metaverse experiences can also be discovered as a result of metaverse developers distributing relevant content to the public through outbound channels.

Layer 3: Creator Economy

"Creators receive access to tools, templates, and content marketplaces that reorient development from a bottom-up, code-centric approach to a top-down, creatively-centered one," says Jon Radoff. The creator economy includes design tools, software, and workflow platforms used to create metaverse experiences [14, 42, 43]. Content creators will shape this atmosphere. They have had great success on social media and will continue to be a prominent metaverse development engine. They will create metaverse venues for audiences to interact, socialize, and engage. Creators can offer commercial products, NFTs, and IRL products and showcase and sell NFT collections to make money in the metaverse [15]. Throughout history, creator economies have developed in predictable ways, whether in the metaverse or games, the establishment of websites, or even e-commerce

> ➤ **Pioneer Era:** Because the first people to build experiences for a particular technology lacked the appropriate tools, they were forced to create each experience from scratch. The earliest websites were written in HTML, while users created shopping carts for online stores and game developers wrote code directly to the graphic hardware [16].
> ➤ **Engineering Era:** The initial market tools are meant to help overworked engineers save time by supplying SDKs and middleware. In games, the introduction of graphics frameworks such as OpenGL and DirectX enables developers to create 3D visuals without using low-level programming. Ruby on

Rails has facilitated the creation of data-driven websites by developers. In the current period, the number of creative individuals is expanding at an alarming rate. Creators are provided with tools, templates, and content marketplaces that transform development from a code-centric, bottom-up process to an aesthetically-driven, top-down one. Using game engines such as Unity and Unreal, it is possible to create 3D visuals without having to rely on the fundamental rendering of their studios' visual interfaces [15].

> *Creator Era:* The experiences that content creators have within the metaverse are now primarily focused on centralized platforms such as Roblox, Rec Room, and Manticore. An unprecedented number of people have been given the ability to create user experiences as a result of these platforms' complete sets of integrated tools and discovery, social network, and monetization functions [44].

Layer 4: Spatial Computing

Combining the real and the virtual, spatial computing blurs the boundaries between the actual and ideal worlds. Spatial computing has evolved into a large category of technology that enables the exploration and modification of 3D locations and the addition of extra data and experiences to the real environment. The key characteristics of this layer include 3D engines such as Unity and Unreal. In addition to mapping and analyzing the inner and outside worlds, geospatial mapping with Cesium, Descartes Labs, and Niantic Planet-Scale AR also aids in mapping the inner world. Integration of device data (Internet of Things) and human biometrics is already prevalent in the health and fitness industries. Incorporating speech and gesture recognition into spatial computing software is the final step [17, 45].

Level 5: Decentralization

In a perfect scenario, the metaverse would be decentralized, open, and diffuse - administered by a single entity and belonging to no one and everyone simultaneously. Choices are maximized when systems are interoperable and developed in a competitive market, which increases experimentation and development. Moreover, creators have ownership over their data and products. Decentralization encompasses the blockchain, smart contracts, open-source platforms, and, eventually, the possibility of a digital identity that is fully autonomous. Developers may use online capabilities more easily using distributed computing and microservices. The most famous decentralized metaverse is Decentraland. It's a blockchain-based virtual world administered by a Decentralized Autonomous Organization whose laws may be changed by voting. In the metaverse's decentralized regions, people and businesses are buying land [18, 46–48].

Layer 6: Human Interface

Human interaction is a crucial aspect of the hardware layer of the metaverse. Moreover, biosensors and neurological links between brains and computers are currently being evaluated. However, neural networks and haptic technologies are also included. This layer also contains haptics, which enable the transmission of information via touch even when no physical items are present. Using haptics, it is possible to control electronic devices in mid-air without touching buttons or a display [18, 46–48].

Layer 7: Infrastructure

The seventh layer 'infrastructure' consists of the technology that makes the preceding items possible. 5G and 6G networks, Wi-Fi, cloud architecture, AI, AR/VR/MR, blockchain, and graphics processing units enable the metaverse (GPUs). 5G networks will exponentially increase capacity while simultaneously reducing competition and latency.

1.1.5   Look into the Metaverse Technologies

The metaverse world is made up of seven main technologies.

Technology 1: VR, AR, and XR

Virtual Reality (VR): VR is by far the most well-known and used of Metaverse Technologies. This is an experience that makes you feel like you're in the real world. This technology is used in the real world for things like online games, social media, education, and job training, among other things. The Metaverse has the potential to upend several businesses by making available VR-based technologies that can whisk people away from their living rooms and into an alternative virtual world. Facebook Horizons lets users meet new people from around the world, participate in exciting activities, and construct their virtual worlds. It's a global gathering area where individuals may collaborate in real-time. The finest VR headsets are Oculus Quest, HTC Vive, Cosmos, Sony, Playstation VR, and Valve Index [19].

Augmented Reality (AR): The real world is made clearer to us through the use of a technology known as AR, which superimposes information generated by a computer on top of what we see. These days, augmented reality apps for smartphones rely heavily on the user holding the device in front of them. The software can show contextual information or provide real-world gaming and social activities by processing the camera image in real-time. Smartphone AR has progressed greatly in the previous decade, but its applications are still limited. Wearable smart glasses are becoming an increasingly important tool for giving an AR experience that is more comprehensive. These devices need to have a form factor that is light enough to be worn for long periods, as well as a processor that uses a very minimal amount of power. Additionally, they need to have several sensors, including ones for depth perception and tracking [19, 49].

Extended Reality (XR): The term "XR" refers to the metaverse in which AR, VR, and MR exist. Popular Extended Reality Metaverse games on TVs include Fortnite, Roblox, and ZEPETO. In addition to its use in video games, extended reality has many other applications. Evidence-based examples of educational materials that take advantage of augmented and virtual reality simulations and tools with Artificial Intelligence, location services, and language translation capabilities have been developed. For example, the United States Army has been using a VR dome for years to teach soldiers. 120,000 HoloLens augmented reality devices were purchased by the military for use in both training and battle [20].

Technology 2: AI and ML
Artificial Intelligence (AI): AI may help create Metaverse elements including characters, landscapes, buildings, character routines, and more. Unreal Engine may soon have sophisticated AI. AI could automate software development, allowing users to generate more complex Metaverse items with less effort. On the blockchain, smart contracts may also be created, audited, and protected with the assistance of AI. Without artificial intelligence, it will be difficult to develop a Metaverse experience that is appealing, lifelike, and scalable. To lessen the risks of artificial intelligence while maintaining its potential, businesses like Meta collaborate with think tanks and ethics organizations.

Metaverse Uses AI in Various Forms
Avatars: The concept of an avatar is one of the most intriguing and hotly debated topics in the Metaverse. Artificial intelligence can analyze 2D user images or 3D scans to build Avatars that are very accurate and lifelike. Artificial intelligence is already being used by some companies, such as Ready Player One, to help in the creation of Avatars for the Metaverse.

Digital Human: In the Metaverse, digital humans are three-dimensional chatbots that respond to users in virtual reality. It's made of AI technology and is fundamental to the Metaverse's architecture. NPCs are non-playing characters in virtual reality and games. NPCs are scripted, unlike user-controlled characters [21].

Language Processing: Individuals will have unrestricted access to the Metaverse once artificial intelligence is implemented and put to use for this purpose. An artificial intelligence system can understand human languages such as English and translate them into a format that a machine can read. Following the completion of an analysis, the output, also known as the answer, is translated back into English and delivered to the user.

Technology 3: Blockchain
The Metaverse, which is built on the blockchain, allows users to visit any virtual area without going through any kind of centralized server. The six metaverse categories of digital ownership, collectibility, value transfer, governance, accessibility, and interoperability are where blockchain shines. The metaverse is a good fit for blockchain technology since it is open and affordable. Blockchain technology in the Metaverse may be applied to in-game real estate, virtual currency, non-fungible tokens (NFTs), self-identity authentication, and virtual currency [50–53]. A digital economy can flourish thanks to the existence of virtual currencies in the metaverse. Assets in blockchain games are often validated cryptocurrencies, like NFTs or crypto tokens, and are held on the chain in a decentralized way due to the games' decentralized and Web3-oriented nature. Each participant independently controls and owns their copy of the game. In the gaming Metaverse, MetaBlaze stands out as a GameFi x Defi utility coin with broad applicability across the entire web3 ecosystem. Players may build and immerse themselves in a high-level, 3D, play-to-earn RPG with unique content, stunning visuals, and incredibly thrilling gameplay, all within the first Blockchain-gaming Metaverse to offer players permanent rewards [22, 54–56].

Technology 4: IoT
Metaverse IoT apps collect and share data. IoT can connect a huge number of real-world devices to 3D. Metaverse simulations are real-time. AI and machine learning may help IoT manage data and improve the Metaverse. Metaverse will analyze and interact with the real world using IoT. Metaverse will customize IoT user experiences in 3D. Metaverse and the Internet of Things will enable data-driven decisions with minimal mental effort and training.

Technology 5: Brain-Computer Interfaces (BCI)

Technological advancements in the field of brain-machine interfaces In the Metaverse, technology can take the reins from the human brain, allowing for the control of avatars, a wide variety of digital products, and digital transactions. Markets for video games and employee efficiency are seen as early adopters of this technology. In the early stages of the Metaverse, this technology will not be crucial. However, early adopters may start employing brain-computer interfaces by the mid-2030s to link up with the neocortex. The human brain's neocortex is where advanced thought is processed. A brain-computer interface device, like the one used in the virtual reality game Awakening by Neurable, uses an electrode-laden helmet connected to an HTC Vive head-mounted display to track brain activity. The software examines game data to identify the proper course of action. The most well-known businesses are Neurolink and Nextmind [23, 57].

Technology 6: Three-Dimensional Reconstruction

Users will be able to virtually tour new constructions from anywhere in the world using 3D models reconstructed in the metaverse. The major problems of the metaverse are solved by this method, which employs 3D reconstruction to build realistic and natural-looking landscapes in a digital environment that mimics the real world as nearly as possible.

By using high-resolution 3D cameras, internet users can digitize their environments in stunning realism. To create a virtual replica for metaverse viewing, the 3D spatial data and 4K HD photos are sent to computers where they are processed. Some people also use the term "digital twin" to refer to these simulations of physical objects [24].

Technology 7 – 5G

Metaverse is the future of real-time communication. The Metaverse requires high bandwidth, latency, and internet connections to join a vast virtual environment with realistic graphics and polygon counts. With 5G's extremely high millimeter-wave frequencies, users can have immersive, real-time dialogues with artificially intelligent characters in virtual reality (VR) and augmented reality (AR). Roaming features improved render LOD, user-friendly API integration and Developer Platforms would all contribute to a wider audience.

1.1.6   Six Characteristics of the Metaverse

Realistic immersive experience: It gives sensory, object, and environment realism and has fueled Metaverse interest.

A complete world structure: The Metaverse will be an exact duplicate of the physical universe, mimicking all ten of its constituents.

UGC (User-Generated Content): Residents of the Metaverse generate material and apps in their virtual worlds using UGC, a new creative arena.

Huge economic value: Metaverse platform architects will use technology to create scarcity and tamper-proof data. The Metaverse's lower scarcity allows it to outperform the actual world economically.

Reforms: As a parallel universe, the Metaverse must reduce "central privilege" in the real world.

Significant uncertainty: Governance structure is the central question in the Metaverse, more specifically, who will lead its future governance system. All designers of the Metaverse will have to determine who has the last word in the virtual world and who owns its economic benefits [3].

1.1.7   Accessing the Metaverse

If we accept that the Metaverse is an inevitable extension of our highly linked world and the subsequent iteration of the World Wide Web, then the crucial question will be how to access the Metaverse. Unknowingly, you may be a part of the in-development version of the Metaverse. For instance, if you are a Web3 user, have a crypto wallet, or have purchased an NFT, you are already a part of the Metaverse [7]. Currently, there is no unified Metaverse; rather, platforms like The Sandbox, Decentraland, and Axie Infinity are experimenting with independent Metaverse-based initiatives. The bulk of extant Metaverse projects operate on Ethereum and employ their coins. Axie Infinity's native governance token is AXS. Sandbox utilizes SAND, whereas Decentraland uses MANA. Although different Metaverse platforms may require different processes to enter, all platforms share three fundamental requirements: creating an account, a digital wallet, and an avatar. Currently, the most popular Metaverse wallets are MetaMask, Coinbase, Enjin Wallet, and Math Wallet [5].

1.1.8   What Can We Do in the Metaverse?

As stated previously, a complete and unified Metaverse is limitless and provides its members with a vast array of unique experiences and opportunities. Even though the current version of the Metaverse is not yet complete, it already provides users with unique virtual activities.

Virtual land: In platforms such as The Sandbox and Decentraland, for instance, you can purchase virtual land that you can resell or use to create digital structures. Virtual land can also be utilized for a variety of social, commercial, and entertainment activities, including meetings, gallery exhibitions, and more.

Gaming: Additionally, the virtual space actively pursues gaming potential. Others, such as Illuvium, are also pulling players to the Metaverse, even though we've already mentioned some of the leading names.

Social interactions: Social interactions, events, and even corporate activities are additional virtual activities that people may pursue in the Metaverse. A corporation seeking to attract new talent, for instance, can set up a virtual booth in the Metaverse to learn more about applicants regardless of their location.

Earning possibilities: There are also significant prospects associated with asset trading and other economic activities that could help you make a side income or – one day – a reliable income.

The future to come: Even if the first steps have been taken, a fully functional virtual universe is still a distant goal. As we continue to evolve and include sophisticated technologies such as VR and AR to reach a higher level of complexity and broader digitization of the world, we will likely be able to create worlds that are superior to those shown in science fiction films. It is impossible to predict when a true Metaverse will arise and whether it will have the interconnection that matches our expectations, but we may appreciate the experiences offered by metaverse-like and blockchain-based projects currently in development [9].

1.1.9   Applications of Metaverse

The Metaverse is a publicly accessible virtual shared space. It is an umbrella term for the whole virtual and digital universe. To provide an immersive experience for end-users, several projects are currently developing digital twins of the physical world we live in and accessing this digital world via the network. This will allow users to meet, interact, and conduct business in a virtual environment, or a metaverse. This is because Metaverse applications continue to cover a broad range of use cases.

Healthcare: When you ask, "What are the uses of metaverse?" one of the first things you might hear is that it can be used in the healthcare field. The use of augmented reality is the most prominent illustration of how the metaverse can be applied in the medical field. Augmented reality (AR) has become an indispensable tool for enhancing medical students' abilities and knowledge. Surgeons use surgical assistive tools like Microsoft Hololens to perform various surgeries [58–60].

Military: Applications of augmented and virtual reality in military settings have also made significant strides in recent years. Tactical Augmented

Reality, also known as TAR, is a technology that gives the impression of being very similar to night-vision goggles (NVG), but it has a great deal more functionality. It can show exactly where a soldier is, as well as where friendly and enemy forces are. You can use the system day or night because it attaches to your helmet the same way your goggles do [15, 61].

Real estate: The field of real estate would appear to be the next most promising entry on the list of potential applications for the metaverse. Virtual reality is a significant technology for driving metaverse experiences. It can provide clients with experiences that are realistic and immersive, which is a strength that can work in favor of the applications of the metaverse in real estate. The power of virtual reality (VR), for instance, can be leveraged by real estate agents so that buyers can experience immersive virtual tours of properties [13, 62].

Applications for teaching: The amazing thing about virtual reality is that it opens the door to new worlds and experiences for us to have. When you put on a virtual reality headset, you get to experience accurate depictions that can change your life for the better. The effectiveness of conventional teaching methods in drawing attention to key concepts through the use of visuals will never reach the level that can be achieved by more modern approaches. Most students, regardless of age, would rather watch a video than read the material. The incredible things that can be "experienced" through VR technology are fascinating because they could never be "experienced" in real life. Students will be more invested in their education when they have access to this technology.

Manufacturing: Virtual reality applications, which are rapidly becoming one of the most promising areas of metaverse research, have the potential to improve workplace safety by increasing employee engagement with and knowledge of risk. Because of this, metaverse applications can make a significant impact in lowering accident rates. The most widely used metaverse applications in production could help improve product quality over time [11, 63].

1.2   Related Works and Contributions

Due to the popularity of the Metaverse, several polls on related topics have lately been conducted. [16] Is it one of the earliest attempts to provide a map of the Metaverse? In [16], the writers discuss the Metaverse's benefit to society. The architecture of the Metaverse is then described, along with some examples of recent developments in the field. According to Dionisio *et al.* [25], there are four qualities of successful 3D virtual worlds (or metaverse): ubiquity, realism, scalability, and interoperability. Highlight the continual development of the underlying technology for virtual worlds. Eight essential technologies that make up the metaverse are reviewed and examined by Lee *et al.* [28] together with the prospects it presents from six user-centric aspects. Huynh-The *et al.* [29]'s investigation on the basis and growth of the metaverse uses AI methods. Yang *et al.* [27]'s investigation looks into the possibilities of blockchain and AI technologies for the creation of a future metaverse. In terms of national policies, industrial projects, infrastructures, supporting technologies, VR, and social metaverse, Ning *et al.* [26] give a survey of the development state of the metaverse. Park *et al.* [30] evaluate the user interaction, implementation, and representative applications in the metaverse and describe three components of the metaverse (i.e., hardware, software, and content). An extensive study of the edge-enabled metaverse from the perspectives of communication, networking, computation, and blockchain is presented by Xu *et al.* in [31]. The analysis of [7] delves more deeply into the Metaverse's technological foundations. The concepts of blockchain, the Internet of Things (IoT), robotics, UI design, and extended reality (XR) are all introduced. Other Metaverse surveys cover more niche topics. In [10], AI is used to create intelligent chatbots and AR/VR gadgets that accurately scan and understand the user environment. The study analyses how blockchain and AI convergence can speed Metaverse service delivery. AI can train Metaverse characters, and blockchain can enable commerce. The report discusses Metaverse industry applications and achievements and predicts future industrial possibilities.

These studies do not address Metaverse implementation challenges at mobile edge networks from resource allocation [8], communication, networking, or computing perspectives. Understand the Metaverse's enabling technologies before examining how these technologies can be employed on mobile edge networks. While analyses AR/VR applications that can improve a user's immersion in the Metaverse, an equally important concern is how to overcome communication and networking constraints to reach potentially millions of edge devices while meeting rigorous latency and data rate requirements. AR/VR surveys focus on 5G mobile edge networks and processing and offloading architectures. These polls don't focus on the Metaverse specifically, thus they don't address some of the major issues we raised in our survey. For instance, the Metaverse will have many people simultaneously accessing and engaging with the virtual worlds through AR/VR. Additionally, since these users will be interacting with one another, the round-trip communication latency will be severely constrained. In this review, we will cover significant issues such as the difficulties of interoperability, heterogeneity, and large simultaneous stochastic network needs. Additionally, the supply of AR/VR services is the main focus of [30, 76]. Our survey, in contrast, takes a comprehensive approach to the implementation of various Metaverse enablers at the edge, such as blockchain and AI model training. As a result, our strategy generates more debate and presents new difficulties than the supply of AR/VR services as it is now practiced.

The polls also neglect the role of blockchain in controlling edge communication and networking resources. The Metaverse cannot become the "successor to the mobile Internet" without solving these key implementation issues and providing solutions "beyond the concept's validation [22]." This inspires us to publish a survey that examines difficulties faced by mobile edge networks in terms of communication and networking, computation, and blockchain. Our study offers crucial insights and practical advice for the readers to better understand how these implementation concerns could be overcome to realize an immersive, scalable, and omnipresent Metaverse through exploring plausible solutions for the challenges.

1.3   The Metaverse Architecture, Developments, and Tools

We outline the architecture, use cases, and development resources for the Metaverse in this section.

1.3.1   Architecture and Definition

Incorporating user avatars with open, interactive, and interoperable virtual ecosystems, the Metaverse is an embodied version of the Internet. In the sections that follow, we define each major term in this definition.

> *Embodied:* In the Metaverse, where users can "physically" interact with virtual environments, the distinction between the two is blurred. Use a physical experience, such as 3D visual, aural, kinesthetic, or haptic input, to engage with virtual environments. The Metaverse can use AR to extend virtual worlds into the physical realm [23, 64].
> *Seamless/interoperable:* Just like in the real world, users' avatars from one virtual world should have their value when seamlessly transferred to another, even if the two virtual worlds were made by various entities. The Metaverse is not "owned" by any one organization, to put it another way.

> ➤ *Immersive:* The Metaverse can be "experienced" "beyond 2D interactions that allow individuals to communicate with one another in a way that is similar to that found in the real world.
> ➤ *Shared:* Like in real life, hundreds of users should be able to share a server session instead of being split among virtual servers. Since users can access the Metaverse and immerse themselves at any moment, their lifelike engagement is shared globally, rather than simply on a specific server.
> ➤ *Ecosystem:* The Metaverse's ecosystem will provide end-to-end services for digital identities (DIDs), including content creation, social entertainment, and in-world value transfer regardless of nationality. These physical services will merge the real and virtual worlds. Blockchain-enabled Metaverse ecosystems are viable due to their closed-loop independent economic structure and open operational principles [26, 65].

Physical–Virtual Synchronization

The physical world's non-exclusive stakeholders each have authority over elements that affect the virtual realms. Stakeholder behavior has effects in the virtual world that could have an impact on the real world as well. Users can enter virtual worlds as avatars using a variety of devices, including Head Mounted Displays (HMDs) or augmented reality goggles [4]. In online communities. The users can then carry out actions to communicate with real or virtual things or with other users.

> ➤ *IoT and sensor networks:* it's collect real-world data. The conclusions are used to maintain the virtual world physical entity Digital Twin (DT) s, among other things. SSPs, which send live data to VSPs to develop and administer virtual worlds, may own sensor networks.
> ➤ *Virtual service providers (VSPs):* Virtual service providers build and maintain Metaverse worlds (VSPs). Like user-generated videos, games, art, and social apps will be added to the Metaverse [2]. (e.g., on YouTube). The Metaverse produces exchanges and consumes UGC.
> ➤ *Physical Service Providers (PSPs):* PSPs manage the Metaverse engine's physical infrastructure and process Metaverse transactions. This includes edge network communication and computer resources and Metaverse product delivery logistics.

Figure 1.3 describes the metaverse architecture, tools, and certain important enabling technologies.

Metaverse Engine

Entities and their activities in the real and virtual worlds generate, maintain, and improve data that is obtained by the Metaverse engine from stakeholder-controlled components.

> ➤ **AR/VR:** AR/VR lets users view the Metaverse, unlike haptics, which lets users feel the Metaverse using haptic gloves. This facilitates user interactions like global handshakes and allows Metaverse services like remote surgery.

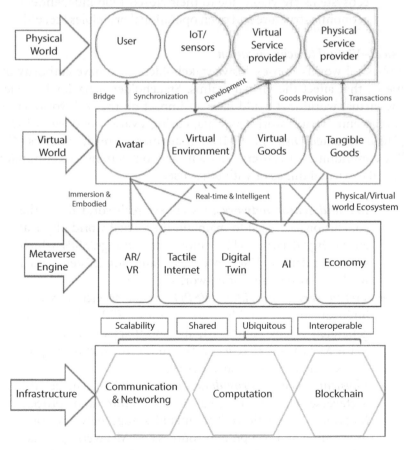

Figure 1.3 The metaverse architecture tools and technology.

Interoperability standards like VRML regulate the properties, physics, motion, and rendering of virtual assets and enable seamless user movement inside the Metaverse.

> *Tactile Internet:* Tactile Internet: Metaverse users can transfer haptic and kinesthetic data with a 1 ms round-trip delay. Meta's haptic glove project5 employs tactile Internet and haptic feedback to let real-world users engage with virtual things and other avatars like their avatars.

> *Digital twin:* Real-time physical world modeling is possible in some Metaverse virtual worlds thanks to digital twin technology. Modeling and data fusion are used to achieve this [27]. The Metaverse becomes more realistic because of DT, which also makes new service and social interaction facets possible [6].

> *AI:* AI can be used to introduce intelligence into the Metaverse to enhance user experiences, such as through effective 3D object rendering, cognitive avatars, and AIGC. For instance, machine learning (ML) is used in Epic Games' MetaHuman project7 to create lifelike digital characters quickly. The produced characters could be used by VSPs to fill the Metaverse as talkative virtual assistants.

> *Economy governs:* The Metaverse ecosystem's economy controls incentives for content generation, the exchange of user-generated content, and the provision of services. VSP can pay SSP for data streams to synchronize real and virtual worlds. For clients with limited resources, metaverse service providers can purchase computing resources from cloud services. The economy also drives Metaverse digital assets and DID growth.

The infrastructure layer makes it possible to access the Metaverse from the edge.

> *Communication and Networking:* AR/VR and haptic traffic must adhere to strict rate, reliability, and latency standards to avoid breaks in the presence or interruptions that make a user aware of the real-world environment [28]. Due to the anticipated enormous expansion in data traffic, ultra-dense networks installed in edge networks may be able to relieve the limited system capacity. Additionally, the B5G/6G communication infrastructure will be crucial in enabling post-Shannon communication to ease bandwidth restrictions and control the skyrocketing increase in communication prices.

> *Computation:* Modern MMO games can support over one hundred players concurrently, necessitating high-spec GPU requirements. The foundational VRMMO games that make up the Metaverse system are still hard to come by. VRMMO games demand strong computers and HMDs to render immersive virtual worlds and hundreds of player interactions. The cloud edge-end computation may enable widespread Metaverse access. Edge devices can do local computations for low-resource tasks like the physics engine's avatar movement and positioning. Edge servers can perform expensive foreground rendering with less graphical fidelity but lower latency to improve cloud scalability and end-to-end latency [5]. Cloud servers can do computationally intensive yet delay-tolerant tasks like background rendering. Additionally, distributed learning and model pruning and compression AI approaches help to lighten the load on backbone networks.

> *Blockchain:* The DLT that the blockchain offers will be essential for developing the Metaverse's economic ecology and for proving ownership of virtual items. Present-day virtual goods struggle to have worth outside of the platforms where they are manufactured or sold. Blockchain technology will be crucial in lessening reliance on this type of centralization. A Non-fungible Token (NFT) verifies a virtual asset's ownership and uniqueness [1]. Decentralized peer-to-peer trading protects virtual product value with this method. The user data may be managed individually because different parties are responsible for creating the numerous virtual worlds in the Metaverse. Multiple parties will require access to and control over such user data to enable seamless travel between virtual worlds. Cross-chain technology is essential to enabling secure data interchange since several blockchains exhibit value separation. The management of edge resources has also been a recent accomplishment for blockchain technology [2].

1.3.2   Present-Day Developments

The Metaverse is still under development, so there is much to do. The Metaverse will use physical-virtual synchronization (P2V and V2P) to bring the digital experience to life. The Metaverse can also simulate physicality in virtual worlds. Communication, networking, computational, and blockchain infrastructures support its operation. For instance, by creating AR/VR gadgets that are more costly, affordable, and lightweight and conquering the difficulties involved in making them a reality. There are two ways to look at how the Metaverse is evolving [30]. How acts in the virtual world can impact the real world is the first point of view. The virtual items in the Metaverse will be worth actual money. Second, how might virtual world actions reflect physical world actions? Digitalization and intelligentization of physical objects are driving this. For remote work, socializing, and education, a virtual 3D environment will accurately mirror the real world [3, 66, 67].

Companies from the entertainment, financial, healthcare, and educational sectors can create the Metaverse. In the actual world, theme parks are expensive to construct, but in the Metaverse, they can be erected swiftly and safely. Disney announced a 2020 Metaverse theme park. The 2021 Q4 earnings call statement reiterated this vision [4]. This section discusses Metaverse's "early forms" advancements. Two main groups describe these advancements.

Hugely Popular Online Role-Playing Games

Video games have long used the Metaverse, according to many. In Massively Multiplayer Online Role Playing Games (MMORPG), players can enter the game as their avatars. These avatars have roles for gamers, like real-world jobs. MMORPGs let many players play in a 3D virtual world. Here are some crucial examples:

> *Second Life:* One of the earliest attempts to build a fully realized virtual setting in which players might reside. Players may nearly do anything they can in the real world in second life, from looking for a job to getting married [31]. In addition, players can alter the surroundings in which they reside. The Linden Dollar9, a virtual currency that can be exchanged for actual money, underpins the Second Life economy. Minecraft: This well-known game offers user access through VR headsets like the Oculus Rift and lets users create their content using 3D cubes in an infinite virtual universe. Any user can view digital replicas of several cities that have been created using Minecraft, such as Kansas City and Chicago10.

> *DragonSB:* Terra Protocol and Binance Smart Chain Platform are used by DragonSB, the first Metaverse MMORPG. SB tokens will be accepted as payment from participants in both centralized and decentralized markets.

Other MMORPGs include Pokemon Go, Animal Crossing: New Horizons, Grand Theft Auto Online, Final Fantasy XIV, and World of Warcraft.

Metaverse Applications

Uses for the Metaverse Beyond the gaming sector, several organizations, including governments and IT firms, have expressed an interest in setting up shop in the Metaverse. This encompasses intelligent cities [20], the entertainment sector, educational institutions, workplaces, and healthcare.

> ➤ **Metaverse Seoul:** According to Seoul Vision 2030 [8], the Seoul Metropolitan Government intends to publish Metaverse Seoul. A virtual city hall, tourist attractions, social service facilities, and many other elements can be found on this platform. Avatar officials are available for meetings with local users for advice and the delivery of government services. Wearing VR headsets, foreign users can explore faithfully duplicated locales and participate in holiday celebrations. The goal of this is to grow the tourism sector.

> ➤ **Barbados Metaverse Embassy:** By creating a Metaverse embassy, the island nation of Barbados is preparing to declare digital real estate to be sovereign property [8]. To help the country acquire land, build virtual embassies and consulates, develop the infrastructure required to provide services like "e-visas," and construct "teleporters" that will allow users to move their avatars between worlds, the government works with many Metaverse companies.

> ➤ **AltspaceVR:** It's an OS-compatible virtual conference room for both live and virtual events. In essence, AltspaceVR users are permitted to interact and meet online while using avatars. Recently, a safety bubble function was added to help lessen the possibility of harassment and inappropriate behavior.

> ➤ **Decentraland:** based on the Ethereum blockchain [5], Decentraland. Users can purchase and sell virtual land in this decentralized virtual environment. Users can create custom micro-worlds that include virtual aircraft, trees, and other elements. Decentraland has everything available in the real world, including hotels and transit networks.

> ➤ **Xirang:** Baidu's Metaverse app, Xirang, means "land of hope." Smartphones and VR headsets can explore virtual worlds with them. User photos can also be used to automatically

create avatars. In 2021, Xirang held a three-day virtual AI developers' conference for 100,000 users. This is crucial to realizing the shared Metaverse.

➢ *The Chinese University of Hong Kong, Shenzhen (CUHKSZ):* The metaverse simulates the campus. Chinese University of Hong Kong, Shenzhen is CUHKSZ. Blockchain technology gives students access to the Metaverse, a hybrid environment where their real-world actions can affect their virtual-world actions and vice versa.

➢ *Telemedicine:* A virtual connection between patients and medical experts enables them to communicate when they are geographically separated [6]. Through virtual reality (VR), doctors and their patients can confer over telemedicine. The data can be sent to any doctor, and physical follow-ups, medical scans, and testing can be scheduled and done near the patient.

1.3.3   Instruments, Frameworks, and Platforms

This section will discuss several Metaverse-creating platforms, frameworks, and tools.

➢ *Unity:* A 3D engine and studio layout are completely integrated into Unity. These components make it possible to experience Metaverse, virtual reality, and augmented reality. The Unity components shop for Metaverse decentralization includes edge computing, AI agents, microservices, and blockchain.

➢ *Unreal Engine:* An unreal Engine is a development tool for the Metaverse. It features asset marketplaces and designing studios, such as MetaHuman Creator [4]. By using MetaHuman Creator, the time needed to create a user avatar may be cut from months to hours while maintaining an unmatched level of quality, fidelity, and realism.

➢ *Roblox:* Although many people only know Roblox as a game, it has gradually developed into a platform that offers a wide range of development tools, including avatar generation11 and teleportation systems. Roblox provides a design platform, a 3D engine, and a marketplace for assets and code.

➢ *Nvidia Omniverse:* Nvidia, a manufacturer of graphics and AI chips, plans to develop the Omniverse Metaverse

platform [9]. Omniverse is a real-time reference development platform that is scalable, supports multiple GPUs, and
is used for 3D simulation and design collaboration. Content
creators may connect and speed current 3D workflows utilizing the Omniverse platform, while developers can swiftly
create new tools and services by plugging them into the
platform layer. Nvidia will copy every Omniverse factory to
reduce waste [75].

➤ **Meta Avatars:** It supports Quest, Rift, and Windows-based
VR devices for Unity developers. A platform-integrated editor lets users customize their Meta Avatars, ensuring that
they are appropriately and consistently displayed in all apps
that use the SDK. Meta avatars communicate by using hand
tracking, controller tracking, and audio input.

➤ **Meta Haptics Prototype:** Meta's haptic glove controls virtual reality and lets users feel objects (VR). Plastic cushions
inflate and fit the palm, fingertips, and underside of the
glove. When running the VR software, the system controls
inflation and applies pressure to specific hand locations.
Touching an object causes a virtual object to press against
the user's flesh. Long finger actuators tighten when a user
grasps a virtual object, giving them a resistive sensation.

➤ **Hololens2:** This mixed reality headset, which has an inbuilt
computer and built-in Wi-Fi, is for sale. In comparison to
its predecessor, it boasts superior sensors, a longer battery
life, and higher computer capability. Microsoft Mesh can be
combined with Hololens2 to link users all over the world.
The user can interact with others, keep eye contact, and see
the facial expressions of individuals who are farther away.

➤ **Oculus Quest2:** Made by Meta [8], the Oculus Quest2 is a
head-mounted virtual reality (VR) device that may be used
with compatible desktop software when connected through
USB or Wi-Fi.

1.3.4   Lessons Discovered

A solitary technology cannot achieve the Metaverse: According to the
aforementioned definition, the Metaverse is created by the fusion of many
engines for its physical synchronization, including AR and VR, the tactile internet, deep learning, artificial intelligence, and blockchain-based

economies. The Metaverse, however, cannot be regarded as just one of them. The following is a detailed list of the lessons discovered:

> **AR/VR:** During the V2P synchronization of the Metaverse, AR/VR is just one of the most often used techniques for submerging users in 3D virtual worlds. Users of the Metaverse will be able to access 3D virtual and audio content thanks to AR and VR. *Tactile Internet:* Users can access tactile and kinesthetic content via tactile Internet, another well-liked technique for submerging people in three-dimensional virtual worlds during V2P synchronization of the Metaverse [15].

> **Digital twin (DT):** The Metaverse's P2V synchronization architecture is DT. The Metaverse, based on real-world DT, can improve V2P synchronization but not provide an immersive experience.

> **AI:** The Metaverse, where pervasive AI exists in both the real and virtual worlds, is thought to be AI-native. The physical-virtual synchronization can be improved by AI. It cannot, however, immediately assist in synchronization.

> **Blockchain-based economy:** The decentralized Internet is what is meant by the term "blockchain-based economy," also known as "Web 3.0." After the read-only Web 1.0 and the read/write Web 2.0, Web 3.0 is read/write/own. The distinct description of Web 1.0, 2.0, and 3.0 is less informative than the Metaverse, which is the next significant stage and long-term vision of the continual digital transformation [22].

Standardized Protocols, Frameworks, and Tools: Each company is creating its Metaverse by combining various protocols, frameworks, and tools. To standardize the Metaverse protocols, structure, and tools, cooperative efforts are required. Once standardized, it will be simpler for content producers to produce content because it may be shared across a variety of virtual worlds, even if they were created by different companies. Additionally, when users are "teleported" between various virtual worlds in the Metaverse, the transition can be seamless. The key distinction/advantage between the Metaverse and the previously mentioned MMORPG games will be the interconnected virtual worlds [18].

The Ecosystem and Economy of the Metaverse: A lot of the illustrations in this part rely on and make use of user-generated content (UGC) and open-source contributions. For instance, Roblox enables anyone to create games, and Meta Avatars helps intuitive game production. As a result, the

Metaverse ecosystem will benefit from user contributions from throughout the world. As a result, user-generated content (UGC) and services can be maintained and valued through cryptocurrency-promoted transactions without the need for outside partners. The majority of transactions in the Metaverse are made using cryptocurrency for safety and security concerns. However, the public finds the present payment gateway interface to be difficult to use. A straightforward user interface may be better supported for digital currency transactions and cross-currency payments. Then, we go over issues with and remedies for blockchain technology [1].

1.4   Advantages and Disadvantages of Metaverse

1.4.1   Advantages of Metaverse

➢ *Connecting the world and eliminating physical separation:* The metaverse eliminates geographical restrictions, its main value. Your location is irrelevant in the virtual world. The metaverse will provide a level playing field for all parties. Discovering and meeting others with similar interests and beliefs will make meeting new acquaintances from home easier, more real, and more comfortable [2, 68].

➢ *Immersive experience:* The metaverse is a 3D internet. A more immersive way to explore the Internet and all its features. The metaverse helps you focus on your work. Immersive experiences increase personal and professional opportunities. Top VR headsets let you exercise, socialize, play games, and have virtual business meetings [4].

➢ *Improved online social connections:* Internet communication was the only option during the COVID quarantine, notwithstanding its lack of engagement. In the metaverse, social interactions and events are more immersive, allowing people to connect with friends and family. Metaverse meetups, parties, and performances are possible. Attending family gatherings or functions no longer requires physical proximity [5, 69].

➢ *Improve social media:* The decade's most prevalent term is social media. Twitter and Facebook depend on social media. Three-dimensional virtual reality will benefit them. The power to build virtual environments in the metaverse and social media's ability to create shared online worlds will transform social media.

➢ *New business prospects:* Like social media, the metaverse will create new business opportunities and marketing and promotion methods. The metaverse uses virtual stores, curated shows, highly interactive interaction, and customer care to promote and consume items and services instead of watching everything on a smartphone screen. Using haptic technology, you can see, grip, and feel it (experience of touch through vibration, forces, and motion). This type of engagement improves the user experience for both consumers and businesses.

➢ *Enhancements to online education and learning:* Since almost 90% of students were unable to finish their studies, the COVID-19 pandemic hindered schooling. Zoom-based online learning become standard. Metaverse learning will be easier than ever. Classroom location no longer matters. Global learners will collaborate in a hands-on setting. Visual learning helps students understand topics because we control what they see in the metaverse. Instead of studying history academically, kids could experience it. Imagine walking around Ancient Rome to understand life [6, 70].

➢ *Positive effect on cryptocurrencies and non-fungible tokens:* Blockchain technology's security, trust, transparency, and decentralization will make cryptocurrencies and NFTs vital to the metaverse. Cryptocurrency is the metaverse's currency, but its currencies will change. However, you cannot buy digital goods and services with real money, which protects virtual environments. The metaverse may use NFTs more. NFTs prove digital or physical ownership. They allow NFT holders to prove ownership and transfer assets between the physical and digital worlds. NFTs are important in the huge metaverse. NFT metaverse brands will market NFTs as deeds to tangible and digital assets [8].

➢ *Advancements in gaming:* VR and AR technology first benefit gaming. In 2021, many VR games launched, and as technology improves, so do the games. Game developers are merging their games into the metaverse. Epic is a frontrunner in metaverse gaming, investing $1 billion by early 2021. Meta (formerly Facebook) also reinvented itself as the metaverse's leader. This is true for Microsoft's Xbox metaverse and Roblox, among others [9].

> *New possibilities for monetary gain:* New technologies will
> always be exploited. People are already finding methods to
> make a life using the metaverse's resources. Some people
> invest in metaverse pieces of land, hoping their value would
> rise. Others create metaverse assets and structures for a liv-
> ing, while others are trained to help build the metaverse
> and its usefulness. Metaverse cryptocurrency trading might
> make early investors rich. Many metaverse players gener-
> ate money by playing games that award tokens and non-
> fungible tokens that can be swapped for cash. Renting real
> properties, hosting concerts, and opening art galleries are
> other metaverse-friendly businesses [10].
> *Enhancements to the working conditions:* Mark Zuckerberg
> introduced the endless office when he revealed the metaverse,
> promising to make working from home easier and more
> productive. Workplaces have always used cutting-edge tech.
> Metaverse and virtual reality won't fix it. VR eyewear and
> logging into a three-dimensional virtual office from home is
> a novel and potentially valuable idea.

1.4.2   Disadvantages of Metaverse

Online crime: Cybercrime has plagued the Internet since its beginnings.
Governments have spent millions of dollars and years fighting it, improving internet security. The metaverse lacks these cyber security safeguards
because it's new. It is vulnerable to fraud, money laundering, child abuse,
illegal goods, services, and cyberattacks. Another problem is that governments cannot fight cybercrime in the metaverse due to its decentralization.
Effects detrimental to cultures and societies: Bringing everyone together
and blending cultures into one loses the world's exquisite cultural diversity.
People who spend most of their time in the metaverse won't feel connected
to their civilization or love their local culture. This may result in the demise
of many ancient customs and the formation of a bland, unified culture [11].
Gaming and addiction problems: Because you're entirely immersed in
the metaverse, some think it's more addictive. You can stay in your VR
setup save for eating and sleeping. Experts say exposing under-18s to the
metaverse and letting them spend too much time there will harm their
development. Living in a virtual world may make it hard to tell reality from
fiction. Offering teenagers and adults enough metaverse time while preventing addiction will be difficult [12].

Without physical contact: Many people worry about the metaverse's ease of time loss. Your senses are linked to the virtual world because they are inhibited. Long-term metaverse exposure can make people lose touch with reality and refuse to acknowledge a physical universe. The average American spends 5.4 hours a day staring at a screen.

Privacy and safety concerns: Many users are unaware that their data is collected and sold to advertisers. Meta's leadership of the emerging metaverse exacerbates these concerns. Despite their name change, their user privacy issues remain.

Mental health issues: Beyond social connection, entertainment, and finances, the metaverse poses a serious mental health risk. Virtual reality can help schizophrenia patients in controlled conditions, but the metaverse is neither regulated nor built to help them. Psychological research has indicated that immersing oneself in this digital realm and isolating oneself from reality might lead to psychotic-like symptoms. The metaverse can impair self-esteem and create depression.

Virtual harassment: Strangers online are often cruel and intolerant of others. The Internet, including social media and video games, is full of malicious behavior. They persist despite repeated efforts to stop them. These bad actors would benefit from integrating the Internet into a 3D environment and immersing individuals in the metaverse. Because victims can't look away from the computer, they're more exposed to attack. Unfortunately, the metaverse's bad aspects—bullying, harassment, and personal assaults—cannot be prevented.

Insufficient moderation: Moderation is difficult. Monitoring that many concurrent users are difficult. Moderation is very impossible, and punishment cannot prevent toxicity. Meta's poor management of undesirable behaviors on "Facebook" suggests there is no way to fix this. The metaverse may be toxic and disastrous [16].

Connection and hardware issues: To make the metaverse as frictionless as possible, it will need a fast and reliable internet connection. Fiber, 5G, and even next-generation wireless networks are needed. It also disadvantages individuals who cannot access the metaverse's technology and digital tools. It will not benefit the poor.

Acquisition: Social media was created for people like us to produce and share content. Before mega corporations took over. Professionally produced and edited videos replaced handmade, honest films. This is perhaps the best example of companies taking over YouTube from individual producers. Instead of individuals interacting, huge companies may take control and use the metaverse as their marketing ground, using metaverse features for their own malicious goals.

1.5   The Metaverse Challenges and Countermeasures

Hardware: Virtual reality, augmented reality, and mixed reality technologies and devices are extremely important to the metaverse. Metaverse cannot be widely adopted because most of these are heavy, expensive, and inconvenient. Providing easy access to the appropriate hardware and developing high-quality, high-performance models with retina display and pixel density for a believable virtual immersion experience is difficult [18].

Identity: Have you ever questioned whether your online friend on social media is also as interesting in real life? As you'll access the metaverse through avatars, the same may happen. Another difficulty lies in establishing your identity, as it is simple for bots to imitate your mannerisms, data, personality, and the entirety of your identity. Authentication will require various verification methods, including facial scans, retinal scans, and voice recognition.

Addiction and Mental Health: Ready Player One shows how the metaverse affects mental health. Addiction to the virtual world may bring sadness, anxiety, obesity, and heart disease due to a sedentary lifestyle.

Privacy and Data Security: We often hear about a data breach at a multinational corporation. Metaverse will store additional information besides your email addresses and passwords. It will also store your behavior. With a massive data mine, the technology must ensure the confidentiality and security of every user's information and personal data. This will necessitate new security measures.

Currency and Digital Payments: The Metaverse won't just be for games. It will be another global marketplace. With so many currencies and cryptocurrencies, quick and easy exchanges are needed. Secure transactions too [19].

Law and Jurisdiction: With virtual crimes already prevalent in social media, the metaverse will also have its share of lawbreakers. Insufficient are rules and regulations that block an account. There must be proper legislation. However, the metaverse will not exist in a physical location. It will be a virtual world that transcends national boundaries. Therefore, countries and authorities must determine their jurisdiction to provide a secure environment for users [31].

1.6   Future Research Directions

When different technologies are adopted in the Metaverse, this section covers the major future paths.

Advanced Multi-Access Immersive Streaming: AR/VR, the tactile Internet, and hologram streaming all need mobile edge networks that are accessible everywhere have high data rates and are reliable, and have low latency. To share virtual worlds well, the shared Metaverse needs complex strategies for multiple access to resource blocks like time, frequency, codes, and power so that many people can use it at the same time [10].

Multi-Sensory Multimedia Networks: The Metaverse offers holographic streaming, AR/VR, and the tactile Internet, unlike the 2D Internet. Mobile edge networks are needed for holographic services like AR/VR and the tactile Internet that use more than one sense. Multi-sensory multimedia services require numerous network resources, making resource allocation methods impractical [30]. The URLLC services are needed for the tactile Internet, while the eMMB services are needed for AR/VR. Augmented reality services employ uplink transmission and computing resources, while VR services use downstream transmission and caching. To support users' immersive experiences, multi-sensory multimedia networks should present effective and suitable resource allocation mechanisms [21].

Multimodal Semantic/Goal-Aware Communication: A large variety of goal-driven and context-aware Metaverse services can be made available through the utilization of semantic communication, which transforms mobile edge networks from data-oriented to semantic-oriented. AI models interpret automatically. Semantic communication models often focus on speech or image extraction, encoding, and decoding. Service models in the Metaverse often include immediate audio and video services [29]. As a result, there are new challenges in the field of semantic communication, such as how to build a multimodal semantic communication model to supply multisensory multimedia services in the Metaverse, how to effectively recover semantics from user-transmitted information, and how to allocate appropriate network resources to support the development and application of semantic communication standards [22].

Communication and Sensing: The edge network integrates communication and sensing from Metaverse development to user access. Future mobile edge networks, however, will make advantage of sensing spectrum (such as mmWave, THz, and visible light). Communication and sensing must be combined for Metaverse production and maintenance. DTs created the Metaverse for physical entities with lots of static and dynamic information. The Metaverse must also enable smooth user-entity communication and instantaneous information delivery to targeted users. Deeper sensor and communication integration will enable additional Metaverse services and real-time digital replication of the world [23].

Digital Edge Twin Networks: Metaverse's best real-time synchronizer (DT). The DT can digitally replicate, watch over, and manage real-world objects on roaming data centers with numerous network edge and Internet of Everything gadgets. Connecting digital things in the Metaverse improves edge network performance in the real world. DT increase mobile edge network operation and maintenance, but they require a lot of communication, computing, and storage, making them difficult for edge networks with low resources. Thus, better DT solutions and mobile edge network operations and maintenance will be studied [31].

Intelligent Edges and Edge Intelligence: Future research should concentrate on the edge intelligence-driven infrastructure layer, a crucial part of future wireless networks, to realize the Metaverse despite its limitations. Edge intelligence uses AI and edge computing. Build Edge and AI. Edge for AI connects data creation, sensing, communication, AI model training, and inference. AI techniques enhance Edge framework orchestration [11].

Resource Management: The Metaverse always needs resources. Cloud computing/fog computing/edge computing services are always needed to give mobile users a great experience on devices with limited storage and processing capability. Thus, the Metaverse will require more energy to communicate and compute, increasing energy consumption and greenhouse gas emissions. Cloud/fog/edge networking and computing must be eco-friendly for sustainability. In the Metaverse, new architectures can support green Cloud computing/fog computing /edge computing networking and computation, energy-efficient resource allocation, and mixing green technologies [24].

Avatars: Metaverse members are immersed in virtual environments as avatars. Setting up dynamic avatar services at mobile edge networks is essential to improve the quality of experience (QoE). Creating and maintaining human-like avatars requires a significant amount of resources. To be able to offer avatar services to users, each avatar must gather and retain a sizable amount of personal biological data from the user as well as from other users who have mapping relationships with the avatar in virtual worlds or related physical items in the real world. To create and use an avatar, you need to have complete control over your privacy settings [25].

Smart Blockchain: Intelligent blockchains use AI to adapt to the network environment during consensus and block propagation. The Metaverse's engine and infrastructure—AI and blockchain—protect users' security and privacy. Dynamic routing algorithms for payment channel networks and adaptive block propagation models are examples of intelligent blockchain research. However, the intelligent blockchain study just seeks to increase virtual blockchain performance. As intelligent blockchain connects the metaverse to the actual world, wireless base stations, cars, and UAVs will operate differently [26].

Quality of Experience: Users and their avatars should enjoy their human-perceived QoE while in virtual worlds and engaging with others. Physiological and psychological QoE data can be utilized to rate and regulate Metaverse services [28].

Market and Mechanism Innovation: Interactive and resource-intensive Metaverse services need it to help service providers and customers manage resources and determine rates. Market and mechanism design for Metaverse services should consider local situations of the physical and virtual submarkets and their interaction effects because the Metaverse may blur the line between them [27].

Industry/Vehicle Metaverse: The industrial Metaverse will merge virtual and real industries for intelligent production. The Industrial Metaverse uses the Industrial Internet of Things (IIoT) to collect data from production and operation lines for data analysis and decision-making, thereby increasing commercial value, decreasing operating costs, and increasing physical space production efficiency. Immersive streaming and real-time synchronization in the automotive Metaverse are expected to increase driving efficiency, safety, and passenger immersion [30].

Conclusion and Future Directions

This paper presents an in-depth analysis of the fundamentals of the Metaverse, focusing specifically on the technologies that are used in the Metaverse. In this study, we focus on the tertiary-world interactions and investigate a novel distributed metaverse architecture and its essential properties. Next, we will discuss the benefits and drawbacks of the metaverse, as well as the most pressing problems that are caused by metaverse systems and the most recent solutions to these problems.

With an eye toward the future, Facebook's R&D team is exploring methods to enable text entry via the peripheral nervous system and brain-computer interface. Neuralink is a technique that involves implanting a chip in a person's brain to facilitate improved communication with various electronic devices. This method is known as a direct connection method. Directly stimulating a brain area while observing a basic EEG is now possible. It's doable now. However, brain-computer interfaces like Neuralink may evolve to give a Metaverse experience that is hard to distinguish from reality (e.g., the method of connecting to the spine from the matrix).

References

1. Yang, Q., Zhao, Y. *et al.*, Fusing blockchain and AI with metaverse: A survey. *Digital Object Identifier*, 3, 2022.
2. Sun, J. and Gan, W., Metaverse: Survey, applications, security, and opportunities. 1–35, 14 Oct 2022, arXiv:2210.07990v1 [cs.DB].
3. Wang, Y. and Zhao, J., Mobile edge computing, metaverse, 6G wireless communications, artificial intelligence, and blockchain: Survey and their convergence. *Proc. 2022 IEEE 8th World Forum Int. Things (WF-IoT)*, 28 Sep 2022, arXiv:2209.14147v1 [cs.DC].
4. Xu, M., Ng, W.C. *et al.*, A full dive into realizing the edge-enabled metaverse: Visions, enabling technologies, and challenges. *Netw. Int. Archit.*, 20 Aug 2022, arXiv:2203.05471v2 [cs.NI].
5. Wang, Y. *et al.*, A survey on metaverse: Fundamentals, security, and privacy. *IEEE Commun. Surv. Tutor.*, 25, 319–352, 2022.
6. Park, S.M. and Kim, Y.G., A metaverse: Taxonomy, components, applications, and open challenges. *IEEE Access*, 10, 4209–4251, 2022, 10.1109/ACCESS.2021.314017.
7. Wangy, Y., Suy, S., Zhang, N., Xing, R., Liu, D., Luan, T.H., Shen, X., A survey on metaverse: Fundamentals, security, and privacy. *IEEE Commun. Surveys & Tutorials*, 319–352, 2023.
8. Yu, Q., Wang, M., Zhou, H., Ni, J., Chen, J., Céspedes, S., Guest editorial special issue on cybertwin-driven 6G: Architectures, methods, and applications. *IEEE Int. Things J.*, 8, 22, 16191–16194, 15 Nov. 15, 2021.
9. Zyda, M., Let's rename everything "the metaverse!". *Digital Object Identifier*, 11 March 2022. 10.1109/MC.2021.3130480Date of current version.
10. Chen, S.C., Multimedia research toward the metaverse. *IEEE Comput. Society, Digital Object Identifier*. March 2022, 10.1109/MMUL.2022.3156185.
11. Laplante, P. *et al.*, Virtual worlds (Metaverse): From skepticism to fear, to immersive opportunities, Paolo Faraboschi and Eitan Frachtenberg. *IEEE Comput. Society*, 100–106, Oct. 2022.
12. Kshetri, N., Web 3.0 and the metaverse shaping organizations' brand and product strategies. *IEEE Comput. Society, Digital Object Identifier*, 11–15 March-April 2022, 10.1109/MITP.2022.3157206.
13. Cheng, R., Wu, N., Chen, S., Han, B., Will metaverse be nextG internet? vision, hype, and reality. pp. 197–204, http://opensimulator.org/ (accessed on 25-August-2022.
14. https://www.innoviusresearch.com/blog/category/metaverse/
15. Overview: Technology roadmap of the future trend of metaverse based on IoT, blockchain, AI technique, and medical domain metaverse activity.
16. https://www2.deloitte.com/cn/en/pages/technology-media-and telecommunications/articles/metaverse-report.html.
17. Suzuki, S.-N., Kanematsu, H., Barry, D.M., Ogawa, N., Yajima, K., Nakahira, K.T., Shirai, T., Kawaguchi, M., Kobayashi, T., Yoshitake, M., Virtual

experiments in the metaverse and their applications to collaborative projects: The framework and its significance. *Proc. Comput. Sci.*, 176, 2125_2132, Jan. 2020.

18. https://www.gartner.com/en/articles/what-is-a-metaverse.

19. https://pixelplex.io/blog/importance-of-blockchain-in-metaverse/.

20. Huggett, J., Virtually real or virtual: Towards a heritage metaverse. *Stud. Digit. Heritage*, 4, 1, 1_15, Jun. 2020.

21. https://cointelegraph.com/metaverse-for-beginners/what-is-metaverse-in-blockchain.

22. Shi, J., Honjo, T., Zhang, K., Furuya, K., Using virtual reality to assess landscape: A comparative study between on-site survey and virtual reality of aesthetic preference and landscape cognition. *Sustainability*, 12, 7, 2875, Apr. 2020.

23. https://www.analyticsinsight.net/challenges-in-metaverse-and-how-to-overcome-them/.

24. Duan, H., Li, J., Fan, S., Lin, Z., Wu, X., Cai, W., Metaverse for social good: A university campus prototype, in: *Proc. 29th ACM Int. Conf. Multimedia*, pp. 153–161, Oct. 2021.

25. Dionisio, J.D.N., Burns, W.G., II, Gilbert, R., 3D virtual worlds and the metaverse: Current status and future possibilities. *ACM Computing Surveys (CSUR)*, USA, 45, 3, 1–38, Jul. 2013.

26. Ning, H., Wang, H., Lin, Y., Wang, W., Dhelim, S., Farha, F., Ding, J., Daneshmand, M., A survey on metaverse: The state-of-the-art, technologies, applications, and challenges, USA, 2021, arXiv preprint arXiv:2111.09673.

27. Yang, Q., Zhao, Y., Huang, H., Zheng, Z., Fusing blockchain and AI with metaverse: A survey, 2022. arXiv preprint arXiv:2201.03201.

28. Lee, L.-H., Braud, T., Zhou, P., Wang, L., Xu, D., Lin, Z., Kumar, A., Bermejo, C., Hui, P., All one needs to know about metaverse: A complete survey on technological singularity, virtual ecosystem, and research agenda, 2021, arXiv preprint arXiv:2110.05352.

29. Huynh-The, T., Pham, Q.-V., Pham, X.-Q., Nguyen, T.T., Han, Z., Kim, D.-S., Artificial intelligence for the metaverse: A survey, 2022, arXiv preprint arXiv:2202.10336.

30. Park, S.-M. and Kim, Y.-G., A metaverse: Taxonomy, components, applications, and open challenges. *IEEE Access*, 10, 4209–4251, Jan. 2022.

31. Xu, M., Ng, W.C., Lim, W.Y.B., Kang, J., Xiong, Z., Niyato, D., Yang, Q., Shen, X., Miao, C., A full dive into realizing the edge-enabled metaverse: Visions, enabling technologies, and challenges. *Netw. Int. Archit.*, 2022, arXiv preprint arXiv:2203.05471.

32. Panda, S.K. and Satapathy, S.C., An investigation into smart contract deployment on ethereum platform using Web3.js and solidity using blockchain, in: *Data Engineering and Intelligent Computing*, Advances in Intelligent Systems and Computing, V. Bhateja, S.C. Satapathy, C.M. Travieso-González,

V.N.M. Aradhya (Eds.), vol. 1, Springer, Singapore, 2021, https://doi.org/10.1007/978-981-16-0171-2_52.

33. Panda, S.K., Rao, D.C., Satapathy, S.C., An Investigation into the usability of blockchain technology in Internet of Things, in: *Data Engineering and Intelligent Computing*, Advances in Intelligent Systems and Computing, V. Bhateja, S.C. Satapathy, C.M. Travieso-González, V.N.M. Aradhya (Eds.), vol. 1, Springer, Singapore, 2021, https://doi.org/10.1007/978-981-16-0171-2_53.

34. Panda, S.K., Dash, S.P., Jena, A.K., Optimization of block query response using evolutionary algorithm, in: *Data Engineering and Intelligent Computing*, Advances in Intelligent Systems and Computing, V. Bhateja, S.C. Satapathy, C.M. Travieso-González, V.N.M. Aradhya (Eds.), vol. 1, Springer, Singapore, 2021, https://doi.org/10.1007/978-981-16-0171-2_54.

35. Nanda, S.K., Panda, S.K., Das, M., Satapathy, S.C., Automating vehicle insurance process using smart contract and ethereum, in: *Advances in Micro-Electronics, Embedded Systems and IoT*, Lecture Notes in Electrical Engineering, V.V.S.S.S. Chakravarthy, W. Flores-Fuentes, V. Bhateja, B. Biswal (Eds.), vol. 838, pp. 237–247, Springer, Singapore, 2022, https://doi.org/10.1007/978-981-16-8550-7_23.

36. Varaprasada Rao, K. and Panda, S.K., Secure electronic voting (E-voting) system based on blockchain on various platforms, in: *Computer Communication, Networking and IoT*, Lecture Notes in Networks and Systems, S.C. Satapathy, J.C.W. Lin, L.K. Wee, V. Bhateja, T.M. Rajesh (Eds.), vol. 459, Springer, Singapore, 2023, https://doi.org/10.1007/978-981-19-1976-3_18.

37. Varaprasada Rao, K., Panda, S.K., Satapathy, S.C., A design model of copyright protection system based on distributed ledger technology, in: *Computer Communication, Networking and IoT*, Lecture Notes in Networks and Systems, J.C.W. Lin, L.K. Wee, V. Bhateja, T.M. Rajesh (Eds.), vol. 459, Springer, Singapore, 2023, https://doi.org/10.1007/978-981-19-1976-3_17.

38. Panda, S.K., Elngar, A.A., Balas, V.E., Kayed, M. (Eds.), *Bitcoin and blockchain: History and current applications*, 1st ed, CRC Press, 2020, https://doi.org/10.1201/9781003032588.

39. Panda, S.K., Jena, A.K., Swain, S.K., Satapathy, S.C. (Eds.), *Blockchain Technology: Applications and Challenges*, Springer, Intelligent Systems Reference Library, 2021, https://doi.org/10.1007/978-3-030-69395-4.

40. Sathya, A.R., Panda, S.K., Hanumanthakari, S., Enabling smart education system using blockchain technology, in: *Blockchain Technology: Applications and Challenges*, Intelligent Systems Reference Library, vol. 203, S.K. Panda, A.K. Jena, S.K. Swain, S.C. Satapathy (Eds.), Springer, Cham, 2021, https://doi.org/10.1007/978-3-030-69395-4_10.

41. Lokre, S.S., Naman, V., Priya, S., Panda, S.K., Gun tracking system using blockchain technology, in: *Blockchain Technology: Applications and Challenges*, Intelligent Systems Reference Library, S.K. Panda, A.K. Jena, S.K. Swain, S.C. Satapathy (Eds.), vol. 203, Springer, Cham, 2021, https://doi.org/10.1007/978-3-030-69395-4_16.

42. Panda, S.K., Daliyet, S.P., Lokre, S.S., Naman, V., Distributed ledger technology in the construction industry using corda, in: *The New Advanced Society: Artificial Intelligence and Industrial Internet of Things Paradigm*, pp. 15–42, https://doi.org/10.1002/9781119884392.ch2.

43. Panda, S.K., Mohammad, G.B., Nandan Mohanty, S., Sahoo, S., Smart contract-based land registry system to reduce frauds and time delay, in: *Security and Privacy*, p. e172, 2021, https://doi.org/10.1002/spy2.172.

44. Panda, S.K. and Satapathy, S.C., Drug traceability and transparency in medical supply chain using blockchain for easing the process and creating trust between stakeholders and consumers. *Pers. Ubiquit. Comput.*, USA, 2021, https://doi.org/10.1007/s00779-021-01588-3.

45. Niveditha, V.R. and K. Sekaran, K.A Sing, S.P Panda, Effective prediction of bitcoin price using wolf search algorithm and bidirectional LSTM on internet of things data. *Int. J. System Syst. Eng.*, 11, 3-4, 224–236.

46. Sri Arza, M. and Panda, S.K., An integration of blockchain and machine learning into the health care system, in: *Machine Learning Adoption in Blockchain-Based Intelligent Manufacturing*, vol. 1, pp. 33–58, 2022.

47. Murala, D.K., Panda, S.K., Swain, S.K., A survey on cloud computing security and privacy issues and challenges. *J. Adv. Res. Dyn. Control Syst.*, 11, 1276–1290, 2019.

48. Murala, D.K., Panda, S.K., Swain, S.K., Secure dynamic groups data sharing with modified revocable attribute-based encryption in cloud. *Int. J. Recent Technol. Eng.*, 8, 4, 2019.

49. Murala, D.K., Panda, S.K., Swain, S.K., A novel hybrid approach for providing data security and privacy from malicious attacks in the cloud environment. *J. Adv. Res. Dyn. Control Syst.*, 11, 1291–1300, 2019.

50. Panda, S.K., Swain, S.K., Mall, R., An investigation into usability aspects of E-Commerce websites using users' preferences. *Adv. Comput. Science: An Int. J.*, 4, 1, 65–73, 2015.

51. Panda, S.K., Swain, S.K., Mall, R., Measuring Web Site Usability Quality Complexity Metrics for Navigability, in: *Intelligent Computing, Communication and Devices*, Advances in Intelligent Systems and Computing, L. Jain, S. Patnaik, N. Ichalkaranje (Eds.), vol. 308, Springer, New Delhi, Springer, Singapore, 2015, https://doi.org/10.1007/978-81-322-2012-1_41.

52. Panda, S.K., A usability evaluation framework for B2C e-commerce websites. *Comput. Eng. Intell. Syst.*, 5, 3, 66–85, 2014.

53. Bhalerao, V., Panda, S.K., Jena, A.K., Optimization of loss function on human faces using generative adversarial networks, in: *Machine Learning Approaches for Urban Computing*, Studies in Computational Intelligence, M. Bandyopadhyay, M. Rout, S. Chandra Satapathy (Eds.), vol. 968, Springer, Singapore, 2021, https://doi.org/10.1007/978-981-16-0935-0_9.

54. Panda, S.K. and Dwivedi, M., Minimizing food wastage using machine learning: A novel approach, in: *Smart Intelligent Computing and Applications*, Smart Innovation, Systems and Technologies, S. Satapathy, V. Bhateja,

J. Mohanty, S. Udgata (Eds.), vol. 159, Springer, Singapore, 2020, https://doi.org/10.1007/978-981-13-9282-5_44.

55. Panda, S.K., Sathya, A.R., Mishra, M., Satpathy, S., A supervised learning algorithm to forecast weather conditions for playing cricket. *Int. J. Innovative Technol. Explroring Eng. (IJITEE)*, India, 9, 1, 2019.

56. Panda, S.K., Fraud-resistant crowdfunding system using ethereum block-chain, in: *Bitcoin and Blockchain*, pp. 237–276, 2020.

57. Panda, S.K., Mishra, V., Balamurali, R., Elngar, A.A., *Artificial intelligence and machine learning in business management concepts, challenges, and case studies*, pp. 237–276, 2022, https://doi.org/10.1201/9781003125129.

58. Joshi, S., Panda, S.K., AR, S., Optimal Deep Learning Model to Identify the Development of Pomegranate Fruit in Farms. *Int. J. Innovative Technol. Exploring Eng.*, 9, 3, 2352–2356, 2020.

59. Puranam, K.S.R., Gaddam, M.C.T., K, V.P.R., Panda, S.K., Reddy, G.S.M., Anatomy and Lifecycle of a Bitcoin Transaction (February 18, 2019). *Proceedings of International Conference on Sustainable Computing in Science, Technology and Management (SUSCOM)*, Amity University Rajasthan, Jaipur - India, February 26-28, 2019, Available at SSRN: https://ssrn.com/abstract=3355106 or http://dx.doi.org/10.2139/ssrn.3355106.

60. Panda, S.K. and Swain, S.K., *Quality assurance aspects of web design, design solutions for improving website quality and effectiveness*, pp. 87–129, IGI Global, USA, 2016.

61. Panda, S.K., Bhalerao, V., AR, S., A Machine Learning Model to Identify Duplicate Questions in Social Media Forums. *Int. J. Innovative Technol. Exploring Eng.*, 9, 4, 370–373, IGI Global, USA, 2020.

62. Ahmareen, S., Raj, A., Potluri, S., Panda, S.K., Book Shala: An android-Based application design and implementation of sharing books, in: *Smart Intelligent Computing and Applications. Smart Innovation, Systems and Technologies*, S. Satapathy, V. Bhateja, J. Mohanty, S. Udgata (Eds.), vol. 1590, Springer, Singapore, 2020, https://doi.org/10.1007/978-981-13-9282-5_28.

63. Panda, S.K., Das, S.S., Swain, S.K., S-Model for service-oriented applications in web engineering. *RCM*, 10, 3, 38–46, 2013.

64. Panda, S.K., *An investigation into usability and productivity of ECommerce websites*, 2016.

65. Panda, S.K., Chandrasekhar, A., Gantayat, P.K., Panda, M.R., Detecting brain tumor using image segmentation: A novel approach, in: *Data Engineering and Intelligent Computing*, Lecture Notes in Networks and Systems, V. Bhateja, L. Khin Wee, J.C.W. Lin, S.C. Satapathy, T.M. Rajesh (Eds.), vol. 446, Springer, Singapore, 2022, https://doi.org/10.1007/978-981-19-1559-8_35.

66. Sanghi, P., Panda, S.K., Pati, C., Gantayat, P.K., Learning deep features and classification for fresh or off vegetables to prevent food wastage using machine learning algorithms, in: *Intelligent Data Engineering and Analytics. Smart Innovation, Systems and Technologies*, S.C. Satapathy, P. Peer, J. Tang,

V. Bhateja, A. Ghosh (Eds.), vol. 266, Springer, Singapore, 2022, https://doi.org/10.1007/978-981-16-6624-7_44.

67. Gantayat, P.K., Mohapatra, S., Panda, S.K., Secure trust level routing in delay-Tolerant network with node categorization technique, in: *Intelligent Data Engineering and Analytics. Smart Innovation, Systems and Technologies,* S.C. Satapathy, P. Peer, J. Tang, V. Bhateja, A. Ghosh (Eds.), vol. 266, Springer, Singapore, 2022, https://doi.org/10.1007/978-981-16-6624-7_45.

68. Panda, S.K., Urkude, S.V., Urkude, V.R., Vairachilai, S., An investigation into COVID 19 pandemic in India, in: *The New Advanced Society: Artificial Intelligence and Industrial Internet of Things Paradigm,* vol. 1, Wiley.

69. Panda, S.K., Das, S., Swain, S.K., Web site productivity measurement using single task size measure. *J. Inf. Sci. Comput. Technologies (JISCT),* 4, 3, October 12, 2015.

70. Hanumanthakari, S. and Panda, S.K., Detecting Face Mask for Prevent COVID-19 Using Deep Learning: A Novel Approach, in: *Smart Intelligent Computing and Applications, Volume 2,* Smart Innovation, Systems and Technologies, S.C. Satapathy, V. Bhateja, M.N. Favorskaya, T. Adilakshmi (Eds.), vol. 283, Springer, Singapore, 2022, https://doi.org/10.1007/978-981-16-9705-0_45.

71. Panda, S.K., Sathya, A.R., Das, S., Bitcoin: Beginning of the Cryptocurrency Era, in: *Recent Advances in Blockchain Technology,* Intelligent Systems Reference Library, S.K. Panda, V. Mishra, S.P. Dash, A.K. Pani (Eds.), vol. 237, Springer, Cham, 2023, https://doi.org/10.1007/978-3-031-22835-3_2.

72. Murala, D.K., Panda, S.K., Sahoo, S.K., Panda, S.K., Securing Electronic Health Record System in Cloud Environment Using Blockchain Technology, in: *Recent Advances in Blockchain Technology,* Intelligent Systems Reference Library, V. Mishra, S.P. Dash, A.K. Pani (Eds.), vol. 237, Springer, Cham, 2023, https://doi.org/10.1007/978-3-031-22835-3_4.

73. Rao, K.V., Murala, D.K., Panda, S.K., Blockchain: A study of new business model, in: *Recent Advances in Blockchain Technology,* Intelligent Systems Reference Library, S.K. Panda, V. Mishra, S.P. Dash, A.K. Pani (Eds.), vol. 237, Springer, Cham, 2023, https://doi.org/10.1007/978-3-031-22835-3_9.

74. Panda, S.K., Mishra, V., Dash, S.P., Pani, A.K., *Recent advances in blockchain technology real-world applications,* in: Intelligent Systems Reference Library (ISRL, volume 237), vol. 1, pp. 1–317, 2023, 978-3-031-22835-3.

75. Panda, S.K., Mohapatra, R.K., Panda, S., Balamurugan, S., *The new advanced society: Artificial intelligence and industrial internet of things paradigm,* vol. 1, pp. 1–512, Wiley.

76. Nanda, S.K., Panda, S.K., Das, M., Satapathy, S.C., Bhateja, V., *Decentralization of car insurance system using machine learning and distributed ledger technology,* X.S. Yang, J. Chun-Wei Lin, R. Das (Eds.), vol. 327, Springer, Singapore, 2023, https://doi.org/10.1007/978-981-19-7524-0_52.

2

Metaverse and Blockchain

Vaishnavi Raj. K.A., Shresta Rongali, Bathula Jaya Teja and Shaik Himam Saheb*

*Faculty of Science and Technology
The ICFAI Foundation for Higher Education, Hyderabad, India*

Abstract

The emergence of metaverses, or 3D virtual worlds, has given rise to a new standard for social networks and online communities. One such example is Facebook's recent rebranding as Metaverse, which aims to provide users with immersive and personalized experiences through the use of various technologies. However, with the increasing popularity of these virtual environments comes the need to ensure the protection of users' digital data and content. Blockchain technology offers a promising solution in this regard, as it is decentralized, immutable, and transparent. These characteristics make it well-suited for use in the metaverse, where it can help to secure user information and facilitate transactions within the virtual world. In this research, we aim to delve into the technical aspects of using blockchain in the metaverse; we will examine the application of blockchain technology in augmenting reality (AR), virtual reality (VR), and mixed reality (MR). We will also delve into the possibilities for future innovation and advancement in the integration of blockchain for the metaverse, as well as potential avenues for further investigation in this field. Ultimately, our objective is to furnish a thorough understanding of how blockchain can safeguard and improve the metaverse experience for users.

Keywords: Blockchain technology, applications of blockchain technology, metaverse, Web3 gaming, augmented reality, virtual reality, mixed reality

Corresponding author: himam.mech@gmail.com

Chandrashekhar A, Shaik Himam Saheb, Sandeep Kumar Panda, S. Balamurugan and Sheng-Lung Peng (eds.)
Metaverse and Immersive Technologies: An Introduction to Industrial, Business and Social Applications, (43–70) © 2023 Scrivener Publishing LLC

2.1 Introduction

Blockchain technology was first introduced in a white paper by Satoshi Nakamoto in 2008 [10–12]. It is a decentralized, distributed ledger that consists of a series of blocks that are connected to each other through the use of cryptographic hash values [13–16]. Each block in the blockchain contains a timestamp, a nonce, and transaction data, as well as the hash value of the previous block.

To ensure the integrity of the blockchain, the block timestamp is only considered valid if it is more recent than two hours beyond the network-adjusted time and newer than the median timestamp of the preceding eleven blocks. The network-adjusted time represents the average of the timestamps of all the connected nodes on the network [17].

Each node in the blockchain network plays a vital role in the smooth functioning of the network, rather than just a few key nodes. Each new block contains a hash pointer, and the potential applications of blockchain technology are vast, including the storage of information, value transfer and exchange, and the use of digital signatures. In this way, blockchain can be seen as a transparent and tamper-proof database of transaction history that is distributed to all members of the network [18, 19].

2.1.1 Types of Blockchains

The two fundamental kinds of blockchains are public blockchains and private blockchains. With public blockchains, individuals all over can

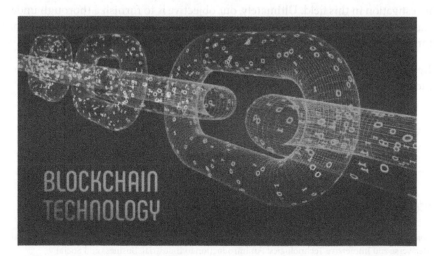

Figure 2.1 Introduction to blockchain technology.

distributed with one another. Private blockchains are more proper for endeavors, and private enterprises who need to limit admittance to the peers. Figure 2.1 demonstrate the introduction to blockchain technology.

1. **Public blockchain** - Anybody can join and take part in the vital tasks of a public blockchain network. The decentralized, self-represented nature of blockchain innovation is created conceivable by the way that anybody can peruse, distribute, and review the ongoing exercises on a public blockchain network. The flexibility of public blockchains as the establishment for many decentralized arrangements makes them profoundly valuable. In expansion, a safe public blockchain is safeguarded against information breaks, hacking endeavors, and other online protection issues because of the enormous number of organization clients that go along with it. The more members a blockchain has, the safer it becomes [20–22].

2. **Private blockchain** - Private blockchain organizations must be joined by greeting and require the member's character or other essential data to be validated and checked. This approval cycle is normally completed by the organization operator(s) or by the actual organization, utilizing savvy contracts or other robotized endorsement techniques that follow a foreordained convention.

Private blockchains have impediments on who can utilize the organization and are commonly confined to a particular gathering of clients. The confidential idea of the organization may likewise limit which clients can take part in the agreement cycle that decides mining privileges and rewards, if material. The common record in a private blockchain may likewise be kept up with by a little gathering of clients, and the proprietor or administrator has the position to change, correct, or eliminate any important blockchain sections depending on the situation [1, 23–25].

2.2 Preparatories of Blockchain

2.2.1 Consensus Protocols

The groundwork of blockchain innovation is the agreement convention, which lays out the guidelines and rules that oversee legitimate activities.

The notable digital currency Bitcoin utilizes a Proof of Work (PoW) method that expects diggers to contribute a lot of handling power to take care of a complex numerical issue. The trouble, otherwise called the nonce, of the following block age is progressively changed in view of a 10-minute span to forestall the centralization of processing power.

While PoW is compelling at forestalling assaults, it likewise has a few disadvantages, for example, a low exchange rate and high energy utilization. In spite of this, it stays a generally involved agreement component in blockchain networks [26–29].

Proof of Stake (PoS) is a consensus mechanism that aims to address the issues associated with Proof of Work (PoW), such as low transaction rates and high energy consumption. In a PoS system, the miner who ultimately wins the right to add a new block to the blockchain is determined by their holdings in the relevant cryptocurrency rather than their processing power [2, 30–32].

Another consensus mechanism that has gained attention in recent years is Proof of Space (PoSpace), which requires participants to provide a certain amount of storage space in order to solve a challenge issued by the service provider. PoSpace is being implemented in the InterPlanetary File System (IPFS), a decentralized storage network.

In addition to these consensus mechanisms, the use of Merkle trees to organize transaction data in blocks can increase the efficiency of the verification process. With a Merkle tree, users can download any branch of the tree for checking without needing to access the full transaction records [3, 33–35].

Digital signatures are used for validation when one or more parties digitally sign any transaction made on blockchain protocol for authentication purposes such as proving identity; digitally signing a contract;

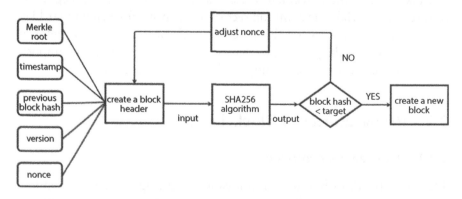

Figure 2.2 Working of consensus mechanism of blockchain.

or guaranteeing that an event happened by proxy if signed on behalf of another person etc. Blockchain has demonstrated to be secure, permanent, and outside misrepresentation. As such it very well may be involved across various fields as a solid distributed approach to putting away records and information. Its capacity to forestall misrepresentation makes it ideal for banking exchanges and different trades. Because of its decentralized nature, blockchain is lined up with the web in numerous ways. Each line of code is introduced on an immensely conveyed record and upheld on over a portion of 1,000,000 hubs internationally. Figure 2.2 shows the working of consensus mechanism of blockchain.

In the present advanced climate, we are encircled by information. Business depends on it to let us know how beneficial they and markets they need to target. Information is something that vows to drive economies all over the planet in a more moderate way, while adding to the sparsity of ecological contamination that plagues many areas of the planet. Blockchain has helped numerous new businesses in investigating arrangements like the assembling business or energy industry where neither had solid information previously [4, 36–38].

2.2.2 Blockchain Through Generations

Bitcoin is considered a first-generation blockchain because it primarily decentralized transaction records. Later, it was discovered that blockchain technology could be used for more than just a ledger, including the management of assets and trusts. While originally developed for Bitcoin transactions, the utility of blockchain technology has been recognized across a variety of industries.

As a result, the second generation of blockchain, based on Ethereum, emerged. One of the major innovations introduced by Ethereum is the use of smart contracts, which are rules encoded in code that can be triggered by transactions. These smart contracts can perform a variety of tasks, such as automatically transferring money or sending notifications to specified accounts.

Smart contracts have a wide range of applications, including increasing the security of the voting process and assisting businesses in making quick claims for patient settlements in the insurance industry. A derivative of smart contracts, called non-fungible tokens (NFTs), has also gained popularity in recent years. NFTs are unique digital assets that cannot be exchanged on a one-to-one basis and are often used to represent ownership of digital art, collectibles, and other types of digital content. Ethereum has released two standards, ERC-721 and ERC-1155, to describe the properties of assets created on NFTs. The NFT industry is now valued at over $7 billion and encompasses a variety of industries, including art, games, sports, copyright, insurance, and more [5, 39, 40].

2.3   Technical Understanding of Blockchain

Blockchain innovation comprises of a progression of blocks that, similar to a customary public record, contain a far reaching rundown of exchange records. Each block in the blockchain has a solitary parent block, which is distinguished by the presence of the past block's hash esteem in the block header. It is quite significant that the hashes of "uncle" blocks, or blocks that are not piece of the principal chain, are additionally recorded on the Ethereum blockchain. The primary block in the blockchain, called the beginning block, has no parent block.

Each block in the blockchain is made up of two components. The exact nature of these components may vary depending on the specific implementation of the blockchain, but they typically include some combination of transaction data and metadata, such as timestamps and cryptographic hashes.

These transactions and communications are verified and validated by specialized nodes known as miners. The data structure known as a block contains the legitimate transactions. The preceding committed transactions are necessary for the present transaction to be carried out. This technology is useful in preventing or limiting double spending in the bitcoin system.

2.3.1   Block Header

The block header in a blockchain comprises of three principal parts. The main component is the hash code of the past block, which connects the ongoing block to the one preceding it. The subsequent component is

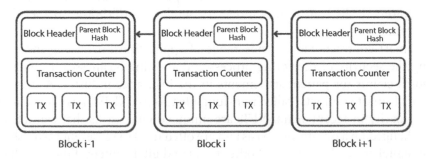

Figure 2.3 Architecture of each block in a blockchain.

the mining measurements used to make the block, like the nonce, time-stamp, and mining trouble. The last component is the Merkle tree root, which is just the hash code of the ongoing block and fills in as the establishment for confirming the precision of the multitude of exchanges contained in the block [41–43]. Figure 2.3 shows the architecture of each block in a blockchain.

To make a hash code for the ongoing block, we utilize the hash code of the first block. In the event that an aggressor attempts to modify the items in a block, they would likewise need to change the hash codes of the multitude of blocks in the chain, which is essentially difficult to do. This makes the blockchain sealed. The information blocks in a Merkle tree are hashed and joined to leaf hubs, while the non-leaf hubs contain the cryptographic hash of their kid hubs [6, 44–46].

2.3.2   List of Transactions

The second component of a block in a blockchain is a rundown of genuine exchanges. The size of the block and the exchanges held inside it decide the quantity of exchanges that can be remembered for a block. Uneven cryptography is utilized for the approval and verification of exchanges, and when an exchange has been added to the chain, it can't be erased or changed [47].

A chain of blocks, or blockchain, is made by connecting blocks together, with each block containing the hash of the past block. To be added to the chain, a block should have confirmation of work, which is a computationally

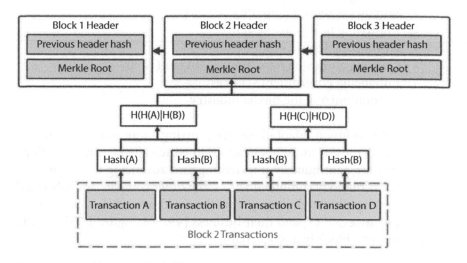

Figure 2.4 Merkle tree in blockchain.

difficult hash delivered during the mining system. This evidence of work guarantees that assuming any of the blocks in the chain are changed, all resulting blocks should be recomputed because of the utilization of a safe hashing strategy, (for example, SHA-256) with secure hash pointers highlighting the past hash. The scientific categorizations connected with blocks and blockchain are recorded underneath [7, 48]. Figure 2.4 shows the Merkle tree in blockchain.

2.4   Advanced Applications of Blockchain in Various Sectors

Blockchain technology has gained widespread attention and popularity in the past decade, and it has a vast array of potential uses across a wide range of industries, including identity management, government, finance, and healthcare. It is perhaps best known for its role in the creation and use of Bitcoin, but its capabilities extend far beyond this single application.

Due to its decentralized design, which makes it highly secure and resistant to attacks, blockchain is being embraced for a variety of applications around the world. Some of the most common and top uses for blockchain technology include:

- Transferring money
- Creating and executing smart contracts
- Enhancing personal identity security
- Improving healthcare systems
- Optimizing logistics
- Creating and using non-fungible tokens (NFTs)
- Enhancing government services
- Revolutionizing the media industry

While the common adaptations are growing more popularity in the technical field, the advanced applications in which blockchain technology stepped into are continuously improvising and advancing their game up. Blockchain technology combined with some other complex and advanced domains are rapidly developing, giving the budding and big companies a scope to enhance and expand their business [49, 50]. Figure 2.5 shows the components of a block in a blockchain.

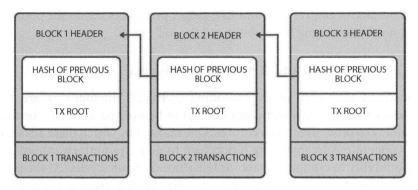

Figure 2.5 Components of a block in a blockchain.

2.4.1 Blockchain and Web of Things (IoT)

Blockchain and Web of Things (IoT): The reconciliation of blockchain innovation with the Web of Things (IoT) permits Web associated gadgets to communicate information to private blockchain networks to make sealed records of shared exchanges. This mix has various applications, for example, working on the effectiveness of transportation by recording the temperature, area, appearance times, and status of delivery holders utilizing IoT-empowered blockchain. All partners can believe the information and make a move to rapidly and really move items because of the permanent idea of blockchain exchanges [8, 51, 55].

Likewise, the capacity to follow the parts that go into planes, vehicles, and different items is fundamental for both security and administrative consistence. By saving IoT information in shared blockchain records, all gatherings can follow the beginning of parts over the lifetime of an item. This data can be effectively and safely imparted to administrative bodies, transporters, and producers, making it more practical and proficient.

IoT gadgets can likewise screen the upkeep and security status of basic hardware, and blockchain empowers an alter free data set of working information and coming about support for everything from motors to lifts. Outsider fix accomplices can utilize the blockchain to follow preventive support and log their work, and government organizations might approach functional archives to affirm consistence.

As sensor and shrewd chip innovation keeps on propelling, making them more versatile and valuable for continuous collaborations with blockchain records, there is major areas of strength for a for a commercial center of administrations to interface gadgets and permit organizations to benefit from information assortment. The developing number of new blockchain conventions, organizations, and IoT gadget producers shows the potential for a nearby fit among blockchain and the IoT area.

2.4.2   Blockchain and Artificial Intelligence (AI)

Blockchain and man-made reasoning (artificial intelligence) are two advances that certainly stand out enough to be noticed as of late for their capability to upset different ventures. One manner by which these advances can cooperate is by involving blockchain to give straightforwardness and responsibility to computer based intelligence dynamic cycles. At the point when computer based intelligence models are put away and conveyed through a blockchain, it makes a review trail that takes into consideration a superior comprehension of the information and suggestions produced by the computer based intelligence. This can increment trust in the exactness of the information and the artificial intelligence's thinking skills. Moreover, the mix of blockchain and simulated intelligence can further develop information security and lessen contact in multiparty exchanges, prompting expanded effectiveness and efficiency. In the monetary administrations industry, for instance, the utilization of blockchain and artificial intelligence can smooth out the acquiring system, bringing about quicker closings and higher consumer loyalty. Generally speaking, the blend of blockchain and simulated intelligence can possibly carry new worth to business tasks including different gatherings.

2.5   Web3 Technology

At regular intervals, another mechanical advancement changes the interaction by which information is delivered and disseminated among people. Because of the improvement of the web, society has become more interconnected as data is shared and dispersed to billions of clients overall by means of an open and permissionless organization. The development of the web can be sorted into three phases: Web 1.0, Web 2.0, and Web 3.0 [52].

2.5.1   Web 1.0: Study

The expression "Web 1" portrays the first variant of the web. The most ideal way to make sense of this variant is as a "read in particular" network comprised of static pages associated by a substance conveyance organization. Just few members were content suppliers because of the abnormal UI and limited admittance, while the extraordinary larger part latently consumed data. Web 1.0 was exemplified by instruments like Netscape, Britannica On

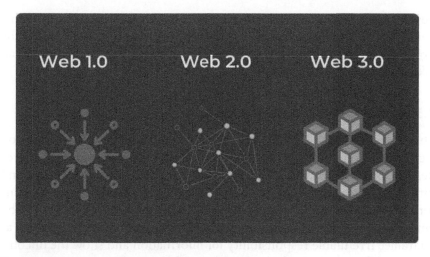

Figure 2.6 Depiction of Web1.0, Web2.0, and Web3.0.

the web, and individual HTML-based sites. Figure 2.6 shows the depiction of Web1.0, Web2.0, and Web3.0.

2.5.2   Web 2.0: Read, Write

The advancement of online entertainment stages, which made it a lot less complex to make and impart your own substance to individuals everywhere, permitted Web 2.0 to beat a portion of the limitations of Web 1.0. The web's outstanding development was made conceivable by the shift from a limited handful distributers to everybody being able to distribute.

With Web2, a little gathering major areas of strength for of, concentrated computerized monsters, as Facebook, Twitter, and YouTube/Google, overwhelm the fundamental stages that permit people to distribute data with the broadest reach. These stages have the power to singularly figure out which distributers can present material on organizations or how much perceivability a piece of content ought to have [9].

Through distributed storage administrations like Amazon Web Administrations (or AWS), which keep a huge number of sites functional, clients are presented to restriction on the application layer as well as on the foundation layer. Web2 has likewise sped up the ongoing power structures inside our worldwide monetary and financial frameworks to turn out to be significantly more incorporated and fit for implementing control. This is because of the digitization of cash.

The basic thought behind Web3 is to make another web from the beginning that utilizes decentralization and open-source innovation to further develop data trade and validation in the computerized age. With Web3, you wouldn't just be a member in the organization yet additionally the proprietor of the substance you make and consume on the web, rather than Web2, which was a "read, state" rendition of the web.

2.5.3 Web 3.0: Read, Write, Own

The expression "Web3" alludes to a gathering of innovations that utilization web conventions and depend on decentralized, conveyed, and open-source designs. Blockchains, advanced monetary forms, shrewd agreements, and different dispersed record structures are models. Using open, straightforward, and carefully designed records known as blockchains, Web3 empowers network gatherings to post and consume information as well as guarantee irrefutable responsibility for information and show the uncommonness of computerized resources [53, 54].

Web3 is as yet an idea that numerous people in the innovation business view as shapeless. From certain perspectives, the concentrated and hierarchical stages will be completely supplanted by decentralized networks in the following period of the web, releasing the maximum capacity of human coordination and joint effort. Others, who hold a more nuanced view, imagine that web3 will not totally supplant web2 however will rather improve it by empowering concentrated organizations to profit from decentralization's straightforwardness, security, unchanging nature, and control opposition while keeping up with their ongoing hierarchical designs, which are intended for execution proficiency. The main part of customary organizations and a rising number of web3 local new businesses seem to pick this model.

To put it another way, web3 frameworks appear to be generally helpful for empowering the gathering to lay out new methods and systems for decision making at the crucial level (i.e., how might choices be made, what are the significant level objectives for the local area or association), while the genuine execution of those choices is best passed on to additional unified and hierarchical authoritative designs that are streamlined for effectiveness.

2.5.4 Web3 Gaming

The overall gaming business is seeing an ascent in web3 gaming. In any case, not every person supports the idea. Truly, most gamers are unyieldingly against bringing in cash by messing around, which is what most of blockchain games guarantee their client base. The more youthful age of gamers acknowledges the compromise as a feature of the fun of gaming.

While tolerating the change in outlook can seem like the reasonable strategy in contrast with the potential for slipping behind the transformative bend, certain gaming firms enjoy taken benefit of the guilelessness of some gamers to sell shoddy items.

The investigator guarantees that some blockchain game makers acquaint new play-with acquire games a very long time in the wake of getting beginning venture. A practical gaming biology should be worked, as indicated by the examination, and some Web3 game designers seem to have ignored this. To draw in gamers to their gaming biological systems, these advanced game makers are involving adapted special strategies as NFT drops.

This postures three critical hardships for Web3 gaming. Most importantly, it builds the expense of joining the gaming local area. Token consuming and compensates are an essential issue. Rewards draw some unacceptable sorts of gamers. The motivations given by Web3 games to attract new players represents a test, especially in the event that new players are principally attracted to the game for the guaranteed prizes. The game can't keep on giving such advantages, subsequently when they run out, there will without a doubt be an enormous channel on the environment as individuals leave looking for higher awards. NFTs and blockchain gaming tokens are still in their outset, making them exceptionally theoretical. They ought not be quickly viewed as the gaming business' future along these lines. All things being equal, they ought to be seen as a part of the impending gaming insurgency, which will embrace vivid gaming among different developments like the metaverse.

2.6 Metaverse and Blockchain Technology

Blockchain: Blockchain innovation is significant for the metaverse in light of the fact that it considers the production of a decentralized and secure stage for putting away and trading computerized resources. With blockchain, clients can claim and control their own computerized resources, as opposed to depending on a focal power.

Computer generated Reality (VR): VR is a vital innovation for the metaverse in light of the fact that it permits clients to encounter a completely vivid computerized world. VR headsets and different gadgets permit clients to collaborate with virtual conditions and items as though they were in reality.

Advanced Twins: Computerized twins are computerized portrayals of actual articles or frameworks, and they can be utilized in the metaverse to reenact and examine certifiable situations. For instance, a computerized twin of a city could be utilized to test new innovations or plan new structures.

6G: The up and coming age of remote innovation, known as 6G, will be a key empowering influence for the metaverse. 6G will give super quick and low-idleness availability, making it workable for clients to encounter the metaverse progressively.

Different advancements that will assume a part in the metaverse incorporate expanded reality (AR), computerized reasoning (man-made intelligence), and the Web of Things (IoT). Together, these innovations will permit the production of a completely intuitive and vivid computerized world that is associated with the actual world.

1. The utilization of expanded reality innovation, including AR and VR, is fundamental for the making of the metaverse. Computer generated reality permits clients to completely submerge themselves in an advanced climate, while expanded reality considers the overlay of computerized data on the actual world. The improvement of the metaverse, a virtual space for human collaboration, intensely depends on both of these innovations.

2. A virtual reproduction of an actual item, made utilizing genuine information to foresee the normal way of behaving of the article, is known as a computerized twin. This innovation is significant in the metaverse, where it can give a virtual portrayal of the actual world. Computerized twins are made utilizing true information to expect the normal way of behaving of the actual item.

3. Blockchain innovation assumes a pivotal part in the metaverse by filling in as both a vault for data and as a method for connecting the virtual universe of the metaverse with this present reality through monetary frameworks. In particular, non-fungible tokens (NFTs) consider the change of virtual items into genuine ones, empowering clients to exchange virtual merchandise as they would actual ones. This assists with overcoming any issues between the actual world and the metaverse through blockchain innovation.

Working from home has turned into a critical way for private ventures to get by during the Coronavirus pandemic, however it misses the mark on eye to eye correspondence that is significant for successful correspondence, as non-verbal communication represents 70% of an individual's expressiveness. Customary up close and personal coordinated effort enjoys many benefits, like better collaboration, prompt commitment, and more clear input. Nonetheless, in the metaverse, clients can utilize a social symbol to connect and carry on with work. Working from home can be improved by utilizing even straightforward non-verbal communication or eye to eye connection to speak with associates according to different points of view in the virtual climate.

Generally, 3D illustrations have been made utilizing displaying programs like Maya and ZBrush. Notwithstanding, the metaverse puts a great deal of spotlight on the showcase layer, opening up new open doors for creative articulation and permitting clients to draw figures with a brush straight-forwardly. The ascent in ubiquity of man-made intelligence painting has additionally made the public more mindful of computerized workman-ship. Moreover, the reception of blockchain innovation has empowered the change of customary disconnected fine arts to a web-based stage. Clients can get to virtual exhibitions in the metaverse and view them from all points.

2.6.1   Blockchain Technology and Metaverse

The metaverse, or virtual world, permits us to imagine different invigorat-ing conceivable outcomes and encounters. Nonetheless, it is likewise like our own existence in that monetary frameworks are a necessary piece of it. Advanced resources, for example, ERC-20 based homogenized tokens and ERC-721 or ERC-1155 based non-homogenized tokens, are key parts of the metaverse and are worked with by blockchain innovation. Blockchain innovation assumes a urgent part in the working of the metaverse by guar-anteeing the smooth activity of its economy.

To offer the most ideal encounters to clients, the metaverse gathers a lot of private information. This information is utilized by organizations or projects to actually fabricate designated frameworks. Nonetheless, assum-ing that some unacceptable people get close enough to this data, they might actually hurt clients in reality. Blockchain innovation assists with safeguarding individual data by giving verification, access control, and agreement techniques that give clients unlimited authority over their infor-mation. The blockchain utilizes procedures, for example, hash calculations and deviated key encryption to protect information inside the metaverse.

The metaverse is fueled by Expanded Reality (AR) and Computer generated Reality (VR) innovation, establishing a more interconnected and vivid climate. The joining of the metaverse with AR on advanced and actual things makes it significant. The metaverse's prosperity relies upon the smooth sharing of AR and VR information, which permits the improvement of inventive, bleeding edge applications that can take care of true issues. The trading of information inside the metaverse is made conceivable by the blockchain's high level data encoding framework.

2.6.2   Blockchain for IoT in the Metaverse

The metaverse stage gathers information from an assortment of Web of Things (IoT) gadgets to work really across different metaverse applications, like medication, instruction, and brilliant urban communities. These IoT gadgets associate the actual world to the metaverse through different equipment, regulators, and articles. IoT gadgets outfitted with explicit sensors consider route in both the physical and virtual universes by connecting to the metaverse. The client's capacity to perform activities inside the metaverse is subject to the capacity of the IoT gadgets to do as such.

The metaverse will comprise of countless interconnected Web of Things (IoT) sensors. With such countless associated gadgets, security and capacity of IoT information is a worry. Ongoing examination of unstructured IoT information can be troublesome because of the volume, exactness, and speed of the information. The nature of metaverse information should likewise be sans mistake to be appropriately investigated. Utilizing a concentrated answer for store information across virtual universes isn't great, as any modification to even one piece of information can think twice about whole arrangement of discoveries produced by the IoT gadgets. Information trade between virtual universes depends on the cross-stage abilities of IoT gadgets. It is essential to follow IoT information for security purposes.

Blockchain innovation empowers IoT gadgets in the metaverse to trade information through cross-chain organizations, making sealed records of shared exchanges in virtual universes. This permits applications and clients to share and access IoT information without the requirement for unified administration or control. Every exchange is archived and approved to limit debates and increment client certainty inside the metaverse. The utilization of IoT-empowered blockchain in the metaverse considers ongoing capacity of information.

2.6.3   Blockchain for Digital Twins in the Metaverse

The modern advanced portrayals of everything in the metaverse, from basic resources for enormous products and conditions, are known as computerized twins. Thus, everything relevant to the client's necessities could be a piece of the environment that utilizes computerized twins. Clients can rejuvenate their picked models while keeping them in a state of harmony with this present reality because of two-way IoT associations. Without an underlying association between the genuine and advanced universes, the metaverse's applications will not have the option to accurately work. To understand how the metaverse climate will change and to assist with future forecast, advanced twins will be essential. It is doable to anticipate when equipment will require upkeep by utilizing computerized twins.

Computerized twins are profoundly cutting-edge advanced portrayals of everything inside the metaverse, from basic resources for enormous products and conditions. Thusly, anything pertinent to the client's requirements can be a piece of the biological system that uses computerized twins. Clients can rejuvenate their picked models while keeping them in a state of harmony with this present reality through two-way IoT associations. Without this association between the genuine and advanced universes, the metaverse's applications won't work as expected. Computerized twins will be fundamental in understanding how the metaverse climate will change and in anticipating future turns of events. They can likewise be utilized to guess when equipment might require support.

Advanced twins are made conceivable by the encryption abilities and straightforwardness of blockchain innovation, which takes into account secure information move between numerous virtual universes. Utilizing a savvy circulated record, information can be moved between advanced twins in virtual universes. Certifiable articles can be put away on the blockchain and synchronized to computerized twins in the metaverse with the assistance of a clever dispersed record. The utilization of advanced twins on the blockchain can likewise resolve issues with information security and protection. By joining blockchain and man-made reasoning (artificial intelligence), it is feasible to follow sensor information and make great advanced twins in the metaverse. There will be an exchange recorded on the blockchain for each computerized twin activity in the metaverse.

2.7   Augmented Reality, Virtual Reality, and Mixed Reality

Increased reality (AR) joins genuine and virtual components, and can be capable on both work area and cell phones. It is one of a kind in that it considers the overlay of computerized components onto the actual world. AR shows different substance inside the genuine climate, which separates it from augmented reality (VR). To actually use AR, specific gear is frequently required, and PC vision, profundity following, and planning are fundamental parts. For instance, cameras can be utilized to gather information continuously and process it right away, permitting the client to see advanced content depending on the situation.

As opposed to AR, VR utilizes virtual experiences to make a realistic portrayal of the real world or a made up universe. This permits the client to completely submerge themselves in the advanced climate utilizing the proper equipment. Thus, there are tremendous contrasts among VR and AR headsets. VR equipment requires tactile parts that convert actual developments into a demonstrated reality, while AR doesn't. VR means to reproduce a totally new reality, and the client sees and connects with the computerized climate through a VR screen, which requires two focal points to decipher eye development and change the client's development inside the VR. Accordingly, VR requires more perplexing stuff to segregate the client from the rest of the world totally.

Blended reality, the mix of expanded reality and augmented reality, is supposed to turn out to be generally embraced by the two buyers and endeavors sooner rather than later. This innovation centers around empowering instinctive information connection and wiping out screen-based work, permitting handheld gadgets to play out similar errands as fixed gadgets. One significant advantage of blended the truth is the capacity to get to incorporated information from any area whenever without any problem.

2.7.1   Holographic Telepresence on the Blockchain and Other XR Applications in the Metaverse

The metaverse offers vivid, reasonable encounters using advances, for example, holographic telepresence and increased reality (AR) applications, which integrate components connected with insight, sound, and video. These projects take into account continuous delivering of both unmistakable and immaterial metaverse items and upgrade the authenticity of the experience by integrating genuine components. Holographic telepresence and multi-tactile AR applications permit clients to encounter both the genuine and virtual universes all the while. Key empowering advancements in the metaverse incorporate computer generated experience (VR), AR, and holographic telepresence, which can possibly raise worries for society and people. These advances can be utilized by organizations to make proposal frameworks utilizing information acquired from them, however the nature of these metaverse suggestion frameworks can be impacted by social information accumulated from various sources. The utilization of these advancements requires a lot of information stockpiling and should be open to clients in the metaverse consistently. Delicate information, for example, biometric data gathered by VR/AR gadgets can be utilized to recognize and accumulate extra data about clients in the virtual climate, raising protection worries that should be tended to by the metaverse.

A blockchain-based disseminated record can approve the records of holographic telepresence and other XR applications in the metaverse and track the wellspring of mistaken information, prompting the making of a more precise suggestion framework. The zero-trust system and cross-chain innovation of the blockchain make it more straightforward for holographic telepresence and other XR applications to send information between virtual universes safely. The interplanetary document framework gave by the blockchain guarantees information respectability for XR applications and holographic telepresence. The agreement technique utilized by these gadgets makes the information they gather and store on the blockchain changeless. Blockchain innovation upholds trust among AR/VR partners by empowering straightforward proprietorship move and resource confirmation.

Blockchain, holographic telepresence, and multi-tangible XR applications will cooperate to coordinate advanced economies into brought together stages that consider effective and clear administration of resources and installments in the metaverse. Later on, VR/AR innovations may not be pretty much as broadly utilized as cell phones or PCs, and the utilization of cutting edge man-made intelligence profound fakes might represent a test for blockchain that should be tended to by new eminent blockchain stages. Figure 2.7 shows the Hologram using the virtual reality and extended reality.

Figure 2.7 Hologram using the virtual reality and extended reality.

2.8   The Metaverse Projects

A concise outline of some famous metaverse projects that use blockchain innovation in the web3 gaming industry. Projects like Decentraland, Sandbox, Axie Vastness, and Illuvium have recognized blockchain as the center innovation of the metaverse, and it fills in as the establishment for the turn of events and execution of different elements and administrations. Blockchain innovation likewise takes into consideration the acquisition of land and different resources inside the metaverse.

2.8.1   Decentraland

Decentraland is a computer generated simulation stage fueled by the Ethereum blockchain that permits clients to encounter, make, and adapt financial resources, hyperreal content, and applications. In Decentraland, the local area forever possesses the land and has full oversight and command over its imaginative undertakings. Virtual land in Decentraland is characterized as an extraordinary, adaptable, and scant computerized resource put away in an Ethereum brilliant agreement and can be guaranteed on the blockchain-based record utilizing ERC20 (Ethereum Solicitation for Remarks 20) tokens called MANA. Figure 2.8 shows the Decentraland theme and logo.

Figure 2.8 Decentraland theme and logo.

Figure 2.9 Axie Infinity logo and theme.

2.8.2   Axie Infinity

Axie Vastness is a metaverse project that joins components of digital currency and Pokémon games, permitting players to gather, raise, breed, and fight dream animals called Axies to construct their Axies realms. This task is one of the spearheading Play-to-Procure metaverse projects, with a client driven economy framework like Decentraland and Sandbox that permits players to really possess, sell, purchase, and trade in-game assets through interactivity activities and biological system commitments. The blockchain-based financial arrangement of the Axie metaverse empowers players to work on their computerized resources by creating in-game capacities to a specific level, which separates it from other customary games. Players can take part in different play types (PvP: player versus player, and PvE: player versus climate) and take part in different rivalries while obtaining in-game assets for exchanging. Also, players can procure AXS tokens by making client produced content and partaking in different Axie Limitlessness Universe games, and they can utilize non-fungible tokens (NFTs) to buy, sell, and trade Axies creatures and other virtual properties on the in-game market. Figure 2.9 shows the Axie Infinity logo and theme.

2.9   Conclusion

Blockchain is a critical creating innovation that will be used in various ventures. The issues encompassing blockchain's business applications are pivotal for both social and scholastic practice, as we would see it. Understanding the components through which blockchain influences business and market productivity is the main urgent review region. Security and protection concerns are the subsequent conceivable review center. In the event that every industry has its own blockchain framework, analysts and engineers should track down better approaches to trade information.

Chiefs and region directors pursue most of critical decisions in conventional associations that follow the customary corporate construction, which are habitually risky and defective because of human blunder. A self-implementing convention is utilized by a gathering of mysterious individuals to share data in DAOs, the up and coming age of hierarchical designs, to tackle these issues. DAOs are overseen by blockchain-based shrewd agreement calculations that give expanded straightforwardness and moral soundness while bringing down exchange the executives costs. A blockchain organization's open-source, straightforward, and secure record fills in as the vault for a DAO's all's administration guidelines.

Strikingly, local symbolic partners can utilize their tokens to decide on recommendations through the DAO's agreement governs however are not permitted to change the standards. As to shared goals of investors, the changelessness of savvy contracts in DAOs would protect any controlled associations' monetary profit and different interests over a sealed common record, where all organization wide movement and exchanges will be 17 recorded. Later on, DAO, whose shrewd agreements and agreement rules will manage every key ability, will actually want to naturally create and keep up with administrations (for instance, DeFi) and items (for instance, NFT) in the metaverse.

References

1. Lee, Y., Moon, C., Ko, H., Lee, S.-H., Yoo, B., Unified representation for XR content and its rendering method, in: *The 25th International Conference on 3D Web Technology*, 25, pp. 1–10, 2020.
2. Lee, L.-H., Braud, T., Zhou, P., Wang, L., Xu, D., Lin, Z., Kumar, A., Bermejo, C., Hui, P., All one needs to know about metaverse: A complete survey on technological singularity, virtual ecosystem, and research agenda, 2021, arXiv preprint arXiv:2110.05352.
3. Kim, T. and Kim, S., Digital transformation, business model and metaverse. *J. Digit. Converg.*, 19, 11, 215– 224, 2021.
4. Guo, J., Ding, X., Wu, W., Reliable traffic monitoring mechanisms based on blockchain in vehicular networks. *IEEE Trans. Reliability*, 2021.

5. https://www.ibm.com/in-en/blockchain.
6. Gadekallu, T.R., Huynh-The, T., Wang, W., Yenduri, G., Ranaweera, P., Pham, Q.-V., da Costa, D.B., Liyanage, M., Blockchain for the metaverse: A review, arXivLabs-Cornell University, 2022.
7. Yang, Q., Zhao, Y., Huang, H., Xiong, Z., Kang, J., Zheng, Z., Fusing blockchain and AI with metaverse: A survey. *IEEE Open J. Comput. Soc.*, 3, 1–15, 2022.
8. Mishra, S., Arora, H., Parakh, G., Khandelwal, J., Contribution of blockchain in development of metaverse. *2022 7th International Conference on Communication and Electronics Systems (ICCES)*, pp. 845–850, Coimbatore, India, 2022.
9. Naik, U. and Shivalingaiah, D., Comparative study of Web 1.0, Web 2.0 and Web 3.0, *Proceedings of International CALIBER*, 2008, pp. 499–507, 2009.
10. Panda, S.K. and Satapathy, S.C., An investigation into smart contract deployment on ethereum platform using Web3.js and solidity using blockchain, in: *Data Engineering and Intelligent Computing*, Advances in Intelligent Systems and Computing, vol. 1, V. Bhateja, S.C. Satapathy, C.M. Travieso-González, V.N.M. Aradhya (Eds.), Springer, Singapore, 2021, https://doi.org/10.1007/978-981-16-0171-2_52.
11. Panda, S.K., Rao, D.C., Satapathy, S.C., An Investigation into the usability of blockchain technology in Internet of Things, in: *Data Engineering and Intelligent Computing*, Advances in Intelligent Systems and Computing, vol. 1, V. Bhateja, S.C. Satapathy, C.M. Travieso-González, V.N.M. Aradhya (Eds.), Springer, Singapore, 563–572, 2021, https://doi.org/10.1007/978-981-16-0171-2_53.
12. Panda, S.K., Dash, S.P., Jena, A.K., Optimization of block query response using evolutionary algorithm, in: *Data Engineering and Intelligent Computing*, Advances in Intelligent Systems and Computing, vol. 1, V. Bhateja, S.C. Satapathy, C.M. Travieso-González, V.N.M. Aradhya (Eds.), Springer, Singapore, 573–579, 2021, https://doi.org/10.1007/978-981-16-0171-2_54.
13. Nanda, S.K., Panda, S.K., Das, M., Satapathy, S.C., Automating vehicle insurance process using smart contract and ethereum, in: *Advances in Micro-Electronics, Embedded Systems and IoT*, Lecture Notes in Electrical Engineering, vol. 838, V.V.S.S.S. Chakravarthy, W. Flores-Fuentes, V. Bhateja, B. Biswal, (Eds.), Springer, Singapore, 237–247, 2022, https://doi.org/10.1007/978-981-16-8550-7_23.
14. Varaprasada Rao, K. and Panda, S.K., Secure electronic voting (E-voting) system based on blockchain on various platforms, in: *Computer Communication, Networking and IoT*, Lecture Notes in Networks and Systems, vol. 459, Satapathy, S.C., J.C.W. Lin, L.K. Wee, V. Bhateja, T.M. Rajesh, (Eds.), Springer, Singapore, 2023, https://doi.org/10.1007/978-981-19-1976-3_18.
15. Varaprasada Rao, K. and Panda, S.K., A design model of copyright protection system based on distributed ledger technology, in: *Computer Communication, Networking and IoT*, Lecture Notes in Networks and Systems, vol. 459,

S.C. Satapathy, J.C.W. Lin, L.K. Wee, V. Bhateja, T.M. Rajesh, (Eds.), Springer, Singapore, 2023, https://doi.org/10.1007/978-981-19-1976-3_17.

16. Panda, S.K., Elngar, A.A., Balas, V.E., Kayed, M., *Bitcoin and blockchain: History and current applications*, 1st ed., CRC Press, 1, 2020, https://doi.org/10.1201/9781003032588.

17. Panda, S.K., Jena, A.K., Swain, S.K., Satapathy, S.C. (Eds.), *Blockchain Technology: Applications and Challenges*, Intelligent Systems Reference Library, Springer, https://doi.org/10.1007/978-3-030-69395-4.

18. Sathya, A.R., Panda, S.K., Hanumanthakari, S., Enabling smart education system using blockchain technology, in: *Blockchain Technology: Applications and Challenges*, Intelligent Systems Reference Library, vol. 203, S.K. Panda, A.K. Jena, S.K. Swain, S.C. Satapathy (Eds.), Springer, Cham, 2021, https://doi.org/10.1007/978-3-030-69395-4_10.

19. Lokre, S.S., Naman, V., Priya, S., Panda, S.K., Gun tracking system using blockchain technology, in: *Blockchain Technology: Applications and Challenges*, Intelligent Systems Reference Library, vol. 203, S.K. Panda, A.K. Jena, S.K. Swain, S.C. Satapathy (Eds.), Springer, Cham, 2021, https://doi.org/10.1007/978-3-030-69395-4_16.

20. Panda, S.K., Daliyet, S.P., Lokre, S.S., Naman, V., Distributed ledger technology in the construction industry using corda, in: *The New Advanced Society: Artificial Intelligence and Industrial Internet of Things Paradigm*, https://doi.org/10.1002/9781119884392.ch2.

21. Panda, S.K., Mohammad, G.B., Nandan Mohanty, S., Sahoo, S., Smart contract-based land registry system to reduce frauds and time delay, in: *Security and Privacy*, p. e172, 2021, https://doi.org/10.1002/spy2.172.

22. Panda, S.K. and Satapathy, S.C., Drug traceability and transparency in medical supply chain using blockchain for easing the process and creating trust between stakeholders and consumers. *Pers. Ubiquit. Comput.*, 2021, https://doi.org/10.1007/s00779-021-01588-3.

23. Niveditha, V.R., Karthik Sekaran, K., Singh, A., Panda, S.K., Effective prediction of bitcoin price using wolf search algorithm and bidirectional LSTM on internet of things data. *Int. J. Syst. Syst. Eng.*, 11, 3-4, 224–236, 2023.

24. Sri Arza, M. and Panda, S.K., An integration of blockchain and machine learning into the health care system, in: *Machine Learning Adoption in Blockchain-Based Intelligent Manufacturing*, vol. 1, pp. 33–58, 2022.

25. Murala, D.K., Panda, S.K., Swain, S.K., A survey on cloud computing security and privacy issues and challenges. *Adv. Res. Dyn. Control Syst.*, 11, 1276–1290, United States, 2019.

26. Murala, D.K., Panda, S.K., Swain, S.K., Secure dynamic groups data sharing with modified revocable attribute-based encryption in cloud. *Int. J. Recent Technol. Eng. (IJRTE)*, 8, India, 2019.

27. Murala, D.K., Panda, S.K., Swain, S.K., A novel hybrid approach for providing data security and privacy from malicious attacks in the cloud environment. *J. Adv. Res. Dyn. Control Syst.*, 11, 1291–1300, United States, 2019.

28. Panda, S.K., Swain, S.K., Mall, R., An investigation into usability aspects of e-commerce websites using users' preferences. *Adv. Comput. Scie. An Int. J.*, 4, 65–73, 2015.
29. Panda, S.K., Swain, S.K., Mall, R., Measuring web site usability quality complexity metrics for navigability, in: *Intelligent Computing, Communication and Devices*, Advances in Intelligent Systems and Computing, vol. 308, L. Jain, S. Patnaik, N. Ichalkaranje, (Eds.), Springer, New Delhi, 2015, https://doi.org/10.1007/978-81-322-2012-1_41.
30. Panda, S.K., A usability evaluation framework for B2C e-commerce websites. *Comput. Eng. Intell. Syst.*, 5, 3, 66–85, 2014.
31. Bhalerao, V., Panda, S.K., Jena, A.K., Optimization of loss function on human faces using generative adversarial networks, in: *Machine Learning Approaches for Urban Computing*, Studies in Computational Intelligence, vol. 968, M. Bandyopadhyay, M. Rout, S. Chandra Satapathy, (Eds.), Springer, Singapore, 189–208, 2021, https://doi.org/10.1007/978-981-16-0935-0_9.
32. Panda, S.K. and Dwivedi, M., Minimizing food wastage using machine learning: a novel approach, in: *Smart Intelligent Computing and Applications*, Smart Innovation, Systems and Technologies, vol. 159, S. Satapathy, V. Bhateja, J. Mohanty, S. Udgata, (Eds.), Springer, Singapore, 2020, https://doi.org/10.1007/978-981-13-9282-5_44.
33. Panda, S.K., Sathya, A.R., Mishra, M., Satpathy, S., A supervised learning algorithm to forecast weather conditions for playing cricket. *Int. J. Innovative Technol. Exploring Eng. (IJITEE)*, 9 , 1, 2019.
34. Panda, S.K., Fraud-resistant crowdfunding system using ethereum blockchain, in: *Bitcoin and Blockchain*, pp. 237–276, 2020.
35. Panda, S.K., Mishra, V., Balamurali, R., Elngar, A.A., *Artificial intelligence and machine learning in business management concepts, challenges, and case studies*, pp. 1–278, 2021, https://doi.org/10.1201/9781003125129.
36. Joshi, S., Panda, S.K., AR, S., Optimal deep learning model to identify the development of pomegranate fruit in farms. *Int. J. Innovative Technol. Exploring Eng.*, 9, 3, 2352–2356, 2020.
37. Puranam, K.S.R., Gaddam, M.C.T., K, V.P.R., Panda, S.K., Reddy, G.S.M., Anatomy and lifecycle of a bitcoin transaction (February 18, 2019). *Proceedings of International Conference on Sustainable Computing in Science, Technology and Management (SUSCOM)*, Amity University Rajasthan, Jaipur - India, February 26-28, 2019, Available at SSRN: https://ssrn.com/abstract=3355106 or http://dx.doi.org/10.2139/ssrn.3355106.
38. Panda, S.K. and Swain, S.K., Quality assurance aspects of web design, in: *Design Solutions for Improving Website Quality and Effectiveness*, pp. 87–129, IGI Global, 2016.
39. Panda, S.K., Bhalerao, V., AR, S., A machine learning model to identify duplicate questions in social media forums. *Int. J. Innovative Technol. Exploring Eng.*, 9, 4, 370–373, 2020.

40. Ahmareen, S., Raj, A., Potluri, S., Panda, S.K., Book Shala: An android-based application design and implementation of sharing books, in: *Smart Intelligent Computing and Applications*, Smart Innovation, Systems and Technologies, vol. 159, S. Satapathy, V. Bhateja, J. Mohanty, S. Udgata, (Eds.), Springer, Singapore, 2020, https://doi.org/10.1007/978-981-13-9282-5_28.

41. Panda, S.K., Das, S.S., Swain, S.K., S-Model for service-oriented applications in web engineering. *Reg. Coll. Manag.*, 10, 3, 38–46, 2013.

42. Panda, S.K., An investigation into usability and productivity of ecommerce websites.

43. Panda, S.K., Chandrasekhar, A., Gantayat, P.K., Panda, M.R., Detecting brain tumor using image segmentation: A novel approach, in: *Data Engineering and Intelligent Computing*, Lecture Notes in Networks and Systems, vol. 446, V. Bhateja, L. Khin Wee, J.C.W. Lin, S.C. Satapathy, T.M. Rajesh, (Eds.), Springer, Singapore, 2022, https://doi.org/10.1007/978-981-19-1559-8_35.

44. Sanghi, P., Panda, S.K., Pati, C., Gantayat, P.K., Learning deep features and classification for fresh or off vegetables to prevent food wastage using machine learning algorithms, in: *Intelligent Data Engineering and Analytics*, Smart Innovation, Systems and Technologies, vol. 266, S.C. Satapathy, P. Peer, J. Tang, V. Bhateja, A. Ghosh, (Eds.), Springer, Singapore, 2022, https://doi.org/10.1007/978-981-16-6624-7_44.

45. Gantayat, P.K., Mohapatra, S., Panda, S.K., Secure trust level routing in delay-tolerant network with node categorization technique, in: *Intelligent Data Engineering and Analytics, Smart Innovation, Systems and Technologies*, vol. 266, S.C. Satapathy, P. Peer, J. Tang, V. Bhateja, A. Ghosh, (Eds.), Springer, Singapore, 2022, https://doi.org/10.1007/978-981-16-6624-7_45.

46. Panda, S.K., Urkude, S.V., Urkude, V.R., Vairachilai, S., An investigation into COVID 19 pandemic in India, in: *The New Advanced Society: Artificial Intelligence and Industrial Internet of Things Paradigm*, vol. 1, pp. 289–305, Wiley, 2022.

47. Panda, S.K., Das, S., Swain, S.K., Web site productivity measurement using single task size measure. *J. Inf. Sci. Comput. Technol. (JISCT)*, 4, 3, October 12, 2015.

48. Hanumanthakari, S. and Panda, S.K., Detecting face mask for prevent COVID-19 using deep learning: A novel approach, in: *Smart Intelligent Computing and Applications, Volume 2*, Smart Innovation, Systems and Technologies, vol. 283, S.C. Satapathy, V. Bhateja, M.N. Favorskaya, T. Adilakshmi, (Eds.), Springer, Singapore, 2022, https://doi.org/10.1007/978-981-16-9705-0_45.

49. Panda, S.K., Sathya, A.R., Das, S., Bitcoin: Beginning of the cryptocurrency era, in: *Recent Advances in Blockchain Technology*, Intelligent Systems Reference Library, vol. 237, S.K. Panda, V. Mishra, S.P. Dash, A.K. Pani, (Eds.), Springer, Cham, 2023, https://doi.org/10.1007/978-3-031-22835-3_2.

50. Murala, D.K., Panda, S.K., Sahoo, S.K., Securing electronic health record system in cloud environment using blockchain technology, in: *Recent Advances*

in Blockchain Technology, Intelligent Systems Reference Library, vol. 237, S.K. Panda, V. Mishra, S.P. Dash, A.K. Pani, (Eds.), Springer, Cham, 2023, https://doi.org/10.1007/978-3-031-22835-3_4.

51. Rao, K.V., Murala, D.K., Panda, S.K., Blockchain: A study of new business model, in: *Recent Advances in Blockchain Technology*, Intelligent Systems Reference Library, vol. 237, S.K. Panda, V. Mishra, S.P. Dash, A.K. Pani, (Eds.), Springer, Cham, 2023, https://doi.org/10.1007/978-3-031-22835-3_9.

52. Panda, S.K., Mishra, V., Dash, S.P., Pani, A.K., *Recent advances in blockchain technology real-world applications*, Intelligent Systems Reference Library, (ISRL, volume 237) vol. 1, pp. 1–317, 978-3-031-22835-3.

53. Panda, S.K., Mohapatra, R.K., Panda, S., Balamurugan, S., *The new advanced society: Artificial intelligence and industrial internet of things paradigm*, vol. 1, pp. 1–512, Wiley.

54. Nanda, S.K., Panda, S.K., Das, M., Satapathy, S.C., Decentralization of car insurance system using machine learning and distributed ledger technology, in: *Intelligent Data Engineering and Analytics. FICTA 2022*, Smart Innovation, Systems and Technologies, vol. 327, V. Bhateja, X.S. Yang, J. Chun-Wei Lin, R. Das, (Eds.), Springer, Singapore, 2023, https://doi.org/10.1007/978-981-19-7524-0_52.

55. Nanda, S.K., Panda, S.K., Dash, M., Medical supply chain integrated with blockchain and IoT to track the logistics of medical products. *Multimed. Tools Appl.*, United States, 2023, https://doi.org/10.1007/s11042-023-14846-8.

3

Blockchain in the Development of Metaverse

Dileep Kumar Murala[1] and Sandeep Kumar Panda[2*]

[1]Computer Science and Engineering, Faculty of Science and Technology, ICFAI Foundation for Higher Education, Hyderabad, Telangana, India
[2]Data Science and Artificial Intelligence, Faculty of Science and Technology, ICFAI Foundation for Higher Education, Hyderabad, Telangana, India

Abstract

The current buzzword, "metaverse", has garnered a lot of interest from both businesses and academics. The goal of the metaverse is to create an immersive virtual environment that will enable users to communicate with the online world and other users in real time, establish a virtual economic system, and increase the virtual space for human activities via the Internet. This will infuse new life into the social, economic, and other fields. Exploring the metaverse allows you to create an exciting digital environment and improve the physical world. In this paper, we review studies on state-of-the-art metaverse, digital currency, and blockchain-enabled technology and explain how these can be combined. Exploitation and transdisciplinary research on blockchain integration into the metaverse will require academic–business collaboration. In this chapter, we provide basic information about blockchain, the consensus algorithms for blockchain, the usage of blockchain in the metaverse, problems in the metaverse, how blockchain technology is useful for solving metaverse issues, and, finally, a conclusion with future directions. We hope this paper will be useful in guiding future metaverse development by scientists, engineers, and educators.

Keywords: Blockchain, metaverse, metaverse economy, layered architecture of blockchain, digital market, digital currency, non-fungible tokens

Corresponding author: drdileepm@ifheindia.org

Chandrashekhar A, Shaik Himam Saheb, Sandeep Kumar Panda, S. Balamurugan and Sheng-Lung Peng (eds.) Metaverse and Immersive Technologies: An Introduction to Industrial, Business and Social Applications, (71–96) © 2023 Scrivener Publishing LLC

3.1   Introduction

"Metaverse" is a virtual environment with a moral code and a different economic system related to the real world. In 1992's Snow Crash, Neal Stephenson defined "metaverse." In this novel, actual individuals use VR technology to create avatars that live in the metaverse. Since its creation, the metaverse has been a second life, 3D virtual environments, and life-logging. Most of the time, the metaverse is thought of as a total immersion, excitable, and conscience-shared virtual environment that brings together the physical, human, and digital [1, 19, 20]. The Metaverse is being used by more individuals as a result of technological advancements, and as more actions that are on par with reality are carried out, a variety of large amounts of data are being produced. The metaverse produces data that is valuable in and of itself. Data volume, value, and reliability are all growing in the Metaverse, as is the significance of security and reliability. For the Metaverse to ensure data dependability, blockchain technology is necessary. After the web and mobile Internet revolutions, the metaverse is considered a blueprint for the next internet. Digital natives can live a different life in the metaverse [2, 21–23].

In a metaverse environment, people can use smart devices like goggles and earbuds to access different virtual spaces, and they can use avatars to take part in different real and virtual activities like learning, traveling, and trading. Another way to put it is that a metaverse setting is a three-dimensional virtual world where avatars can be employed for social, cultural, and business objectives. Since they can offer more immersive experiences than current online environments, the metaverse environments are anticipated to be widely used. Numerous metaverse platforms, like Roblox, Minecraft, and Fortnite, have evolved in response to the growing popularity of the metaverse surroundings and offer virtual reality experiences with avatars. Currently, metaverse platforms use virtual environments and avatars to deliver a variety of services, including education, telecommuting, and gaming. To use platform services, users must register with the proper platform servers [3, 24, 25]. Then, smart devices can transmit physical data like gaze and Metaverseion data to the platform's servers. The platform servers use physical data to render avatars in real-time in a range of virtual situations. Avatars can also trade and talk on the platform server. As a result, users can express their actions and engage in a variety of activities in metaverse settings using their avatars [4, 26–28].

3.2 Related Work

Virtual reality technology could be implemented thanks to advancements in computer vision and graphics after the word "metaverse" first emerged in the book Snow Crash. The client-server Second Life platform, which was introduced in 2003, offers a metaverse environment. Users can take part in a variety of activities in Second Life, including creating avatars, going to virtual classes, and trading virtual goods. Maksymyuk, T., Gazda, J. *et al.* [13] presented illustrative metaverse research in 2007. They claimed to have a roadmap for the metaverse and defined it as having four main parts: AR, lifelogging, mirror worlds, and VR. Their metaverse research led to the creation of many platforms. Several metaverse gaming systems, such as Roblox, Fortnite, and Minecraft, have recently been released, enabling users to build their avatars and communicate with one another [14]. Catak, Murat Kuzlu, *et al.* [2] discuss existing virtual world technologies and list four characteristics of effective 3D virtual worlds (or metaverses): ubiquity, realism, scalability, and interoperability. Eight essential technologies that make up the metaverse are reviewed and examined by Sun, J. and Gan, W. [6] together with the prospects it presents from six user-centric aspects. Platforms for metaverse education have also lately been studied in terms of national policies, industrial projects, infrastructures, supporting technologies, VR, and the social metaverse. To give students an immersive education, The VoRtex platform was proposed by Jovanovic and Wangy, Y. *et al.* [16] in 2022 to offer an educational experience and enable collaborative learning activities in virtual spaces. To achieve decentralization and interoperability in metaverse environments, Panda, S.K. *et al.* [20] suggested utilizing blockchain technology around 2022. They claimed that data can be protected, stored, and shared via blockchain technology. Furthermore,

3.2.1 Blockchain

Blockchain is a decentralized ledger that provides immutability, authenticity, and auditability of transactions. Permissioned and permission-less Blockchains are two different types of Blockchain. Permissionless Blockchain like Bitcoin and Ethereum allow anybody to view, write, and reach an agreement [5, 29–31]. Keep in mind that anyone, even potentially dangerous adversaries, can freely enter or exit the network without authorization. Private permission blockchains (like Hyper ledger Fabric) and public permission blockchains are two types of permission blockchains. Private and public permission Blockchain limit writing and consensus. Here, a chosen collection of reliable nodes carry out the consensus process. Whereas private permission Blockchain limits who can access the data, public permission Blockchain makes it possible for anybody to do. So, in metaverse environments, we use a public permission blockchain to keep track of users' fake identities and public keys in a way that is open to everyone [6, 32, 33].

3.2.2 The Metaverse Economic System

The metaverse's most important element is its economics. From a more utopian standpoint, the metaverse ought to be interoperable so that users can exchange virtual goods like clothing or vehicles between different plat- forms. As shown in Figure 3.1, we will first outline the metaverse economic system in light of popular games and previous studies. The conventional economy will change as a result of the exploitation of the four components that make up the metaverse economic system: digital production, asset, market, and currency [7, 34].

Digital Creation: The metaverse is built on the concept of digital creation. The process of creation is comparable to the production of tangible goods in the physical world. The number of creators determines how the metaverse economy will grow. Digital creation requires a basic authoring tool to swiftly and distinctively create. The Builder and SDK are the Decentraland gaming platform's interactive app writing tools. Without needing to know any code, players can use the Builder to use a straightforward drag-and- drop editor, and the Decentraland SDK gives players enough flexibility to build their applications [8, 35].

Digital Asset: A requirement for trade, exists in digital assets. People's validation of digital assets is thus inextricably linked to the value that the blockchain and its encryption mechanism provide. Because consensus

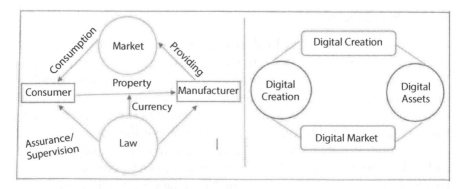

Figure 3.1 Traditional economy and metaverse economy.

techniques enable users to verify and confirm transactions, encryption algorithms can profit from data [9, 36–38].

The digital market: It is the primary location where avatars can trade to earn money just as in the real world. The mature metaverse market that will ensure that genuine trade and the manufacturing of items are performed in the metaverse must be distinct from the current digital market [10, 39, 40].

Digital currency: The medium in the metaverse known as "digital currency" allows avatars to complete transactions and exchanges. The metaverse legal money system is too expensive for fiat currency to meet its development needs. Fiat currency is converted from cash, unlike metaverse currency (such as gold and silver). The Wealth of Nations explains how real-world economics is founded on resource scarcity and self-interest. The people in the metaverse, on the other hand, are illogical and unselfish. These people favor highlighting their own emotions, such as happiness and a sense of accomplishment. This is because there are no traditional industrial structures in the virtual world, just as there are no farming societies or industrial societies that people can experience [11, 41, 42]. Metaverse economic activity will be dominated by the conceptual economy. Precious metals are becoming virtual social currency rather than natural financial currency. The following can be used to summarize the differences between the traditional economy and the economy of the metaverse:

- ✓ Production's marginal benefits will rise in the metaverse.
- ✓ The marginal costs of items will fall in the real world;
- ✓ Transactions are prevalent in the metaverse due to low transaction costs.
- ✓ These are all differences from the traditional economy, where undifferentiated labor decides the value.

Currently, the metaverse economy is still in its early stages because it is only just able to adopt and test new digital economy innovations like different digital currencies, sharing and cooperative economies, and inclusive finance. For an intelligent and safe metaverse, AI and blockchain should be combined. As a result, in the sections that follow, we review the relevant studies that may provide us with ideas [12, 43, 44].

3.3 Consensus Algorithms for Blockchain

Blockchain is a peer-to-peer network without a central hub, allowing all nodes to connect directly. Because it specifies how distributed nodes securely validate each transaction, the consensus algorithm is the crucial step in any blockchain network. The distributed ledger's records matching modifications are indicated by a transaction, which must be validated by many nodes. The distributed ledger must be updated by all nodes (or more than 51%) on the blockchain to reflect the current state, ensuring the immutability and security of every transaction [13, 45–47].

Selecting the best consensus method from the range of options is not an easy undertaking. The consensus method outlines how information is distributed among all nodes of the blockchain, how each node makes choices, and how a new block of validated transactions is added to the blockchain. In the next section, we will compare the most common consensus algorithms, like Proof-of-Work (PoW), Proof-of-Stake (PoS), and Byzantine Fault Tolerance (BFT), as well as their different versions, and how they can be used in the Metaverse [14, 48, 49].

3.3.1 Proof-of-Work (PoW)

The first and most well-known consensus algorithm is PoW. It is used in the blockchain of Bitcoin. The complicated cryptographic challenge (hash), which requires a lot of time and effort to solve, is the core concept of PoW. Mining is the process that is involved. The struggle for mining the following block is more likely to go to the nodes with the most processing power. Additionally, each block has a hash function from the preceding block, which links all of the blocks together. The system is protected by these features if there are enough blockchain nodes, as no one can accommodate enough computer power quickly enough to replace the falsified transactions with the real ones. Ethereum 1.0, Litecoin, Monero, etc. are the largest PoW blockchains after Bitcoin. While Proof-of-Work (PoW) is the most decentralized and secure consensus mechanism, it nevertheless has significant downsides, including low efficiency and high consumption of electricity. Therefore, in a decentralized Metaverse system, the suggested multi-flow service provisioning is incorrect [15, 50, 51].

3.3.2 Proof-of-Stake (PoS)

PoS has evolved as a consensus technique that uses less energy by substituting the validation phase for the mining process. As a result, validators (nodes) compete with one another based on their money stakes invested in the system rather than computing ability. Because the "richest" validator will win the competition, this type of strategy does not necessitate difficult computations. At first look, it could appear to be a hazardous choice because only the most affluent users would be able to afford to own 51% of the network's total stake, centralizing the entire blockchain and modifying transactions to their advantage. In terms of actual risk, a fund loss as a whole would result from this kind of attack. Aside from that, PoS picks validators at random from among all nodes that are eligible and stake a little amount of money. This extra security mechanism requires potential attackers to stake 51 percent of the overall stake and disperse it among more than 50 percent of the validation nodes. Therefore, a large and regularly used PoS blockchain like Ethereum 2.0, Polkadot, and Cosmos would be extremely unlikely to be the target of such an attack, whereas a very small blockchain would be vulnerable. PoS is a strong candidate for Metaverse applications because it offers substantially faster transaction throughput, far reduced latency, and infinite scalability through a sharing method [16, 52, 58].

3.3.3   Delegated Proof-of-Stake

Which replaces the PoS's large number of validators with a small number of delegates chosen by the vast majority of nodes, has emerged as a speedier variant of the PoS. This strategy reduces the minimum number of validators to a few nodes, enhancing transaction speed and blockchain latency. However, this results in a less decentralized structure, which reduces the security of the entire network. EOS, TRON, and Cardano are the three DPoS blockchains with the largest adoption [17, 53, 59].

3.3.4   Proof-of-Stake and Authority (PoSA)

PoSA, where validators are chosen by the central authority, is represented by PoSA consensus. Such a mechanism has clear disadvantages because it centralizes the entire network. However, this feature enables the system to scale up and attain a high throughput. Binance Smart Chain, the first and most popular PoSA implementation, creates a new block every three seconds.

3.4   Practical Byzantine Fault Tolerance (PBFT)

Another popular strategy is the consensus method known as Practical Byzantine Fault Tolerance (PBFT). Similar to DPoS, PBFT has primary and secondary nodes that are ordered sequentially. In PBFT, unlike DPoS, the secondary nodes should confirm the transaction and respond to the primary nodes. The primary node confirms the transaction if at least 2/3 of the secondary nodes do. If at least 2/3 of the primary 3 nodes approve the transaction, the consensus is then reached. Because of this, a Byzantine fault-tolerant blockchain in the real world can still operate properly even with up to one-third of malicious nodes. By adding more nodes, the PBFT blockchain becomes safer. The Hyperledger Fabric and the XRP Ledger are also the most popular PBFT implementations. The latter is typically thought to be the quickest way to establish CBDC (Central Bank Digital Currency), whilst the former has garnered significant interest for industrial IoT applications [11, 54, 60].

3.5   Blockchain in Metaverse

Because it can connect disparate minor sectors and give a solid economic system, blockchain is regarded as one of the metaverse's core infrastructures and helps supply the metaverse with laws that are transparent, open, effective, and dependable. For instance, the traceability and confidentiality of the data might be made available to users of the metaverse using hash algorithms and timestamp technologies, which make up the majority of the data layer of the blockchain. Figure 3.2 shows the typical Blockchain design including data, network, consensus, incentive, contract, and application layers [12, 55, 61].

✓ Data transmission and system verification methods provide the network with a variety of data transmission types and metaverse economic system verification.
✓ The credit issue with metaverse transactions is resolved via consensus procedures.

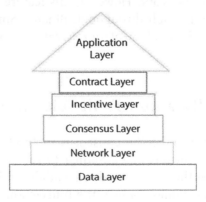

Figure 3.2 Layered architecture of blockchain.

✓ Distributed blockchain storage offers guarantees for user identities and the privacy of virtual assets.

✓ Metaverse cooperators can trust smart contract technology. It realizes the metaverse's pricing group activity and ensures that the system norms outlined in contract codes are followed in a clear and accountable manner. Once smart contracts are launched, their code cannot be altered. Every clause in these smart contracts must be fulfilled in full.

Blockchain technology is needed to value metaverse commodities and resources, especially when they interact with the actual economy. Therefore, it would be wise to investigate blockchain technology in the metaverse [13, 56].

3.5.1 Cryptocurrency for the Metaverse

What role do cryptocurrencies play in the metaverse? How can cryptocurrency be created and used in the metaverse? In light of these concerns, we analyze in this part whether the traditional cryptocurrency issuing rule holds for the metaverse. One of the key uses of blockchain technology that is currently in the spotlight is cryptocurrency. It also increases interest in blockchain. The value system of cryptocurrencies is supported by a broad base of user trust, which also fuels cryptocurrency circulation and trading [14, 57].

Value-adding cryptocurrency circulation, payment, and settlement are inevitable in the future metaverse, just as they are in the real world built on fiat currency. Specifically, blockchain-based systems have been used to implement several cryptocurrency-related functions, including creation, recording, and trading. The metaverse cannot exist without all of these essential operations. Ethereum tracks each account address's balance, which can be checked directly with the Ethereum dataset tools, while Bitcoin tracks bitcoin usage via the UTXO (Unspent Transaction Outputs) transaction model (e.g. Etherscan). Ethereum and UTXO employ PoW. Miners make money by producing blocks. Block generation requires a charge. Miners use a lot of electricity to solve hash puzzles to build blocks in a PoW consensus. According to the Proof-of-Stake (PoS) consensus method for Ethereum 2.0, miners choose which blocks to mine based on their coinage age [15].

There are several approaches to dealing with bitcoin exchanges using blockchain technologies. The great majority of exchanges for cryptocurrencies, like OKEX and AOFEX, are centralized. Low-latency transactions, easy-to-use interfaces, and a certain degree of security are some benefits of centralized exchanges. However, there are issues with centralized exchanges as well, like insiders manipulating prices by exploiting gaps in information. Other cryptocurrency exchanges take place on decentralized exchanges, where peer-to-peer networks or smart contracts automatically execute transactions. As a result, different cryptocurrencies utilized in those smaller metaverses must be traded, much like fiat money in the real world. We believe that the metaverse of the future will support a variety of coins. Users of the metaverse will inevitably need to swap various cryptocurrencies in the manner just mentioned [16].

3.5.2 Metaverse Transaction Characteristics

Financial issues relating to renting goods and services, purchasing real estate, and almost everything else that people do in the actual world are expected to exist in the metaverse. Consequently, token transfers and intra-metaverse situations are not the only transactions that can take place in the metaverse. Users' initial transactions are often broadcast to miners and stored in their transaction pools, as per the standard blockchain implementation [15]. The miner will carry out the hash-based consensus after accumulating a predetermined amount of transactions. The miner who generates an output satisfying the difficulty threshold initially creates the block. Once uploaded to the chain, the block is distributed to all other miners. Given the high number of users who conduct transactions in the virtual world every second using various intra- or inter-metaverse apps, blockchain nodes will handle a lot of metaverse transactions. Full blockchain nodes in the metaverse, as is customary, need to keep a copy of every transaction ever made on their local machines. This places a considerable burden on the entire nodes [1].

Low confirmation latency is a need for metaverse transactions, which is another problem. End-to-end latency for Internet applications that fulfill human behaviors is frequently between tens and hundreds of milliseconds. Furthermore, to prevent vertigo, metaverse apps that use three-dimensional displays and interaction need a delay of fewer than 10 milliseconds. All of those low-latency applications require transactions in the metaverse to have quick confirmation times [2].

The limitations of the current blockchain consensus protocols hinder their direct application to the metaverse. For example, the PoW technique depends on the hashing power of miners to reach consensus on a particular transaction data. The vast amount of data in the metaverse will necessitate extensive mining resources for PoW consensus. To obtain consensus on a proposed set of transactions, the Proof-of-Stake (PoS) mechanism uses the quantity and age of coins held by miner nodes. To reach a consensus, the PoS method relies on miners being completely fair and objective, but this is impossible in the metaverse, where the Matthew effect is much stronger. To achieve the strict requirements of transactions, the metaverse needs novel consensus methods and blockchain systems [3].

3.5.3   A Market in the Metaverse Powered by Blockchain

Before Ethereum, Blockchain like Bitcoin only supported the transfer of tokens. Smart contracts start to support Turing-complete programming before the development of the Ethereum platform. Smart contract codes could be used to run complex commercial operations in a virtual computer. Ethereum enables the transformation of cryptocurrency-based blockchain applications into crypto-businesses. Different blockchain-based market and business reconfiguration strategies could be used. Decentralized finance (Defi), enabled by cutting-edge blockchain technologies, can expand the decentralized market and industry in the metaverse. Here, we examine several illustrative studies about the Defi market and industry. Defi provides a fresh method for developing innovative economic models in the metaverse. It's built with fungible tokens and smart contracts (FT) [14]. Successful existing systems, like Uniswap, an Ethereum-based decentralized exchange (DEX), automatically give customers liquidity for their tokens. The CYB token is also distributed by Cybex. It's important to remember that CYB can only be used on the Cybex market for things like paying transaction fees, exchanging new tokens, and staking to borrow tokens representing crypto assets. The Diem Blockchain, which is run by a network of validator nodes, serves as the payment system's technological foundation. Because the blockchain implementation software is open-sourced, anyone can expand on it and grow it to meet their financial demands [4].

3.5.4   Utilizing Blockchain Validation in the Metaverse

The main sources of income in the metaverse at the moment are land development and leasing, gaming task rewards, and bitcoin investment gains. Auctions are also held for virtual assets like real estate, rare goods, and lands. As a result, the metaverse offers a novel funding scheme that blends elements of the offline and online worlds. But more recently, it has been fusing with the metaverse to build a brand-new digital content business. Non-fungible tokens (NFT) have typically been used to gather digital assets or remember significant occurrences. NFT keeps digital assets unique by storing encrypted transaction history on the blockchain. Identifying each token's unique value allows digital asset ownership. The avatar and other metaverse objects are unique, as shown by the blockchain-enabled NFT [5].

3.6   Blockchain Metaverse

The blockchain metaverse integrates the real and virtual worlds while putting a strong emphasis on a fully functional economy. The internet, augmented reality, and virtual reality are combined in the metaverse. With a focus on a fully functional economy, the blockchain metaverse merges the real and virtual worlds. That is not the only aspect of the blockchain metaverse, though. Additionally, it guarantees that users can go to various locations within the metaverse. The market value of cryptocurrencies is currently over $10 billion. Because cryptocurrencies can only operate on specific platforms, if something goes wrong, a multi-billion dollar industry might vanish. Non-fungible tokens (NFTs) provide a solution to this issue. NFTs can be produced and traded on open markets, and as they are under the ownership and control of a single user, there is no requirement for assistance or approval from centralized organizations. By connecting actual value to digital assets, they may bring about a great deal of revolution [6].

3.6.1   What Function Does the Blockchain Serve in the Metaverse?

Blockchain makes it easier to build the Metaverse, a foundational layer connecting various experiences and apps. The technology also facilitates the development of virtual collectibles like NFTs and utility token-based digital economies. But other factors make blockchain appropriate for the Metaverse. A digital economy, a means of establishing ownership over assets, and access to safe transfers of digital currencies or other valuables to participants are unavoidable if we were to conceive a digital version of our reality. It would also need to be consistently administered and accessible from many locations throughout the world [7].

Although it is still in its infancy, blockchain technology has the potential to enable all of the aforementioned activities. Crypto tokens are used to underpin virtual economies, while digital wallets like MetaMask are used to offer proof of ownership in the form of a digital record. Blockchain also makes it simple to access the Metaverse because anyone may use a public blockchain to create a wallet [8].

The technology also ensures asset ownership, which is a crucial function in a metaverse. A regular game's in-game things are susceptible to theft, but because an NFT has immutable ownership information, it cannot be taken or changed. Blockchain enables safe asset and currency transactions between various applications, which will eventually lead to a unified Metaverse [9].

3.6.2   Properties of the Metaverse Enabled by Blockchain

Blockchain technology enables a decentralized, persistent, social, and limitless metaverse. It is a cosmos that would keep changing as long as its inhabitants contributed to it with innovative ideas and various virtual activities.

Decentralized: Blockchain is fundamentally decentralized and independent of any one company or regulatory agency. Ownership is shared among all users of a blockchain-based Metaverse, who are in charge of their data. Blockchain-based metaverse transactions are transparent, auditable, secure, and immutable [13].

Persistent: A metaverse cannot be stopped or restarted like a game. It is a virtual existence in its most basic and full form that develops as a result of the combined efforts of all users. Anyone can join the Metaverse and contribute to the development and expansion of the virtual universe's shapes and forms.

Social: The needs of its participants will determine how the Metaverse develops. Users can produce original material, establish inventive methods of knowledge exchange, and share experiences through the usage of AI-driven avatars. In certain ways, the way we communicate might be challenged by a blockchain-based Metaverse. For instance, in the early Metaverse, there are already virtual concerts happening [12].

Boundless: Not to mention, a metaverse is limitless in the sense that it creates a connected universe with no restrictions on what is and is not conceivable. Thanks to the 3D virtual environment, the Metaverse may support any kind of activity, industry, and experience without any physical restrictions.

3.6.3   Why Blockchain is the Metaverse Core Technology

1. Hardware and software are the two major parts of any metaverse. Users may comfortably engage with virtual or augmented reality thanks to the hardware component, which incorporates all common controller kinds. In the case

of software, we're referring to a digital setting where the user has access to content.

2. Many industry professionals today agree that software should be created using blockchain technology, which refers to a secure decentralized database where independent nodes can connect in a single, continuously updated network [10].

3. It becomes evident that blockchain technology can meet the needs of the metaverse when you evaluate its most important components. Here is a list of them:

✓ **Security.** Secure transmission, synchronization, and storage issues are raised by the exabyte-scale data storage of the metaverse. According to this perspective, blockchain technology is particularly relevant due to the decentralization of data processing and storage nodes [11].

✓ **Trust.** Tokens, which are secure storage containers with the ability to transmit things like encoded private information, digital material, and authentication credentials, are a prerequisite for blockchain. The metaverse blockchain promotes higher user confidence in the ecosystem because sensitive data won't be available to outside users.

✓ **Decentralization.** For the metaverse to work effectively, everyone's virtual reality must be identical. Decentralized ecosystems built on the blockchain make it possible for thousands of independent nodes to synchronize.

Electronic contracts with the help of these, interactions among ecosystem participants inside the metaverse can be effectively governed in terms of financial, legal, sociological, as well as other aspects. Smart contacts also enable the creation and implementation of the fundamental elements for the government of the metaverse [18].

Interoperability. Blockchain enables the seamless and interoperable operation of multiple systems and interfaces. This is crucial in terms of NFT valuation and turnover.

Financial ties. Cryptocurrency can serve as a dependable replacement for fiat money because it is a crucial part of the blockchain. It can be used to settle disputes between parties in the metaverse.

4. It is evident that there are many problems associated with centralized ecosystems when it comes to the development and operation of the virtual world. These include malware,

hacking, and even centralized decision-making that affects how the metaverse works. However, the dangers are reduced with blockchain technology, making it feasible to create a reliable virtual ecosystem [12].

5. Blockchain technology is needed for the metaverse's essential elements, including electronic asset proofs, financial transactions, administration, transparency, and accessibility.

6. There are various methods to make money in the metaverse, including producing virtual property and buying and selling collections of metaverse NFTs [13, 62, 63].

Code for Blockchain: Based on its blockchain, Ethereum is a platform network intended to run numerous decentralized applications (DApps). RFCs were used to record the fundamental structure and specifics of Internet standards, and the Ethereum Request for Comment (ERC) does the same. DApps must follow the ERC-number protocol if they want to create tokens on the Ethereum network. The initials of Ethereum standard papers include ERC-20, ERC-165, ERC-223, ERC-621, ERC-721, ERC-777, ERC-827, ERC-884, ERC-998, ERC-1155, ERC-1404, and others [11]. One of them is the ERC-20 protocol, which is connected to replaceable tokens. ERC-20 tokens are interchangeable and have the same value and purpose. The Ethereum project issues ERC-20-compliant coins and enables various commercial and investing activities [14].

NFT uses the protocol ERC-721 (Non-Fungible Tokens). NFT makes a guarantee that each transaction is unique by keeping the encrypted transaction history forever on the blockchain. Every token has a unique recognition value that both serves to verify the legitimacy of digital assets and gives the transaction value. The main purposes of NFT have been to commemorate important events or to collect digital assets, but more recently, it has partnered with Virtual world to create a new digital entertainment firm [15].

Ethereum-based Metaverse: In the three-dimensional virtual environment known as the Metaverse, social and commercial interactions are commonplace, just like they are in the real world. NFT allows Metaverse communication and property. CryptoKitties uses NFT. Blockchain-based cat reproduction game. CryptoKitties is a DApp created using the ERC-721 token from Ethereum. In the game CryptoKitties, players are only given access to one cat worldwide. Because they differ from other virtual assets in having a distinct recognition value, cat digital assets are rare. Most online games have the issue that when the service is stopped, the character generated in the game can no longer be owned. NFT technology, however, enables users enrolled in the network to distribute and store digital assets to prove ownership [16].

Blockchain and VR helped Decentraland build Metaverse real estate. MANA, an ERC-20 token, allowed Decentraland users to own land. On land they have purchased from Decentraland, users are free to erect buildings as they choose, generate money by mounting billboards to buildings, or host exhibitions by gathering exclusive digital content. ERC-721 non-fungible tokens include collectibles and ownership of the real estate. Owners of these special assets may validate their ownership on the blockchain ledger thanks to Ethereum smart contracts, which are used to create them. MANA cryptocurrency can be bought on exchanges and used all around the world to pay for digital goods and services. Enjin Coin was created to trade in-game stuff. Ethereum-based smart contract platform. Enjin Coin protects all game items' ownership and value. Enjincoin can be used for Metaverse and real-world payments [17].

3.7 Obstacles and Unresolved Problems

We discovered through the prior review that blockchain is a key technology for the metaverse. We are conscious that the metaverse is still in its infancy, despite the technologies' potential to create a scalable, dependable, and effective metaverse. The difficulties, unresolved problems, and recommendations for the metaverses are thus covered in this section.

3.7.1 Unresolved Issues in the Metaverse's Digital Economy

Digital creativity in the virtual world may be limitless, unlike in the physical world. In the digital economy, identification rather than the uniformity of labor as in the traditional economy determines value. To help users create original material quickly and profitably at a low cost, authoring tools must be developed in the field of digital creation. These tools might increase the motivation of metaverse content creators. Instead of decreasing, the marginal gains of output in the physical world will increase in the metaverse. A value conversion mechanism is necessary to close the gap between the real and virtual worlds' disparate marginal benefits [1].

In the future, when corporations begin selling virtual skins, virtual clothing, and even virtual estates at high prices that will prevent a large number of players from joining the metaverse, people will prefer to select a digital outfit from their virtual wardrobe. Therefore, it is vital to suggest specific governance methods with the assistance of multinational corporations. How to create a metaverse-real-world digital currency system is also unclear [12].

3.7.2   Concerns with Blockchain

Even though blockchain technology has made significant advancements, merging blockchain with the metaverse still presents difficulties and unresolved problems. To encourage readers to seriously delve into the pertinent technical studies, we present several questions in the section below.

❖ Are real-world NFT platforms capable of handling metaverse transaction volumes? With blockchain technology, NFTs are special cryptographic tokens that are used. NFTs, digitalize physical objects like artworks and real estate by giving them non-reproducible properties. The NFT platforms available today, however, are still in their infancy. To support future metaverse apps' high traffic, NFT platforms must improve their service.

❖ What regulations are necessary for a thriving blockchain-powered digital market and economy in the metaverse? From a policy standpoint, the market for digital blockchain technology may benefit from a combination of decentralization and regulation. The DAO paradigm is recognized as a successful, decentralized, and promising paradigm that collaborates with like-minded individuals worldwide. DAO members each have their internal treasuries that can only be accessed with the group's consent. Smart contracts, which are transparent scripts that anybody can verify, are used to carry out DAOs. So that every person in the metaverse has a countable voice, decisions can be made via DAOs and governed by proposals and voting.

❖ Is it possible to immediately import the real-world blockchain-powered application paradigm into the metaverse? Today's massive cryptocurrency speculations and initial coin offering (ICO) scams have cast serious questions on the meaning of metaverse. The current blockchain-powered application models also fall short of the high throughput and low latency performance standards set by the metaverse.

❖ Is the metaverse going to demand new blockchain technologies and consensus mechanisms? Consensus building blocks like PoW and PoS are used in blockchain technology.

The present consensus algorithms, however, suffer from a significant amount of hash processing and a variety of security issues [3].

3.7.3   Metaverse Governance

Companies like Roblox and Metaverse are currently the leading users and proponents of the concept of the metaverse (Facebook previously). Naturally, these massive companies build and manage the most well-known ecosystems quite quickly. Tiny metaverse has a limited number of applications. On the other hand, all of the user-necessary scenarios would be present in the macro metaverse. Such a vision requires large firms to collaborate to create a broad, unified metaverse. But how are you going to convince those big corporations to cooperate? Once it has been established, how are universal rules for the entire united metaverse created? In the future metaverse, however, there will be risks related to market fraud and financial fraud. Thus, metaverse regional jurisdiction will value market governance more [4].

3.7.4   Metaverse Applications Powered by Blockchain

Numerous applications, including blockchain-enabled ones for social media platforms, administrative work, NFT markets, entertainment financing, etc., will strengthen the metaverse's virtual economy. Axie Infinity, a blockchain-based game, lets players fight, breed, and trade Axis. Players can transfer money from Ethereum to Ronin wallets using the Ronin Bridge. Players can buy ETH on Binance, Coinbase, or Ronin with fiat or cryptocurrency and have it transferred to their address. In other words, the game permits the interchange of fiat and cryptocurrency. Although some nations may not accept this blockchain-based game financing, we think that the metaverse of the future will embrace a much more transparent, equitable, and logical physical world [5].

3.7.5   Metaverse Privacy and Security

Privacy and security in the metaverse are important considerations from the perspectives of metaverse organizations, producers, and consumers together. Failure to do so could lead to privacy violations, identity theft, and other types of fraud.

The identity of virtual objects, bitcoin spending histories, and other private user data are only a few examples of the many private attributes in the metaverse that must be protected. Metaverse-oriented encryption techniques are hence unproven suggestions for the metaverse's privacy protection [6].

3.8   What Other Problems in the Metaverse Can Blockchain Help With?

In the preceding sections, we talked about the inescapable connection between blockchain and the metaverse. We will now see how blockchain aids in overcoming some potential difficulties in creating a metaverse environment.

3.8.1   Acquiring Transactional Data

❖ *Difficulties in the collecting of transactional data*
Since there will be tons of unstructured, real-time transactional data, the dependability and integrity of the services provided in the Metaverse might be determined by the quality of the data. The amount of data that will be gathered will be so massive that the data-collecting systems may become overburdened. Additionally, duplicate and erroneous data may accumulate, impairing the data's quality [1].

❖ *How does the blockchain approach the problem?*
Different applications will find it simpler to obtain verified and legitimate transactional data as a result of the distributed ledger in the blockchain validating the transaction records and tracing the metaverse data. Each block of data collected using blockchain technology is secured by including a cryptographic hash of the block before it, as well as a timestamp and metadata, making the data resistant to hacking. Thus, the unique validation process supported by multiple processes in blockchain technology prohibits data that is now being processed from being duplicated or altered. As a result, the data obtained in the Metaverse through the use of blockchain-enabled acquisition tools will be completely trustworthy [2].

3.8.2   Interoperability of Data

❖ *Data interoperability issues in the metaverse*
The transfer of a user's digital belongings, such as NFTs and avatars, from one digital environment to another is restricted. It is challenging to move to the virtual world

because of the lack of openness. For instance, it is not feasible to log into Roblox and Decentraland using the same account. The ability to govern the interactions across virtual worlds in an appropriate manner, which is a severe restriction of the conventional approach, is necessary for metaverse interoperability [3].

❖ *How blockchain addresses the problem?*
A cross-chain protocol that enables the exchange of goods like avatars, NFTs, and payments between the virtual worlds would be the ideal solution. Therefore, companies can use cross-blockchain technology to do away with the necessity for middlemen in the metaverse [4].

3.8.3   Data Privacy

❖ *Obstacles to maintaining privacy in the metaverse include:*
Personal information can be used by attackers to deceive other users. As a result, it is important to address the issue of protecting personally identifiable information. Although we corporate validity data in the metaverse. It would make managing enormous amounts of data more difficult and present new difficulties [5].

❖ *Blockchain's approach to the problem:*
The best way to safeguard sensitive data is to employ blockchain technology. By using private and public keys, users may manage their data. Therefore, it is prohibited for third-party intermediaries to misuse or get data from other parties. Additionally, Blockchain has a feature that lets data owners choose when and how third parties can access their data.

By implementing zero-knowledge proof on the blockchain, people can easily access identifying information that is crucial to the metaverse while also keeping their privacy and control over their belongings. The blockchain's zero-knowledge proofs mechanism allows users to convince others of something about them without revealing the information. Blockchain thus completely safeguards the privacy of sensitive data [6].

3.9   Conclusion and Future Research Directions

We aim to provide a thorough assessment to professionals from academia and industry by reviewing the most relevant works across metaverse components, digital currencies, and blockchain-enabled technologies. We also anticipated significant difficulties and unresolved problems when building the core components of the metaverse using blockchain technology. Collaboration between academics and business is necessary for further metaverse exploitation and multidisciplinary study to work toward an open, just, and logical metaverse of the future.

The Metaverse is a controversial Internet concept and cutting-edge technology. The Metaverse requires these technologies. The Metaverse needs AI to monitor information to stop hazardous information from spreading. A fully developed blockchain system, data computing (including edge and cloud computing), a 5G or 6G network, data transport, and virtual reality technologies are needed to store and validate identities. The Metaverse needs 3D rendering, XR, BCI, wearable tech, robots, and more. Despite their unimplementation, these technologies are evolving swiftly. Metaverse uses cutting-edge information technology to create a more open and immersive digital environment to assist Internet growth and digital economy modernization. This approach may dominate the digital economy's development. As it evolves, this idea will affect global politics, society, the economy, the global landscape, and international relations.

References

1. Nguyen, C.T., Hoang, D.T., Nguyen, D.N., Dutkiewicz, E., MetaChain: A novel blockchain-based framework for metaverse applications. *2022 IEEE 95th Vehicular Technology Conference (VTC2022-Spring)*, 2022.
2. Catak, F. O., Kuzlu, M., Catak, E., Cali, U., and Guler, O., Defensive distillation-based adversarial attack mitigation method for channel estimation using deep learning models in next-generation wireless networks, in: *IEEE Access, 10*, 98191–98203, 2022.
3. Xu, H., Li, Z., Li, Z. *et al.*, Metaverse native communication: A blockchain and spectrum prospective, 16 Mar 2022. arXiv:2203.08355v1 [cs.DC].
4. Chen, H., Lu, Y., Cheng, Y., consid, FileInsurer: A scalable and reliable protocol for decentralized file storage in blockchain, 24 Jul 2022. arXiv: 2207.11657v1 [cs.CR].
5. Kang, J. *et al.*, Blockchain-based federated learning for industrial metaverses: incentive scheme with optimal AoI, in: *IEEE International Conference on Blockchain (Blockchain)*, pp. 71–78, Espoo, Finland, 2022.
6. Sun, J. and Gan, W., Metaverse: Survey, applications, security, and opportunities, 14 Oct 2022. arXiv:2210.07990v1 [cs.DB].

7. Ryu, J., Son, S., Lee, J., Park, Y., Design of secure mutual authentication scheme for metaverse Environments using blockchain, in: *IEEE Access,* 10, 98944–98958, 2022.

8. Sun, X., Lu, Y., Sun, J., Matrix syncer - a multi-chain data aggregator for supporting blockchain-based metaverses, 8 Apr 2022. arXiv:2204.04272v1 [cs. MM].

9. Xu, M., Ng, W.C. *et al.*, A full dive into realizing the edge-enabled metaverse: Visions, enabling technologies, and challenges, 20 Aug 2022. arXiv: 2203.05471v2 [cs.NI].

10. Wang, Q., Li, R., Wang, Q., Chen, S. *et al.*, Exploring Web3 From the View of Blockchain, 17 Jun 2022. arXiv:2206.08821v1 [cs.CR].

11. Yang, Q. *et al.*, Fusing blockchain and AI with metaverse: A survey. *IEEE Open J. Comput. Soc.,* 3 122–136, 2022.

12. Park, S.-M. and Kim, Y.-G., A metaverse: Taxonomy, components, applications, and open challenges. *IEEE Access,* 10, 4209–4251, 2022.

13. Maksymyuk, T., Gazda, J., Bugár, G., Gazda, V., Liyanage, M., Dohler, M., Blockchain-empowered service management for the decentralized metaverse of things. *IEEE Access,* 10, 99025–99037, 2022.

14. Gadekallu, T.R. *et al.*, Blockchain for the metaverse: A review. *Future Gener. Comput. Syst.,* 143 401–419, 2022.

15. Wang, Y. and Zhao, J., Mobile edge computing, metaverse, 6G wireless communications, artificial intelligence, and blockchain: Survey and their convergence. ArXiv abs/2209.14147, 2022, n. pag.

16. Wang, Y. *et al.*, A survey on metaverse: Fundamentals, security, and privacy. *IEEE Commun. Surv. Tutor.,* 25, 319–352, 2022.

17. Cao, Z., Zhen, Y., Fan, G., Gao, S., TokenPatronus: A decentralized NFT anti-theft mechanism, 10 Aug 2022. arXiv:2208.05168v1 [cs.CR].

18. Wang, Z., Hut, Q., Xu, M., Jiang, H., Blockchain-based edge resource sharing for metaverse, in: *2022 IEEE 19th International Conference on Mobile Ad Hoc and Smart Systems (MASS)*, pp. 620–626, Denver, CO, USA, 2022.

19. Panda, S.K. and Satapathy, S.C., An investigation into smart contract deployment on ethereum platform using Web3.js and solidity using blockchain, in: *Data Engineering and Intelligent Computing, Advances in Intelligent Systems and Computing*, V. Bhateja, S.C. Satapathy, C.M. Travieso-González, V.N.M. Aradhya (Eds.), vol. 1, Springer, Singapore, 2021, https://doi.org/10.1007/978-981-16-0171-2_52.

20. Panda, S.K., Rao, D.C., Satapathy, S.C., An investigation into the usability of blockchain technology in Internet of Things, in: *Data Engineering and Intelligent Computing, Advances in Intelligent Systems and Computing*, V. Bhateja, S.C. Satapathy, C.M. Travieso-González, V.N.M. Aradhya (Eds.), vol. 1, Springer, Singapore, 2021, https://doi.org/10.1007/978-981-16-0171-2_53.

21. Panda, S.K., Dash, S.P., Jena, A.K., Optimization of block query response using evolutionary algorithm, in: *Data Engineering and Intelligent Computing, Advances in Intelligent Systems and Computing*, V. Bhateja, S.C. Satapathy,

C.M. Travieso-González, V.N.M. Aradhya (Eds.), Springer, Singapore, 2021, https://doi.org/10.1007/978-981-16-0171-2_54.

22. Nanda, S.K., Panda, S.K., Das, M., Satapathy, S.C., Automating vehicle insurance process using smart contract and ethereum, in: *Advances in Micro-Electronics, Embedded Systems and IoT*, Lecture Notes in Electrical Engineering, V.V.S.S.S. Chakravarthy, W. Flores-Fuentes, V. Bhateja, B. Biswal (Eds.), vol. 838, Springer, Singapore, 2022, https://doi.org/10.1007/978-981-16-8550-7_23.

23. Varaprasada Rao, K. and Panda, S.K., Secure electronic voting (E-voting) system based on blockchain on various platforms, in: *Computer Communication, Networking and IoT*, Lecture Notes in Networks and Systems, S.C. Satapathy, J.C.W. Lin, L.K. Wee, V. Bhateja, T.M. Rajesh (Eds.), Springer, Singapore, 2023, https://doi.org/10.1007/978-981-19-1976-3_18.

24. Varaprasada Rao, K. and Panda, S.K., A design model of copyright protection system based on distributed ledger technology, in: *Computer Communication, Networking and IoT*, Lecture Notes in Networks and Systems, S.C. Satapathy, J.C.W. Lin, L.K. Wee, V. Bhateja, T.M. Rajesh (Eds.), vol. 459, Springer, Singapore, 2023, https://doi.org/10.1007/978-981-19-1976-3_17.

25. Panda, S.K., Elngar, A.A., Balas, V.E., Kayed, M. (Eds.), *Bitcoin and blockchain: History and current applications*, (1st ed.), CRC Press, 2020, https://doi.org/10.1201/9781003032588.

26. Panda, S.K., Jena, A.K., Swain, S.K., Satapathy, S.C. (Eds.), *Blockchain Technology: Applications and Challenges*, Springer, Intelligent Systems Reference Library, https://doi.org/10.1007/978-3-030-69395-4.

27. Sathya, A.R., Panda, S.K., Hanumanthakari, S., Enabling smart education system using blockchain technology, in: *Blockchain Technology: Applications and Challenges*, Intelligent Systems Reference Library, S.K. Panda, A.K. Jena, S.K. Swain, S.C. Satapathy (Eds.), vol. 203, Springer, Cham, 2021, https://doi.org/10.1007/978-3-030-69395-4_10.

28. Lokre, S.S., Naman, V., Priya, S., Panda, S.K., Gun tracking system using blockchain technology, in: *Blockchain Technology: Applications and Challenges*, Intelligent Systems Reference Library, S.K. Panda, A.K. Jena, S.K. Swain, S.C. Satapathy (Eds.), vol. 203, Springer, Cham, 2021, https://doi.org/10.1007/978-3-030-69395-4_16.

29. Panda, S.K., Daliyet, S.P., Lokre, S.S., Naman, V., Distributed ledger technology in the construction industry using corda, in: *The New Advanced Society: Artificial Intelligence and Industrial Internet of Things Paradigm*, https://doi.org/10.1002/9781119884392.ch2.

30. Panda, S.K., Mohammad, G.B., Nandan Mohanty, S., Sahoo, S., Smart contract-based land registry system to reduce frauds and time delay, in: *Security and Privacy*, p. e172, 2021, https://doi.org/10.1002/spy2.172.

31. Panda, S.K. and Satapathy, S.C., Drug traceability and transparency in medical supply chain using blockchain for easing the process and creating trust

between stakeholders and consumers. *Pers. Ubiquit Comput.*, 2021, https://doi.org/10.1007/s00779-021-01588-3.

32. Niveditha, V.R., Sekaran, K., Singh, K.A., Panda, S.K., Effective prediction of bitcoin price using wolf search algorithm and bidirectional LSTM on internet of things data. *Int. J. Syst. Syst. Eng.*, 11, 3–4, 224–236.

33. Sri Arza, M. and Panda, S.K., An integration of blockchain and machine learning into the health care system, in: *Machine Learning Adoption in Blockchain-Based Intelligent Manufacturing*, vol. 1, pp. 33–58, 2022.

34. Murala, D.K., Panda, S.K., Swain, S.K., A survey on cloud computing security and privacy issues and challenges. *J. Adv. Res. Dyn. Control Syst.*, 11, 1276–1290, 2019.

35. Murala, D.K., Panda, S.K., Swain, S.K., Secure dynamic groups data sharing with modified revocable attribute-based encryption in cloud. *Int. J. Recent Technol. Eng. (IJRTE).*, 8, 4, 9508–9512, 2019.

36. Murala, D.K., Panda, S.K., Swain, S.K., A novel hybrid approach for providing data security and privacy from malicious attacks in the cloud environment. *J. Adv. Res. Dyn. Control Syst.*, 11, 1291–1300, 2019.

37. Panda, S.K., Swain, S.K., Mall, R., An investigation into usability aspects of E-Commerce websites using users' preferences. *Adv. Comput. Sci.: An Int. J.*, 4, 1, 65–73, 2015.

38. Panda, S.K., Swain, S.K., Mall, R., Measuring web site usability quality complexity metrics for navigability, in: *Intelligent Computing, Communication and Devices*, Advances in Intelligent Systems and Computing, L. Jain, S. Patnaik, N. Ichalkaranje (Eds.), vol. 308, Springer, New Delhi, 2015, https://doi.org/10.1007/978-81-322-2012-1_41.

39. Panda, S.K., A usability evaluation framework for B2C e-commerce websites. *Comput. Eng. Intell. Syst.*, 5, 3, 66–85, 2014.

40. Bhalerao, V., Panda, S.K., Jena, A.K., Optimization of loss function on human faces using generative adversarial networks, in: *Machine Learning Approaches for Urban Computing*, Studies in Computational Intelligence, vol. 968, M. Bandyopadhyay, M. Rout, S. Chandra Satapathy (Eds.), Springer, Singapore, 2021, https://doi.org/10.1007/978-981-16-0935-0_9.

41. Panda, S.K. and Dwivedi, M., Minimizing food wastage using machine learning: A novel approach, in: *Smart Intelligent Computing and Applications*, Smart Innovation, Systems and Technologies, S. Satapathy, V. Bhateja, J. Mohanty, S. Udgata, (Eds.), vol. 159, Springer, Singapore, 2020, https://doi.org/10.1007/978-981-13-9282-5_44.

42. Panda, S.K., AR, S., Mishra, M., Satpathy, S., A supervised learning algorithm to forecast weather conditions for playing cricket. *Int. J. Innovative Technol. Exploring Eng. (IJITEE)*, 9, 1, 1560–1565, 2019.

43. Panda, S.K., Fraud-Resistant Crowdfunding System Using Ethereum Blockchain, in: *Bitcoin and Blockchain*, pp. 237–276, 2020.

44. Panda, S.K., Mishra, V., Balamurali, R., Elngar, A.A., *Artificial intelligence and machine learning in business management concepts, challenges, and case studies*, pp. 1–278, https://doi.org/10.1201/9781003125129.

45. Joshi, S., Panda, S.K., AR, S., Optimal deep learning model to identify the development of pomegranate fruit in farms. *Int. J. Innovative Technol. Exploring Eng.*, 9, 3, 2352–2356, 2020.

46. Puranam, K.S.R., Gaddam, M.C.T., K, V.P.R., Panda, S.K., Reddy, G.S.M., Anatomy and lifecycle of a bitcoin transaction (February 18, 2019). *Proceedings of International Conference on Sustainable Computing in Science, Technology and Management (SUSCOM)*, Amity University Rajasthan, Jaipur - India, February 26-28, 2019, Available at SSRN: https://ssrn.com/abstract=3355106orhttp://dx.doi.org/10.2139/ssrn.3355106.

47. Panda, S.K. and Swain, S.K., *Quality assurance aspects of web design, design solutions for improving website quality and effectiveness*, pp. 87–129, IGI Global, 2016.

48. Panda, S.K., Bhalerao, V., AR, S., A machine learning model to identify duplicate questions in social media forums. *Int. J. Innovative Technol. Exploring Eng.*, 9, 4, 370–373, 2020.

49. Ahmareen, S., Raj, A., Potluri, S., Panda, S.K., Book Shala: An android-based application design and implementation of sharing books, in: *Smart Intelligent Computing and Applications, Smart Innovation, Systems and Technologies*, S. Satapathy, V. Bhateja, J. Mohanty, S. Udgata (Eds.), vol. 159, Springer, Singapore, 2020, https://doi.org/10.1007/978-981-13-9282-5_28.

50. Panda, S.K., Das, S.S., Swain, S.K., S-model for service-oriented applications in web engineering. *Reg. Coll. Manag.*, 10, 3, 38–46, 2013.

51. Panda, S.K., *An investigation into usability and productivity of ecommerce websites*.

52. Panda, S.K., Chandrasekhar, A., Gantayat, P.K., Panda, M.R., Detecting brain tumor using image segmentation: A novel approach, in: *Data Engineering and Intelligent Computing*, Lecture Notes in Networks and Systems, V. Bhateja, L. Khin Wee, J.C.W. Lin, S.C. Satapathy, T.M. Rajesh (Eds.), vol. 446, Springer, Singapore, 2022, https://doi.org/10.1007/978-981-19-1559-8_35.

53. Sanghi, P., Panda, S.K., Pati, C., Gantayat, P.K., Learning deep features and classification for fresh or off vegetables to prevent food wastage using machine learning algorithms, in: *Intelligent Data Engineering and Analytics, Smart Innovation, Systems and Technologies*, S.C. Satapathy, P. Peer, J. Tang, V. Bhateja, A. Ghosh (Eds.), vol. 266, Springer, Singapore, 2022, https://doi.org/10.1007/978-981-16-6624-7_44.

54. Gantayat, P.K., Mohapatra, S., Panda, S.K., Secure trust level routing in delay-tolerant network with node categorization technique, in: *Intelligent Data Engineering and Analytics, Smart Innovation, Systems and Technologies*, S.C. Satapathy, P. Peer, J. Tang, V. Bhateja, A. Ghosh, (Eds.), vol. 266, Springer, Singapore, 2022, https://doi.org/10.1007/978-981-16-6624-7_45.

55. Panda, S.K., Urkude, S.V., Urkude, V.R., Vairachilai, S., An investigation into COVID 19 pandemic in India, in: *The New Advanced Society: Artificial Intelligence and Industrial Internet of Things Paradigm*, vol. 1, Wiley.

56. Panda, S., Das, S., Swain, S., Web site productivity measurement using single task size measure. *J. Inf. Sci. Comput. Technol.*, 4, 3, 347–353, 2015.

57. Hanumanthakari, S. and Panda, S.K., Detecting face mask for prevent covid-19 using deep learning: A novel approach, in: *Smart Intelligent Computing and Applications, Volume 2*, Smart Innovation, Systems and Technologies, S.C. Satapathy, V. Bhateja, M.N. Favorskaya, T. Adilakshmi, (Eds.), vol. 283, Springer, Singapore, 2022, https://doi.org/10.1007/978-981-16-9705-0_45.

58. Panda, S.K., Sathya, A.R., Das, S., Panda, S.K., Mishra, V., Dash, S.P., Pani, A.K., Bitcoin: Beginning of the cryptocurrency era, in: *Recent Advances in Blockchain Technology. Intelligent Systems Reference Library*, vol. 237, Springer, Cham, 2023, https://doi.org/10.1007/978-3-031-22835-3_2.

59. Murala, D.K., Panda, S.K., Sahoo, S.K., Securing electronic health record system in cloud environment using blockchain technology, in: *Recent Advances in Blockchain Technology*, Intelligent Systems Reference Library, S.K. Panda, V. Mishra, S.P. Dash, A.K. Pani, (Eds.), vol. 237, Springer, Cham, 2023, https://doi.org/10.1007/978-3-031-22835-3_4.

60. Rao, K.V., Murala, D.K., Panda, S.K., Blockchain: A study of new business model, in: *Recent Advances in Blockchain Technology*, Intelligent Systems Reference Library, S.K. Panda, V. Mishra, S.P. Dash, A.K. Pani, (Eds.), vol. 237, Springer, Cham, 2023, https://doi.org/10.1007/978-3-031-22835-3_9.

61. Panda, S.K., Mishra, V., Dash, S.P., Pani, A.K., *Recent advances in blockchain technology real-world applications*, Intelligent Systems Reference Library (ISRL, volume 237), vol. 1, pp. 1–317, 978-3-031-22835-3, .

62. Panda, S.K., Mohapatra, R.K., Panda, S., Balamurugan, S., *The new advanced society: Artificial intelligence and industrial internet of things paradigm*, vol. 1, pp. 1–512, Wiley.

63. Nanda, S.K., Panda, S.K., Das, M., Satapathy, S.C., Decentralization of car insurance system using machine learning and distributed ledger technology, in: *Intelligent Data Engineering and Analytics, FICTA 2022. Smart Innovation, Systems and Technologies*, V. Bhateja, X.S. Yang, J. Chun-Wei Lin, R. Das, (Eds.), vol. 327, Springer, Singapore, 2023, https://doi.org/10.1007/978-981-19-7524-0_52.

4

Revolution of the Metaverse and Blockchain Technology

Sandeep Kumar Panda

Department of Data Science and Artificial Intelligence, Faculty of Science and Technology, ICFAI Foundation for Higher Education, Hyderabad, Telangana, India

Abstract

A Google Trends search revealed that 'non-fungible tokens (NFTs)' and the 'metaverse' were some of the most popular tech terms in 2021. It is broadly acknowledged that the metaverse is a fully realized virtual environment that serves as the hub for all kinds of activities in business, education, and leisure. The metaverse, which is depicted in literature, film, and video games, has the potential to not only complement real-world experiences but also significantly replace them. Blockchain technology, along with many other technologies, is used to quickly implement the newest technologies in the metaverse, a digital virtual environment where you can safely and freely engage in social and economic activities that go beyond the bounds of the actual world. By implementing blockchain technology, resource trades, data storage, and other activities might be made fair and secure. Our review aims to describe the metaverse and its reliance on blockchain technology and components of blockchain technology such as data acquisition, data interoperability, data storage, and privacy and security. This chapter also provides insight into the preliminaries of metaverse and blockchain and the overview of blockchain applications in the metaverse.

Keywords: Web 3.0, metaverse, NFTs, decentralization, smart contracts, cryptocurrency, blockchain technology

Email: sandeeppanda@ifheindia.org

Chandrashekhar A, Shaik Himam Saheb, Sandeep Kumar Panda, S. Balamurugan and Sheng-Lung Peng (eds.) *Metaverse and Immersive Technologies: An Introduction to Industrial, Business and Social Applications*, (97–126) © 2023 Scrivener Publishing LLC

4.1   Introduction

The terms Metaverse, Blockchain, and NFTs are a few of the most searched and spoken about topics of this generation. All these technologies exist due to the development of the internet and hardware devices which lead to increased computational power. The Internet quickly evolved from a small collection of services, such as email reading and web page browsing, to a highly broad and complex service based on connectivity that places individuals in a spatial and temporal context. Email and one-on-one interactions are no longer the only modes of communication available on the Web. An individual has a wide range of alternatives for exteriorizing thoughts, feelings, sentiments, and ideas in the present and in a selected manner [36, 45]. A crucial component of what's being hyped as "web3," or third generation of the internet, which follows the world wide web which is web1 and social media which comes under web2. With the use of virtual and augmented reality (VR/AR), which combine to create 3D environments, this next iteration of the internet is intended to be more engaging and experiential [3].

Web 1.0, commonly referred to as the informational web, is the first generation of the internet which was prevalent from around 1991 until 2004. Information on web pages can only be read and shared by users. Websites can display information thanks to the Content Delivery Network (CDN) of Web 1.0. One can use it as their own personal webpage. Here, users can simply read information; they are unable to engage with the pages' content. Web1.0 was built entirely on the client-pull model (HTTP), which can only be initiated by the client, and does not permit two-way communication [45]. Few authors and many readers made up web 1.0, which slowed down the network and left the users famished for resources.

Worldwide websites that emphasize user-generated content, usability, and interoperability for end users are referred to as "Web 2.0." In contrast to web 1.0, web 2.0 allows users to collaborate and gain collective intelligence by enabling them to produce, change, and update material online. Instead than referring to any specific technical advancement, "Web 2.0" describes a change in how people utilize the internet. Another name for Web 2.0 is the social participatory web. Web 2.0 is the era of centralization, during which a significant portion of communication and trade occurs on closed platforms that are held by a small number of extremely powerful businesses. Major Web 2.0 features enable users to categories and locate dynamic information that flows back and forth between site owners and site users via assessment, comments, and reviews. One can assume that an improved version of Web 1.0 is Web 2.0 [37, 38]. Figure 4.1 shows the evolution of the web.

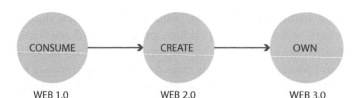

Figure 4.1 Evolution of the web.

The web was divided into many versions due to distinct stages of evolution. According to some, the Web 3.0 stage is the point at which the internet offers the conditions needed for people and organizations to use information in ways that encourage the flow of material, irrespective of the devices and networks [44]. Web 3.0 can be looked at as transforming the Web into a database with the incorporation of DLT (a blockchain is an example of distributed ledger technology), and that data can assist in the creation of Smart Contracts tailored to the needs of the individual [39, 46]. The fundamental ideas of decentralization, openness, and increased consumer usefulness form the foundation of Web 3.0. Decentralization and permission less systems, two key components of Web 3.0, will also allow users far more control over their personal data. Online content, digital assets, and the online identities of users are within their control and ownership. Now the major question among the public is what exactly is the Metaverse and how is it related to web 3.0.

METAVERSE as stated by various intelligent minds is the next inevitable step in the evolution of the internet. The term metaverse originates from Snow Crash, a science fiction novel written by Neal Stephenson [1]. The book represents the metaverse as a second, computer-generated virtual reality world that individuals from all around the world could connect to and access using goggles and earphones. The metaverse roadmap overview team has established that the metaverse mainly encompasses four scenarios-augmented reality, lifelogging, virtual worlds, and mirror worlds [2, 40, 41]. The Metaverse is envisioned as a 3D immersive world where we will spend a lot of time socializing, working, amusing ourselves, learning, etc., it is not yet a tangible reality yet. It combines various technologies, including social media, gaming, virtual reality (VR), augmented reality (AR), and mixed reality (MR). By converting from 2D to 3D, the Metaverse offers users a new way to interact with the internet. Web content is turned into three-dimensional objects so that users can interact with it in three dimensions rather than simply clicking and paging through multiple pages and tabs on 2D screens on desktops or mobile devices. Numerous businesses that have jumped on the metaverse bandwagon also have plans for a brand-new digital economy in which users will be able to produce, purchase, and sell items. Leading tech companies are embracing the metaverse craze. Tech powerhouses like Microsoft and Meta aren't the only ones developing technology for interfacing with virtual worlds. Numerous other significant corporations, such as Nvidia, Unity and Roblox are setting up the necessary framework to build better virtual worlds that more closely resemble our real world. Nonfungible Tokens (NFTs) from consumer brands like Gucci and Coca-Cola are being sold on metaverse marketplaces like Decentraland. Additionally, Nike and Roblox collaborated on "Nikeland," a virtual environment where Nike fans can play games, interact, and outfit their avatars in clothing. Samsung, a major technology company, opened its first store in the metaverse in Decentraland in January 2022. Not just tech and consumer companies but the decentralized nature of web3 and Metaverse has won over many musicians. Lil Nas X performed four times over the course of two days for a 33 million-person crowd in one of the earliest Roblox virtual concerts. There were 27.7 million Fortnite players who watched Ariana Grande's Rift Tour [42–45, 47]. NFTs allow artists the chance to have more control over their professional futures. They make it possible for musicians and artists to interact with their listeners and have more control over their music and image. As stated by Roblox's vice president of product management, Metaverse is "not just about taking money out of the ecosystem, it's also about using the same virtual currency and spending it across the ecosystem." The metaverse cannot be controlled by a single organization; rather, a constellation of businesses, groups, and individual innovators working together under some set rules and guidelines will likely emerge. Where exactly does Web3 come into the picture? The most ideal Metaverse is the one where no single entity controls the data and assets of users in this "open and decentralized" metaverse. This is majorly where Web 3.0 comes into the picture i.e., it might provide the Metaverse's foundation for connectivity. On the other side, the Metaverse's creator economy can complement Web 3.0's ambition by creating an entirely new financial system through the use of decentralized solutions. Blockchain technology and ideas, such as digital identification, smart contracts, and decentralized apps, are the focus of Web3. This chapter further discusses how blockchain technology acts as one of the pillars in realizing the Metaverse.

4.2   Blockchain

In recent times Blockchain technology has gained immense popularity. It can also be said that Blockchain is the newest buzzword, and practically all Fintech enthusiasts and professionals are discussing its potential on a worldwide scale. Blockchain technology was initially introduced as the backbone technology of Bitcoin in the whitepaper written by Satoshi Nakamoto in 2008. Blockchain can be defined as a public ledger that stores all transactions made in a chain of blocks. Each block in the blockchain has a cryptographic hash similar to the fingerprint of a human being that is unique to every human. The previous block's hash links all blocks in the blockchain. The chain expands as new blocks are appended to it. One of the machines that run the blockchain's software to verify and store the whole history of transactions on the network is referred to as a node. Each node on the blockchain network has the entire blockchain on its system. Blockchain technology operates on peer-to-peer protocol also known as P2P protocol i.e., each node serves as a server, eliminating the need for a network's central server, therefore, making it a decentralized network which is one of the primary reasons blockchain technology is favored. A block in a blockchain network consists of cryptographic hashes – both parent block and Merkle tree, timestamp, nonce, and transaction data [4, 46, 47].

To establish trust and reliability among the nodes, all the peers in the network reach an agreement about the present state of the data in the network such as verification and addition of new blocks using a consensus mechanism which is a method for helping a decentralized network reach consensus on specific issues [5]. A blockchain update protocol is said to attain consensus if the following four criteria are satisfied: Validity, agreement, liveness, and total order [6, 48–50]. The famous cryptocurrency Bitcoin implements Proof of work also known as PoW protocol to reach consensus. In order to authenticate PoW, a challenging computational technique is needed. In POW, each node in the network computes a hash value of the block header, which is continually updating. According to the consensus, the estimated value must be less than or equal to a specific given value. To reach the aim of the decentralized network, all members must continuously calculate the hash value using various nonces. All other nodes must mutually verify the accuracy of the value when one node obtains the pertinent value. Then, in the event of fraud, the transactions in the new block would be verified. Then, a new block is added to the blockchain to represent the authenticated result, which was determined from the collection of transactions utilized for the calculations. The POW mechanism is known as mining, and the nodes that calculate the hashes are known as miners. An incentive system is necessary since calculating the authentication takes time. For bitcoin, the incentive is in form of a block reward. The amount of Bitcoin awarded for each block that is cleared and added to the blockchain is known as the block reward. The system is designed in such a way that the block reward for the miners is said to be halved every four years or 2016 blocks mined. The Last halving happened in 2020 and, as of then for every block a miner solves, they are rewarded with 6.25 bitcoins. Figure 4.2 shows the flow of proof of work protocol.

Another prominent consensus mechanism is known as the Proof of Stake protocol or PoS. The blockchain revolution around the globe was primarily sparked by Proof of work, however, due to the nature of proof of work, a crypto-currency is dependent on energy consumption, introducing considerable operating costs that are passed on to users in the form of inflation and transaction fees [7]. Proof of Work enables consensus on the next block to add by asking network users to invest a significant amount of time and energy in creating new valid blocks. On the other hand, proof of stake utilizes less energy than proof of work while performing the same function for which it was designed. However, PoS requires users to stake cryptocurrency as collateral in order to add a new block to the block-chain-based digital record. Users staking cryptocurrency are known as validators. These validators are chosen pseudo- randomly by the algorithm. The system ensures the validator's honesty by using the staked cryptocurrency i.e., can be destroyed if the validator behaves dishonestly or lazily [8]. When a predetermined number of validators confirm that a block is accurate, it is finalized and closed.

There are many other important consensus mechanisms such as delegated proof of stake, proof of burn, Practical Byzantine fault tolerant Mechanisms, etc. All of these mechanisms are used in different block-chains as per the requirement of the network to ensure a safe, secure, and tamper-free network.

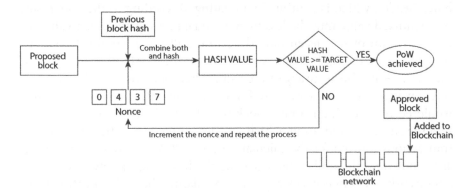

Figure 4.2 The flow of proof of work protocol.

A blockchain network is majorly comprised of four layers i.e., L0 is the primary layer and this is where the hardware, internet, and connections exist. Next, come the L1s, Blockchains that are considered layer 1s, such as Bitcoin and Ethereum, process and complete transactions on their own blockchain [51–53]. Consensus (PoW, PoS) and all the technical aspects, such as block time and dispute resolution, take place here. L2 solutions are the overlapping networks that are positioned above the base layer. Integrations with third parties are utilized in conjunction with layer one to boost scalability and the number of transactions per second at layer 2. Layer three, or L3, is frequently used to refer to the application layer. The L3 projects serve as a user interface while hiding the communication channel's technical details. Blockchains' real-world usability is a result of L3 applications. The metaverse applications such as Decentraland, cryptokitties, etc. which will be discussed in further sections are all L3 Dapps.

A few important concepts in Blockchain technology are:

4.2.1 Distributed Architecture

In a distributed system, two or more nodes collaborate with one another to achieve a common goal. The model is constructed so that end users perceive the system as a single logical platform. The blockchain is replicated on each node in the network and updated in real-time whenever a transaction occurs thanks to distributed computing. Blockchain is made secure, transparent, and irreversible through the use of distributed computing and peer-to-peer architecture, both of which eliminate the need for a central authority to run the network. As each node must connect with its neighbor node in order to reach a consensus decision, distributed computing is crucial to maintaining this consensus protocol [54, 55].

4.2.2 Tokens

Tokens are digital assets created on a particular blockchain and defined by a project or smart contract. Tokens come in utility and security varieties. Consumer or incentive tokens are other names for utility tokens [43]. Tokens represent commodities or assets that can be traded and live on their own blockchains. Although crowd sales are commonly financed with cryptocurrency tokens, they can also be used in other scenarios. Cryptocurrencies are frequently used as the basis for transactions on blockchains built using standardized templates, such as the Ethereum network, which enables the creation of tokens. These blockchains work on the basis of "smart contracts" or "decentralized apps," in which the various transactions that occur on the ledger are processed and handled using programmable, self-executing programming. There are certain standards followed by the Ethereum blockchain to generate a token such as, the technical standard for fungible tokens produced on the Ethereum network is called ERC-20. Contrary to the well-established non-fungible tokens (NFTs), which cannot be done so, a fungible token is one that can be traded for another token. A sort of token is distinct and may have a different value from another token from the same Smart Contract thanks to the introduction of the NFT standard in the ERC-721. ERC-777 is a fungible token standard improving the existing ERC-20 standard [44, 56].

4.3   The Metaverse

As established in section 4.1, Metaverse is a virtual world where users can communicate with each other and a computer-generated environment through a virtual reality headset and can navigate through the world through specially designed technologies, the user can feel the physical sensation of being in the computer- generated universe. One can assume that Metaverse is a virtual world where one can find all physical things, services, friends and family, buildings, world maps, and the Universe there.

According to [9] the metaverse architecture designed by Pietro [10] can be majorly classified into seven layers as shown in Figure 4.3.

As shown in Figure 4.4, the seven layers of the Metaverse are namely:

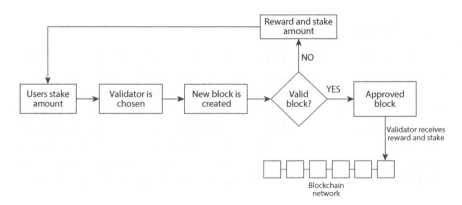

Figure 4.3 The flow of proof of stake protocol.

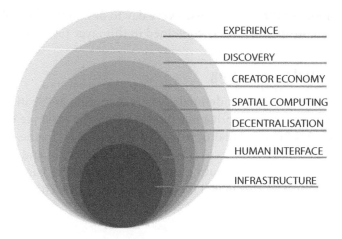

EXPERIENCE

DISCOVERY

CREATOR ECONOMY

SPATIAL COMPUTING

DECENTRALISATION

HUMAN INTERFACE

INFRASTRUCTURE

Figure 4.4 The seven layers of Metaverse.

4.3.1 Experience

The closest layer to human beings which enables humans to experience the Metaverse. The limitations that physicality imposes will be removed as physical space is dematerialized. As a result, the metaverse will provide us with a wide range of experiences that we cannot currently enjoy for example in general all the customers prefer the front row in concerts but in the physical world, it is not possible whereas in the virtual world of the Metaverse all the customers could be given front row seats by designing the universe as such. A few examples of this layer are games, social events, theatre, concerts, etc.

4.3.2 Discovery

Jon Radoff describes Metaverse as push and pull that introduces people to new experiences. The inbound and outbound discovery systems are still present in the metaverse ecology. Inbound discovery occurs when people are seeking those experiences whereas Outbound refers to the strategy of trying to reach individuals with communications whether or not they requested it [57, 58].

4.3.3 Creator Economy

As the Metaverse's popularity increases and the experiences in the Metaverse become immersive, The number of creators also grows exponentially. All of the technology that creators use every day to design the enjoyable experiences that consumers have is contained in this layer [59, 60].

4.3.4   Spatial Computing

In 2003, Simon Greenwold defined spatial computing as "Spatial computing is human interaction with a machine in which the machine retains and manipulates referents to real objects and spaces" [11]. In the Metaverse, spatial computing enables us to travel through 3-D spaces and manipulate them. In short Spatial computing proposes to break the barrier between physical and ideal worlds which includes technologies such as AR, VR, etc. [61, 62, 75, 76, 81].

4.3.5   Decentralization

Decentralization is the process through which authority and decision-making are transferred from a centralized entity (an individual, an organization, or a collection of such entities) to a distributed network. In decentralization, the users rather than basing their trust in a centralized entity, trust is based on software or distributed networks. This is where Blockchain also comes into the picture. Decentralization in the metaverse can be achieved by the implementation of blockchain technology which includes smart contracts, open-source platforms, and eventually the possibility of self-sovereign digital identity [63].

4.3.6   Human Interface

Human intervention is a crucial component of the hardware layer of the metaverse. This layer consists of technologies that allow humans to experience the metaverse such as VR headsets, smart glasses, etc. This layer also allows humans to gather Intel on the real world and make versions of the 3-dimensional spaces [64, 65].

4.3.7   Infrastructure

The infrastructure layers enable devices to connect to the internet and deliver the content required. As of this year, the 4G network is prevalent all over the world. Without 5G and 6G networks in the picture, Metaverse is still a distant dream. 5G computing reduces the network latency while increasing the bandwidth by great extents, such kind of functionality is required by next-generation mobiles, headsets, and smart wearables [66–68, 77].

Now that we have discussed the 7 layers of the metaverse architecture and a few underlying technologies in the layers, we come across the question of what exactly are the main enabling technologies of the metaverse.

The key enabling technologies in the metaverse are AR and VR, Artificial intelligence, Internet of things (IoT), spatial and edge computing, 3-D reconstruction, and Blockchain technology.

1. Augmented reality (AR) and Virtual reality (VR) essentially come under Extended Reality or Cross Reality (XR) which consists of immersive technologies, and digital environments. Augmented reality provides simulations that are superimposed on the actual physical world with real- time interaction [12]. One of the most widespread examples of Augmented reality is Snapchat, the popular social messaging application which uses AR technology to project a variety of really cool and fashionable filters onto users' faces. Virtual reality or VR without any physical restrictions can replicate any 3D environment and experience for the user [12]. The usage of smart wearables such as VR headsets, immersion helmets, etc. is enhanced by the pre-existing human senses such as sight, sound, and natural interaction with virtual objects. The combination of both these realities and making a reality layer for humans to experience and interact with is one of the most important steps in realizing the metaverse.

2. Artificial intelligence facilitates the content creation process, For instance, some AI components, such as GANverse3D from NVIDIA, allow designers and makers to take photographs of objects and then turn them into virtual reproductions. Avatars may interact with a variety of real-world modalities, including voice recognition and sentiment analysis, which are supported by AI in terms of accuracy and processing speed [13]. By giving these avatars the ability to pick up on human body language and conversational nuances, AI further enhances their realism. Internet of things or IoT is defined as the global network of machines and devices capable of interacting with each other [14]. IoT gives the metaverse access to real-time information gathered from the outside world. By making use of such information, the metaverse can improve the veracity of the events taking place in its virtual world and make them pertinent to the circumstances or environment in the actual world [69, 78].

3. 3-D reconstruction consists of an important technology called Digital twins. The most accurate modeling of physical items is provided by digital twins (DTs), which can precisely identify and forecast all physical output from the computer [15]. A digital twin in the metaverse can reflect the physical world into the virtual one. Therefore by having a digital twin real-world problems can be solved by performing simulations on the DTs.

4. Blockchain technology provides many uses in the Metaverse such as storage, security, trust, decentralization, and many more which will be discussed in further sections. This chapter has discussed the architecture of the metaverse and how the metaverse works i.e., its underlying technologies. A question raised by various smart minds of the world is that is the Metaverse still a distant dream. As discussed in the earlier sections it will take up a considerable amount of time for the entire Metaverse to come into action as the enabling technologies required for the Metaverse are being developed, but there are already a few applications in the field of the Metaverse in the real world which are:

1. **Healthcare:** Metaverse combined with the Medical internet of things, integrated with AR and VR glasses enable doctors or medical professionals to interact in the metaverse for medical education, science popularization, consultation, graded diagnosis and treatment, and clinical research [16]. Adaptation of the Metaverse can already be seen in telemedicine, virtual medicine, remote care and monitoring, data-driven medicine, and other fields [17]. Ever since the beginning, healthcare meant physical interaction between the patients and the doctors. To get treated or to get diagnosed, the whole process was hands-on. But the pandemic has changed the situation and more people chose teleconsultations and home-based health care. This is when the Metaverse has taken the charge to revolutionize this forever. Breaking down the physical barriers by Metaverse is one of the major wins for both medical professionals and patients. Metaverse in the pharma world, one can increase the time spent on ethical scientific education. The consultations with the doctor could be more personalized, and the doctors

can really join in, where people can feel the physical presence without actually turning on the camera, it also helps people to demonstrate things in a more immersive and 3D way. One of the use cases of Metaverse in Healthcare would be to remove Phobias. The phobia from the perspective of fear of heights or water etc., and it could be a lot to do with the different therapy areas. For example, a lot of companies are using the Metaverse to enable public speaking, this could help People who have a phobia of speaking in public. Also, a recent study shows that VR-trained Surgeons are a 200% boost in overall performance compared to a traditionally trained surgeon. For example, a major company called META or previously known as Facebook group acquired OCULUS VR Technology. And during the years 2012-2014, the Oculus VR Headset was in total awe. One of their notable collaboration was with the WHO Academy when a mobile application was developed during the pandemic, which helped healthcare workers to develop skills for more efficient management of COVID-19 patients using Virtual Reality. But the biggest problem for healthcare in the metaverse is Accessibility, it is very much important to make it accessible to everyone in a much easier way and that is why digital healthcare focuses so much on easy access. Now, this could make you question whether it is really worth having access to consultations from the comfort of your house without actually knowing how to use the headset. We can't ask a patient in need to get into an hour-long conversation just to get into the Metaverse for a medical consultation [70].

2. **Education:** When we look at the traditional delivery of Education where you read the content that you're trying to learn, we tend to retain just 5% of that knowledge whereas if you experience something in Virtual Reality, the retention goes to over 75%. The online education system that was used by students during the pandemic has paved the way for the Metaverse to change the way we learn. During the pandemic, we had no choice but to adapt to online education where many visual aids were introduced to make it better. But it came with several drawbacks like lack of social interaction and strain of screentime. But another way to look at this online education system was, as a training ground for being able to study on Metaverse. The Metaverse classrooms

make it more interesting and exciting for the students to learn. Because, here students are not taught with the help of PowerPoint Presentations or through books, but are taught by experiencing it virtually. For example, biology students can learn the anatomy of a frog in a more efficient and interesting way without actually touching or cutting it. Another way of using Metaverse in Education is using Holograms for Teaching, where a teacher being anywhere in the world can be projected as a Hologram into any classroom. This shows that there's a huge level of opportunity for how Metaverse can change the Education system. But the major challenges of Metaverse in Education would be Accessibility, Affordability, and quality. Because, more than 40% of the people in India do not have an access to the internet, which makes it impossible for them to join metaverse classrooms [71].

3. **Gaming:** Gaming in the Metaverse is going to span from immersive experiences in the fantasy world by bringing simple games into our everyday lives using holograms, you would play old games in new ways. It is no surprise that video games are serving as the testing grounds for Metaverse. The Metaverse wants to create video games that are more social and more decentralized. Yet Gamers are still suspicious of the metaverse or at least the way in which it's currently being discussed by the big companies. Every major publisher's announcement of some sort of web3 initiatives like Metaverse or a decentralized currency has been met with a strong unanimous reaction from the community. The Metaverse is designed to fascinate users by giving them real-life experiences in the virtual world. The Metaverse is here to take those collaborative possibilities beyond 2D screens. This collaboration is a great technique to make games more interactive in the 3D world. The Gaming industry is one of the major sectors that is utilizing the metaverse features to take the gaming experience to the next level. Gaming in the Metaverse is inherently social and interactive which sets it apart from the traditionally known VR gaming experience where the players were playing alone. Multi-player gaming will be set on an additional dimension where the players would be able to invite their friends from all over the world and make the gaming experience more interactive. In

the metaverse, gamers can make an addition to the virtual world, they can create their own content, and even build sub-games. Here, assets or avatar enhancements acquired in one game could be portable to another game, leading to the Asset Portability in Metaverse. The players can also experience the physical sense of touch using haptic gloves and jackets. The Metaverse does not only indulge towards immersive gaming but also an individual can get access to Web3, Crypto and so much more. Blockchain and Cryptocurrency help developers to develop decentralized metaverse projects, While, the blockchain is indulged towards the technology, Crypto assets help in exchanging gaming assets. While Age-appropriate services, control, and experiences would be the concern to be addressed regarding Gaming in Metaverse [72].

4.4   Blockchain-Powered Metaverse

4.4.1   What is the Need for Blockchain in the Metaverse?

Data security and privacy: How to ensure users' security and privacy in the metaverse, where there is a risk of privacy invasion, identity theft, and other forms of fraud, is a natural concern from the perspectives of metaverse businesses, developers, and users. Threats in Data security and privacy: Firstly looking at data privacy issues there are a few major issues in data privacy in the Metaverse for example:

Internet 2.0 has made it possible for advertisers to track how users move their cursor, where they gaze on a screen, how long they spend looking at a particular image, and which individuals or items they like. Web 3.0 or Metaverse is a huge step up from the previous kind of data collection, in the Metaverse the platform will be able to track our body movements, physiological responses such as breath count, eyeball movements, perspiration, etc., likely even brainwaves, and real and virtual interactions with the surrounding environment [18, 73, 74].

Doxing i.e., the act of disclosing a victim's private information in order to obtain money or for online shaming is already being done in web 2.0 based on personal information gathered via social media sites and other mediums. Coming to the Metaverse, numerous real-world details about user habits and physiological traits will be among the personal and sensitive information, with this kind of information how can doxing be prevented? Due to the enormous growth in data generation in the metaverse, applications' insufficient security protocols will increase the risk of a data breach [19]. In the Metaverse, concerns exist over the protection of the confidentiality of personal data when it comes to personally identifiable information (PII).

How Blockchain Tackles This Issue

Blockchain technology makes use of asymmetric cryptography for encryption and decryption i.e., it consists of two different keys, a public key - for validating signatures and encrypting data and a private key - for signing messages and decrypting data. Therefore Blockchain will be able to grant the ownership of the data to the respective user through public and private keys or asymmetric cryptography. Blockchain makes use of another cryptographic technique known as zero-knowledge proof or ZKP which can be used to check whether the prover has enough transactions without disclosing any private transaction information in a blockchain setting [20]. The use of zero-knowledge proof on the blockchain enables people to easily identify crucial data in the metaverse while keeping their privacy and ownership over their assets [21]. Smart contracts in the blockchain enable secure, permissionless, and tamper-free transactions. Some rules or codes can be applied before for example Each participant will be required to confirm that user PII has not been hacked, for instance, if integrated metaverse platforms offer Initial Coin Offerings (ICO) [22, 79, 80].

Data Acquisition: The process of digitizing data from the environment so that it may be presented, examined, and saved in a computer is known as data acquisition, or DAQ as it is frequently abbreviated. Data acquisition is a very important step in the metaverse. Recently, artificial intelligence has increasingly replaced actual people in the development of creative activities in the Metaverse. Artificial intelligence (AI) artists learn about the trends and styles of their works before expressing what they have discovered in their works [23]. In order to train the Artificial intelligence agents and make the metaverse systems autonomous, an immense amount of data is required for training, testing, and validation. Acquiring large amounts of data and practicing regularly increases the accuracy and reduces the time taken by the artificial intelligence agents in play. Applications will be able to develop superior insights and evolve over time and adapt to new scenarios with the help of data collection in the metaverse. A new breed of Metaverse applications will change the way we live, work, and engage with the real environment through data collecting, information processing, and experience delivery [24].

Challenges in Data Acquisition

Since there will be tons of unstructured, real-time transactional data, the dependability and integrity of the services provided in the Metaverse might be determined by the quality of the data. Data can be obtained through various sources such as web forms, etc. and if data is obtained from unknown sources, this may damage the reliability. As the metaverse offers top-notch digital services employing VR headsets, the amount of data generated will soar [25]. The amount of data that will be gathered will be so massive that the data-collecting systems may become overburdened.

How Blockchain Tackles this Issue

Since we have established that searching for required data amongst the tons of massive unstructured data is an issue. When looking for a particular kind of data, using blockchain meta-information will allow you to narrow your search to the pure information that learning requires, resulting in higher-quality learning. The essential high-quality data is made judiciously available thanks to metadata that is kept within the blockchain block [23]. Data can be readily chosen and reused by being stored in the distributed ledger. Every piece of information gathered in the metaverse is validated using a blockchain-specific process that is driven by consensus mechanisms [26]. There will be no repetition in the data-collecting process because the likelihood of creating a duplicate block is virtually zero. The data obtained by blockchain-enabled acquisition mechanisms in the metaverse will be trustworthy since every block in the blockchain is authorized [27].

Data Storage

This chapter has discussed that immense amounts of data are required for the realization of the metaverse. All the data obtained must be stored in someplace accessible to the system when required. The products, locations, and experiences that can be accessed online will make up the metaverse. Huge data storage is necessary for the metaverse. Not just the data related to experiences but there must be a place to store information regarding the user's avatar's appearance. Aspects that can be changed include accessories, height, skin tone, and hair color. The digital property represented by NFTs, such as digital items and land parcels, will also need a secure storage facility. Based on this we can come to the conclusion that data storage is one of the top priorities in the metaverse.

Challenges with Data Storage

As a result of the creation of files, the metaverse will produce extensive information. The amount of data that can be stored physically is pushed to its breaking point once the metaverse is completely functional [21]. Data sovereignty, interoperability, and security are all problems with current centralized storage services. First of all, they establish a single point of failure due to centralized servers, which puts our information at risk of security breaches. Centralized storage finds it challenging to adapt to changes in capacity, read/write speed, security, and data relationships brought on by the exponential development of online data due to the high cost and factors like pre-required storage settings. The potential of the metaverse to offer biometric data, vocal inflexions, and vital signs that depend on sensitive data is jeopardized by the high likelihood of data loss and corruption in centralized applications [28].

How Blockchain Tackles this Issue

Using blockchain-based decentralized storage is beneficial as compared to traditional centralized storage because, Unstoppability, a feature of decentralized storage, ensures that the data you upload cannot be removed. Since anyone can develop anything in the metaverse, from NFTs to entire decentralized universes, this is very important. With decentralized storage, only individuals who own the decryption keys have access to the data instead of the people who manage the servers, this improves security without a single point of failure and ensures continuous uptime. The actual data is dispersed among a network of peers or users who are compensated financially for their storage space. In the blockchain, data is stored along the chain as a copy of the original blocks, increasing data dependability and transparency in the metaverse. Strong scalability, high security, high efficiency, automatic fault tolerance, high dependability, and low costs are all benefits of integrating decentralized storage with blockchain technology [29]. Data scientists in the metaverse may collaborate and work on data cleansing because of the decentralized nature of blockchain technology, which drastically cuts the time and expenses involved in labeling data and getting datasets ready for analyses [21, 30].

Data Interoperability

Jon Radoff defines Interoperability as the capacity to harmonize economies, avatars, and systems between worlds, which is frequently cited as one of the key characteristics of the metaverse. A platform for social and cultural interaction between virtual worlds will be the metaverse. Virtual bridges will be developed gradually to enable users to easily transfer their assets between virtual worlds while maintaining their avatars [21]. An identity standard is used to offer the user a special set of credentials that may be utilized outside of the boundaries of virtual worlds, such as our real-life license numbers and other identification numbers [31, 48, 49]. Interoperability is essential to link various metaverse initiatives so that users can have a consistent experience when taking part in various socio-cultural activities, exactly like it does in the real world. Interoperability is essential if Web3 platforms and the metaverse are to be widely adopted and into the mainstream since we require mobility and connectedness.

Challenges with Data Interoperability
The existing centralized traditional digital platforms are fragmented and disorganized. To engage in various realms, people must set up their accounts, avatars, hardware, and payment infrastructure. Lack of interoperability limits users' access to the Metaverse by preventing them from freely navigating across various virtual worlds integrated into the 3D horizon of Metaverse, but instead restricting their travel to a single project. The commonality and interoperability we encounter in our real world are equally significant even when we are in the virtual environment since the Metaverse represents the real world. Because there is little transparency in virtual worlds, moving there might be difficult; for instance, using the same account in two different virtual worlds is not possible. Digital world applications should be able to easily exchange information with one another regardless of their location or the technology being used.

How Blockchain Tackles This Issue
Ecosystems may communicate, share any data, and use each other's features and services thanks to blockchain-based interoperability. A cross-chain protocol is an ideal approach to guarantee compatibility between virtual worlds in the metaverse [32].

By implementing such protocols, users will be able to transfer their avatars, nfts, storage space, assets, game collectables, etc. [50, 51]. The metaverse in the picture must be based on an open blockchain ecosystem if compatibility is necessary. One example of virtual currencies is users should be able to use a single wallet to store money and conduct transactions across many Metaverse projects, eliminating the need to manage several wallets. Utilizing cross-blockchain technology will make it possible for virtual worlds to communicate with one another thus removing the necessity for middlemen in the metaverse [33, 52, 53].

4.5 Overview of Blockchain Use Cases in the Metaverse

A few of the accomplished use cases of blockchain in the Metaverse are as follows:

4.5.1 NFTs

The Metaverse offers an open and just economic system supported by the transparency and immutability of the blockchain. Numerous analysts predict that non-fungible tokens also known as NFT's will play a significant part in the metaverse. These tokens, which are currently often used in digital art transactions, will serve as evidence of ownership of digital assets. NFT digital avatars serve as access tokens for various metaverse places by representing real-world identities. To enter and swap between various areas in the metaverse, players could enter and exit using their NFT avatars as access tokens. With full ownership, control, and flexibility for creating virtual identities, NFTs can be seen as an extension of users' real-life identities. According to many blockchain specialists, gaming will soon be the sector where the idea of the metaverse really takes off. They forecast that non-fungible metaverse tokens will be used to represent the virtual assets players use and that games will allow users to amass real money that can be used as payment inside a particular ecosystem over time. NFT owners with comparable inclinations could connect with one another and create communities for communicating, exchanging ideas, and cooperating [35, 54, 55]. Avatar NFT ownership enables virtual access to a wide range of exclusive experiences in the metaverse and the real world, promoting social and communal interactions. Nonfungible Tokens (NFTs) from top consumer brands like Gucci and Coca-Cola are being sold on metaverse marketplaces like Decentraland [34, 56]. NFTs are essential to owning a specific area of the metaverse due to their capacity to demonstrate proof of ownership and their application in various metaverse ecosystems. It is believed that any metaverse crypto project involving the purchase of avatars, gaming assets, or other items has a huge potential for integrating NFTs. The use of NFTs as a deed to virtual property would be made possible through NFT metaverse projects. Prices are set by the basic rule of supply and demand, which eliminates the possibility of pumps and artificial value inflation. It is based on the scarcity and on-chain value of an NFT according to its applicability. Through the use of infrastructure that supports location-based engagement and augmented reality, NFTs could provide interoperability beyond the metaverse. One of the established examples is Sandbox-On NFT LAND, Sandbox enables players to make their own in-game characters, engage in trades, and sell goods. Anyone may develop, share, and earn money from assets on SandBox [36, 57]. It's interesting to note that some of the most well-known businesses from the actual world are already part of the Sandbox metaverse ecosystem. An NFT's assets can be copied by anyone, but blockchain technology is necessary to preserve the NFT's original ownership. The fact that blockchain enables transparency and immutability makes the role of NFT in the metaverse abundantly clear.

4.5.2   Virtual Currencies

A number of elements, such as mobile-based always-on access and virtual currency interaction with reality, are strengthening the metaverse [42]. One of the most obvious applications of blockchain technology in the metaverse is settlements. The time when consumers shop online is quickly approaching. We can be confident that cryptocurrencies will soon find use in a decentralized ecosystem because consumption is continually rising and offline trading is progressively giving place to internet businesses. Because it is utilized as a genuine product in a virtual environment, the virtual money of the Metaverse differs from virtual currencies used in the real world and can eventually take on a combined form [42]. Substantial infrastructure of banks and regulators are needed to serve as custodians, mediators, and clearinghouses in order to conduct transactions using traditional money. On the other hand, cryptocurrency transactions typically merely call for software that runs on regular PCs. Cryptocurrencies possess great potential for scalability. Instant, direct, cost-free peer-to-peer transactions over the internet are what cryptocurrencies promise. Cryptocurrency is the way to go because it solidifies the notion of interoperability, or operating across different blockchain systems, fast transfer of value, and digital, permanent proof of ownership in the metaverse.

4.5.3   Sandbox

The in-game virtual currency in the game Sandbox is called SAND, and it is based on the Ethereum blockchain network. On a number of cryptocurrency exchanges, these tokens can be purchased and traded. As NFTs, SAND can be used to buy virtual land, buildings, equipment, and other commodities. The native token MANA, which serves as the virtual currency in Decentraland, allows users to buy virtual land and develop it for games and other experiences as well as for avatars and digital accessories.

The native token of Axie Infinity, which enables users to buy virtual pets, is the Axie Infinity Shard. Cryptocurrency becomes more of a requirement than a choice in a world where efficiency, openness, and security are practically important. In addition to acting as a link between the actual world and the Metaverse, the virtual money also promotes a healthy ecology.

4.5.4   Self-Identity Authentication

The creation of the metaverse's own digital identity is another crucial first step. It is crucial to establish an identity verification method within the metaverse to prevent illegal access and malpractices because metaverse applications would contain avatars of real individuals. With the use of identification certificates built on the blockchain, businesses can implement user identity verification. By requiring user identity verification, it is impossible for anyone to use a fraudulent identity to commit crimes within the virtual environment. In [37] the authors have combined knowledge-based and biometric-based methods to build a two-factor authentication framework. [37] has mentioned the development of an iris-based and blockchain-based avatar authentication system that enables virtual-physical tracking of avatars which avoids malpractices related to avatars in the Metaverse such as Disguise i.e., the attacker poses as a malevolent avatar who resembles the target avatar in order to trick the interactor, Impersonation i.e., in order to manipulate the associated avatar in the real world, the attacker poses as a malicious manipulator and uses a device that has been authenticated by a real player and Replay i.e., The attacker gathers the out-of-date identification parameters associated with an honest avatar in both the metaverse and the real world and gives them to the interactor who poses as the target avatar. Their system uses blockchain to ensure that the identity of the avatar can be publicly verified, and stores the records in a secure database to ensure that the player's real identity can be tracked. In [38], the authors constructed a secure blockchain-based authentication and key agreement mechanism. The protocol constructed by them offers a distributed method for securely storing the data of all subscribers. Authentication-related items are hashed digests that function similarly to public keys by using the once-only hash secret. In order to reduce key management overhead costs and get rid of the issue of relying on a trusted third party, an effective blockchain-assisted secure device authentication technique for cross-domain IIoT was presented in [39]. Without the assistance of a reliable third party, these public key-based authentication techniques enable one-party authentication [37, 39, 58, 59].

4.5.5   Digital Real Estate

In the future, ownership of digital assets would generally be referred to as "digital real estate," and each NFT holder would have a place in the metaverse. There is a lot of virtual real estate and space in virtual worlds. NFTs could be used to take full control of virtual areas in the metaverse. Users might simply establish ownership of the object and create virtual real estate with the aid of the blockchain. The NFT's smart contract features may be used to facilitate the sale of property in the metaverse. Along with building other structures like online stores or event venues, you can also rent out land to generate passive revenue. Reselling property, renting it out for passive income, installing other structures like online stores on the current land, or hosting social gatherings are some uses for virtual real estate in the metaverse.

The most well-known illustration of the metaverse's digital real estate situation is Decentraland. Decentraland was created using the Ethereum Blockchain network. The site claims that its users own the virtual world, and they can build, explore, and earn money from their creations [40]. LAND (virtual content) can be purchased by users using MANA, an ERC-20 token created and only supported by Ethereum. Land parcels are digital intangible goods that only exist because of their ownership history on the Ethereum network. On the decentralized ledger found within the Ethereum platform, smart contracts are executed and take place in their entirety [41, 60, 61]. Since LAND ownership operates on a blockchain, each transaction must be verified on Ethereum. A virtual fashion exhibition was recently held by Decentraland in association with Adidas. The exhibition featured the NFT fashion design auction. Musicians or pop stars are interested in virtual real estate because it allows them to claim ownership of their creations. Therefore, there is no hesitancy in considering the potential for future auctions for virtual locations in the metaverse.

4.6   Conclusion

The Metaverse is still in the early stages of development but is continually changing. There are many potential growth and application areas for the metaverse. The development of blockchain technology is having a significant impact on the current state of the digital asset market. This chapter provides an overview of the technologies being discussed i.e., The metaverse, Blockchain technology, Metaverse's reliance on blockchain technology, overview of blockchain use cases in the Metaverse and much more. We can confidently say that without blockchain technology, it is difficult to construct a full-fledged virtual environment. We can see the inevitable role of blockchain technology in the metaverse thanks to aspects like digital proof of ownership, money transfer, governance, accessibility, interoperability, etc.

References

1. Radoff, J., *The Metaverse Value-Chain*, United States 2021, Access Date: 15/12/2021, https://medium.com/building-the-metaverse/the-metaversevalue-chain-afcf9e09e3a7.
2. Greenwold, S., *"Spatial Computing"* (PDF), MIT Graduate Thesis, United States, June 2003. Retrieved 22 December 2019.
3. Koutitas, G., Smith, S., Lawrence, G., Performance evaluation of AR/VR training technologies for ems first responders. *Virtual Reality*, 25, 1, 83–94, 2021.
4. Huynh-The, Thien *et al.*, Artificial intelligence for the metaverse: A survey, *Eng. Appl. Artif. Intell.*, 117, 105581, 2022. arXiv preprint arXiv:2202.10336.
5. Lee, I. and Lee, K., The Internet of Things (IoT): Applications, investments, and challenges for enterprises, *Business Horizons*. 58, 431–440, 2015.
6. Far, S.B. and Rad, A.I., Applying digital twins in metaverse: User interface. *Secur. Privacy Challenges*, 2, 8–16, 2022.
7. Yang, D., Zhou, J., Chen, R., Song, Y., Song, Z., Zhang, X., Wang, Q., Wang, K., Zhou, C., Sun, J., Zhang, L., Bai, L., Wang, Y., Wang, X., Lu, Y., Xin, H., Powell, C.A., Thüemmler, C., Chavannes, N.H., Chen, W., Wu, L., Bai, C., Expert consensus on the metaverse in medicine. *Clin. eHealth*, 5, 1–9, 2022.
8. Ning, H. *et al.*, A survey on metaverse: The state-of-the-art, technologies. in: *IEEE Internet of Things Journal.*
9. Applications, and Challenges, 2021, ArXiv abs/2111.09673.
10. Di, P.R. and Cresci, S., Metaverse: Security and privacy issues, *2021 Third IEEE International Conference on Trust, Privacy and Security in Intelligent Systems and Applications (TPS-ISA)* 2021, 281–288, 2021.
11. Kostenko, O., Electronic jurisdiction, metaverse, artificial intelligence, digital personality, digital avatar, neural networks: Theory, practice, perspective. *World Sci.*, 1, 73, 2022.
12. Sun, X., Yu, F.R., Zhang, P., Sun, Z., Xie, W., Peng, X., A survey on zero-knowledge proof in blockchain. *IEEE Network*, 35, 4, 198–205, July/August 2021.
13. Gadekallu, T.R., *et al.*, Blockchain for the metaverse: A review, *Future Gener. Comput. Syst.*, 143, 401–419, 2022.
14. https://www.tcs.com/content/dam/tcs/pdf/discover-tcs/Research-and-Innovation/user-privacy-protection-metaverse-experience.pdf.
15. Jeon, H-j. *et al.*, Blockchain and AI meet in the metaverse. Blockchain potential in AI, IntechOpen, 12 Jan. 2022. Crossref, 73, 2022.

16. Yang, C. *et al.*, Compute- and data-intensive networks: The key to the metaverse, 2022, arXiv preprint arXiv:2204.02001.
17. Brunschwig, L., Campos-Lopez, R., Guerra, E., de Lara, J., Towards domain-specific modelling environments based on augmented reality, in: *IEEE/ACM 43rd International Conference on Software Engineering: New Ideas and Emerging Results (ICSE-NIER)*, pp. 56–60, 2021.
18. Bouraga, S., A taxonomy of blockchain consensus protocols: A survey and classification framework. *Expert Syst. Appl.*, 168, 114384, 2021.
19. Guo, J., *et al.* Reliable traffic monitoring mechanisms based on blockchain in vehicular networks. *IEEE Transactions on Reliability*, 71, 1219–1229, 2020.
20. Kiong, L.V., *Metaverse made easy: A beginner's guide to the metaverse: Everything you need to know about metaverse, NFT and GameFi*, 2022, Liew Voon Kiong.
21. https://www.jinse.com/news/blockchain/835473.html.
22. Can blockchain do AI and data labeling. Effect.AI thinks they can, and will. Accessed on 08.03.2022. The Effect.AI Newsletter, January 2019, Available: https://medium.com/@lawrence.effect/can-blockchain-do-ai-and-data-labeling-effect-ai-thinks-they-can-and-will-9ea94229dbf1.
23. Sparkes, M., What is a metaverse. *New Scientist*, 251, 3348, 18, 2021.
24. Belchior, R., Vasconcelos, A., Guerreiro, S., Correia, M., A survey on block-chain interoperability: Past, present, and future trends. *ACM Computing Surveys (CSUR)*, 54, 8, 1–41, 2021.
25. Jabbar, R., Fetais, N., Krichen, M., Barkaoui, K., Blockchain technology for healthcare: Enhancing shared electronic health record interoperability and integrity, in: *IEEE International Conference on Informatics, IoT, and Enabling Technologies (ICIoT)*, pp. 310–317, 2020.
26. Kim, J., Advertising in the metaverse: Research agenda. *J. Interactive Adver.*, 21.3, 141–144, 2021.
27. Usmani, S.S., Sharath, M., Mehendale, M., Future of mental health in the metaverse. *Gen. Psychiatr.*, 35, e100825, 2022.
28. Kaur, M. and Gupta, B., Metaverse technology and the current market, Insights2Techinfo, pp.1, 2021.
29. Yang, K. *et al.*, A secure authentication framework to guarantee the traceability of avatars in metaverse, 2022, arXiv preprint arXiv:2209.08893.
30. Chow, M.C. and Maode, M., A secure blockchain-based authentication and key agreement scheme for 3GPP 5G networks. *Sensors*, 22, 4525, 2022. MDPI AG.
31. Shen, M., Liu, H., Zhu, L., Xu, K., Yu, H., Du, X., Guizani, M., Blockchain assisted secure device authentication for cross-domain industrial IoT. *IEEE J. Sel. Areas Commun.*, 38, 5, 942–954, 2020.
32. https://docs.decentraland.org/.
33. Goanta, C., *Selling LAND in decentraland: The regime of non-fungible tokens on the ethereum blockchain under the digital content directive*, A. Lehavi, and R. Levine-Schnur, (Eds.), 2020.

34. Levine-Schnur, R. (Ed.), *Disruptive Technology, Legal Innovation, and the Future of Real Estate*, Springer, Cham, pp 1–181.
35. Park, S.-M. and Kim, Y.-G., A metaverse: Taxonomy, components, applications, and open challenges. *IEEE Access*, 10, 4209–4251, 2022.
36. Panda, S.K. and Satapathy, S.C., An investigation into smart contract deployment on ethereum platform using Web3.js and solidity using blockchain, in: *Data Engineering and Intelligent Computing, Advances in Intelligent Systems and Computing, vol. 1*, V. Bhateja, S.C. Satapathy, C.M. Travieso-González, V.N.M. Aradhya (Eds.), Springer, Singapore, 2021.
37. Panda, S.K., Rao, D.C., Satapathy, S.C., An investigation into the usability of blockchain technology in Internet of Things, in: *Data Engineering and Intelligent Computing, Advances in Intelligent Systems and Computing, vol. 1*, V. Bhateja, S.C. Satapathy, C.M. Travieso-González, V.N.M. Aradhya (Eds.), Springer, Singapore, 2021.
38. Panda, S.K., Dash, S.P., Jena, A.K., Optimization of block query response using evolutionary algorithm, in: *Data Engineering and Intelligent Computing, Advances in Intelligent Systems and Computing, vol. 1*, V. Bhateja, S.C. Satapathy, C.M. Travieso-González, V.N.M. Aradhya (Eds.), Springer, Singapore, 2021.
39. Nanda, S.K., Panda, S.K., Das, M., Satapathy, S.C., Automating vehicle insurance process using smart contract and ethereum, in: *Advances in Micro-Electronics, Embedded Systems and IoT, Lecture Notes in Electrical Engineering, vol. 838*, V.V.S.S.S. Chakravarthy, W. Flores-Fuentes, V. Bhateja, B. Biswal (Eds.), Springer, Singapore, 2022.
40. Varaprasada Rao, K. and Panda, S.K., Secure electronic voting (E-voting) system based on blockchain on various platforms, in: *Computer Communication, Networking and IoT, Lecture Notes in Networks and Systems, vol. 459*, S.C. Satapathy, J.C.W. Lin, L.K. Wee, V. Bhateja, T.M. Rajesh (Eds.), Springer, Singapore, 2023.
41. Varaprasada Rao, K. and Panda, S.K., A design model of copyright protection system based on distributed ledger technology, in: *Computer Communication, Networking and IoT, Lecture Notes in Networks and Systems, vol. 459*, S.C. Satapathy, J.C.W. Lin, L.K. Wee, V. Bhateja, T.M. Rajesh (Eds.), Springer, Singapore, 2023.
42. Panda, S.K., Elngar, A.A., Balas, V.E., Kayed, M. (Eds.), *Bitcoin and Blockchain: History and Current Applications*, 1st ed, CRC Press, 2020.
43. Panda, S.K., Jena, A.K., Swain, S.K., Satapathy, S.C. (Eds.), *Blockchain Technology: Applications and Challenges*, Springer, Intelligent Systems Reference Library, 1–300.
44. Sathya, A.R., Panda, S.K., Hanumanthakari, S., Enabling smart education system using blockchain technology, in: *Blockchain Technology: Applications and Challenges, Intelligent Systems Reference Library, vol. 203*, S.K. Panda, A.K. Jena, S.K. Swain, S.C. Satapathy (Eds.), Springer, Cham, 2021.

45. Lokre, S.S., Naman, V., Priya, S., Panda, S.K., Gun tracking system using blockchain technology, in: *Blockchain Technology: Applications and Challenges,* Intelligent Systems Reference Library, vol. 203, S.K. Panda, A.K. Jena, S.K. Swain, S.C. Satapathy (Eds.), Springer, Cham, 2021.

46. Panda, S.K., Daliyet, S.P., Lokre, S.S., Naman, V., Distributed ledger technology in the construction industry using corda, in: *The New Advanced Society: Artificial Intelligence and Industrial Internet of Things Paradigm.*

47. Panda, S.K., Mohammad, G.B., Nandan Mohanty, S., Sahoo, S., Smart contract-based land registry system to reduce frauds and time delay, in: *Security and Privacy,* p. e172, 2021.

48. Panda, S.K. and Satapathy, S.C., Drug traceability and transparency in medical supply chain using blockchain for easing the process and creating trust between stakeholders and consumers. *Pers. Ubiquit. Comput.,* 2021.

49. Niveditha, V.R. and Karthik Sekaran, K., Singh, A, Panda, SK, effective prediction of bitcoin price using wolf search algorithm and bidirectional LSTM on internet of things data. *Int. J. Syst. Syst. Eng.,* 11, 3-4, 224–236.

50. Sri Arza, M. and Panda, S.K., An integration of blockchain and machine learning into the health care system, in: *Machine Learning Adoption in Blockchain-Based Intelligent Manufacturing,* vol. 1, pp. 33–58.

51. Murala, D.K., Panda, S.K., Swain, S.K., A survey on cloud computing security and privacy issues and challenges. *J. Adv. Res. Dyn. Control Syst.,* 11, 1276–1290, 2019.

52. Murala, D.K., Panda, S.K., Swain, S.K., Secure dynamic groups data sharing with modified revocable attribute-based encryption in cloud. *Int. J. Recent Technol. Eng. (IJRTE),* 8, 4, 9508–9512, 2019.

53. Murala, D.K., Panda, S.K., Swain, S.K., A novel hybrid approach for providing data security and privacy from malicious attacks in the cloud environment. *J. Adv. Res. Dyn. Control Syst.,* 11, 1291–1300, 2019.

54. Panda, S.K., Swain, S.K., Mall, R., An investigation into usability aspects of E-commerce websites using users' preferences. *Adv. Comput. Sci.: An Int. J.,* 4, 1, 65–73, 2015.

55. Panda, S.K., Swain, S.K., Mall, R., Measuring web site usability quality complexity metrics for navigability, in: *Intelligent Computing, Communication and Devices, Advances in Intelligent Systems and Computing,* vol. 308, L. Jain, S. Patnaik, N. Ichalkaranje, (Eds.), Springer, New Delhi, 2015.

56. Panda, S.K., A usability evaluation framework for B2C E-commerce websites. *Comput. Eng. Intell. Syst.,* 5, 3, 66–85, 2014.

57. Bhalerao, V., Panda, S.K., Jena, A.K., Optimization of loss function on human faces using generative adversarial networks, in: *Machine Learning Approaches for Urban Computing, Studies in Computational Intelligence, vol. 968,* M. Bandyopadhyay, M. Rout, S. Chandra Satapathy, (Eds.), Springer, Singapore, 2021.

58. Panda, S.K. and Dwivedi, M., Minimizing food wastage using machine learning: A novel approach, in: *Smart Intelligent Computing and Applications,*

Smart Innovation, Systems and Technologies, vol. 159, S. Satapathy, V. Bhateja, J. Mohanty, S. Udgata, (Eds.), Springer, Singapore, 2020.

59. Panda, S.K., Sathya, A.R., Mishra, M., Satpathy, S., A supervised learning algorithm to forecast weather conditions for playing cricket. *Int. J. Innovative Technol. Exploring Eng. (IJITEE),* 9, 1, 1561–1565, 2019.

60. Panda, S.K., Fraud-resistant crowdfunding system using ethereum blockchain, in: *Bitcoin and Blockchain,* pp. 237–276, 2020.

61. Panda, S.K., Mishra, V., Balamurali, R., Elngar, A.A., *Artificial intelligence and machine learning in business management concepts, challenges, and case studies,* pp. 1–278, CRC Press, Boca Raton, 5 November 2021.

62. Joshi, S., Panda, S.K., AR, S., Optimal deep learning model to identify the development of pomegranate fruit in farms. *Int. J. Innovative Technol. Exploring Eng.,* 9, 3, 2352–2356, 2020.

63. Puranam, K.S.R., Gaddam, M.C.T., K, V.P.R., Panda, S.K., Reddy, G.S.M., Anatomy and lifecycle of a bitcoin transaction. *Proceedings of International Conference on Sustainable Computing in Science, Technology and Management (SUSCOM),* Amity University Rajasthan, Jaipur - India, February 26-28, 2019, February 18, 2019, Available at SSRN: https://ssrn.com/abstract=3355106.

64. Panda, S.K. and Swain, S.K., *Quality assurance aspects of web design, design solutions for improving website quality and effectiveness,* pp. 87–129, IGI Global, 2016.

65. Panda, S.K., Bhalerao, V., AR, S., A machine learning model to identify duplicate questions in social media forums. *Int. J. Innovative Technol. Exploring Eng.,* 9, 4, 370–373, 2020.

66. Ahmareen, S., Raj, A., Potluri, S., Panda, S.K., Book Shala: An android-based application design and implementation of sharing books, in: *Smart Intelligent Computing and Applications, Smart Innovation, Systems and Technologies, vol. 159,* S. Satapathy, V. Bhateja, J. Mohanty, S. Udgata, (Eds.), Springer, Singapore, 2020.

67. Panda, S.K., Das, S.S., Swain, S.K., S-model for service-oriented applications in web engineering. *Reg. Coll. Manag.,* 10, 3, 38–46, 2013.

68. Panda, S.K., An investigation into usability and productivity of ecommerce websites (https://shodhganga.inflibnet.ac.in:8443/jspui/handle/10603/123505).

69. Panda, S.K., Chandrasekhar, A., Gantayat, P.K., Panda, M.R., Detecting brain tumor using image segmentation: A novel approach, in: *Data Engineering and Intelligent Computing, Lecture Notes in Networks and Systems, vol. 446,* V. Bhateja, L. Khin Wee, J.C.W. Lin, S.C. Satapathy, T.M. Rajesh, (Eds.), Springer, Singapore, 2022.

70. Sanghi, P., Panda, S.K., Pati, C., Gantayat, P.K., Learning deep features and classification for fresh or off vegetables to prevent food wastage using machine learning algorithms, in: *Intelligent Data Engineering and Analytics, Smart Innovation, Systems and Technologies, vol. 266,* S.C. Satapathy, P. Peer, J. Tang, V. Bhateja, A. Ghosh, (Eds.), Springer, Singapore, 2022.

71. Gantayat, P.K., Mohapatra, S., Panda, S.K., Secure trust level routing in delay-tolerant network with node categorization technique, in: *Intelligent Data Engineering and Analytics, Smart Innovation, Systems and Technologies, vol. 266,* S.C. Satapathy, P. Peer, J. Tang, V. Bhateja, A. Ghosh, (Eds.), Springer, Singapore, 2022.

72. Panda, S.K., Urkude, S.V., Urkude, V.R., Vairachilai, S., An investigation into COVID 19 pandemic in India, in: *The New Advanced Society: Artificial Intelligence and Industrial Internet of Things Paradigm,* vol. 1, Wiley.

73. Panda, S.K., Das, S., Swain, S.K., Web site productivity measurement using single task size measure. *J. Inf. Sci. Computing Technol. (JISCT),* 4, 3, October12, 2015.

74. Hanumanthakari, S. and Panda, S.K., Detecting face mask for prevent COVID-19 using deep learning: A novel approach, in: *Smart Intelligent Computing and Applications, Volume 2, Smart Innovation, Systems and Technologies, vol. 283,* S.C. Satapathy, V. Bhateja, M.N. Favorskaya, T. Adilakshmi, (Eds.), Springer, Singapore, 2022.

75. Panda, S.K., Sathya, A.R., Das, S., Bitcoin: Beginning of the cryptocurrency era, in: *Recent Advances in Blockchain Technology, Intelligent Systems Reference Library, vol. 237,* S.K. Panda, V. Mishra, S.P. Dash, A.K. Pani, (Eds.), Springer, Cham, 2023.

76. Murala, D.K., Panda, S.K., Sahoo, S.K., Securing electronic health record system in cloud environment using blockchain technology, in: *Recent Advances in Blockchain Technology, Intelligent Systems Reference Library, vol. 237,* S.K. Panda, V. Mishra, S.P. Dash, A.K. Pani, (Eds.), Springer, Cham, 2023.

77. Rao, K.V., Murala, D.K., Panda, S.K., Blockchain: A study of new business model, in: *Recent Advances in Blockchain Technology, Intelligent Systems Reference Library, vol. 237,* S.K. Panda, V. Mishra, S.P. Dash, A.K. Pani, (Eds.), Springer, Cham, 2023.

78. Panda, S.K., Mishra, V., Dash, S.P., Pani, A.K., *Recent advances in blockchain technology real-world applications,* Intelligent Systems Reference Library (ISRL, volume 237), vol. 1, pp. 1–317, Springer, Switzerland, 2023, 978-3-031-22835-3.

79. Panda, S.K., Mohapatra, R.K., Panda, S., Balamurugan, S., *The new advanced society: Artificial intelligence and industrial internet of things paradigm,* vol. 1, pp. 1–512, Wiley, 2022.

80. Nanda, S.K., Panda, S.K., Das, M., Satapathy, S.C., Decentralization of car insurance system using machine learning and distributed ledger technology, in: *Intelligent Data Engineering and Analytics, FICTA 2022. Smart Innovation, Systems and Technologies,* vol. 327, V. Bhateja, X.S. Yang, J. Chun-Wei Lin, R. Das, (Eds.), Springer, Singapore, 2023.

81. Nanda, S.K., Panda, S.K., Dash, M., Medical supply chain integrated with blockchain and IoT to track the logistics of medical products. *Multimed. Tools Appl.,* 2023.

5

Metaverse: The New Era in Medical Field

M. Sreedhar[1], Shaik Himam Saheb[2*] and Kona Ravi Sandeep Kumar[3]

[1]Guru Nanak University, Ibrahimpatnam, Hyderabad, India
[2]Department of Mechatronics Engineering, ICFAI Foundation for Higher Education, Hyderabad, India
[3]Vignan's Institute of Management and Technology for Women, Hyderabad, India

Abstract

Metaverse technologies have recently become a reality and have gained the interest of scientific companies, the educational environment, and the medical industry. Given the prevalence of screen time, particularly among children and adolescents, meta versions should serve as a venue for health promotion. The goals of this study were to find publications that connected meta versions to prevention as well as medical treatment, engineering education with practical training, and simulation and the research environment, and to review recent literature. Rapid developments in automation and digitization have expedited the expansion of the healthcare industry and developed new models that open up new avenues for providing care at lower costs. An innovative digital technique called the metaverse has a huge potential in the healthcare industry that can help all stakeholders of medical facilities such as doctors, patients, and medical students. The metaverse is the connection of many supporting technologies, together with artificial intelligence (AI), augmented reality (AR), virtual reality (VR), mixed reality, Internet of Things (IoT), medical devices, medical robots, among others., and it allows for the exploration of new possibilities for the delivery of good healthcare facilities and medical services. The mixture of these technologies offers patients individualized, intimate, and immersive care. In addition to this, it offers clever adaptive solutions that break down barriers between patients and healthcare providers. This review provides a clear understanding about the metaverse in the healthcare industry and day-to-day healthcare applications, with an emphasis on state-of-the-art, enabling technology. The importance of the metaverse in healthcare innovations,

Corresponding author: himam.mech@gmail.com

Chandrashekhar A, Shaik Himam Saheb, Sandeep Kumar Panda, S. Balamurugan and Sheng-Lung Peng (eds.) *Metaverse and Immersive Technologies: An Introduction to Industrial, Business and Social Applications*, (127–158) © 2023 Scrivener Publishing LLC

for example, spectacle frame selection in the field of ophthalmology, is easier in online applications, namely, Lenskart using the metaverse technology for spectacle frame selection. There are many medical problems that can be addressed easily with the advancement in metaverse technology.

Keywords: Metaverse, medical field, healthcare, artificial intelligence, virtual reality, augmented reality, quantum computing

5.1   Introduction

The "Metaverse" term was coined by professor Neal Stephenson in the year of 1992 in Snow Crash novel, and the sci-fi novel Snow Crash is deals with the immersive and alternate virtual reality and the universe connected to the Internet becomes reality. Since 2021, the applications of Metaverse technologies in various fields has been identified widely and discussed. These technologies include the AR, MR, and VR glasses, used in various industries like entertainment, 3D imaging, construction, education, medical and social media applications. The virtual space has become a real world for alternate life in which avatars or digital profiles participates in social media activities in the virtual cultural events, but they also have a monetary life [1].

In terms of the various technologies backside of meta version, Metaverse technologies are divided into major four different types: augmented reality (AR), Virtual Reality (VR), life logging and mirror world. The Metaverse is used in various medical fields such as surgeries, mental health, radiology, pain diagnosis and management, wellness, fitness, disease diagnosis and plastic surgeries the detailed flowchart is shown in the Figure 5.1.

Figure 5.1 Metaverse key applications in medical fields.

The metaverse is a virtual reality space that combines physical reality and cyberspace, where people can interact with each other and digital objects in a shared, immersive environment. The term "metaverse" was popularized by Neal Stephenson's 1992 science fiction novel "Snow Crash," in which the metaverse was a virtual reality network where people conducted business, socialized, and played games.

The idea of the metaverse has evolved since then, with various companies and organizations exploring the potential of creating a fully-realized metaverse. The metaverse is often described as a three-dimensional space that people can access through virtual reality headsets, where they can interact with other people's avatars, engage in activities, and own virtual assets.

The metaverse has the potential to revolutionize many aspects of our lives, including entertainment, commerce, education, and social interaction. However, creating a functional metaverse that is accessible to everyone and scalable is a complex and challenging task that requires significant technological advances and cooperation between various stakeholders.

Augmented Reality is the technology as a part of Metaverse technologies. AR works in a real-time graphics environment to the physical as well as real-world using glasses, contact lenses, and smart phones. Metaverse technology is about bringing more information into the real world. Examples of VR include PokemonGo game and 3D medical animation. Life logging is an extension of the inner word. In fact, smart devices are used for data activities, for example the smart watch record the heartbeat and walking minutes. The augmented reality helps to get in real time experience in the virtual environment.

Virtual reality (VR) is an online mature 3D virtual reality, a communiqué device that simulate the inner environment of avatars and moments. Avatars are customizable and have realistic cultural, physical, and social characteristics. Avatars can converse with other units and accomplish objectives. Examples include online multiplayer video games, virtual hospitals, and doctor's offices. The Metaverse can therefore be seen as a place where the real world is augmented, connected and replicated with virtual reality, resulting in another world. It's also important to remember that for the generation of digital natives, The ,Metaverse is helping the users to relax the situations and helping the society to refresh and continue their thoughts with the virtual world. This aspect that especially need to be considered since his 2019 coronavirus pandemic that accelerated and implemented Meta-version development. Pandemic situation restricts real physical life.

5.1.1   Metaverse in Medical Surgeries

The perception of the metaverse refers to a virtual world where people can interact with each other and digital objects in a shared space. One potential use case for the metaverse in medical surgeries is in surgical planning. Surgeons could use a virtual model of a patient's anatomy to plan and practice surgical procedures before performing them in the physical world. This could help reduce the risk of errors during surgery and improve patient outcomes [17–22].

Another potential application is in surgical training. Surgeons could use the metaverse to practice surgical procedures in a safe and controlled environment, without putting real patients at risk. This could be especially useful for complex procedures that are difficult to simulate in a traditional training environment. The metaverse could also be used to provide remote assistance during surgical procedures. For example, a surgeon in one location could use a virtual reality headset to provide guidance and support to a surgeon in another location who is performing a procedure. This could help improve access to surgical expertise in areas where it is limited. Overall, while the use of the metaverse in medical surgeries is still in its early stages, there is significant potential for this technology to improve surgical outcomes and expand access to surgical expertise [23–26].

5.1.2   Metaverse in Medical Education and Training

The metaverse has high probability to transform medical education and training in many ways, making it more interactive, immersive, and accessible. Here are some potential applications of the metaverse in medical studies, research, and training:

- Simulation-based learning: Medical students and trainees can use the metaverse to simulate complex medical procedures and learn from their mistakes without putting patients at risk. This can help improve the quality and safety of medical care [27–30].
- Virtual collaboration: The metaverse can enable medical students and trainees to collaborate with their peers and instructors in virtual environments. They can practice teamwork and communication skills, and learn from each other's experiences [31–34].
- Remote learning: The metaverse can enable remote medical education and training, allowing students and trainees to

participate in courses and workshops from anywhere in the world. This can help improve access to medical education, particularly in areas where it is limited [35–37].

- Lifelike anatomy: The metaverse can provide realistic, three-dimensional models of the human body, allowing students and trainees to explore and understand complex anatomical structures in greater detail [38–42].
- Interactive learning: Metaverse can facilitate interactive learning experiences, where students and trainees can explore virtual environments, interact with objects, and engage in problem-based learning activities [43–46].

The metaverse has the capabilities to revolutionize medical education and training, making it more immersive, interactive, and accessible. As the technology evolves, we can expect to see more innovative applications of the metaverse in the field of medicine.

5.1.3   Metaverse Applications in Pain Diagnosis and Management

The metaverse is a collective virtual united space formed by the union of physical and virtual reality. In recent days, there has been a growing interest in the potential of the metaverse to transform many aspects of healthcare, including pain diagnosis and management.

Here are some potential applications of the metaverse in pain diagnosis and management:

- Virtual reality (VR) and augmented reality (AR) for pain distraction: Virtual reality and augmented reality technologies have been shown to be effective in reducing pain by providing distraction from the sensation. By immersing the user in a virtual world or overlaying digital information onto the real world, these technologies can take the user's mind off their pain and help them relax.
- Telemedicine and remote consultations: The metaverse could allow healthcare professionals to provide consultations and support remotely, without the need for physical travel. This could be particularly useful for patients with chronic pain who may struggle to attend appointments in person [47, 48].
- Personalized pain management programs: By collecting data on a patient's pain levels and responses to different

treatments, the metaverse could enable the development of personalized pain management programs. These programs could incorporate a range of interventions, such as physical therapy, mindfulness exercises, and medication, tailored to the individual's needs [49–51].

- Virtual support groups: Chronic pain can be an isolating experience, and virtual support groups could provide a way for patients to connect with others who are going through similar experiences. By creating a virtual space where people can chat, share experiences, and offer support, the metaverse could help combat the sense of social isolation that can often accompany chronic pain [52–55].

- Education and training: The metaverse could also be used as a tool for education and training in pain diagnosis and management. For example, healthcare professionals could use virtual simulations to practice different diagnostic techniques or to learn about new treatments [56–59].

The metaverse has the potential to transform many aspects of pain diagnosis and management, offering new tools for healthcare professionals and patients alike. However, it's important to note that these technologies are still in their early stages of development, and further research is needed to fully understand their potential and limitations.

5.1.4   Metaverse Applications in Radiology

The metaverse has many potential applications in radiology, which is the medical specialty that uses medical imaging to diagnose and treat diseases. Here are some potential applications of the metaverse in radiology:

- Virtual imaging simulations: The metaverse can be used to create virtual simulations of medical imaging procedures, such as X-rays, CT scans, and MRIs. Medical students and radiology trainees can practice interpreting these images in a safe and controlled environment.

- Three-dimensional imaging: The metaverse can provide three-dimensional images of anatomical structures, which can help radiologists and other medical professionals better visualize and understand complex medical conditions [60, 61].

- Virtual reality imaging: The metaverse can be used to create immersive virtual reality experiences that allow medical professionals to interact with medical imaging data in new ways. For example, they could manipulate 3D images of medical conditions to better understand them.

- Remote consultations: The metaverse can enable radiologists to provide remote consultations to other medical professionals or patients. This can help improve access to specialized medical expertise, particularly in areas where it is limited.
- Collaborative learning: The metaverse can enable radiologists and other medical professionals to collaborate in virtual environments, sharing knowledge and expertise with each other. This can help improve the quality of medical care and the accuracy of medical diagnoses.

Metaverse has the potential to transform radiology by making medical imaging data more interactive, immersive, and accessible. As the technology evolves, we can expect to see more innovative applications of the metaverse in the field of radiology in coming future.

5.1.5   Metaverse Applications in Mental Health

Metaverse in mental health is still in its nascent stages, and its potential applications in mental health are yet to be fully explored. However, some possible ways in which the metaverse could be used to support mental health include:

- Virtual Reality Exposure Therapy: Virtual reality can be used to simulate real-life scenarios that trigger anxiety, such as public speaking, heights, or flying. Exposure therapy in virtual reality has shown promise in reducing symptoms of anxiety disorders, and the metaverse could provide a more immersive and interactive environment for such therapy.
- Social Support Networks: Social isolation and loneliness can have a significant impact on mental health. The metaverse could provide a virtual space where people can connect with others who share similar experiences or interests, providing social support and reducing feelings of isolation.
- Mindfulness and Relaxation: The metaverse could be used to create virtual environments that promote relaxation and mindfulness, such as virtual beaches, gardens, or forests. These environments could be used for meditation, breathing exercises, or other relaxation techniques.

- Therapeutic Games: Games can be a fun and engaging way to learn coping skills and reduce stress. The metaverse could provide a platform for developing and delivering therapeutic games that address specific mental health issues.
- Teletherapy: The metaverse could provide a platform for delivering teletherapy services, allowing people to connect with mental health professionals in a virtual environment.

These are just a few possible applications of the metaverse in mental health. As the technology evolves, there will likely be many more innovative ways in which the metaverse can be used to support mental health and well-being.

5.1.6   Metaverse Applications in Plastic Surgeries and Cosmetics

Plastic surgery is a medical specialty that involves the reconstruction, restoration, or alteration of the human body. In the context of the metaverse, plastic surgery could have a range of potential applications. Here are a few real time applications

- Avatar customization: In virtual worlds, users often create avatars that represent them. Plastic surgery could be used to allow users to customize their avatars in ways that more closely resemble their real-life appearance or desired appearance. For example, someone who is self-conscious about their nose in real life could use virtual plastic surgery to alter their avatar's nose.
- Roleplaying: In some metaverse applications, users may engage in roleplaying activities where they take on the persona of a different character. Plastic surgery could be used to allow users to change their avatar's appearance to match the character they are playing. For example, someone playing a vampire might use virtual plastic surgery to give their avatar fangs or pale skin.
- Cosmetic enhancements: Some users may want to make cosmetic enhancements to their avatars purely for aesthetic reasons. For example, they may want their avatar to have larger breasts or a smaller waist. Plastic surgery could be used to make these changes.
- Body modifications: In some metaverse applications, users may want to modify their avatar's body in ways that are not

possible in the real world. For example, they may want their avatar to have wings or tentacles. Plastic surgery could be used to create these modifications.

It's worth noting that there are potential ethical concerns around the use of plastic surgery in the metaverse. For example, there may be pressure to conform to certain beauty standards or to alter one's appearance in ways that are not healthy or sustainable. Additionally, there may be concerns around the impact of virtual plastic surgery on real-world body image and self-esteem. As with any technology, it's important to approach the use of virtual plastic surgery thoughtfully and responsibly (Figure 5.2).

Industries, individual firms, and organizations are dynamically investing to develop virtual entity in the metaverse, ranging from social connections to fashion, from technical engineering to business, painting to construction industries. Now that the healthcare industry is involved in the Metaverse, there are countless opportunities for research, education, training, and prevention and treatment in clinical settings. Due to these factors, this study's goal is to: The goal was to comprehend the development of the scientific creative writing on the Metaverse related to health and to make suggestions for improvement in terms of clinical condition anticipation and action, education and training, and research. The use of the Metaverse was also taken into account. Therefore, it is crucial and fascinating to evaluate the existing public health literature. The study of literature gives him a clear idea of what he has done and needs to do.

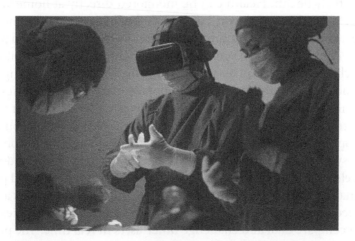

Figure 5.2 Doctors using Metaverse technology in operation theatre.

5.2   Discussion

The Metaverse has the capabilities to become the subsequently generation Internet 3.0. Thanks to this three-dimensional space of these techniques, the real presence of the user is connected, ensuring the opportunity of interaction and collaboration in circumstance.

5.2.1   Metaverse Used in the Prevention and Treatment

The primary aspect needed to be analyzed is the relationship among the metaverse and disease avoidance and treatment. Literature analysis of virtual and augmented reality shows that Metaverse can be used for diagnosis and rehabilitation of surgical procedures, pain, stroke, anxiety, depression, anxiety, cancer and neurodegenerative diseases with satisfactory results and became clear. Especially for cancer treatment, AI technology can help prevent and diagnose cancer, treat and rehabilitate patients. Health 4.0 is a widely accepted concept that integrates innovative technologies into healthcare. Health 4.0 examples include Internet of Health Things, medical cyber-physical systems, health cloud or fog, big data analytics, machine learning, blockchain, intelligent algorithms, and even virtual reality. This not only allows us to monitor the population, but also educates people on their involvement in community activities. Digital innovation has been embraced as an alternative model of care delivery, with methods of creating avatars enabling consultation and personalized care. In the Metaverse, doctors can use telemedicine services and home devices such as wearable sensors and smartphone apps to visit patients in her 3D virtual clinic and monitor their health. Health can be monitored directly at home and connect real life to the virtual world using a variety of devices. With the help of 12-lead heart electrocardiogram, cardiovascular assessment blood pressure monitor, cardiovascular oxygen saturation monitor, remote monitoring of human clinical aspects can be adopted, and then health monitoring system and blood glucose calculator can be adopted, perfect for diabetics. Heart rate monitors are also widely used on the Internet in connection with the assessment of physical performance. Another tool that has become especially popular in recent years is smart watches that integrate a global positioning system (GPS) as well as heart rate, blood saturation, pedometers and accelerometers. Data not only allows us to monitor health and physical performance, but also treat chronic diseases. These smart watches are often connected to smartphones, which are connected to communities where you can compare data and challenge other users in real time. The potential of smart watches in health promotion programs is enormous. Real-time monitoring allows you to join online communities and get expert guidance, increasing opportunities to participate in fitness programs and adopt healthy lifestyles around the world. This smart watch could be a tool for creating living humans in the Metaverse. In addition, his 24-hour monitoring of health parameters enables rapid prevention or intervention for problems such as atrial fibrillation, and also allows service providers to improve the safety of interventions. In addition to monitoring, another important aspect to consider is the presence of virtual AI-based avatars or agents in the Metaverse that can provide personalized feedback and motivation. In this way, interventions are more effective in supporting behavior change. These considerations can also be made when considering how avatars react realistically with words, facial expressions and body language thanks to new technology. preoperative planning by analyzing and obtaining the opinions of other connected experts via the Internet. Additionally, virtual reality can be integrated into a variety of therapeutic modalities, is an effective intervention for a variety of health conditions, and offers benefits in terms of compliance, cost, availability, motivation, and convenience. Virtual reality can also be used as a rehabilitation technique. Mirror therapy is used to create the illusion that the affected limb is functioning properly in order to re-educate cognitive patterns of movement.

5.2.2 Emerging Digital Techniques

Society must keep up with the fast development of non-technology and the possible of digital changes. Global tech start-ups are rapidly advancing digital health research and development. Digital technology is becoming pervasive in the pharmaceutical and biotech industries. The increasing use of smart phones, along with wearable devices is opening up new opportunities to measure the impact of health interventions in real time. Digital literacy has become an essential skill for governments, industry leaders and the general public. The Metaverse technologies helps the needy persons in terms of disable persons for better society [2, 3].

An experiment conducted by Donna Banakou attempted to capture a group of subjects into Albert Einstein's digital body. By changing their bodies, they became noticeably smarter. The same group used the same technique to change racial attitudes and confirmed that racial prejudice decreased when in the bodies of black subjects. In fact, your brain automatically changes the simulation when you enter another body. It is clear that these possibilities are opening up entirely new scenarios, from the world of health and well-being to the field of education. However, there are two paradoxes. First, the potential for positive applications of the Metaverse is only

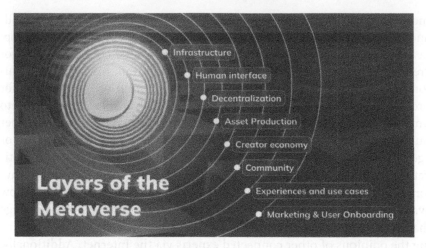

Figure 5.3 Layers of metaverse technology.

one side of the coin. Figure 5.3 shows the layers of metaverse technology. The other side is the risk that this technology poses. With the Metaverse, you can change not only people's behavior, but their emotions and even their perception of reality. What if we used the Metaverse to bring Adolf Hitler to life in my body, and associate gratitude and joy with that experience? In addition, the data collected in the Metaverse allows companies to be more social than his media and can also gather information about users much more efficiently. And that would probably require regulation at the supranational level, which is completely non-existent at the moment [4].

5.2.3   Limitations of the Metaverse

Metaverse's main limitations relate to data supervision, data security and data privacy, cyber security risks, ethical hacking, potential barriers to entry (poor internet connectivity), and visually impaired users. The Metaverse can be a dangerous place, especially where crimes and sophisticated crimes related to identity theft can occur. The first aspect to consider concerns data management and storage. The commercial interest is so great that people may have limited powers to control data sharing, with whom and on what terms. As a result, privacy, security, technical, legal and regulatory issues is essential to address. Privacy, ethics, and security concerns are also being raised by healthcare leaders as healthcare moves online. Therefore, there is a need to strengthen data security and centralize regulatory oversight. Organizational methods Controlled admission to a complex system of records is done via blockchain.

5.2.4   The Metaverse as Integrated Design Space

Formerly represented in fictional literature, the Metaverse is a globally accessible and collectively used multidimensional (3D) virtual space created by the convergence of virtual augmented physical reality and physically persistent virtual space, recently envisioned as a spatial and computing infrastructure (Figure 5.4). Various assumptions about technological, social, legal, economic and other aspects and factors have been made to predict the development and success of metaverse-related developments. In this context, a "progress indicator" has recently been defined. For example: B. Social indicators (such as digital rights management principles, patent law, etc.), business indicators (such as business models), or technical indicators (such as wearable technology) to help assess progress. Rather than think of the Metaverse as an end in itself, think of it as a means of moving cyber-physical development to different levels. In this sense, a first attempt was made to ensure interoperability between existing virtual worlds and their accessibility. It is therefore not surprising that standardization has been identified as a major obstacle or driver to the development of the metaverse, technology trends, and CPS [7, 62].

Other development drivers may prove relevant in the future. B. Take steps to prevent (whether knowingly or unintentionally) unethical or illegal conduct. In our view, a unified design space must be created to sustainably respond to social and business challenges and meet CPS-related expectations for high-value use cases to adapt. This space needs to be integrated, coordinated and coordinated between different layers of technology and

Figure 5.4 Connect to metaverse.

human cognition. We need to put humans in the cycle of automating and adapting technology like never before [8].

5.3   Medical Cloud Plus

The interaction among the virtual cloud experts, doctors (terminal) and real cloud experts is enabled and enhanced with the help of a cloud plus terminal application, this application enhances the quality in medical education as the students able to revise the lesson, easier consultations for passengers, diagnosis into gross root level, medicine and clinical research is effective, these Metaverse and cloud combined platforms helps the all stakes holders of the hospitals and the allied areas of education.

5.3.1   Existing Metaverse Platforms

1. Decentraland: It is a blockchain-based application which creates social environment. Detailed information about the Decentraland can be accessed from https://decentraland. org/
2. The Sandbox: the sandbox is a 3Dimensional virtual reality application used the etherium coins for transactions, it's a meta based game, more detailed information can be accessed from sandbox.

There are various popular Metaverse platforms available in the block chain environment, like metahorizon world, metahero project etc.

5.3.2   A Space for New Social Communication

Due to the ongoing COVID-19 pandemic, it is not easy for many people to have private meetings or eat together in restaurants. But in the Metaverse, hundreds of thousands and tens of millions of people can gather to host festivals and watch concerts of their favorite singers. Virtual reality metaverses like Roblox and Zepeto have provided new social spaces for people who have been unable to leave their homes due to COVID-19 to meet and relax. When schools were closed due to COVID-19 and students were unable to attend school, the most popular of Zepeto's 3D maps was the Classroom Map. The students went to Zepet's classroom instead of the correct classroom. They met with friends and kept in touch. While the idol group BLACK PINK was unable to hold a face-to-face fan signing event due to the influence of the new coronavirus, they held a virtual fan sign-ing event through Zepeto. Blackpink also released a choreographed music video for "Ice Cream" recreated using avatars, with over 46 million users attending his Blackpink virtual fan-signing event to sign autographs with their favorite singers [9].

5.4   The Metaverse's Benefits and Drawbacks

5.4.1   Advantages of Metaverse

We must first gain a basic understanding of the Metaverse and its sup-porting technologies in order to appreciate its advantages. Initially, keep in mind that business managers, entrepreneurs, the media, and researchers all employ various definitions. One common definition is a graphics-in-tensive digital universe that makes use of augmented reality, virtual real-ity, artificial intelligence, and other related technologies to build a virtual environment that facilitates collaboration and immersive user experiences. Due to the ability to navigate, it is a fully immersive virtual environment where people can establish a virtual presence that offers experiences that are nearly identical to those of the real world. Additionally, group commu-nication is more realistic [10].

Enhanced Collaboration: The Metaverse offers new opportunities for col-laboration by enabling people to work together in real-time regardless of their physical location. It could also provide a more immersive and engag-ing platform for remote teams to work together, increasing productivity and efficiency.

New Business Models: The Metaverse could open up new business models and revenue streams for companies. For instance, it could offer new chan-nels for advertising, e-commerce, and virtual goods sales.

Improved Education: The Metaverse could also provide new opportunities for education by creating immersive and engaging virtual learning environ-ments that can facilitate active learning and help students develop new skills.

Enhanced Social Interaction: The Metaverse offers a more social expe-rience compared to traditional online platforms. It can enable people to socialize, meet new friends, and form communities with people who share their interests, regardless of geographical barriers.

Virtual Travel and Tourism: The Metaverse could offer new opportunities for virtual travel and tourism by providing immersive and interactive virtual experiences of real-world locations and attractions, making travel accessible to more people.

Personalized and Customized Experiences: The Metaverse could also provide personalized and customized experiences for users. It could enable users to create their own virtual environments and avatars, and customize their experience according to their preferences.

Overall, the Metaverse offers numerous advantages, and its potential applications are vast and diverse, ranging from entertainment to education to business. However, as with any emerging technology, there are also potential risks and challenges that need to be addressed.

5.4.2   Disadvantages of Metaverse

The creation of digital frameworks that operate as platforms for the deployment of apps that will further alter how people interact and communicate with one another over the Internet is commonly referred to as one of the benefits of the metaverse. Numerous people and organizations have expressed worry about the inherent drawbacks and restrictions, including the need for more dependable Internet connections and the present difficulties [11].

Privacy concerns: As the Metaverse requires users to create digital personas and interact with others, it raises concerns about the privacy of personal information and data. The collection and use of personal data by companies operating in the Metaverse could pose a threat to individuals' privacy.

Addiction and overuse: The immersive and engaging nature of the Metaverse could lead to addiction and overuse, which could negatively impact mental and physical health.

Digital divide: The Metaverse could create a digital divide, where only those with access to the required technology and infrastructure could participate fully. This could create social and economic disparities.

Centralization of power: The development and operation of the Metaverse could be controlled by a few large companies, leading to a concentration of power and potential monopolistic behavior.

Security risks: As with any digital platform, the Metaverse could be vulnerable to security breaches, hacking, and other cyber threats.

Ethical concerns: The creation of a virtual world that mimics reality raises ethical questions around the impact on social behavior and human relationships. There may be issues around censorship, hate speech, and other forms of inappropriate content.

It's essential to consider these potential drawbacks when exploring the possibilities of the Metaverse and work towards addressing them in a responsible and ethical manner.

5.5   Applications of Metaverse in Various Fields

5.5.1   Automobile Applications

There are several advances are happening in the automobile sector these are some of the areas where the Metaverse technologies can be implemented for efficient automobiles

Design and prototyping: The Metaverse can provide a virtual environment where designers and engineers can collaborate to design and prototype new cars, parts, and systems. This can help to reduce the time and cost of physical prototyping while allowing for real-time testing and evaluation.

Manufacturing and assembly: The Metaverse can simulate and optimize manufacturing and assembly processes, helping to identify and eliminate potential issues before production. This can reduce production costs and increase efficiency.

Training and education: The Metaverse can provide a virtual training environment for automotive engineers, technicians, and other professionals. This can allow for hands-on, interactive training without the need for expensive physical equipment.

Sales and marketing: The Metaverse can offer a unique and immersive sales and marketing experience, allowing customers to explore and customize cars and components in a virtual environment. This can help to increase engagement and sales while reducing the need for physical show-rooms and events.

Maintenance and repair: The Metaverse can provide a virtual environment for diagnosing and repairing automotive issues, allowing technicians to access and manipulate digital models of cars and parts. This can increase the accuracy and speed of repairs while reducing downtime and costs.

5.5.2   Applications of Metaverse Technologies in Military Sector

Military AR and VR applications have also seen significant breakthroughs. Tactical Augmented Reality (TAR) is a technology that looks like Night Vision Goggles (NVG) but has a lot more capabilities. It can display the exact location of a soldier as well as the positions of allied and enemy forces. The system is attached to the helmet in the same way as glasses and can be used at any time of the day or night [12].

5.5.3   Educational Application

The Metaverse technologies are used in the education sector for simulation and trainings, in reality there is a huge gap exists between teaching and understanding among student community. We can discover new worlds and sensations thanks to virtual reality. You can expose yourself to excellent representations that can have a good effect on your life by donning a VR headset. The efficiency of using graphics to highlight topics will never be as high in traditional teaching methods. Students always opt to watch something rather than read, regardless of their age. Because it can create amazing experiences that can never be "experienced" in real life, virtual reality technology is fascinating. Students will be more motivated to learn thanks to the employment of this technology.

5.5.4   Manufacturing

As one of the cutting-edge technologies of the metaverse, VR applications can help train employees on security measures along with encouraging participation in the simulation of risk scenarios. As a result, metaverse applications can greatly contribute to reducing accident risks. The most popular applications of the metaverse in manufacturing could facilitate the development of better products in the long run [13].

5.5.5   In Construction Industries

The Metaverse has several potential applications in the construction industry, including:

Planning and Design: The Metaverse can provide a virtual environment for architects, engineers, and contractors to collaborate and plan construction projects. This can allow for real-time feedback and adjustments, reducing the time and cost of physical prototyping.

Safety Training: The Metaverse can provide a safe and controlled environment for training workers in construction safety procedures. This can allow workers to practice hazardous activities without risking their safety and well-being.

Virtual Site Inspection: The Metaverse can provide virtual site inspection capabilities, allowing inspectors to review construction progress and safety compliance without being physically present at the site. This can help reduce travel costs and time, while also improving safety and efficiency.

Virtual Reality Tours: The Metaverse can provide virtual reality tours of completed projects, allowing clients and stakeholders to explore and interact with buildings before they are built. This can help improve communication and collaboration between stakeholders and increase customer satisfaction.

Remote Collaboration: The Metaverse can facilitate remote collaboration among construction teams working on the same project from different locations. This can improve coordination and communication between team members and help reduce travel and lodging expenses.

5.6   Definition and Clinical Significance of Metaverse in Medicine

It addresses the four tiers of performance requirements in the metaverse theory and is based on almost five years of experience as well as recent research. However, no one in the medical field has proposed a metaverse, nor is there a concept of a medical metaverse. Her use of IoT in medicine while using AR glasses is known as metaverse. Since 2017, we have been engaged in related work. BRM All-in-One, a device that could be considered the medical equivalent of the Metaverse, was created by H. In-depth investigations on how to conduct metaverse medicine using holographic building, holographic simulation, virtual real merging, and virtual real bonding have just been completed by our team. Holographic simulation, virtual-real integration, and virtual-real connection are used, all of which have high-tech connotations.

The medical metaverse We suggest extending holographic building to "holographic construction + complex perception" in order to better and more effectively utilize Metaverse in medicine; to increase holographic simulation "Extend virtual-real integration to "virtual-real integration + quality control"; holographic simulation plus intelligent processing "Virtual-real connection + human-machine connection" should be included to the virtual-real connection" [14].

At some point, you will come to the realization that "complicated problems are simplified, simple problems are digitalized, digital problems are programmed, and programming difficulties are systematized." This can solve the issue that current telemedicine and Internet medicine platforms, particularly in metropolitan hospitals, are challenging to manage at the county level. The current model of diagnosis and treatment in the craft workshop style of various levels can be easily updated to a modern assembly line project that meets national and even worldwide requirements since hierarchical diagnosis and treatment technology is more practical to use.

The great complexity of human anatomy, etiology, pathological and pathophysiological changes, and pharmacodynamic efficacy of the same drug in different patients makes the study and practice of the metaverse in medicine extremely difficult. However, it is based on the successful research results of the metaverse. In pulmonary nodule medicine, we discovered that even if we divide the medical metaverse by disease, we can find the law of resolution. This allows for "broad simplification," the simplification of complex issues of medical importance through consensus guidelines. According to complex perception and holographic structure solutions, to transfer holographic design information to the Metaverse of the Medical Cloud for the next step in the Intelligent Holographic Simulation process [15].

5.6.1   Holographic Simulation Diagnosis - Medical Image Processing

Holographic simulation is a new feature that significantly reduces iteration time when developing holographic applications in Unity. Research shows that developers building applications for Microsoft HoloLens can quickly prototype, debug, and iterate their designs directly from the Unity editor, without the hassle of lengthy build and deployment times. Although current preliminary research indicates that the results do not apply to medicine, holographic simulations hold promise for medical applications. The Figure 5.5 depicts the metaverse integrated design space and Figure 5.6 shows the holographic diagnostic approach flow chart. The addition of intelligent processing would greatly improve the current effectiveness of the Internet of Things in medical applications. Improving the effectiveness of education and increasing the efficiency of teaching and training is one of the goals of the augmented metaverse in medicine. This solves the problem that cloud experts cannot immerse themselves in scientific education and expert lectures anytime and anywhere, and cannot request cloud experts to lead the final doctor's diagnosis and treatment anytime and anywhere. The IOT medicine can be transplanted to AR glasses without any modifications.

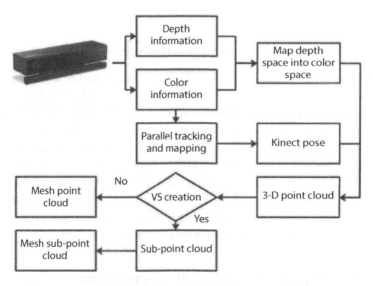

Figure 5.5 Metaverse as integrated design space [23].

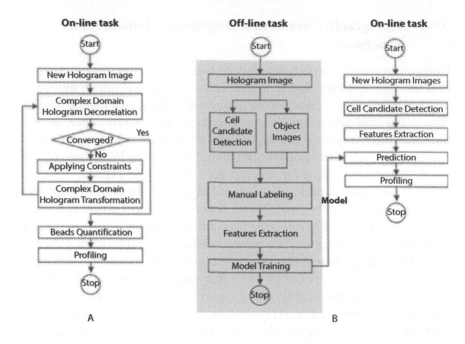

Figure 5.6 Holographic diagnostic approach flow chart, A shows the Regular approach and B indicates Approach with Machine learning and Metaverse.

5.6.2   Virtual-Real Connection – Human-Machine Integration

In clinical work, the Metaverse will be the "integration of virtual and real human-machine connectivity" that best reflects medical value. Current technology reflects virtual reality connectivity, which is very mature, but requires advanced clinical application of human-machine integration to improve diagnostic and therapeutic outcomes. To this end, we propose to systematize the virtual-real man-machine connection problem, either pro-grammatically or via a "man-machine MDT". Based on procedural digital techniques that help integrate virtual and real connections, workshop-style diagnostic and therapeutic models are transformed into modern assembly line projects that meet national and international standards.

5.6.3   Developing the Cardio Verse Application

The cardiovascular community has always looked for effective ways to integrate cutting-edge technological innovations into clinical practice, despite the fact that healthcare and the life sciences have historically been slow to adopt changes to long-established working practices inspired by technology. The creation of a future cardiology-focused meta-version (Cardio-Verse), a theoretical phrase for the adoption of meta-version by cardiovascular medicine, would concentrate on the different ways that cardiology and heart surgery could profit from this digital trend. CardioVerse has a modified model that is based on two axes and four different metaverse types. The possibilities and cutting-edge applications of medicine that CardioVerse provides at first glance seems enormous, but at the same time it raises many safety, technical and moral questions [16].

5.6.4   Enhanced Medical Visits

With a 3D virtual clinic that offers a far better user experience when it comes to telemedicine services, Metaverse wants to increase the number of cardiac doctor visits where patients and medical professionals can consult. A cardiac surgeon or physician to evaluate the disease course and discuss test results, patients can participate in virtual consultations and aftercare talks. Because tactile technology to simulate human touch is still in its infancy, not all cardiovascular disorders are primarily determined through physical examination. This has benefits of its own because numerous physical visits can be made almost regardless of the participant's location. There is no doubting that virtual environments cannot easily simulate physical contact, and Cardio-Verse is not meant to take the place of real-world interactions not intended to replace physical encounters.

However, we are really looking to make better telemedicine visits and create them as close to physical visits as possible. This is a notable advantage, especially for those who live in remote areas or who have difficulty getting to hospitals or clinics (e.g., disability). Patients can measure blood pressure, glucose levels, heart rate, get an electrocardiogram with a 12-lead ECG device (based on a smartphone app), and project all results directly into the Metaverse platform, allowing doctors and patients to ask questions. You can Investigate and discuss results and create virtual diagnoses Avatar-based virtual representations transform existing remote consultations based on video calls into patient and physician interactions using high-resolution illustrations, 3D reconstructions of people and the environment. (Facial scanning applications are used by younger patients, who are also accustomed to gamification of different aspects of their daily lives, so it is important to adopt and follow such technology for younger generations.) Hospitals are already built to deliver care in this new way of providing concurrent opportunities for adaptation-based disease education, prevention and diagnosis.

5.6.5   Virtual Training for Surgeries and Biomedical Devices

Doctors may find the process challenging since surgery calls for specialized abilities that require extensive experience and training. To overcome this issue, VR gives medical trainees the chance to practice a low-risk operation before doing surgery on a patient. Virtual reality simulators like RASimsAs, AnatomyX, and SimSurgery helped students get ready for unforeseen circumstances that may arise during medical procedures. These simulations are becoming more and more common in medical schools, helping students learn skills like quick thinking, problem-solving in the real world, and task performance under pressure. Some of the above simulators encourage collaboration by using pointers to let others see what one is pointing to in the virtual world, even when VR programs discourage it owing to segregated headsets. Together, students and teachers can use a pointer to point to an object that their peers would see in the virtual environment instead of specifically stating the object or body part they are referring.

5.6.6   Real-Time Trending Applications of VR and AR in Mental Health

There haven't yet been any studies on the use of therapeutic tools in the metaverse to treat psychiatric problems. However, the diagnosis and treatment of mental health illnesses are increasingly being done using VR, AR, and MR. Virtual reality simulations have the advantage of allowing users to virtually reproduce scenarios that are challenging to replicate in real life. The lack of mental health specialists can also be controlled because some VR simulations can allow providers to engage remotely from remote regions without having to be physically there. The following mental health conditions could have benefited from using simulations in the metaverse in VR treatment.

5.6.7   Eating Disorders

VR technologies used in food industries, the food industries are developing variety of foods, the food industry is mainly depends of taste, whereas health needs taste and hygiene quality. The human beings ate these foods without any calculations of calories burnt and calories consumed. The VR enabled technologies show how much food to be consumed and what type of food healthier as per hotel and area the customized foods can be suggested with metaverse technologies. The patients get benefitted mostly with these technologies.

5.6.8   Possible Extensions of Metaverse Technologies

The following areas are not limited to

- ✓ Standardization of VR, AR and MR applications in medical devices, medical applications and education
- ✓ User manual and health assistance for Metaverse medical application systems
- ✓ Sensor assisted Metaverse technologies in ophthalmology surgery studies
- ✓ CT image capturing with Metaverse technologies medical application systems
- ✓ Surgical simulation based on Metaverse technologies medical application systems
- ✓ Medical robotics based on Metaverse technologies medical application devices
- ✓ Metaverse technologies condition analysis aid
- ✓ Metaverse technologies medical live telecasting and remote treatment
- ✓ Metaverse technologies psychological intervention therapy
- ✓ Metaverse technologies-based virtual medical community
- ✓ Metaverse technologies treatment of childhood autism
- ✓ Metaverse technologies assisted Rehabilitation
- ✓ Pain studies with Metaverse technologies
- ✓ Metaverse technologies games for medical purposes
- ✓ Metaverse technologies treatment of mental disorder fear
- ✓ Data privacy for Metaverse technologies and image processing prediction and other analytics
- ✓ Solution to dizziness reduction with Metaverse technologies.

5.6.9   Alzheimer's Disease Solutions

VR is being used to identify the navigation skills and highlight the cognition in Alzheimer's patients. However, in some patients experienced boredom, sacredness and anxiety when applying VR applications [17]. The VR equipments are in Alzheimer disease the patients get accurate information about the disease and the medication levels and other related issues of Alzheimer disease.

5.7   Conclusions

The application of Metaverse technologies specifically augmented reality, as a add on method, which plays major role to improve efficacy and effectiveness of various divisions of the medical industries. The Metaverse technologies used as an educational tool in addition to the current education, the current technologies of medical education are inferior, without addition of the Metaverse technologies. The laparoscopic surgeries ENT surgeries and critical heart diseases surgeries also can be taught with the help of these technologies, there are implications on the real life precision surgeries by internship medical students, with the Metaverse technologies, the medical students get hands on training and effective medical education. it is further recommended that Metaverse technologies should be used in practicals and trainings such in laparoscopic surgeries, orthopedic surgeries, ligament surgeries Gynecology surgeries, suturing, ultrasound surgeries, various nursing procedures and paramedical applications. The Metaverse technologies can be extended to various engineering and non-engineering fields in training and other potentials areas.

References

1. Petrigna, L. and Musumeci, G., The metaverse: A new challenge for the healthcare system: A scoping review. *J. Funct. Morphol. Kinesiology*, 7, 3, 63, 2022. https://doi.org/10.3390/jfmk7030063.
2. Agarwal, R., *et al.,* Cardiovascular and kidney outcomes with finerenone in patients with type 2 diabetes and chronic kidney disease: The Fidelity pooled analysis. *Europ. Heart J.,* 43, 6, 7, 474–484, February 2022. https://doi.org/10.1093/eurheartj/ehab777
3. Chavannes, N.H. and Bai, C., Welcome to the new era of metaverse in medicine. *Clin. EHealth*, 5, 37–38, 2022. https://doi.org/10.1016/j.ceh.2022.06.001.
4. Huvila, I., Sorting out the metaverse and how the metaverse is sorting us out, in: *The Immersive Internet*, Teigland, R., Power, D. (eds.), Palgrave Macmillan, London, 2013. https://doi.org/10.1057/9781137283023_17
5. Sintowoko, D.A.W., Resmadi, I., Azhar, H., Gumilar, G., Wahab, T. (Eds.), Sustainable development in creative industries: Embracing digital

culture for humanities, in: *Proceedings of the 9th Bandung Creative Movement International Conference On Creative Industries (BCM 2022)*, (1st ed.), Routledge, Bandung, Indonesia, 1 SEPTEMBER 2022, 2023. https://doi.org/10.1201/9781003372486

6. Falchuk, B., Loeb, S., Neff, R., The social metaverse: Battle for privacy. *IEEE Technol. Soc. Magazine*, 37, 2, 52–61, 2018. https://doi.org/10.1109/MTS.2018.2826060.

7. Rehm, S.-V., Goel, L., Crespi, M., The metaverse as mediator between technology, trends, and the digital transformation of society and business. *Futures J. Virtual Worlds Res.*, 8, 2, 2015. http://jvwresearch.org.

8. Ning, H. *et al.*, A survey on metaverse: The state-of-the-art, technologies, applications, and challenges, *IEEE Internet of Things Journal.*

9. Kye, B., Han, N., Kim, E., Park, Y., Jo, S., Educational applications of metaverse: Possibilities and limitations, in: *Journal of Educational Evaluation for Health Professions*. Korea Health Personnel Licensing Examination Institute, vol. 18, 2021. https://doi.org/10.3352/jeehp.2021.18.32.

10. Kumar, A.V. *et al.*, Design, analysis and fabrication of human external ear by using fused film fabrication. *IOP Conference Series: Materials Science and Engineering*, vol. 988, IOP Publishing, 2020.

11. Samadbeik, M., Yaaghobi, D., Bastani, P., Abhari, S., Rezaee, R., Garavand, A., The applications of virtual reality technology in medical groups teaching. *J. Adv. Med. Educ.Prof.*, 6, 3, 123–129, 2018.

12. Raajan, N.R. *et al.*, Augmented reality based virtual reality. *Proc. Eng.*, 38, 1559–1565, 2012.

13. Saheb, S.H. and Babu, G.S., Kinematic analysis of 3RRR planar parallel manipulator by using adaptive neuro fuzzy inference system (ANFIS). *Solid State Technol.*, 64.2, 01–12, 2021.

14. Usmani, S.S., Sharath, M., Mehendale, M., Future of mental health in the metaverse, in: *General Psychiatry*. vol. 35, issue 4, BMJ Publishing Group, 2022. https://doi.org/10.1136/gpsych-2022-100825.

15. Thomason, J., Metaverse, token economies, and non-communicable diseases. *Glob. Health J., KeAi Communications Co.*, 6, 3, 164–167, September 2022. https://doi.org/10.1016/j.glohj.2022.07.001.

16. Zhou, H., Gao, J.Y., Chen, Y., The paradigm and future value of the metaverse for the intervention of cognitive decline. *Front. Public Health*, 10, 1016680, 2022.

17. Panda, S.K. and Satapathy, S.C., An Investigation into Smart Contract Deployment on Ethereum Platform Using Web3.js and Solidity Using Blockchain, in: *Data Engineering and Intelligent Computing*, Advances in Intelligent Systems and Computing, V. Bhateja, S.C. Satapathy, C.M. Travieso-González, V.N.M. Aradhya (Eds.), vol. 1, Springer, Singapore, 2021. https://doi.org/10.1007/978-981-16-0171-2_52.

18. Panda, S.K., Rao, D.C., Satapathy, S.C., An investigation into the usability of blockchain technology in Internet of Things, in: *Data Engineering and*

Intelligent Computing, Advances in Intelligent Systems and Computing, V. Bhateja, S.C. Satapathy, C.M. Travieso-González, V.N.M. Aradhya (Eds.), vol. 1, Springer, Singapore, 2021. https://doi.org/10.1007/978-981-16-0171-2_53.

19. Panda, S.K., Dash, S.P., Jena, A.K., Optimization of block query response using evolutionary algorithm, in: *Data Engineering and Intelligent Computing, Advances in Intelligent Systems and Computing*, V. Bhateja, S.C. Satapathy, C.M. Travieso-González, V.N.M. Aradhya (Eds.), vol. 1, Springer, Singapore, 2021. https://doi.org/10.1007/978-981-16-0171-2_54.

20. Nanda, S.K., Panda, S.K., Das, M., Satapathy, S.C., Automating vehicle insurance process using smart contract and ethereum, in: *Advances in Micro-Electronics, Embedded Systems and IoT*, Lecture Notes in Electrical Engineering, V.V.S.S.S. Chakravarthy, W. Flores-Fuentes, V. Bhateja, B. Biswal (Eds.), vol. 838, Springer, Singapore, 2022. https://doi.org/10.1007/978-981-16-8550-7_23.

21. Varaprasada Rao, K. and Panda, S.K., Secure electronic voting (E-voting) system based on blockchain on various platforms, in: *Computer Communication, Networking and IoT*, Lecture Notes in Networks and Systems, S.C. Satapathy, J.C.W. Lin, L.K. Wee, V. Bhateja, T.M. Rajesh (Eds.), vol. 459, Springer, Singapore, 2023. https://doi.org/10.1007/978-981-19-1976-3_18.

22. Varaprasada Rao, K. and Panda, S.K., A design model of copyright protection system based on distributed ledger technology, in: *Computer Communication, Networking and IoT*, Lecture Notes in Networks and Systems, S.C. Satapathy, J.C.W. Lin, L.K. Wee, V. Bhateja, T.M. Rajesh (Eds.), vol. 459, Springer, Singapore, 2023. https://doi.org/10.1007/978-981-19-1976-3_17.

23. Panda, S.K., Elngar, A.A., Balas, V.E., Kayed, M. (Eds.), *Bitcoin and blockchain: History and current applications*, 1st ed, CRC Press, 2020 https://doi.org/10.1201/9781003032588.

24. Panda, S.K., Jena, A.K., Swain, S.K., Satapathy, S.C. (Eds.), *Blockchain Technology: Applications and Challenges*, Springer, Intelligent Systems Reference Library, pp. 1–300, 2021 https://doi.org/10.1007/978-3-030-69395-4.

25. Sathya, A.R., Panda, S.K., Hanumanthakari, S., Enabling smart education system using blockchain technology, in: *Blockchain Technology: Applications and Challenges*, Intelligent Systems Reference Library, S.K. Panda, A.K. Jena, S.K. Swain, S.C. Satapathy (Eds.), vol. 203, Springer, Cham, 2021. https://doi.org/10.1007/978-3-030-69395-4_10.

26. Lokre, S.S., Naman, V., Priya, S., Panda, S.K., Gun tracking system using blockchain technology, in: *Blockchain Technology: Applications and Challenges*, Intelligent Systems Reference Library, S.K. Panda, A.K. Jena, S.K. Swain, S.C. Satapathy (Eds.), vol. 203, Springer, Cham, 2021. https://doi.org/10.1007/978-3-030-69395-4_16.

27. Panda, S.K., Daliyet, S.P., Lokre, S.S., Naman, V., Distributed ledger technology in the construction industry using corda, in: *The New Advanced Society: Artificial Intelligence and Industrial Internet of Things Paradigm*. https://doi.org/10.1002/9781119884392.ch2.

28. Panda, S.K., Mohammad, G.B., Nandan Mohanty, S., Sahoo, S., Smart contract-based land registry system to reduce frauds and time delay. *Security and Privacy*, e172, 2021. https://doi.org/10.1002/spy2.172.

29. Panda, S.K. and Satapathy, S.C., Drug traceability and transparency in medical supply chain using blockchain for easing the process and creating trust between stakeholders and consumers. *Pers. Ubiquit. Comput.*, 2021. https://doi.org/10.1007/s00779-021-01588-3.

30. Niveditha, V.R., Karthik Sekaran, K., Singh, A., Panda, S.K., Effective prediction of bitcoin price using wolf search algorithm and bidirectional LSTM on internet of things data. *Int. J. System Syst. Eng.*, 11, 3–4, 224–236, 2021.

31. Sri Arza, M. and Panda, S.K., An integration of blockchain and machine learning into the healthcare system, in: *Machine Learning Adoption in Blockchain-Based Intelligent Manufacturing*, vol. 1, pp. 33–58, 2009.

32. Murala, D.K., Panda, S.K., Swain, S.K., A survey on cloud computing security and privacy issues and challenges. *J. Adv. Res. Dyn. Control Syst.*, 11, 1276–1290, 2019.

33. Murala, D.K., Panda, S.K., Swain, S.K., Secure dynamic groups data sharing with modified revocable attribute-based encryption in cloud. *Int. J. Recent Technol. Eng. (IJRTE)*, 8, 4, 2019.

34. Murala, D.K., Panda, S.K., Swain, S.K., A novel hybrid approach for providing data security and privacy from malicious attacks in the cloud environment. *J. Adv. Res. Dyn. Control Syst.*, 11, 1291–1300, 2019.

35. Panda, S.K., Swain, S.K., Mall, R., An investigation into usability aspects of E-commerce websites using users' preferences. *Adv. Comput. Science: An Int. J.*, 4, 1, 65–73, 2015.

36. Panda, S.K., Swain, S.K., Mall, R., Measuring web site usability quality complexity metrics for navigability, in: *Intelligent Computing, Communication and Devices*, Advances in Intelligent Systems and Computing, L. Jain, S. Patnaik, N. Ichalkaranje (Eds.), vol. 308, Springer, New Delhi, 2015. https://doi.org/10.1007/978-81-322-2012-1_41.

37. Panda, S.K., A usability evaluation framework for B2C E-commerce websites. *Comput. Eng. Intell. Syst.*, 5, 3, 66–85, 2014.

38. Bhalerao, V., Panda, S.K., Jena, A.K., Optimization of loss function on human faces using generative adversarial networks, in: *Machine Learning Approaches for Urban Computing*, Studies in Computational Intelligence, vol. 968, M. Bandyopadhyay, M. Rout, S. Chandra Satapathy (Eds.), Springer, Singapore, 2021. https://doi.org/10.1007/978-981-16-0935-0_9.

39. Panda, S.K. and Dwivedi, M., Minimizing food wastage using machine learning: A novel approach, in: *Smart Intelligent Computing and Applications*, Smart Innovation, Systems and Technologies, S. Satapathy, V. Bhateja, J. Mohanty, S. Udgata (Eds.), vol. 159, Springer, Singapore, 2020, https://doi.org/10.1007/978-981-13-9282-5_44.

40. Panda, S.K., A.R, S., Mishra, M., Satpathy, S., A supervised learning algorithm to forecast weather conditions for playing cricket. *Int. J. Innovative Technol. Exploring Eng. (IJITEE)*, 9, 1, 2019.

41. Panda, S.K., *Fraud-resistant crowdfunding system using ethereum blockchain, bitcoin and blockchain*, pp. 237–276, CRC Press, Boca Raton, 2020.

42. Panda, S.K., Mishra, V., Balamurali, R., Elngar, A.A., *Artificial intelligence and machine learning in business management concepts, challenges, and case studies*, pp. 1–278, CRC Press, Boca Raton, 2021, https://doi.org/10.1201/9781003125129.

43. Joshi, S., Panda, S.K., AR, S., Optimal deep learning model to identify the development of pomegranate fruit in farms. *Int. J. Innovative Technol. Exploring Eng.*, 9, 3, 2352–2356, 2020.

44. Puranam, K.S.R., Gaddam, M.C.T., K, V.P.R., Panda, S.K., Reddy, G.S.M., Anatomy and lifecycle of a bitcoin transaction. *Proceedings of International Conference on Sustainable Computing in Science, Technology and Management (SUSCOM)*, Amity University Rajasthan, Jaipur-India, February 26-28, 2019, February 18, 2019. https://ssrn.com/abstract=3355106orhttp://dx.doi.org/10.2139/ssrn.3355106.

45. Panda, S.K. and Swain, S.K., *Quality assurance aspects of web design, design solutions for improving website quality and effectiveness*, pp. 87–129, IGI Global, 2016.

46. Panda, S.K., Bhalerao, V., AR, S., A machine learning model to identify duplicate questions in social media forums. *Int. J. Innovative Technol. Exploring Eng.*, 9, 4, 370–373, 2020.

47. Ahmareen, S., Raj, A., Potluri, S., Panda, S.K., Book Shala: An android-based application design and implementation of sharing books, in: *Smart Intelligent Computing and Applications, Smart Innovation, Systems and Technologies*, S. Satapathy, V. Bhateja, J. Mohanty, S. Udgata (Eds.), vol. 159, Springer, Singapore, 2020. https://doi.org/10.1007/978-981-13-9282-5_28.

48. Panda, S.K., Das, S.S., Swain, S.K., S-model for service-oriented applications in web engineering. *Regional Coll. Manag.*, 10, 3, 38–46, 2013.

49. Panda, S.K., An investigation into usability and productivity of ecommerce websites. https://shodhganga.inflibnet.ac.in:8443/jspui/handle/10603/123505.

50. Panda, S.K., Chandrasekhar, A., Gantayat, P.K., Panda, M.R., Detecting brain tumor using image segmentation: A novel approach, in: *Data Engineering and Intelligent Computing*, Lecture Notes in Networks and Systems, V. Bhateja, L. Khin Wee, J.C.W. Lin, S.C. Satapathy, T.M. Rajesh (Eds.), vol. 446, Springer, Singapore, 2022. https://doi.org/10.1007/978-981-19-1559-8_35.

51. Sanghi, P., Panda, S.K., Pati, C., Gantayat, P.K., Learning deep features and classification for fresh or off vegetables to prevent food wastage using machine learning algorithms, in: *Intelligent Data Engineering and Analytics, Smart Innovation, Systems and Technologies*, S.C. Satapathy, P. Peer, J. Tang, V. Bhateja, A. Ghosh (Eds.), vol. 266, Springer, Singapore, 2022. https://doi.org/10.1007/978-981-16-6624-7_44.

52. Gantayat, P.K., Mohapatra, S., Panda, S.K., Secure trust level routing in delay-tolerant network with node categorization technique, in: *Intelligent Data Engineering and Analytics*, Smart Innovation, Systems and Technologies,

S.C. Satapathy, P. Peer, J. Tang, V. Bhateja, A. Ghosh (Eds.), vol. 266, Springer, Singapore, 2022. https://doi.org/10.1007/978-981-16-6624-7_45.

53. Panda, S.K., Urkude, S.V., Urkude, V.R., Vairachilai, S., An investigation into COVID 19 pandemic in India, in: *The New Advanced Society: Artificial Intelligence and Industrial Internet of Things Paradigm*, vol. 1, pp. 289–305, Wiley.

54. Panda, S.K., Das, S., Swain, S.K., Web site productivity measurement using single task size measure. *J. Inf. Sci. Computing Technol. (JISCT)*, 4, 3, October12, 2015.

55. Hanumanthakari, S. and Panda, S.K., Detecting face mask for prevent COVID-19 using deep learning: A novel approach, in: *Smart Intelligent Computing and Applications, Volume 2*, Smart Innovation, Systems and Technologies, S.C. Satapathy, V. Bhateja, M.N. Favorskaya, T. Adilakshmi (Eds.), vol. 283, Springer, Singapore, 2022. https://doi.org/10.1007/978-981-16-9705-0_45.

56. Panda, S.K., Sathya, A.R., Das, S., Bitcoin: Beginning of the cryptocurrency era, in: *Recent Advances in Blockchain Technology*, Intelligent Systems Reference Library, vol. 237, S.K. Panda, V. Mishra, S.P. Dash, A.K. Pani (Eds.), Springer, Cham, 2023. https://doi.org/10.1007/978-3-031-22835-3_2.

57. Murala, D.K., Panda, S.K., Sahoo, S.K., Securing electronic health record system in cloud environment using blockchain technology, in: *Recent Advances in Blockchain Technology*, Intelligent Systems Reference Library, vol. 237, S.K. Panda, V. Mishra, S.P. Dash, A.K. Pani (Eds.), Springer, Cham, 2023. https://doi.org/10.1007/978-3-031-22835-3_4.

58. Rao, K.V., Murala, D.K., Panda, S.K., Blockchain: A study of new business model, in: *Recent Advances in Blockchain Technology*, Intelligent Systems Reference Library, S.K. Panda, V. Mishra, S.P. Dash, A.K. Pani (Eds.), vol. 237, Springer, Cham, 2023. https://doi.org/10.1007/978-3-031-22835-3_9.

59. Panda, S.K., Mishra, V., Dash, S.P., Pani, A.K., *Recent advances in blockchain technology real-world applications*, Intelligent Systems Reference Library (ISRL, volume 237), vol. 1, pp. 1–317, 2023.

60. Panda, S.K., Mohapatra, R.K., Panda, S., Balamurugan, S., *The new advanced society: Artificial intelligence and industrial internet of things paradigm*, vol. 1, pp. 1–512, John Wiley & Sons, 2022.

61. Nanda, S.K., Panda, S.K., Das, M., Satapathy, S.C., Decentralization of car insurance system using machine learning and distributed ledger technology, in: *Intelligent Data Engineering and Analytics. FICTA 2022, Smart Innovation, Systems and Technologies*, V. Bhateja, X.S. Yang, J. Chun-Wei Lin, R. Das (Eds.), vol. 327, Springer, Singapore, 2023. https://doi.org/10.1007/978-981-19-7524-0_52.

62. Nanda, S.K., Panda, S.K., Dash, M., Medical supply chain integrated with blockchain and IoT to track the logistics of medical products. *Multimed. Tools Appl.*, 2023. https://doi.org/10.1007/s11042-023-14846-8.

6

The Role of Immersive Reality (AR/VR/MR/XR) in Metaverse

Dileep Kumar Murala[1] and Sandeep Kumar Panda[2*]

[1]Computer Science and Engineering, Faculty of Science and Technology, ICFAI Foundation for Higher Education, Hyderabad, Telangana, India
[2]Data Science and Artificial Intelligence, Faculty of Science and Technology, ICFAI Foundation for Higher Education, Hyderabad, Telangana, India

Abstract

People often use the terms augmented reality (AR), virtual reality (VR), mixed reality (MR), and extended reality (XR) to talk about technologies that make or change reality. However, the way that academics and professionals have been using these phrases has varied. There has recently been a lot of interest in the metaverse, a network that connects devices based on AR, VR, and other virtual world technologies. VR and AR technologies can modify users' views of reality by combining virtual items with the real environment. These advantages of VR and AR technologies include the fact that they are immersive, simple to use, reasonably priced, and possibly extendable. These applications include video gaming, online shopping, and architectural and interior design. In this chapter, we discuss the shortcomings of 2D learning settings; a brief overview of the metaverse and its characteristics; immersive reality; the functions of VR, AR, and MR on the metaverse; why extended reality serves as the metaverse's foundation; how to access the metaverse right now; open issues with the metaverse; the creation of metaverse apps; and obstacles inside the metaverse. In its final section, the study suggests a future research agenda that will be helpful to academics, industry experts, and decision-makers alike.

Keywords: Immersive reality, metaverse, augment reality, virtual reality, mixed reality, extended reality, reality–virtuality continuum, digital reality

Corresponding author: skpanda00007@gmail.com

Chandrashekhar A, Shaik Himam Saheb, Sandeep Kumar Panda, S. Balamurugan and Sheng-Lung Peng (eds.)
Metaverse and Immersive Technologies: An Introduction to Industrial, Business and Social Applications, (159–190) © 2023 Scrivener Publishing LLC

6.1 Introduction

Technology is radically altering how we connect with the physical world to this day. Everyone has access to the shared virtual environment known as the Metaverse. It is a word that can be used to describe the whole digital and virtual world. What we have here is the convergence of augmented, virtual, and physical worlds in a shared digital environment. The main industries in the Metaverse are healthcare, entertainment, military, real estate, manufacturing, and education. In a metaverse, each user sees the virtual world from their perspective, yet the environment stays the same. Metaverse Innovative VR and AR technologies are entering the healthcare and medical professions to improve medical education, training, and workflows. Virtual reality (VR) uses hardware and software to simulate the actual world [7]. AR merges virtual and real worlds. It recognizes real-world surfaces and objects using computer vision techniques such as object recognition, plane detection, facial recognition, and movement tracking. Virtual and augmented reality are combined under the umbrella of "mixed reality." Doctors create their ideal smart digital operating room using VR, AR, and MR technology, allowing everyone to view live patient procedures that closely resemble real operations.

The introduction of 5G and mobile immersive computing has pushed research and development on the Metaverse greatly in both industry and academia at this moment [1]. The Metaverse, widely viewed as a collection of 3D virtual worlds linked over the Internet [2] and enabled by several immersive technologies such as AR, VR, and MR, which are frequently referred to together as extended reality, has now entered its open development phase XR. Even though there is no broadly acknowledged description of the Metaverse, it is widely assumed to represent a hypothetical next-generation (NextG) Internet.

Users of XR devices frequently use the Metaverse to participate in its many social activities, whose flawless implementation is made possible by technologies like 5G and HCI (Human Computer Interaction). Users are free to plan social events in the Metaverse using their original 3D-modeled content. Non-Fungible Tokens (NFTs) can be used to trade the content using a decentralized blockchain. Consuming digital twins of real-world things that were developed through 3D modeling and presented in the Metaverse can be done with the help of artificial intelligence-assisted XR gadgets [3].

6.1.1 The Drawbacks of 2D Learning Environments

Online distance learning has long been associated with open education. After the 1960s, open education spawned open universities worldwide. Later, computer and Internet technology enabled Open Courseware, Open Educational Resources, and Open Educational Practices. More recently, it catalyzed the growth of Massive Open Online Course (MOOCs). Tens of thousands of students enroll in free, publicly accessible online courses known as MOOCs each year. They often last a few weeks and are cost-free [18]. Higher education and adult continuing education are increasingly using online learning. COVID-19 disrupted attendance-based activities at all educational levels, accelerating this tendency. Health-related physical separation limits have made remote emergency teaching mandatory [19–22]. The two major system types employed in online education have been synchronous and asynchronous e-learning since its beginnings [20]. Both techniques use software or internet programmers in two-dimensional digital settings that span in-plane digital windows with width and height but no depth. Asynchronous online learning resources include LMSs, social networks, and collaborative web programs. Asynchronous tools let teachers, students, and materials interact anytime, anyplace. Synchronous e-learning platforms bring educators and students together online. Zoom, WebEx, Microsoft Teams, and user stress enable synchronous online learning. The following 2D platform restrictions have a big impact on education: Low sense of self Users have a very limited feeling of who they are in 2D environments. A live or static headshot represents them as ethereal creatures. Web conferencing sessions are seen as video calls rather than virtual group meetings because there is no physical presence [4]. Participants in lengthy sessions frequently slump and lose interest. Passivity: There are few options for user interaction on 2D platforms. Only when professors initiate learning activities may students take a passive part in them. Beyond smileys and emoticons, users have very few other alternatives for expressing their feelings. Crude emotional expression. It is possible to get over all of these limitations using 3D immersive spatial environments [5].

6.2 Related Works

6.2.1 Summary of the Metaverse

Intuitively, it is difficult to distinguish between the metaverse and VR, AR, and MR. The metaverse can be best described as a super virtual-reality ecosystem based on the Internet, which is made up of cross-disciplinary technologies like blockchain, VR, AR, MR, Artificial Intelligence (AI), Machine Learning (ML), computer vision, speech recognition, and the Internet of Things (IoT) [6]. Contrarily, despite being a significant part of the metaverse, VR/AR/MR is merely a type of virtualized and digitized technology and does not require a whole ecosystem, laws, or the Internet. The word "ecosystem" suggests that the metaverse constituent parts interact with and constrain one another and that they are in a relatively stable dynamic equilibrium condition that results in a permanent and cohesive virtual reality. The ecosystem is built on a big number of users, nevertheless. No matter how excellent it is, if there are no users, it can only be described as a 3D virtual vision system and not as "verse". It can only be referred to as a warehouse rather than a retail mall, similar to a location that sells a variety of things but has no paying customers. In actuality, users generate demand to encourage the growth of the metaverse, which in turn draws users in and creates a healthy ecosystem.

To put it another way, a metaverse devoid of users is bound to failure, suggesting that only a select few metaverse platforms would survive the long run while the others will perish. This trend is already seen on existing Internet platforms. For instance, despite the availability of alternatives, people still favor Instagram and Tiktok for sharing photographs and brief films, respectively. After this idea was put forth for many years, there are two key reasons why the metaverse can now be polygenesis. First, the COVID-19 pandemic has taught people how to navigate the virtual world of technology and, to a certain extent, encouraged socialization to move from offline to online [4]. Second, it is now conceivable to create a metaverse thanks to recent significant advancements in the aforementioned associated technologies, such as Big Bang. Technically.

6.2.2   Immersive Reality (IR)

Give people an immersive experience, immersive reality is often referred to as "immersive technology." It is a form of reality technology that either improves or substitutes a virtual or simulated environment for the real world. VR, AR, MR, and/or XR are all types of immersive reality [7]. Figure 6.1 Explains the relationship between Immersive Reality in Metaverse.

> ➤ **Augmented Reality (AR):** AR might be viewed as a compromise between virtual reality and the real world. With augmented reality (AR), users can observe any physical environment in real-time, complete with all of its aspects,

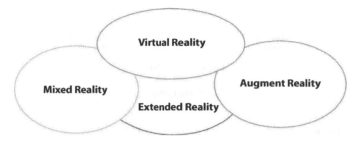

Figure 6.1 Metaverse extended reality.

by using digital sensory input like images, videos, audio, or GPS data. In other words, augmented reality exists in the real world by allowing users to view the real environment through the screens of their smartphones, tablets, smart glasses, or other similar sorts of devices, and allowing them to make virtual modifications to the environment on those screens. The gadgets' built-in cameras enable augmented reality applications to projecting digital content onto the physical world. AR can be explained using the Reality-Virtuality Continuum (RVC). Figure 6.2 shows the timeline for the continuum. RVC shows how reality enters virtual space. By superimposing computer-generated data on top of what we see, augmented reality improves how we see the outside world. Many smartphone AR apps employ this technology and require users to hold their phones in front of them. By collecting a camera image and analyzing it in real time, the program can deliver contextual information or real-world gaming and social experiences. Despite substantial advancements in smartphone augmented reality over the past ten years, there are still few uses for it. More and more, the goal is to provide wearable smart glasses with a more complete AR experience. These gadgets must incorporate an ultra-low-power processor with numerous sensors, such as tracking and depth perception, all in a lightweight design that is comfortable to wear for extended periods. AR smart glasses demand always-on, simple, and safe navigation while moving. This requires considerable advancements in in-depth, occlusion (when one object in a 3D space blocks the view of another), semantics, location, orientation, position, pose, gesture, and eye tracking. In 2021,

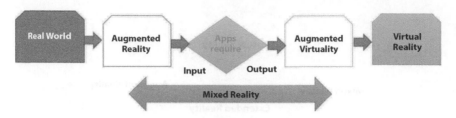

Figure 6.2 The reality–virtuality continuum of AR and VR.

Snap Spectacle, Lenovo ThinkReality A3, and Vuzix Next Gen Smart Glass were released. Future developments in AR smart glasses are expected to improve everyone's lives. They'll probably serve as entrances to the metaverse, where virtual and actual worlds collide.

➢ ***Virtual reality (VR):*** A realistic simulation of any kind is considered virtual reality. The term "virtual reality" refers to a three-dimensional virtual environment created by computers, either to replicate an actual environment or just an imaginary world. Virtual reality is created by blending realistic sights, sounds, and a range of other sensations utilizing specialized equipment, such as VR or virtual reality headsets, gloves, helmets, and other body detectors that come with sense detectors. When using virtual reality, the user is completely immersed in a made-up virtual world. Although it is primarily used for recreational pursuits such as gaming, concerts, and sports, it is rapidly expanding into the realm of social interaction. Virtual reality (VR) entertainment requires experiences like high-definition (HD) rendering pipelines, volumetric capture, six degrees of freedom (DoF) motion tracking, and facial expression capture [6]. VR is also utilized to teach in healthcare settings like rehabilitation. Virtual reality technology prioritizes high-quality video and graphics and low latency. This makes these encounters seamless and imaginable for the end user. Lastly, VR technology is already enhancing video conferencing with services such as RecRoom that offer virtual meetings in a variety of virtual spaces. RecRoom, which supports the Oculus Quest, was featured in episode three of Arm's 2020 New Reality series on immersive VR experiences. The Oculus Quest 2 in the image is an example of a standalone VR device that can give AAA gaming and metaverse experiences, in contrast to some VR systems that need to be connected to a PC. These portable standalone VR systems are powered by top-tier Arm CPUs. Standalone VR headsets will eventually function as portals to the metaverse [6].

➢ **Mixed Reality (MR),** which combines the actual and virtual worlds, is a type of reality that falls between AR and VR. MR, also known as hybrid reality, is the blending of the virtual and real worlds to create a new setting where real-time interactions between virtual and real-world items are possible. MR devices always get new information about what's going on around them, unlike VR, which completely immerses the user in a virtual world, or AR, which just adds digital content on top of the real world without taking into account its unique and changing structure [8]. Such knowledge is essential for integrating digital content with the physical world so that consumers may engage with it. In situations when the virtual and the physical are entangled, MR combines both worlds.

➢ **Digital reality (DR)/Extended reality (XR):** The term "extended reality" refers to all the different technologies that improve our senses, whether they do so by giving us more information about the real world or by constructing unreal, virtual, or simulated worlds for us to experience. XR encompasses a wide range of technologies, such as VR, AR, and MR (MR). The three "realities" may share certain common characteristics and criteria, but they are nevertheless distinct in their overarching goals and enabling technologies [9]. It is anticipated that XR will have a significant impact on the metaverse. It is also known as "Digital Reality (DR)" in general. All real-and virtual worlds created by computer/mobile technology and wearables are referred to as "XR" environments. Any letter can be used as the variable 'X' in XR. "Extended reality" is a catchall term for technology that alter or enhance how we perceive the world. Computer-generated text and graphics are sometimes used to superimpose, envelop, or combine with both actual and virtual environments to achieve this effect. In the "next generation of the Internet," Arm-powered "gateway" devices like VR headsets or AR smart glasses will integrate real, digital, and virtual worlds to create new realities. The following are some important similarities between XR technologies: The ability

to explore the world and display information that is relevant to the current context can be accomplished by the use
of many forms of visual input, such as tracking of objects,
gestures, and gaze. This ability is an essential component
of all XR wearable technology. Both depth perception and
mapping are made possible by the location and depth attributes. However, XR devices vary depending on the type of
augmented reality, mixed reality, and virtual reality experiences that they enable as well as the level of difficulty of the
use case [10].

6.2.3   Features of the Metaverse

The Metaverse, an online, shared virtual reality world, coexists with and
engages with the actual world. Through individualized 3D virtual avatars,
users can simulate the real world in the Metaverse [11]. In the Metaverse,
for instance, avatars can engage in a variety of human activities like video
conferencing, telecommuting, and shopping. The Metaverse has the following characteristics in particular:

Immersive: Screens and mobile devices have been limiting users' ability to
interact with virtual worlds for the past ten years. However, the blending
of the real and virtual worlds has greatly lessened this restriction because
of the ongoing development of Metaverse technology. The "stimulus" that
the avatar in the Metaverse received can be faithfully replicated for the
user in the real world using XR technologies and intelligent wearables like
brain-computer interfaces (BCI). Remote video conferencing users with
VR and AR headsets can access the Metaverse, completing the transition
from the 2D application interface of the real world to the 3D simulation
environment of the virtual world. These elements enhance immersion [10].

Multi-technology: The Metaverse hosts a broad variety of cutting-edge
AI and digital technologies, some of which include digital twin, extended
reality, blockchain, and computer vision, amongst others. Digital twin
technology lets users replicate and test physical objects in the Metaverse,
XR technology immerses users in MR and AR, and blockchain technology
powers the Metaverse's economy [11].

Compatibility: Multiple application scenarios are integrated into the metaverse,
and some of the functionalities between the scenarios are compatible [12]. For
instance, user-purchased services like virtual clothing and sensations can be
used in a variety of Metaverse settings, demonstrating interoperability.

Social Skills: A new phase in the evolution of human social forms is the
metaverse. In the Metaverse, humans can pursue higher-level needs beyond

those of the physical world, such as social interactions, virtual work environments, and entertainment. As a result, sociality is a crucial component of user interaction in the Metaverse [13].

6.3   VR, AR, and MR's Responsibilities in the Metaverse

As we have all come to realize, the term "metaverse" encompasses a lot more than just virtual games. It also includes blockchain, web3, cryptocurrency, social media, and a variety of other technologies. Because VR, AR, and MR are some of the most significant components of the metaverse and provide users with a 3D immersive virtual experience, let's examine what exactly they are.

Virtual Reality: According to some, the immersive quality of VR can occasionally be isolating, both for the users themselves and for those around them. However, virtual reality (VR) can also shorten distances between people, even those who are far apart physically (at least virtually). By using body sensors in addition to the VR headset to operate your avatar in virtual reality environments, you may increase the level of immersion [14]. Here are a few well-known VR products now on the market

Vulcan Quest 2, Acer Vive, the PlayStation VR, Galaxy Gear VR.

Real-world VR examples: Famous fashion brands like Tommy Hilfiger provide 360-degree fashion demonstrations in-store using virtual reality headsets. The shoe company Toms launched a digital contribution campaign called "Virtual Giving Trip" using VR technology. To kick off the initiative, for every pair of shoes purchased, one new pair was donated to a child in need. The company's employees and partners will then embark on a charitable journey throughout the globe and deliver shoes to the kids there in person. Toms can encourage its consumers to join the philanthropic outing by collaborating with the VR technology company within. Customers may use virtual reality headsets in-store to watch the kids receive their shoes and observe the kids' emotions. Customers were also able to virtually interact with the receivers and view their living spaces. With the help of programs like Tilt Brush and popular VR devices, users can paint in 3D space using virtual reality, allowing them to express their creativity without being constrained by a 2D canvas. The Web3 Metaverse environments like Decentraland and the Sandbox are my personal favorite use cases [15].

Augmented Reality: Real-time observation of a physical world that has aspects that have been improved by digital sensory input like music, images, videos, or GPS data. AR is a technology that superimposes Computer-Generated Imagery (CGI) onto a user's perspective of the actual world as seen through a mobile device or smart glasses. Using the cameras on smartphones, tablets, and smart glasses, apps may superimpose digital material in the real environment. This technology rests on top of any surface, using our real environment as a static backdrop and not taking into account the surroundings of users or requiring interaction with their space. Pokemon Go, Snapchat filters, virtual makeup, and furniture fits are a few of the well-known AR examples. The following list of popular augmented reality smartglasses is current: Magic Leap One, Microsoft HoloLens 2, and Vuzix Blade [16].

AR Real-World Examples: IKEA has made a piece of software for smartphones called "Ikea Place" that lets people use augmented reality to place IKEA furniture in their own homes. This allows people to visualize the products in their environments. Probably the most well-known application of AR is Pokemon Go. Since its initial release in 2016, the game has become extremely well-liked by players of all ages. The basic objective of the game is for players to explore the real world to find and "capture" the game characters that have been virtually positioned throughout. You've probably seen individuals using their phones to play Pokemon Go while assembling in groups at specific spots where the cartoon figure is visible. However, the user experience is significantly more authentic and compelling with the aid of AR [17].

Customers can customize the BMW Individual 7 Series following their preferences and represent their styles thanks to an augmented reality app created by BMW called the BMW Individual AR App. Customers can then inspect the vehicle in life-size and even walk around it to see all of its intricacies. Here, discover more about the app. The well-known American messaging app Snapchat uses augmented reality (AR) technology to project a variety of cool and fascinating filters onto users' faces. The filters are digitally applied to the users' faces once artificial intelligence has detected their faces. It's a lot of fun to use the filters because they may make users into a variety of characters, such as a cat or even a strawberry [10].

Mixed Reality: MR, also known as hybrid reality, is the blending of the virtual and real worlds to create a new setting where real-time interactions between virtual and real-world items are possible devices always get new information about what's going on around them, unlike VR, which completely immerses the user in a virtual world, or AR, which just adds digital content on top of the real world without taking into account its unique and changing structure. Such knowledge is essential for integrating digital content with the physical world so that consumers may engage with it. In situations when the virtual and the physical are entangled, MR combines both worlds. The following are some common MR products on the market: Hololens 2 by Microsoft, and One Magic Leap [15].

MR Examples From Real Life

Education: By engaging them in learning through real-world experiences rather than the conventional visual or audio learning approaches, MR improves student learning experiences and efficacy.

Medivis: Surgeons and physicians can increase surgical accuracy and provide better patient outcomes thanks to Medivis the MR technology. With Medivis, surgical visualization will advance, surgical results will be improved, and medical institutions will experience incremental cost reductions [16].

Angry Birds: Magic Leap has released various notable MR games featuring well-known properties like Angry Birds. Up until now, the perception of virtual things has frequently only been available to the player using the headset, making for a completely isolated gaming experience. This can be improved with MR by setting up a shared virtual environment by having numerous users wear different headsets. As a result, they can enjoy gaming together. However, MR games also enable players to fully immerse themselves in their current surroundings while interacting with the virtual world without taking off their headphones. Although there are many unanswered questions regarding the future operation of the metaverse, we are confident that VR/AR/MR technologies will unquestionably play a crucial part in its creation and anticipate active market growth in the next few years. Since the metaverse is a collection of virtual worlds, VR, AR, and MR technologies are how we can access it [14].

6.4 The Contribution of AR/VR to the Metaverse Development

Users can converse via technology in the metaverse. Hardware and software are used in tandem to achieve this. Although each business has a different vision for this idea, they all envision a network of 3D worlds that are produced in real-time and that many people can enter at once. In the metaverse, you can work, learn, chat, relax, go to virtual concerts, and do other activities. It is designed to be a simulation of the real world. Brand interest in the metaverse is significantly shaped by the fact that a large portion of it is connected to the digital economy, where users can transact in commodities just like they would in the real world. The metaverse can be a terrific way for businesses to grow their revenue by promoting their products on such virtual platforms because modern individuals spend a significant portion of their time online [12, 57].

There are numerous explanations. AR/VR, 5G, and remote work due to the COVID-19 pandemic have made the metaverse easier to grasp. All of this, together with the fact that a company the size of Facebook started working on the metaverse, generated interest from investors and regular Internet users worldwide, adding the metaverse to the year's top trending topics. Facebook has bought multiple VR firms with more than $1 billion in funding since 2014, demonstrating that it is committed to creating the metaverse and that it will be more than just another one of Facebook's current tools. Snap, Nvidia, Unity, and Roblox are also building infrastructures for such applications [10].

6.4.1   Does Metaverse Need AR/VR?

AR and VR are strongly related to metaverse VR. AR may bring virtual items to life. VR combines 3D computer modeling, one of the most exciting visual concepts, to immerse you in a 3D virtual world. Virtual reality technology isn't required in the metaverse, but experts believe it will be essential. AR glasses, VR headsets, and desktop and mobile apps can access the Facebook metaverse. "Project Cambria" is the company's high-end VR/AR headset. According to Meta, the gadget will support mixed reality and have new sensors that enable the virtual avatar to maintain eye contact and replicate the facial emotions of actual people. With the aid of more advanced technology, avatars will be able to better express human emotions and employ body language, giving the impression of real dialogue in virtual environments. The combined market for augmented reality and virtual reality is anticipated to be worth up to $300 billion by 2024 and $100 billion by 2030, as estimated by Morgan Stanley, according to Statista [9].

6.4.2   Where Do Virtual Reality and the Metaverse Part?

How the metaverse varies from the virtual reality we are familiar with today is one of the primary concepts that make it difficult to comprehend. In conclusion, the metaverse is much bigger than virtual reality (VR), even though it may be a part of it. It includes components from various digital fields, including social networking, virtual reality, augmented reality, online gaming, and cryptocurrencies. In contrast to the video conferencing we are used to, VR can guarantee true telepresence. The metaverse is intended to transform the way we consume media, taking it from a static 2D environment to a completely immersive, dynamic 3D one. The metaverse, which connects the virtual and physical worlds, is anticipated to revolutionize how people interact with one another as a shared virtual area [7].

In a remote workplace, it can greatly boost virtual team collaboration. Regular video chats can likewise be transformed by the metaverse into meetings that feel as though a real person is there. The metaverse is a huge, multipurpose realm that is fully exposed when using VR or AR, even though many questions remain. The metaverse has been called the next version of the internet, delivering a better user experience. VR is one way to reach it [5].

6.4.3   Use Cases for AR/VR in the Metaverse

Even though the majority of people only think of gaming when they think of the metaverse, there is a ton of other applications that it can be used for. The creation of virtual environments has so far brought the most tangible benefits to the gaming sector. World of Warcraft founder Activision Blizzard has made over $8 billion from this virtual world. In addition to gaming, other businesses and brands are attempting to keep up with the craze and figure out how to apply it to their ends. For instance, the decentralized platform Decentraland recently sold a virtual plot of land to a Canadian investment firm for 2.5 million dollars. Blockchain-based Decentraland sells non-fungible tokens for real estate (NFT) [23–27, 58]. This area hosts VR fashion shows and fashion brand e-commerce partnerships. This shows how companies can leverage virtual platforms to find new marketing opportunities.

The idea of a virtual workplace space that might change as the metaverse develops has already been brought up. With this technology, as opposed to the more common Zoom and Skype, the team feels more physically present together. The metaverse goes beyond the functionality provided by the services listed, such as picture masking, which enables you to modify the background of a conference. It provides 3D-rendered avatars that accurately reflect your movements and even facial expressions in virtual meetings [3, 28, 29, 59].

Many products with similar functions already exist. Virtuworx is a company that offers VR and mixed reality solutions, and they have flexible alternatives for the office, virtual meetings, and other gatherings. Many different fields, including tourism, education, entertainment, retail, design, and engineering, can benefit from the metaverse. The metaverse can become contaminated by anything happening in the real world [1].

6.4.4   Metaverse Building Blocks

Extended Reality
How does extended reality fit into this new internet view?
The Metaverse and Web 3 creation may have caught your attention recently. Extended reality provides the building blocks for the Metaverse, which, like Web 2.0, allows shared experiences but also mixes that with an "open-world" or "worlds," as some of the world's greatest IT corporations invest heavily in the next phase of the internet. Imagine wearing a headset and entering a fully virtual office where you can effortlessly switch between virtual meetings, engage with coworkers without Zoom, and then attend a virtual museum mixer. You may already be using Extended Reality in Web 2.0 [2, 30–35, 60].

Extended Reality tools and platforms, whether VR, AR, or MR, make up the metaverse and allow us to blend our real world with digital ones in surprising ways. The Internet, a network of places, things to do, and data that can be accessed in many ways, may be called the "metaverse" shortly. Tony Parisi from Unity explains how we utilize the internet today as a prototype for the Metaverse: "The Internet is not the Metaverse yet. The current Internet, which is growing in power, will form the future Metaverse. It has pioneered real-time 3D, rich media, and virtual worlds for years. It's already a Metaverse prototype. More work is needed. What's required? It begins with us collaboratively exploring Extended Reality's current applications. We'll connect the possible Metaverse to the future by investigating virtual team training, designing buildings digitally to interact with a space before it's completed, or corporations establishing digital office spaces for workers to communicate [3].

6.5   How to Use the Metaverse Right Now

Many people may be curious about the Metaverse today and how to reach it.

6.5.1   Shared Virtual Environments

The Metaverse's virtual worlds can generate fictional environments or replicate any real-world environment. Many technology companies once believed that their unique platform and product ecosystems gave them a competitive edge. They made an effort to get clients into their space and nowhere else. For instance, Apple and Microsoft made it challenging for users to use iOS apps on Microsoft hardware or the Microsoft Office package on Apple devices. Companies have worked together to create an open ecosystem that best serves customers as they have come to understand that a rising tide lifts all ships [4, 36–38].

As the aforementioned meanings of the term suggest, the current stage of Metaverse technology development and adoption is following suit and has not yet enabled a single overarching Metaverse that everyone can access. Instead, several distinct Metaverses, or "Microverses," have been created. These walled-garden Metaverses were developed by firms like Meta, Microsoft, Roblox, Epic Games, and others and are their settings or private platforms. Similar to how people use various social media sites, users must first register accounts on each Metaverse platform to access them. Depending on customer expectations, businesses may decide to keep these immersive worlds separate and isolated or choose interconnectivity between them. It may resemble the social media platform environment in many aspects, where there is connectivity between them all but different content and influencers are present in each. There might be separate users for various Metaverses, much as there might be different users for TikTok, Twitter, and Facebook - however, they can still move across environments with ease. Specific surroundings have helped to characterize the early Metaverse eras. However, we anticipate that this will change when Metaverse users demand a decentralized and interoperable architecture that allows them to travel easily between platforms and virtual worlds [6, 39–41, 62].

6.5.2   Avatars of Virtual Humans

Since virtual human avatars have become the norm for how humans assume a presence and communicate in VR and AR experiences, people also have realistic digital representations in the metaverse. Through laptop computers, mobile devices, and VR headsets like the Oculus, users may build their avatars and access virtual settings. In addition to mimicking actual humans visually, virtual human figures also speak and move with realism. Users have the option of controlling virtual people or interacting with them as non-playable characters (NPCs) in immersive experiences. Organizations and individuals can predetermine the speech and physical actions of NPCs in virtual experiences thanks to no-code authoring tools [8, 42].

6.5.3   Hardware Equipment

Both standard 2D devices like desktop computers, laptops, and mobile devices as well as XR technology like virtual reality headsets can access metaverse platforms. For instance, virtual conferencing platforms let people join the same conference call using VR or 2D devices and depending on the gear they use, they provide varying degrees of immersion. With a VR headset, users can, for instance, turn their heads to control their point of view or walk about in their real world to control where their avatar travels in the virtual world when they log into a multi-user encounter in the Metaverse. The same is true for Metaverse simulations, where immersive learning sessions can be broadcast via a web browser or experienced while wearing a VR headset. Because the user's complete point of view is contained within the virtual world and their head movements enable them to "see about" the virtual environment, the VR experience gives a deeper level of immersion. A desktop user, however, would utilize a mouse to manage the experience and would still be able to see their real surroundings through their peripherals.

Since most people will first use devices they currently own, like their computer or smartphone, to encounter metaverse technology, enabling access to the Metaverse via a variety of devices is essential for its growth and adoption. Accessing the Metaverse will only grow simpler and more interesting when VR and AR hardware becomes more affordable and our current devices receive additional XR features [10].

6.5.4   XR: Facts and Figures on AR, VR, and the Metaverse

"Extended reality" encompasses all immersive technologies, including AR, VR, MR, and those in development XR. XR technologies expand our reality by combining the virtual and "real" worlds or creating an immersive experience. In the upcoming years, it is anticipated that the worldwide XR market will expand significantly. The United States, Asia, particularly Japan and China, as well as Europe Germany, and the United Kingdom, are projected to lead the way in XR innovation [11, 61].

Companies That Make XR Headsets: While VR creates an artificial experience, AR uses the existing environment by superimposing additional information on top of it. In both AR and VR, the user is often provided with information or visuals through a headset. Vendors of XR headsets include Microsoft, Magic Leap, and Vuzix for AR headsets and glasses, as well as Meta (Oculus), Pico, Sony, and HTC for VR devices. Along with these companies, LG and Qualcomm have been rated as the top holders of XR patents. Chipmaker Qualcomm has formed the Global XR Content Telco Alliance with a group of international telecom companies to create 5G-based AR/VR content [13].

Applications XR: According to experts, advancements in software applications and connectivity, along with changes in XR hardware like the advent of smaller and more comfortable devices, will enable the expanding acceptance of XR across a variety of industries. The industries that XR technologies are predicted to affect the most include healthcare, manufacturing, and the auto sector. The use cases for XR will expand and increase as technology advances, and its economic advantages should be recognized on a global scale [15, 43].

Metaverse: The metaverse is where the real world and the virtual world meet. It is thought to be the next version of the internet. As a result of the growth of social technology, avatars, which are digital representations of humans, are now capable of interacting with one another in a wide variety of settings. The metaverse provides a setting for an infinite number of interconnected virtual communities, which can exist everywhere, such as at work or in an office, while going to a concert or a sporting event, or even while just putting on clothing. Many companies have already invested in their own metaverses, including Meta, Microsoft, Roblox, and Epic. However, cooperation between businesses, creators, and legislators will be necessary for the metaverse's development.

The Metaverse's Future: Although the concept of the metaverse appears intriguing, it is difficult to predict what the future may hold for it. The development of 5G and the rising popularity of VR and AR technologies may truly help to provide the right conditions for something like this. But there will be many difficulties for the metaverse's designers. Digital object compatibility is vital to metaverse development. To utilize a metaverse-bought digital object across several games and platforms, you must preserve your rights to it. Additionally, establishing a currency is necessary for the metaverse economy to grow [17, 44]. Real-time data synchronization is another necessity of the metaverse, which at scale can be very difficult and expensive. For businesses that offer data synchronization services, this poses a new problem because the metaverse will need to support heavy loads and broadcast-quality data while also catering to the unique security requirements of every user. Additionally, a low-quality Internet connection in many areas and expensive hardware that enables you to fully utilize this technology raise the bar for entry into the metaverse. Despite these difficulties, businesses like Microsoft, Google, Zoom, and others are prepared to contribute to the advancement of metaverse technology in line with Facebook's ambitions. As an illustration, Microsoft Teams will introduce mixed reality in 2022, including holograms and virtual avatars. The future of AR/VR businesses appears promising given how strongly the metaverse relies on these technologies. Businesses that want to develop augmented reality applications or virtual reality features have a great opportunity of satisfying the market's expanding demand [17, 45].

Bringing Everything Together: Tech enthusiasts believe the metaverse will open up the Internet and immerse us in the virtual world. Metaverses require VR/AR technologies, hence the market will grow rapidly. VR is a means of accessing the metaverse if it is a virtual environment. Contemporary hardware, which is pricy and burdensome for long-term usage, tends to limit VR capabilities. Regarding AR, it is now widely available thanks to contemporary smartphones, making it a preferred technology for the extensive creation of the metaverse. We still have a lot of questions about the metaverse's operation, the significance of the advantages it offers, and how easily common users will be able to access it. But there's no denying that, when used properly, the metaverse can be a better platform for global online communication [16, 46].

6.6   Unresolved Issues

6.6.1   The Interaction Issue

The Metaverse's interface technology, which connects the virtual and real worlds, must be lightweight, convenient to use, wearable, and portable. Users can overlook the signs of technology and become more fully immersed in the virtual world because of its transparency. Somatosensory, brain-computer interface and XR (VR, AR, MR) technologies are widespread interactive technologies. "XR technology" uses computer and wearable technology to simulate human-computer interaction. Immersive real-world-virtual technologies are called "XR." VR, AR, MR, and other immersive technologies may emerge as technology advances. Somatosensory technology lets people engage with electronics and the environment around them without complicated control apparatus. These two technologies now have the issue that interactive gadgets are too heavy, opaque, and expensive, which makes it hard for them to become widely accepted. There are three types of technology for connecting the brain to a computer: invasive, semi-invasive, and non-invasive. Invasive procedures include surgically inserting electrodes into the cerebral cortex. Semi-invasive electrode implantation involves cranial cavity placement outside the cerebral cortex. Non-invasive EEG signal interpretation uses a scalp-mounted device. Invasive EEG collecting is accurate yet risky. The non-invasive approach avoids surgery but collects signals poorly. Another downside of the brain-computer interface is that it is difficult to propagate [15].

6.6.2 Computer Problems

Data processing requires calculation, storage, and transfer. Computer power and infrastructure drive technological advancement in the digital economy. Metaverse relies on a larger user population, stronger network resources, and more processing power. New business models and the Metaverse platform's cloud computing have increased computer resource demand and growth potential. Heavy demands are placed on client device speed and server reliability by cloud storage, processing, rendering, and other Metaverse technologies. Complexity, power consumption, and speed of processing in the Metaverse must be continuously improved [14, 47–49].

6.6.3 Moral Concerns

People now live and interact in the metaverse. Relationships are more complicated. To maintain a healthy ecological environment, the Metaverse, a next-generation network, must regulate user behavior and establish ethical and moral guidelines. The Metaverse's ethical and moral difficulties arise from the absence or confusion of moral rules that contrast with real society's. Metaverse moral issues include:

- ✓ Problems with honesty, such as publishing and spreading false information and committing fraud;
- ✓ An unfavorable environment;
- ✓ Violating the rights to intellectual property.

With Metaverse interactive technology, brain awareness may be manipulated, stored, and copied like computer data, making science fiction movie sequences less innovative. Nowadays, ethics are far more crucial than ever. The Metaverse is growing faster than the new code of ethics, which has been damaged. Thus, the Metaverse should be better regulated and maintained [13, 50, 51].

6.6.4   Privacy Concerns

Metaverse and true identity are linked. Like its predecessor, the Metaverse must protect users' data privacy while it builds new networks.

6.6.5   Cyber-Syndrome

Internet addiction causes "cyber-syndrome," a physical, social, and mental illness. Interactive approaches have downsized and lightened electronics. Equipment simplicity is increasing Internet use. The Metaverse and the real world are interconnected at the same time. The problem of the cyber syndrome is made even more problematic by the blending of the real and the virtual and by the extent of Metaverse immersion [12, 52].

6.6.6   Standardization and Compatibility

It is essential to create guidelines for the Metaverse because it is a multidimensional virtual world with strong ties to reality. There are two sides to the Metaverse's compatibility and standards problems: compatibility problems between Metaverses produced by various businesses.

Relationship between the real world and metaverses.

6.7   Application for XR

Here, we give a quick review of XR tools while concentrating on the advantages of employing them in the Metaverse.

> ➢ **Examples of Images:** The 3D visualization capabilities of XR are particularly suited to image-based applications, where the ability to interact with 3D objects quickly and easily can increase speed and accuracy. Opportunities for XR visualization arise when 3D tissue data processing and reconstruction in spatial biology become practical. Programs like ConfocalVR, Spyglass, volume, Genuage, and DIVA can load volumetric images and point cloud data from the microscope and 3D medical data [11].
> ➢ **Examples without Images:** Transcriptional and epigenetic profiling of cell populations can now be performed with the use of single-cell technologies. Using tools like UMAP/tSNE, data is reduced to two or three dimensions to create

cell "maps." For big and complex datasets, 3D reductions can help resolve overlapping clusters, and simultaneously displaying many reductions can be very helpful. In addition to doing this, CellexalVR is a VR program that offers additional capabilities for thoroughly visualizing and analyzing single-cell data. Others include single-celled, which allows visualization using Google Cardboard, and Theia, which will also handle volumetric data. The broad biological and protein interaction network study made possible by VRNetzer avoids the common "hairballs" that are present in such analyses. A web-based program called ProteinVR uses WebXR to see PDB protein structures on a variety of devices while providing important biological context and allowing users to position themselves in 3D space. XR makes it considerably easier to comprehend the arrangement of biological protein structures than a traditional 2D depiction. iMD-VR shows that VR is a versatile tool for interactive observation of small molecule drugs docking into their protein targets. Cynthia is a web-based application for chromatin visualization that enables de novo modeling of intricate 3D chromatin connections in various disease tissues to comprehend how genomic structure affects gene expression [10].

✓ **Combining Domains in the Metaverse:** Due to the abundance of dashboards, statistics, and information while dealing with multi-modal datasets, screen space is quickly consumed. This is less confined to XR applications and space, and if used in tandem in the metaverse, they might work better. Physicians, biologists, mathematicians, and computational biologists worldwide might communicate using an evidence wall or Anacapa chart-based technique. Anacapa charts show criminal evidence, timing, and relationships. Biological visualization can use this concept to gather, arrange, and explain information about a disease process or biological phenomenon [10].

6.7.1 Applications and Exciting Uses of AR/VR/MR

Businesses are adopting AR/VR/MR technology in new ways. A recent Forbes article featuring the Forbes Technology Council calls out various exciting uses of VR including an interesting outlook for the use of this technology in mental health applications.

What advantages will AR/VR/MR offer across all industries?
Human Resources: VR training is growing as more professions are remote.
Maintenance and Service: Remote service enabled by AR/VR/MR technology has contributed to cost savings and enhanced throughput without negatively impacting client happiness.
Design and Production: Before manufacturing begins, parts and mechanisms can be developed digitally and tested in AR, VR, and MR devices. As a result, R&D takes less time, which eventually lowers expenses. AR, VR, and MR can be used in other ways that can directly affect the costs and output of a business. As more money is put into the technology and more people use it, the benefits will keep growing [9].

6.8   Challenges in the Metaverse

The challenges in metaverse are given below
Infrastructure and Connectivity: The metaverse concept emphasizes collaborative working with colleagues from around the globe, which calls for a high-quality communications infrastructure. Latency is minimized to preserve natural communication and social interactions, which are greatly damaged by lag. This affects all institutions using old Wi-Fi or Ethernet, not just developing nations. A multi-vendor Metaverse system's single sign-on process is challenging to create. Microsoft may benefit from the Hololens 2's Windows OS, which allows enterprise single sign-on.
Upcoming Legislation: Early issues involving minors using Meta's platform as well as numerous accusations of verbal and "physical" abuse of people have been widely publicized in the media. To combat this, Meta has instituted a minimum 2-meter rule between participants. However, it is unclear whether legislation will be created to police this (and other rules), and if so, whether STEM-centric metaverses will also require the enforcement of these laws [8].
Equipment and Design: Data processing and visualization may be demanding, therefore a well-designed VR environment is essential for comfort. Some people can stay in VR for hours at a time, while others can only do so for a short time before getting sick or tired. However, this is frequently a sign of an environment that is badly designed and illuminated. The frame rate is crucial and needs to be at least 72 FPS (preferably between 90 and 120 FPS) to provide a fluid experience. Additionally, it will be necessary to address the issue of making the hardware accessible to all users, including disabled groups, but doing so holds great promise for ensuring that everyone in the metaverse has equitable access [7]. HMDs are gradually getting

smaller and lighter while adding functions like eye and facial expression monitoring to achieve this. Additionally, it should be made sure that every environment is built such that people can use it while seated. A low-cost untethered experience is best, but all untethered XR devices have limited CPU/GPU power, which makes visualization difficult as data sets to rise. A single-cell experiment may have hundreds of thousands of data points with several metadata columns. Displaying such data on a portable, low-powered device is problematic. On-demand application streaming may help. 3D "remote desktops" will render and deliver large datasets on low-powered devices. Cloud XR renders application pictures on cloud-based GPUs and streams them to any HMD with a client across fast, low-latency networks like WiFi6/5G. An application can be used as a local machine with a powerful network. This strategy presents difficulties since, if the latency is not controlled below 20 ms, the user may develop immersion sickness. The Hololens 2 supports a Microsoft technique called Azure Remote Rendering (ARR), however, it is customized for specific objects [6].

Software Design: The various software environments that each specific HMD offers room for innovation, but this adaptability also carries the risk that users may need to become familiar with a variety of operating systems for each application. When combined with a 3D environment, the user experience could be challenging and perplexing for new users. React, for instance, is frequently used to create Javascript front-ends for bioinformatics browser-based applications. This enables the rapid development of specific features in a consistent style. Dashboards may crowd the user's surrounding 3D area. More study is needed on automated layout techniques based on machine learning that extract features from dashboards and use human-in-the-loop algorithms to organize, conceal, and eliminate unimportant information. Despite the existence of growing standards like IEEE SAA, there is no clear-cut leader in the 3D industry. To remedy this, applications might need to offer interactive tutorials that walk users through the functionalities. The optimal way to build these interfaces needs to be outlined in much clearer rules and style manuals. Additionally, user testing may be more constrained because there are fewer HMDs than there are conventional computers. Developers will need to make sure their software is compatible with new XR systems when they are introduced to the market. Hand controllers and software/runtime are the biggest examples (SteamVR, Windows Mixed Reality, Oculus link). New button/touchpad layouts may require updated virtual models for aesthetics. OpenXR is in progress to address these difficulties [5].

Release of XR Tools: Most academic academics need peer-reviewed publications to get funding. Journals often need reviewers to install and test the source code or application. However, not all reviewers will have HMDs, making it harder for them to evaluate XR applications. Authors frequently offer in-depth supplemental films to demonstrate the functionality of their product to aid in evaluation, although this still calls for some creative license on the part of the reviewers. To protect reviewer anonymity until XR is more widely used, publications must make the review process easier by providing XR equipment to authors and reviewers via their editorial office. In the interim, it is up to the authors to ascertain whether their preferred publication will do this before submission. As XR application development progresses, it may be important for journals/publishers to have set standards stating how they will handle XR submissions. The authors of this article have found that while some people are naturally suspicious of XR and what else it can offer, they frequently change their minds after using it [4].

Assessment of XR Tools: Benchmarking is still another problem. Speed, repeatability, and accuracy are three areas where XR may be superior to conventional methods, but a systematic, unbiased comparison of these factors necessitates careful thought. When 11 experts were questioned and training and testing times were compared between XR-experienced users and nonexperienced users, AR for head and neck cancer was used as an excellent example of a quantitative method for evaluating the efficacy of an XR application. The System Usability Scale (SUS) was also employed in this investigation. Non-Spatial Data It will be necessary to access non-spatial data in the metaverse, such as descriptive text, tables, 2D images, and multimedia sources. The outside environment can be viewed and possibly enhanced with MR and AR devices. For instance, in AR or MR, selecting a 2D term like "SARS-CoV-2 variant" may cause a 3D overlay to appear over the text, displaying the virus's structure and appearance. Schol-AR is an illustration of how linked images can be displayed utilizing an AR framework. Reading comprehension of 2D screens when immersed in VR has been proven to be unaffected, however, response times to multiple-choice questions have been demonstrated to be 10% slower. To boost comprehension, it's necessary to create new ways to consume information [3, 53]. For instance, Rapid Serial Visual Presentation (RSVP), which presented text word-by-word at a fixed location, was tested in virtual reality. Since the user may concentrate in one place while traveling in a virtual space, comprehension was found to be improved. On the other hand, a vast wall of connected images might be viewed in VR without the limitations of a small 2d screen, allowing for the simultaneous viewing of more data. Given its significance, additional research is required to determine the cognitive load in various use cases as well as how to grasp and retrieve non-spatial data sets.

New Methods of Data Interaction: The obvious alternative to typing is speech-to-text, but it might also be used to activate things in the VR world rather than utilizing a menu. A tantalizing hint that data selection and querying could be accomplished by thought power is provided by wrist-based "Brain-Computer Interfaces," or BCI, such as Neuralink. Motor neuron signals from the wrist are sensed by electromyography (EMG) devices and converted into motions and commands [2, 54, 55].

Haptic Equipment: The development of haptics gloves is still in its early stages, but they would enable physical interaction with metaverse items. Physically isolate a 3D scatter plot cluster for further analysis. Mixed reality systems can provide haptic feedback on walls and tables. These interactions enhance immersion and selection precision, similar to painting in the air [1, 56].

6.9   Conclusion and Future Directions

Academics are debating the metaverse's benefits and capacity to revolutionize civilization. While the metaverse offers new and exciting levels of connection between the virtual and real worlds, creating new opportunities and potential business models, widespread adoption faces several issues related to governance, ethics, safety and security, acceptable behavior, privacy, and potential disenfranchisement of those without the necessary infrastructure to enter it. The promise of XR is fuelling expectations for a slew of previously inconceivable possibilities within the rapidly evolving metaverse. By the year 2030, we may spend more time in the metaverse than in the real world. People will use the virtual features of the metaverse to look for jobs, make money, hang out with friends, shop, and even get married. Brain-computer interfaces (BCIs) that enable the tracking, recording, and sharing of the human mind are anticipated to emerge by 2030. These XR capabilities may enable us to truly relive the experiences and memories of another person. Meanwhile, synthetic data collected from simulated worlds will most likely aid robots in problem-solving and will likely replace people performing high-risk work.

References

1. Al-Ghaili, A.M., Kasim, H., Al-Hada, N.M., Hassan, Z.B., Othman, M., Tharik, J.H., Kasmani, RMd, Shayea, I., A review of metaverse's definitions, architecture, applications, challenges, issues, solutions, and future trends. *IEEE Access*, 10, 125835–125866, 2022.

2. Wang, Y. and Zhao, J., *Mobile edge computing, metaverse, 6G wireless communications, artificial intelligence, and blockchain: Survey and their convergence.* ArXiv abs/2209.14147, 2022.

3. Cassidy, K.C., Šefčík, J., Raghav, Y., Chang, A., Durrant, J.D., ProteinVR: Web-based molecular visualization in virtual reality. *PLoS Comput. Biol.*, 16, 3, e1007747, 2020. doi:10.1371/journalPCBs.1007747.

4. Park, S.-M. and Kim, Y.-G., A metaverse: Taxonomy, components, applications, and open challenges. *IEEE Access,* 10, 4209–4251, 2022.

5. Makamara, G. and Adolph, M., A survey of Extended Reality (XR) standards, in: *2022 ITU Kaleidoscope-Extended reality – How to boost quality of experience and interoperability,* pp. 1–11, Accra, Ghana, 2022.

6. Vichare, P., Cano, M., Dahal, K., Siewierski, T., Gilardi, M., Incorporating extended reality technology for delivering computer aided design and visualisation modules, in: *2022 14th International Conference on Software, Knowledge, Information Management and Applications (SKIMA),* pp. 114–119, Phnom Penh, Cambodia, 2022.

7. Gupta, R. *et al.*, Augmented/mixed reality audio for hearables: Sensing, control, and rendering. *IEEE Signal Process. Mag.*, 39, 3, 63–89, May 2022.

8. Abrash, M., Creating the future: Augmented reality, the next human-machine interface. *2021 IEEE Int. Electron. Devices Meeting (IEDM).* 2021, DOI: 10.1109/IEDM19574.2021.9720526.

9. Patil, S., Gaikwad, G., Hiran, S., Ikhar, A., Jadhav, H., metaAR – AR/XR shopping app using unity, in: *2023 International Conference for Advancement in Technology (ICONAT),* pp. 1–11, Goa, India, 2023.

10. Xi, N., Chen, J., Gama, F. et al., The challenges of entering the metaverse: An experiment on the effect of extended reality on workload. *Inf. Syst. Front.*, 25, 659–680, 202, https://doi.org/10.1007/s10796-022-10244-x.

11. Ahsen, T., Dogar, F.R., Gardony, A.L., Exploring the impact of network impairments on remote collaborative augmented reality applications, in: *Extended Abstracts of the 2019 CHI Conference on Human Factors in Computing Systems (CHI EA '19),* 2019, Association for Computing Machinery.

12. Flavián, C., Ibáñez-Sánchez, S., Orús, C., The impact of virtual augmented and mixed reality technologies on the customer experience. *J. Business Res.*, 100, 547–560, 2019.

13. Wang, Q., Li, R., Wang, Q., Chen, S., Ryan, M.D., Hardjono, T., Exploring Web3 from the view of blockchain. *ArXiv*, abs/2206.08821, 2022.

14. Chen, H., Lu, Y., Chengx, Y., FileInsurer: A scalable and reliable protocol for decentralized file storage in blockchain, 24 Jul 2022. Consid, arXiv: 2207.11657v1 [cs.CR].
15. Sun, X., Lu, Y., Sun, J., Matrix syncer - A multi-chain data aggregator for supporting blockchain-based metaverses, 8 Apr 2022. arXiv:2204.04272v1 [cs.MM].
16. Gadekallu, T.R., Yenduri, G., Ranaweera, P., da Costa, D.B., Blockchain for the metaverse: A review, 21 Mar 2022. arXiv:2203.09738v2 [cs.SI].
17. Calvelo, M., Piñeiro, Á., Garcia-Fandino, R., An immersive journey to the molecular structure of SARS-CoV-2: Virtual reality in COVID-19. *Comput. Struct. Biotechnol. J.*, 18, 2621–2628, 2020. doi:10.1016/j. csbj.2020.09.018.
18. Panda, S.K. and Satapathy, S.C., An investigation into smart contract deployment on ethereum platform using Web3.js and solidity using blockchain, in: *Data Engineering and Intelligent Computing*, Advances in Intelligent Systems and Computing, V. Bhateja, S.C. Satapathy, C.M. Travieso-González, V.N.M. Aradhya (Eds.), vol. 1, Springer, Singapore, 2021, https://doi. org/10.1007/978-981-16-0171-2_52.
19. Panda, S.K., Rao, D.C., Satapathy, S.C., An investigation into the usability of blockchain technology in Internet of Things, in: *Data Engineering and Intelligent Computing*, Advances in Intelligent Systems and Computing, V. Bhateja, S.C. Satapathy, C.M. Travieso-González, V.N.M. Aradhya (Eds.), vol. 1, Springer, Singapore, 2021, https://doi.org/10.1007/978-981-16-0171-2_53.
20. Panda, S.K., Dash, S.P., Jena, A.K., Optimization of block query response using evolutionary algorithm, in: *Data Engineering and Intelligent Computing*, Advances in Intelligent Systems and Computing, V. Bhateja, S.C. Satapathy, C.M. Travieso-González, V.N.M. Aradhya (Eds.), vol. 1, Springer, Singapore, 2021, https://doi.org/10.1007/978-981-16-0171-2_54.
21. Nanda, S.K., Panda, S.K., Das, M., Satapathy, S.C., Automating vehicle insurance process using smart contract and ethereum, in: *Advances in Micro-Electronics, Embedded Systems and IoT*, Lecture Notes in Electrical Engineering, V.V.S.S.S. Chakravarthy, W. Flores-Fuentes, V. Bhateja, B. Biswal (Eds.), vol. 838, Springer, Singapore, 2022, https://doi.org/10.1007/978-981-16-8550-7_23.
22. Varaprasada Rao, K. and Panda, S.K., Secure electronic voting (E-voting) system based on blockchain on various platforms, in: *Computer Communication, Networking and IoT*, Lecture Notes in Networks and Systems, S.C. Satapathy, J.C.W. Lin, L.K. Wee, V. Bhateja, T.M. Rajesh (Eds.), vol. 459, Springer, Singapore, 2023, https://doi.org/10.1007/978-981-19-1976-3_18.
23. Varaprasada Rao, K. and Panda, S.K., A design model of copyright protection system based on distributed ledger technology, in: *Computer Communication, Networking and IoT*, Lecture Notes in Networks and Systems, S.C. Satapathy, J.C.W. Lin, L.K. Wee, V. Bhateja, T.M. Rajesh (Eds.), vol. 459, Springer, Singapore, 2023, https://doi.org/10.1007/978-981-19-1976-3_17.

24. Panda, S.K., Elngar, A.A., Balas, V.E., Kayed, M. (Eds.), *Bitcoin and Blockchain: History and Current Applications*, 1st ed, CRC Press, Boca Raton, 2020, https://doi.org/10.1201/9781003032588.

25. Panda, S.K., Jena, A.K., Swain, S.K., Satapathy, S.C. (Eds.), *Blockchain technology: Applications and challenges*, Intelligent Systems Reference Library, Springer, pp. 1–300, 2021, https://doi.org/10.1007/978-3-030-69395-4.

26. Sathya, A.R., Panda, S.K., Hanumanthakari, S., Enabling smart education system using blockchain technology, in: *Blockchain Technology: Applications and Challenges*, Intelligent Systems Reference Library, S.K. Panda, A.K. Jena, S.K. Swain, S.C. Satapathy (Eds.), vol. 203, Springer, Cham, 2021, https://doi.org/10.1007/978-3-030-69395-4_10.

27. Lokre, S.S., Naman, V., Priya, S., Panda, S.K., Gun tracking system using blockchain technology, in: *Blockchain Technology: Applications and Challenges*, Intelligent Systems Reference Library, S.K. Panda, A.K. Jena, S.K. Swain, S.C. Satapathy (Eds.), vol. 203, Springer, Cham, 2021, https://doi.org/10.1007/978-3-030-69395-4_16.

28. Panda, S.K., Daliyet, S.P., Lokre, S.S., Naman, V., Distributed ledger technology in the construction industry using corda, in: *The New Advanced Society: Artificial Intelligence and Industrial Internet of Things Paradigm*, 2022, https://doi.org/10.1002/9781119884392.ch2.

29. Panda, S.K., Mohammad, G.B., Nandan Mohanty, S., Sahoo, S., Smart contract-based land registry system to reduce frauds and time delay, in: *Security and Privacy*, p. e172, 2021, https://doi.org/10.1002/spy2.172.

30. Panda, S.K. and Satapathy, S.C., Drug traceability and transparency in medical supply chain using blockchain for easing the process and creating trust between stakeholders and consumers. *Pers. Ubiquit. Comput.*, 2021. https://doi.org/10.1007/s00779-021-01588-3.

31. Niveditha, V.R., Karthik Sekaran, K., Singh, A., Panda, S.K., Effective prediction of bitcoin price using wolf search algorithm and bidirectional LSTM on internet of things data. *Int. J. System Syst. Eng.*, 11, 3–4, 224–236, 2021.

32. Sri Arza, M. and Panda, S.K., An integration of blockchain and machine learning into the health care system, in: *Machine Learning Adoption in Blockchain-Based Intelligent Manufacturing*, vol. 1, pp. 33–58, 2022, DOI: 10.1201/9781003252009-3.

33. Murala, D.K., Panda, S.K., Swain, S.K., A survey on cloud computing security and privacy issues and challenges. *J. Adv. Res. Dyn. Control Syst.*, 11, 1276–1290, 2019.

34. Murala, D.K., Panda, S.K., Swain, S.K., Secure dynamic groups data sharing with modified revocable attribute-based encryption in cloud. *Int. J. Recent Technol. Eng. (IJRTE)*, 8, 4, 9508–9512, 2019.

35. Murala, D.K., Panda, S.K., Swain, S.K., A novel hybrid approach for providing data security and privacy from malicious attacks in the cloud environment. *J. Adv. Res. Dyn. Control Syst.*, 11, 1291–1300, 2019.

36. Panda, S.K., Swain, S.K., Mall, R., An investigation into usability aspects of E-commerce websites using users' preferences. *Adv. Comput. Sci.: An Int. J.*, 4, 1, 65–73, 2015.

37. Panda, S.K., Swain, S.K., Mall, R., Measuring web site usability quality complexity metrics for navigability, in: *Intelligent Computing, Communication and Devices*, Advances in Intelligent Systems and Computing, vol. 308, L. Jain, S. Patnaik, N. Ichalkaranje (Eds.), Springer, New Delhi, 2015, https://doi.org/10.1007/978-81-322-2012-1_41.

38. Panda, S.K., A usability evaluation framework for B2C E-commerce websites. *Comput. Eng. Intell. Syst.*, 5, 3, 66–85, 2014.

39. Bhalerao, V., Panda, S.K., Jena, A.K., Optimization of loss function on human faces using generative adversarial networks, in: *Machine Learning Approaches for Urban Computing*, Studies in Computational Intelligence, vol. 968, M. Bandyopadhyay, M. Rout, S. Chandra Satapathy (Eds.), Springer, Singapore, 2021, https://doi.org/10.1007/978-981-16-0935-0_9.

40. Panda, S.K. and Dwivedi, M., Minimizing food wastage using machine learning: A novel approach, in: *Smart Intelligent Computing and Applications*, Smart Innovation, Systems and Technologies, S. Satapathy, V. Bhateja, J. Mohanty, S. Udgata (Eds.), vol. 159, Springer, Singapore, 2020, https://doi.org/10.1007/978-981-13-9282-5_44.

41. Panda, S.K., A.R, S., Mishra, M., Satpathy, S., A supervised learning algorithm to forecast weather conditions for playing cricket. *Int. J. Innovative Technol. Exploring Eng. (IJITEE)*, 9, 1, 2019.

42. Panda, S.K., Fraud-resistant crowdfunding system using ethereum blockchain, in: *Bitcoin and Blockchain*, pp. 237–276, 2020.

43. Panda, S.K., Mishra, V., Balamurali, R., Elngar, A.A., *Artificial intelligence and machine learning in business management concepts, challenges, and case studies*, pp. 1–278, CRC Press, Boca Raton, 2021, https://doi.org/10.1201/9781003125129.

44. Joshi, S., Panda, S.K., AR, S., Optimal deep learning model to identify the development of pomegranate fruit in farms. *Int. J. Innovative Technol. Exploring Eng.*, 9, 3, 2352–2356, 2020.

45. Puranam, K.S.R., Gaddam, M.C.T., K, V.P.R., Panda, S.K., Reddy, G.S.M., Anatomy and lifecycle of a bitcoin transaction. *Proceedings of International Conference on Sustainable Computing in Science, Technology and Management (SUSCOM)*, Amity University Rajasthan, Jaipur-India, February 26-28, 2019, February 18, 2019, Available at SSRN: https://ssrn.com/abstract=3355106orhttp://dx.doi.org/10.2139/ssrn.3355106.

46. Panda, S.K. and Swain, S.K., *Quality assurance aspects of web design, design solutions for improving website quality and effectiveness*, pp. 87–129, IGI Global, 2016.

47. Panda, S.K., Bhalerao, V., AR, S., A machine learning model to identify duplicate questions in social media forums. *Int. J. Innovative Technol. Exploring Eng.*, 9, 4, 370–373, 2020.

48. Ahmareen, S., Raj, A., Potluri, S., Panda, S.K., Book shala: An android-based application design and implementation of sharing books, in: *Smart Intelligent Computing and Applications*, Smart Innovation, Systems and Technologies, S. Satapathy, V. Bhateja, J. Mohanty, S. Udgata (Eds.), vol. 159, Springer, Singapore, 2020, https://doi.org/10.1007/978-981-13-9282-5_28.

49. Panda, S.K., Das, S.S., Swain, S.K., S-model for service-oriented applications in web engineering. *Regional Coll. Manag.*, 10, 3, 38–46, 2013.

50. Panda, S.K., An investigation into usability and productivity of E.commerce websites.

51. Panda, S.K., Chandrasekhar, A., Gantayat, P.K., Panda, M.R., Detecting brain tumor using image segmentation: A novel approach, in: *Data Engineering and Intelligent Computing*, Lecture Notes in Networks and Systems, V. Bhateja, L. Khin Wee, J.C.W. Lin, S.C. Satapathy, T.M. Rajesh (Eds.), vol. 446, Springer, Singapore, 2022, https://doi.org/10.1007/978-981-19-1559-8_35.

52. Sanghi, P., Panda, S.K., Pati, C., Gantayat, P.K., Learning deep features and classification for fresh or off vegetables to prevent food wastage using machine learning algorithms, in: *Intelligent Data Engineering and Analytics*, Smart Innovation, Systems and Technologies, S.C. Satapathy, P. Peer, J. Tang, V. Bhateja, A. Ghosh (Eds.), vol. 266, Springer, Singapore, 2022, https://doi.org/10.1007/978-981-16-6624-7_44.

53. Gantayat, P.K., Mohapatra, S., Panda, S.K., Secure trust level routing in delay-tolerant network with node categorization technique, in: *Intelligent Data Engineering and Analytics*, Smart Innovation, Systems and Technologies, S.C. Satapathy, P. Peer, J. Tang, V. Bhateja, A. Ghosh (Eds.), vol. 266, Springer, Singapore, 2022, https://doi.org/10.1007/978-981-16-6624-7_45.

54. Panda, S.K., Urkude, S.V., Urkude, V.R., Vairachilai, S., An investigation into COVID 19 pandemic in India, in: *The New Advanced Society: Artificial Intelligence and Industrial Internet of Things Paradigm*, vol. 1, Wiley.

55. Panda, S.K., Das, S., Swain, S.K., Web site productivity measurement using single task size measure. *J. Inf. Sci. Computing Technol. (JISCT)*, 4, 3, October12, 2015.

56. Hanumanthakari, S. and Panda, S.K., Detecting face mask for prevent COVID-19 using deep learning: A novel approach, in: *Smart Intelligent Computing and Applications, Volume 2*, Smart Innovation, Systems and Technologies, S.C. Satapathy, V. Bhateja, M.N. Favorskaya, T. Adilakshmi (Eds.), vol. 283, Springer, Singapore, 2022, https://doi.org/10.1007/978-981-16-9705-0_45.

57. Panda, S.K., Sathya, A.R., Das, S., Bitcoin: Beginning of the cryptocurrency era, in: *Recent Advances in Blockchain Technology*, Intelligent Systems Reference Library, S.K. Panda, V. Mishra, S.P. Dash, A.K. Pani (Eds.), vol. 237, Springer, Cham, 2023, https://doi.org/10.1007/978-3-031-22835-3_2.

58. Murala, D.K., Panda, S.K., Sahoo, S.K., Securing electronic health record system in cloud environment using blockchain technology, in: *Recent Advances in Blockchain Technology*, Intelligent Systems Reference Library, S.K. Panda, V. Mishra, S.P. Dash, A.K. Pani (Eds.), vol. 237, Springer, Cham, 2023, https://doi.org/10.1007/978-3-031-22835-3_4.

59. Rao, K.V., Murala, D.K., Panda, S.K., Blockchain: A study of new business model, in: *Recent Advances in Blockchain Technology*, Intelligent Systems Reference Library, S.K. Panda, V. Mishra, S.P. Dash, A.K. Pani (Eds.), vol. 237, Springer, Cham, 2023, https://doi.org/10.1007/978-3-031-22835-3_9.

60. Panda, S.K., Mishra, V., Dash, S.P., Pani, A.K., *Recent advances in blockchain technology real-world applications*, Intelligent Systems Reference Library (ISRL, volume 237), vol. 1, pp. 1–317, 978-3-031-22835-3.

61. Panda, S.K., Mohapatra, R.K., Panda, S., Balamurugan, S., *The new advanced society: Artificial intelligence and industrial internet of things paradigm*, vol. 1, pp. 1–512, Wiley, DOI:10.1002/9781119884392.

62. Nanda, S.K., Panda, S.K., Das, M., Satapathy, S.C., Decentralization of car insurance system using machine learning and distributed ledger technology, in: *Intelligent Data Engineering and Analytics. FICTA 2022*, Smart Innovation, Systems and Technologies, V. Bhateja, X.S. Yang, J. Chun-Wei Lin, R. Das (Eds.), vol. 327, Springer, Singapore, 2023, https://doi.org/10.1007/978-981-19-7524-0_52.

Advances in Design and Manufacturing of VR Headset

Chandrashekhar Bendigeri[1]* and Devaraj E.[2]†

[1]University of Visvesvaraya College of Engineering, Bengaluru, Karnataka, India
[2]CMR University, Bengaluru, Karnataka, India

Abstract

Modern artificial cognitive technology is a result of how people interact with computer systems to feel like they are in the real world. Virtual reality (VR) is one of the developing technologies that allow for improvements in human–computer interaction (HCI) based on a variety of inputs in the current trend. VR, which uses a human–computer interface to simulate a virtual environment in real time, makes multidisciplinary engineering possible. One of the most significant and essential functional processes in the manufacturing and construction industries is welding. With high-strength welded joints, the structure's mechanical strength improves. Typically, welding instructors in undergraduate institutions and businesses lack the necessary knowledge, which reduces the number of qualified welders and has an impact on the education of instructors in undergraduate programs, manufacturing, and various construction sectors. These are caused by high material costs, equipment upkeep, training costs, and significant carbon emission with environmental damage. In contrast to conventional welding, VR technology offers an appropriate solution for the aforementioned issues, resulting in trained instructors, and a decrease in material waste, time savings, and self-learning practice. However, welding characteristics in VR are reported as weld speed and execution time. To study the experience of presence in a virtual environment while seeing, hearing, and feeling the welding process, the design and development of a user-fixed VR system called Virtual Reality Metal Arc Welding (VRMAW) are emerging. To enjoy the immersive virtual environment, which is typically challenging in a traditional context, VRMAW leverages HCI. The design includes

Corresponding author: uvce.csb@gmail.com
Corresponding author: devaraj.e@cmr.edu.in

Chandrashekhar A, Shaik Himam Saheb, Sandeep Kumar Panda, S. Balamurugan and Sheng-Lung Peng (eds.)
Metaverse and Immersive Technologies: An Introduction to Industrial, Business and Social
Applications, (191–216) © 2023 Scrivener Publishing LLC

computer-aided design (CAD) modeling of welding, creating virtual objects, changing coordinate systems, creating a VR environment, and integrating an application with smartphone sensors. The new track, which addressed the design interface, demonstration, and usability, comes to reality virtually. It allows users to engage with computers or smartphones in an environment as similar to real-world metal arc welding as possible. The field of welding is fast advancing in VR technology. Its user-fixed VRMAW is a one-of-a-kind, cutting-edge welding solution that promotes digital technology to teach inexperienced welders how to use metal arc welding while also being cost-effective, environmentally friendly, and clean.

Keywords: VRMAW, human-computer interaction, CAD

7.1   Introduction

The term "virtual" was widely used in every field that used technology to simulate the real world. Because of the virtual "integration dimension," artificial cognitive technology used today makes it possible for people to engage with computers as though they were in the real world.

Virtual reality is a modern example of an emerging technology that advances human-computer interaction based on a variety of inputs. In the fields of computer graphics, medical research, surgery, engineering, mining, and construction, mechanical and manufacturing engineering, three-dimensional (3D) scientific visualization, and education for cognitive learning, virtual reality is one of the most promising and potential research applications.

Input, application, rendering, and output are the four main divisions of a user and a VR system in Figure 7.1. The user's eyes, hands, and button pushes are only a few examples of the information that input gathers from the user. The program incorporates non-rendering features of the virtual environment, such as dynamic geometry updating, user interaction, physics simulation, etc. Visual rendering, auditory rendering, and haptic rendering (the feeling of touch) are all examples of rendering, which is the conversion of a computer-friendly format into a user-friendly one that creates the illusion of some type of reality. Drawing a sphere is an example of rendering. Other than high-level descriptions and components that directly impact the user experience, rendering is already fully defined. The physical representation known as output is what the user can see and feel (e.g., a display with pixels or headphones with sound waves).

Visual displays, audio, haptics, and motion platforms are the main VR output devices. Olfactory (smell), wind, heat, and even taste displays are

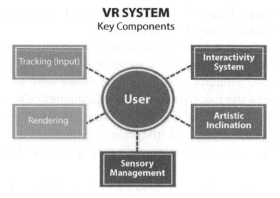

Figure 7.1 A VR system consists of input from the user, the application, rendering, and output to the user.

some of the more unusual exhibits. Designing VR experiences requires careful consideration of the hardware to be used. For some designs, some hardware could be a better fit than others. For instance, for big audiences gathered at the same physical area, enormous screens are preferable overhead mounted displays. The sections that follow give an overview of various

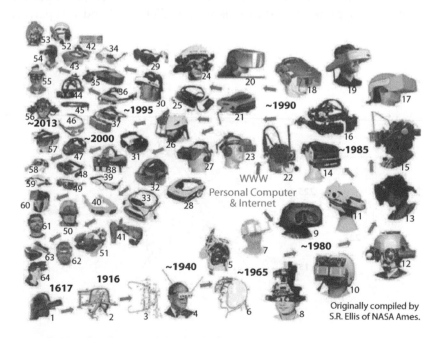

Figure 7.2 Some head-mounted displays and viewers over time [44].

popular VR devices. Figure 7.2 represents the sections that follow and give an overview of various popular VR devices.

In 1860, self-assembled cardboard stereoscopes with manually operated moving images were among the stereoscopes that were popular during the first 3D craze. Millions of stereoscopic views were sold by one business in 1862. Brewster's design for headset is theoretically similar to both the Google Cardboard of today and the View-Master of the 20th century. Instead of using actual physical images, a cell phone is utilized to display the images in the case of Google Cardboard and other phone-based VR systems.

Many years later, at the 1995 Midwinter Fair in San Francisco, a 360⁰ VR-type display known as the Haunted Swing was presented. It is still one of the most captivating technological illusion displays to this day. The demonstration was held in a room with a huge swing that could accommodate about 40 people. The swing was started after the audience had taken their seats, and as it oscillated, users unintentionally grasped their chairs as if they were in an elevator. In reality, the swing barely moved at all, but the area around it moved significantly, giving the sensation of self-motion.

The development of VR technology went beyond just showing visual visuals in the 1900s. Beginning to emerge were new interaction ideas that even today's VR systems could seem unique. A head-worn pistol pointing and shooting system, for instance, is seen in Figure 7.3 and was patented

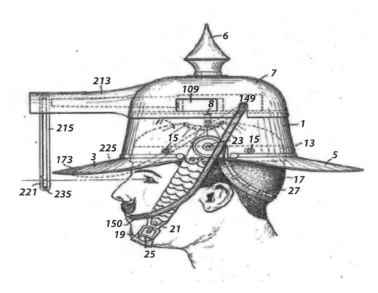

Figure 7.3 Albert Pratt's head-mounted targeting and gun-firing interface [44].

by Albert Pratt in 1916 [Pratt 1916]. This weapon can be fired without the need for hand tracking because the operator blows through a tube that serves as the interface.

VR, which uses a human computer interface to simulate a virtual environment in real time, also makes multidisciplinary collaborative engineering easier. Due to its strong resemblance to reality, virtual reality technology produces an engaging environment that encourages active learning as opposed to passive learning. The majority of beginning learners are drawn to VR's increased multimedia and three-dimensional visualization techniques, which also improve learning outcomes. One key benefit of VR technology is repetition, which enables users to practice certain welding procedures and scenarios in a virtual setting, emphasizing the learning outcome. By removing the possibility of exposure to potentially harmful risks present in other teaching interfaces, VR technology aids novices in reducing their financial and societal costs.

By utilizing Virtual reality along with Augmented Reality (AR), and Mixed Reality (MR) as technically advanced advance computation technology, the concept of the "smart factory" has opened up new opportunities for the industrial sector. Implementing VR technology has improved process monitoring, control, and precise manufacturing. As a result, manufacturers may be able to produce high-quality, efficient, and precise products to meet demand. Key dimensions of VR technology include highly interfaced communication systems, sensor technologies, and automation functions.

One of the most crucial and essential functional processes in the industrial industry is welding. The number of experienced welders has declined because most welding instructors in undergrad institutions and the workplace lack experience. It affects the manufacturing, many construction businesses, and the training of instructors for undergrads. This is a result of the high cost of training, supplies, and equipment upkeep. The afore mentioned issues can be effectively solved by VR technology, which also results in qualified trainers, a reduction in material use, time savings, cost savings, and compatibility.

Before realizing the science fiction dreams, virtual reality is successfully applied in numerous fields. A lot of work has been put into developing virtual reality assisted welding processes for various working environments due to its effectiveness and crucial significance. However, creating VR mechanisms for various welding processes where there may be a variety of working restrictions, such as angle, mass control, arc rod elongation, etc. Creating a VR model under these circumstances is a very time-consuming undertaking. However, the current study was motivated by the rapid growth of virtual manufacturing processes to identify an appropriate welding process that made a significant contribution to modern applications and to create a cutting-edge, reliable, android-based virtual reality metal arc welding or training module for resource augmentation that would ultimately guarantee higher productivity and accuracy. Understanding welding and related structures is crucial because the proposed effort aims to establish a VR assisted welding process. Virtual Reality Metal Arc Welding may make learning and practicing metal arc welding simple, green, affordable, and quick.

7.2   Literature Survey

By choosing the right software and hardware equipment, virtual reality metal arc welding aims to close the gap between traditional and cutting-edge virtual reality technologies. To determine the present state and extent of the research effort, a thorough survey, and study of the literature in the field of virtual reality is conducted in this direction.

a) CAD/CAM
b) Welding
c) Virtual reality
d) Virtual manufacturing
e) Mathematical modeling and computer graphics
f) Virtual reality in welding and training

Yang Zheng *et al.* [1] demonstration of a variety of computer-based design tools for use in design activities (CAD). Due to its capability for Boolean operations like the addition and deletion of surfaces, this method is efficient for design tasks.

According to Kun Yang *et al.* [2], the conceptual design of the triple helix is an inventive and creative problem-solving model for computer-aided creative design systems. The three types of space established for computer-aided creative design systems are design flow space, knowledge inspiration space, and solution operating space. This paradigm uses cognitive stimulation to model design types like variant, adaptable, and unique.

Holger Graf *et al.* [3] novel approach to preparing computer-aided design data for virtual reality model was described. By using tessellation as an intermediate representation, computer-aided design models are transformed into various virtual reality examples models. Data interface and scene configuration make up virtual design data preparation.

The framework for the representation of matrices is provided by an object-oriented approach to geometry algebra. Virtual reality modeling relies on human visual perception, and the foundation for it is digital modeling appearance. Shape, material, and incident light all work together to produce a visual image. When building models for virtual environments, other factors such as material appearance, encoding appearance, and rendering appearance are just as crucial.

The process of creating detailed scenes in three dimensions takes a significant amount of data storage and is challenging. To develop simple visual representations, a tool building technique using a command language and algorithm is applied. A process based and organized strategy is necessary to obtain high quality training and cognitive learning strategies for the development of welding skills.

When welding students are trained using virtual reality technology rather than traditional welding, A. Preston Byrd et al. [4] look at how much their social anxiety and phobias decrease. The manufacturing sector demonstrates the lack of skilled welders, from apprentices to engineers, which has an influence on output and product quality. The development of productivity is greatly aided by the exchange of knowledge about effective working methods. Artificial cognitive technology training reduces welding training costs and increases welding production following the training of novice welders.

The cognitive learning framework, which provides a touchstone for discussion with four dimensional parameters pedagogical consideration, style of representation, context, and learner specifications is highlighted by Sara de Freitas et al. [5].

Fully immersive and virtual reality integrated technology is used in welding by Richard T. Stone et al. [6] to track the use of weld patterns in various welding locations for improved visual aid.

In order to view the evolution of a medical operation that shortens the procedure completion time and increases cost efficiency, Kevin Kunkler [7] examined the use of virtual reality simulation in medical applications.

According to Davide Manca et al. [8], the chemical process sector should integrate and combine a dynamic accident simulator with a virtual reality simulator of a dynamic process to provide learners with a customized, efficient learning experience. The virtual chemical industry offers users a completely immersive virtual setting with three-dimensional audio effects that let them feel the challenging conditions of a manufacturing operation.

Virtual reality training is an innovative cognitive tool that offers rich educational context with high levels of immersion, graphic fidelity, and multi-sensory indications to boost interest and motivation in the trainees for skill acquisition and learning processes within experiential framework, according to Fabrizia Mantovani *et al.* [9].

The phrase "virtual reality" or "manufactured reality" was first used by Howard Rheingold [10]. A middle range of human interfaces to computer graphics systems use artificial reality. The use of position trackers and helmet mounted displays to visualize synthetic (virtual) surroundings and images is also common.

In order to transform the traditional manufacturing system into an information-oriented manufacturing system that has the potential to integrate manufacturing resources and processes in cloud networking, Kazuaki Iwata *et al.* [11] place special emphasis on advanced information technology with cloud networking and 3D computer graphics.

According to Abdulrahman M. Al-Ahmari *et al.* [12], virtual reality technology offers the manufacturing sector an efficient and affordable option for the design, plan, and prototype of machine parts and assembly for training and decision-making. The collaborative interaction modules with visual, acoustic, and tactile feedback offered by the virtual assembly system provide an immersive environment for the user.

Current industrial industries need two new technologies: virtual reality and internet communications. Full-scale 3D models can be viewed in synthetic environments using artificial cognitive technology, which boosts designer efficiency and transparency in 3D model examination. The two database managers are the universal database manager and the knowledge-base manager. Data transferred to virtual environments through user interface environments and data for 3D graphics are kept in knowledge base managers in universal database managers.

Customized product creation in mass production employing virtual prototype and design by manufacturing simulation approaches was provided by Mitchell M. Tseng *et al.* in their study [13]. By using virtual prototyping, bespoke products can be designed more effectively. The primary tenet of virtual prototyping of customized product development is concept development for design and concept evaluation for simulation environment inside the single domain.

The synergistic marriage of 3D computer graphics and touch screen display soft controls results in greater interactivity. The location and angle of approach are both detected by a multidimensional touchscreen with sensing position of six (6) degrees of force vector information and sensor frame. Virtual reality describes the user's interaction with an artificial environment as well as the media used to create it. The main components of virtual reality include a fully immersive virtual world, affordances for depth perception, tracking the user's direction of motion, motion parallax, and a spatialized audio system.

According to Samar K. Saha [14], virtual manufacturing is particularly effective for enhancing the current manufacturing process, creating cutting-edge process technology, and increasing the product's potential to be manufactured. The two main developments of an efficient manufacturing process are product development and technology development.

A closed-loop environment that may be utilized online to control and automate a manufacturing organization is discussed by Bin Wu *et al.* in their discussion of the conceptual framework and implementation of an integrated, computer-aided manufacturing system design environment [15].

Virtual manufacturing, which employs modeling, simulation, product optimization, synthesis, knowledge capitalization, analysis, and the processes involved in its manufacturing domain, is highlighted by Philippe Depince *et al.* [16]. Virtual manufacturing (VM) is the term used to describe manufacturing done on a computer utilizing CAD tools for modeling and simulation. A decision-making tool, virtual manufacturing functions as a foundation for three-dimensional facility layout with both static and dynamic production system behavior.

System architecture with virtual-real interactions and system infrastructure were proposed by K. Iwata *et al.* [17] for usable development. Seven functional blocks that can be used to create virtual objects using modeling approaches are identified, along with the informational dependencies that exist between them.

Hyper-realism technology for three-dimensional model projection with interactive and audiovisual systems in digital applications. The advantages of virtual prototyping include cost savings during pre-build, a decrease in the number of prototypes, and a reduction in the number of physical prototypes and manufactured goods. Through modeling and simulation, the kernel technique is used to implement the virtual manufacturing concept in next-generation manufacturing systems.

Two production systems are described by Masahiko Onosato *et al.* [18]. While virtual manufacturing systems are broken down into virtual and informational systems in information systems and virtual and physical systems in physical systems, real manufacturing systems are divided into real and informational systems in information systems and real and physical systems in information systems. The configuration of the Virtual Works system includes a solid model editor, a class manager, a simulation manager, and a report reader.

The three modeling approaches for determining the center of subjectively formed objects are the polygon centroid method, selection center, and optimal center. While human-computer interaction designers use models to assess and enhance interaction strategies, interface designers employ models to forecast and optimize the performance of user interfaces. Transformation matrices are rotated and oriented using quaternions.

The significance of mathematics and algorithms for computer graphics and geometric modeling was summarized by Max K. Agoston [19]. The three different kinds of geometric modeling are global, local, and intrinsic. The virtual reality model is created using intrinsic geometric modeling. For the transformation of the matrices, the fundamentals of quaternions are also given.

Computer-aided design heavily relies on solid geometric modeling. It consists of a geometric modeling algorithm, mathematical theories for the algorithms, software and hardware systems, and solid modeling of the geometry (face, surfaces, vertices, and solids) and transformations such rigid motion and Boolean operations. The art of creating interactive computer visuals using mathematical objects and their change is known as mathematical visualization. By using visuals that are logically helpful, it offers new understanding into the objects of pure geometry.

According to W. R. DeVries et al. [20], computer graphics can give a simulation in the time domain by animating and visualizing a dynamic process model using a transformation matrix.

According to Jixiang Lu et al. [21], human computer interaction makes it possible and amenable for people to engage with virtual objects. Because they are in direct contact with users, mobile internet gadgets promote improved interaction and user happiness.

A collaborative handheld computer is designed with virtual reality in mind for educational purposes. The outcome demonstrates an efficient method for combining collaborative and cognitive learning with mobile computers. Mobile technology is becoming more and more popular in the modern period because to its simplicity of use, small size, and parity with laptop or desktop technology. Human-computer communication on mobile devices uses a model-based temporal method. Using mathematical models at the keystroke and movement levels, user interface designers can more affordably evaluate input technique.

For mobile handheld interaction, Ken Hinckley et al. [22] proposed voice memo detection, scrolling of the joystick, and display mode identification in addition to touch sensors, tilt sensors, and proximity sensors as hardware sensor solutions.

By focusing on cutting-edge tools like proximity snapping and collision snapping, Richard G. Dewar *et al.* [23] help users of virtual environments reuse the design product database and interact with virtual objects.

Positive transfer training effectiveness ratio is achieved during welding instruction using integrated virtual reality. The three main components of interaction and team learning are collaborative learning, open communication, and continuous development.

Santosh N. Nair *et al.* [24] demonstrate cognitive feedback training that enhances visual inspection performance by gathering and analyzing eye movements using a 3D binocular eye tracker.

For the weld beads, Dongsik Jo *et al.* [25] created a mathematical model. The actual welding process served as the basis for creating the database of bead height, width, angle, and penetration. The mathematical model consists of a numerical equation for calculating bead shape and height as well as a curve equation.

According to Sakol Teeravarunyou *et al.* [26], a computer-based welding training system improves fundamental skills by transferring information from creation to coding, leading to an increase in welding skills.

By adjusting the welding parameters, particularly arc length, weld rate, and arc time, the effectiveness of welding training can be increased. For the straight travel of the electrode, the arm movement's trajectory is set. The use of virtual reality in welding has decreased the cost of training [27].

The benefits of virtual reality in welding training were discussed by Laurent Da Dalto *et al.* [28] as the technology aids in enhancing a better training quality with flexibility, minimizing the training cost, and increasing the training pace. To conceptualize and simplify the scene model for improved learning and understanding, counterintuitive design techniques are applied.

According to J. Kreindl *et al.* [29], virtual welding systems can teach beginning welders the fundamentals of welding as well as safety techniques without the need for an expensive testing welding room and its associated equipment. The concepts for instruction are provided via virtual welding, which improves the effectiveness of the learning process.

An intelligent welder training system with the use of neural networks and scriptable information was presented by Yeong-Do Park *et al.* [30] to enhance hand-eye coordination, welding postures, various weldment shapes, and welding diagnostics. For weldment structure and postures, a script based on Extensible Markup Language (XML) is employed.

In order to assess the cognitive level of learning among the undergraduates, Richard T. Stone *et al.* [31] make a distinction between virtual reality integrated weld training and traditional weld training. With the established skills of virtual reality technology, skilled welders are generated quickly.

According to Faizal Amin Nur Yunus *et al.* [32], a virtual reality welding simulator can redo welding sessions without wasting any material and improve comprehension of welding processes.

With design factors taken into account, computer graphics techniques are employed for high-quality visualization techniques, and a way of implementation is used for user-computer interaction with the virtual objects. Multimodal interfaces for realistic experience and three-dimensional weld bead visualization are used to create interactive training. The database for generating the shape of the weld bead is created with the aid of real-time visualization from experiential sources [32–35].

Technical training, problem-solving, decision-making, communication, and interpersonal skills are all areas where Benjamin Knoke *et al.* [36] deemed physical and simulation fidelity to be essential for experienced trainers. Training with simulations focuses on developing three types of skills: cognitive (thinking), psychomotor (doing), and emotional (interacting).

According to A. P. Byrd *et al.* [37], a virtual reality simulator is utilized as a tool for evaluating beginning welders. Five welding characteristics are taken into account while assessing simple and complex welded locations.

Erik Engh [38] emphasizes the use of virtual reality technology in active-based welding instruction to improve skills and competency in welding process. In order to close the communication gap between students and teachers, the structure of the learning design process is examined.

Welder education that is on par with emerging technologies is suggested by Luisa Quintino *et al.* [39] as a way to improve weld quality. Robotized welding uses control systems and sensor technology.

For beginning welders, virtual reality technology improves their psychomotor skills during the welding process. Additionally, it shortens the training period for welders and improves their proficiency in a single welding operation [40].

With the use of RobCAD, Yongkang Ma *et al.* [41] demonstrate 3D visible welding simulation for optimizing the weld path to lower design costs and increase welding process dependability.

The efficiency and logic of the welding operation were improved by LI Yanping *et al.* [42] mathematical model for multi-robot welding task utilizing hill climbing algorithm and genetic algorithm coded using Matlab and Visual C++.

The findings from the literature survey are as follows:

- The core of developing new products for future technologies like digital manufacturing, VR, extended VR, and AR is modeling utilizing a proper CAD tool.
- A brief overview of the various welding procedures and their corresponding functional properties was done. To support ongoing development and improvement in the new product design process, new systems using virtual reality technology are being introduced, such as VR based system for product (model) based assembly, human integrated simulation and visualization in manufacturing, web-based system for combined e-learning, rule based system for virtual prototypes, and united structure for model design review.
- Computer graphics techniques are essential for rendering CAD models, creating multimodal interfaces for realistic environments, and product design. The technique of interactive virtual model creation using computer graphics and manipulation algorithms is known as mathematical modeling and visualization.
- Virtual reality is employed in a variety of industries, including aerospace, automotive, medicine, heavy engineering, training, and educational learning, albeit this use is still in its infancy. Users of virtual reality have the chance to learn well, practice often, and do so without using any electricity, consumables, or raw materials.
- Virtual reality metal arc welding requires the cooperation of CAD, reverse engineering, and virtual reality technologies. The use of advanced virtual reality equipment, such as HTC virtual reality glasses, virtual reality systems, and cameras, has been used to train surgeons before to surgery and train pilots in aerospace. However, despite having less expensive equipment, android-based virtual reality technology is still uncommon in the engineering field. As a result, prospects in the field of mechanical engineering are more skill-based.
- The areas to be focused for immersion and interaction include designing the CAD platform in a virtual world using CAD tools, converting CAD models to virtual models, identifying virtual reality software, and mathematical modeling. Present-day difficulties with e-training for novices in

welding using virtual reality metal arc welding, which is healthy, clean, and economical.

- Overall, it paints a picture that there is still much study to be done in fields like metal arc welding, coding, and virtual reality for computers and android-based smartphones. Other areas include solid modeling utilizing an appropriate CAD tool.

The advances in design and manufacturing of VR headset include:

- Virtual reality is an essential component of people's daily lives all around the world. Virtual reality products are used to research product design and replicate user interaction in a virtual setting. In a virtual environment, the user activates their senses to see, hear, and touch the virtual items as if they had never actually been. The majority of virtual environments are created on computers. Real world and virtual world collaboration is the vision and goal of VR.
- Virtual reality is a representation of the imaginary worlds that humans can imagine. By giving the user a sense of presence and total immersion, virtual reality aims to make any scenario they may imagine seem realistic. Virtual reality offers a completely interactive experience that allows users to walk freely throughout the scene, interact with numerous items, and make the best choice after familiarizing themselves with (or mastering) the material.
- The majority of research work have been launched in the areas of medical surgery, safety, aerospace, education, and training. There are therefore many chances to use virtual reality in the field of engineering design and development. Android smartphones are used to display this virtual environment to the user.

7.3   Technically Enriched Advance Computation Technologies

Virtual reality and augmented reality, the industrial internet of things, big data, and block chain, robotics with artificial intelligence, additive manufacturing, cybersecurity, and cloud computing are some of the emerging technologies associated with the fourth industrial revolution.

- Industry 1.0: Existence of small-scale mechanical industries and power generation industries with the aid of water, steam, and coal.
- Industry 2.0: Assembly line production, manufacturing of goods in large quantities, and Mega Watt electric power generation.
- Industry 3.0: Application of robotics for automation using CAD/CAM/CAE tools.
- Industry 4.0: Usage of smart technologies between computerization and exchange of data in mechanical, automobile, cyber systems, aerospace, and electronic manufacturing sectors.

Data analysis, manipulation, and exploitation are made more efficient by 3D visualization, simulation, interaction, and immersion. The advances in manufacturing, healthcare, education, sciences, finance, and energy that use 3D visualization, virtual reality, and immersion tools assist teams (human resources) develop technically and achieve higher success rates.

7.4 Arc Welding

The method of arc welding involves permanently connecting two pieces of metal together with the help of filler material under the effect of heat and maybe pressure. The welder must practice making straight movements with the electrode holder to improve the weld bead. Continuous welding practice improves a welder's ability to produce the right weld bead at junctions. Shielded metal-arc welding is the most common form of welding procedure. The focus of the current research is on creating a reliable and effective virtual reality metal arc welding learning mechanism for the most efficient use of resources and the safe implementation of the green training idea.

7.5 Virtual Manufacturing

Manufacturing, which includes the steps of materials, processes, manufactured items, labor, and assembly, is a crucial component of the economy. Due to international rivalry, industries are currently experiencing serious problems and difficulties. Fast reaction and flexibility are currently more popular in manufacturing than mass-produced proto-types. One can achieve resource design, process, integrated goods, quality, cost-effective products, technology optimization, and cost reduction through virtual manufacturing (VM).

Through greater process understanding and the creation of a platform to educate and train aspiring machine operators on a particular machine and machine time, VM helps to reduce material waste and flawed design. On desktop computers and smart phones, virtual production is the exact opposite of traditional manufacturing. Virtual reality is the foundation of virtual manufacturing because it allows customers to experience the benefits and drawbacks of a product realistically, cutting costs, and saving time.

7.6   Virtual Reality

VR emerged as a unique area of human-computer interfaces, and its use began in the early twenty-first century. Due to the early stages of development of VR tools and technology, evaluation of this technology is difficult; to date, little research has been done on this technology's implications for education and training. Researchers are currently gathering useful information about VR hardware and software for applications in the aerospace, automotive, construction, and educational sectors. Figure 7.4 represents the vision of virtual manufacturing.

Virtual reality is a human-computer interaction that gives the user an immersive experience in a 3D virtual world filled with movable,

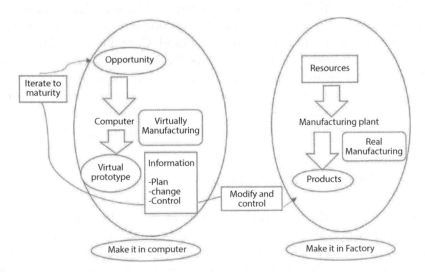

Figure 7.4 Vision of virtual manufacturing [43].

interactive items. With the use of virtual reality technology, a user can engage and become fully immersed in 3D virtual objects, experiencing them intuitively and simulating their actions in a real-world setting. A virtual reality environment gives the user a 3D sense of presence, immersion, and instinctual engagement with the virtual environment.

The user investigates the quickening pace of VR technology development while immersed in the virtual environment. Interaction between the smartphone and the virtual reality controller is made possible via collaborative virtual reality. Compared to desktop computer systems, virtual reality speeds up complete immersion. The physical user actions with the interface devices are picked up by VR systems in the visible field of vision surrounding the 3D virtual environment. Virtual reality encourages users to enter perilous situations so they may see actual cases. For instance, simulating intricate industrial installations, developing new structures, visualizing intricate things, invisible matter molecules, and airflow direction.

Virtual reality is classified into three major categories namely

(i) Neural-direct virtual reality: In this type, the database collected from various sources and the present user position and orientation is directly associated.

(ii) Non-immersive virtual reality: In this type, user experience 3D virtual object in the virtual environment programmed for windows-based or mobile (Smartphones) based platforms and is created without any hardware components.

(iii) Sensory-immersive virtual reality: In this type, real environment 3D modeling plays a vital role with various types of sensors attached. The user is encircled by projected pictures (image) in a virtual environment.

7.7 Virtual Welding: An Innovation Towards Virtual Reality for Welding and Training

Welding is a complex manufacturing operation that must be carried out with numerous trials before producing the desired welded junction, as was previously stated. In the assembly and construction of metal structures, welding is essential. The education and manufacturing industries both play a crucial role in the training of new and inexperienced welders, and they place a lot of emphasis on fields like nuclear pipes and navy ships, where the welded connections must pass stringent inspection.

Virtual reality has a wide range of uses, some of which include training surgeons in laparoscopic procedures using haptic screens and gloves in virtual reality simulations. Commercial pilot training takes place in virtual reality-enhanced flight simulators. Because of this virtual reality setting, it is important to train beginners and undergraduates in order to increase the efficiency of the process.

Welders in the beginning stages can receive minimally expensive, material-wastage-free training through virtual reality metal arc welding. The focus of this research is on creating a product-based VR system prototype called Android Based Virtual Reality Metal Arc Welding that will allow people to create virtual metal arc welding in various welding joints. Process parameters like weld duration and weld speed are recorded by the VRMAW and shown after welding for analysis and improvement. In traditional welding, the strength of the actual weld as well as other welding characteristics like visual inspection, guided bend test, free bend test, tensile test, magnetic particle test, and hydrostatic test are computed. However, a world-fixed virtual reality system in virtual reality can analyze the strength and quality of virtual welds. The user-fixed virtual reality system is the subject of the current research. The user-fixed VRMAW introduces a first-of-its-kind welding teaching methodology employing smartphones with Android operating systems and cutting-edge VR technologies. Figure 7.5 represents the flowchart of VR welding.

7.8 Virtual Reality Metal Arc Welding System (VRMAWS)

VRMAW system consists of three sub-systems namely (i) input/output device manager to handle communication with input devices such as virtual reality controllers, VR headset and smart phones, (ii) virtual world manager for interaction, (iii) visual and audio manager for graphical 3D display and surround sound system. Figure 7.6 represents VRMAWS.

7.9 Software's and Hardware Used in VRMAW

VRMAW hardware - Input device: Virtual reality controller, Output devices: Smart phones and virtual reality headset.

A virtual reality controller can be used as an input device to allow users to interact and navigate within the VR world. The VR controller's spherical tracker serves as a controller for the mobility of the electrode throughout the welding process. The virtual keyboard can be selected using the controller buttons, an alphabetic QWERTY keypad, menu icons, and virtual

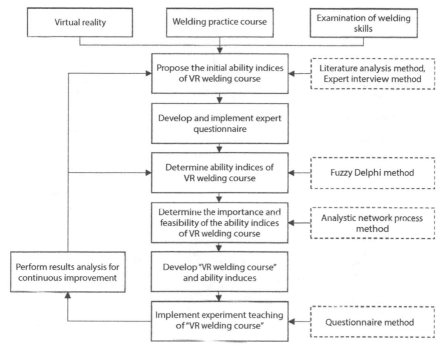

Figure 7.5 Flowchart of VR welding [45].

objects to enter the username. To expose the VR world to consumers and create an immersive experience within the environment, virtual reality headsets and smartphones are employed.

VRMAW software's – 3Ds Max, Autodesk Inventor, Adobe Fuse, Unity 3D, Microsoft Visual Studio, and Android SDK are among the VRMAW software programs (Software Development Kit). Modeling of the welding table, helmet, electrode holder, electrode, and workpieces is done using CAD programs like Autodesk Inventor and 3Ds Max. The CAD models are rendered using Adobe Fuse software to create realistic images. A graphical user interface called Unity 3D is used to create virtual scene models in virtual environments and to interact with CAD models in VR models.

The scripting language utilized in the Microsoft Visual Studio product is C#. Emerging technologies like virtual reality, augmented reality, and the internet of things are all compatible with Android applications. Android applications' adaptability, flexibility, and adaptability enable developers to create interactive, dynamic mobile applications.

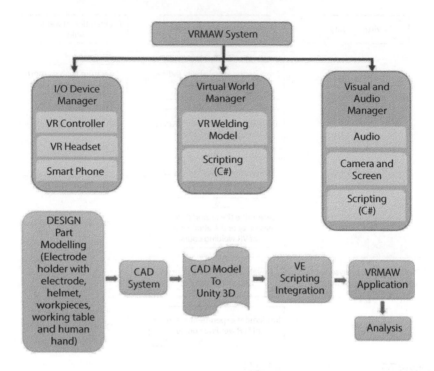

Figure 7.6 Virtual reality metal arc welding system.

7.10   Virtual Design and Manufacturing

First, a research study and expert interviews were used to determine the VR welding course's skill indices. After determining the relative significance of the ability indices and the viability of VR-assisted welding instruction, the teaching approach and course material were developed, and experimental instruction was put into practice to confirm the results. The literature study, expert interviews, and the questionnaire were all conducted using several techniques, including fuzzy Delphi, ANP, and others.

Using virtual reality (VR) technology, instructors can demonstrate the safety regulations for welding in a virtual setting, such as wearing safety goggles, gloves, and masks and verifying the automatic electric shock prevention device, allowing students to practice and implement each requirement one at a time. S0401: In order to experience the proper safety precautions before welding operations. The correct equipment, a slag hammer, should be used to remove slag from the weld bead; otherwise, we would be scalded if we didn't follow the rules and wear protective gloves. Figures 7.7 and 7.8 represents the Protective Leather Gloves for Welding and Tool for Removing Slag from a Weld Bead, a Slag Hammer.

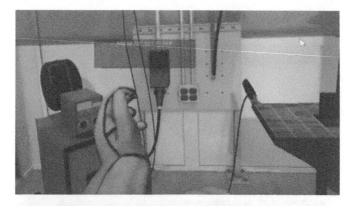

Figure 7.7 Protective leather gloves for welding [45].

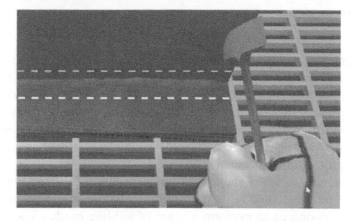

Figure 7.8 Tool for removing slag from a weld bead, a slag hammer [45].

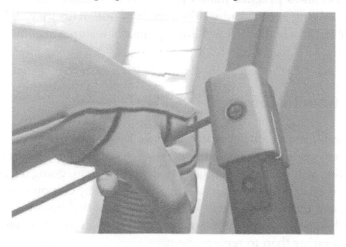

Figure 7.9 VR welding simulation screen [45].

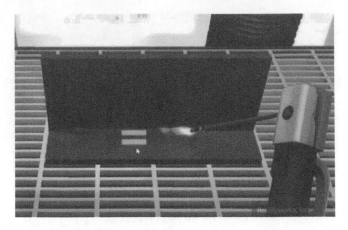

Figure 7.10 VR welding simulation screen [45].

The practice welding operations and become accustomed to welding postures and processes appreciations to VR welding equipment. The most crucial factor was that practice frequently without worrying about being hurt or breaking the equipment. Additionally, the VR welding equipment's practice mode features a prompt feature like welding angle, walking pace, etc. Figures 7.9 and 7.10 represents VR Welding Simulation Screen and VR Welding Simulation Screen.

Additionally, to learn stable welding techniques. "VR welding equipment can set plate thickness in addition to flat welding and horizontal welding, allowing us to perform a range of welding modes. The weld out good works since practice makes perfect when it comes to welding. The stability, walking speed, and welding angle of our welds may all be tested using the test mode that VR welding equipment features in addition to the practice mode.

7.11 Conclusion

Digital realities are getting closer because it is now possible to combine physical environments with computer-based components that add extra information and create engaging virtual worlds. Then, going ahead to the future, it is evident that people will be surrounded by computer-simulated realities, and they do not need to be conscious of that because, in reality, these technologies are here to support people in doing their tasks more effectively rather than to replace them.

The sector is particularly flourishing because to VR. Anyone who has tested a VR experience can witness to its quality and functionality. New uses for this immersive technology have emerged, and new businesses have been established during the past several years, so it is not surprising that it is becoming less science fiction and more science reality.

Despite being in its very early stages of development and being closely linked to gaming, virtual reality is actually reshaping the way that people currently watch sports, design new products, or even teach. Because of this, it is thought that VR will not only disrupt current markets but also create new ones.

If using a headset to experience VR is so simple, the reader would question why there aren't more individuals already residing in virtual reality. There are unfortunately still a lot of problems to fix. The obstacles the VR industry faces today are discussed in this part, along with future trends that are expected.

References

1. Zheng, Y., Shen, H., Sun, C., Collaborative design: Improving efficiency by concurrent execution of Boolean tasks. *Expert Syst. App.*, 38, 1089–1098, 2011.
2. Yang, K., Li, Y., Xiong, Y., Yan, J.-Y., Na, H.-Z., A model for computer-aided creative design based on cognition and iteration. *J. Mech. Eng. Sci.*, 1–18, 2015.
3. Graf, H., Brunetti, G., Stork, A., A methodology supporting the preparation of 3D-CAD data for design reviews in VR, in: *Design-2002*, Dubrovnik, (Ed.), pp. 489–495, 2002.
4. Preston Byrd, A., Stone, R., Anderson, R.G., Integrating virtual reality to reduce anxiety in beginning welders. *Poster presented at the North Central Region – American Association for Agricultural Education Research Conference*, pp. 163–176, Champaign, 2012.
5. de Freitas, S. and Oliver, M., How can exploratory learning with games and simulations within the curriculum be most effectively evaluated? *Comput. & Educ.*, 46, 249–264, 2006.
6. Stone, R.T., McLaurin, E., Zhong, P., Watts, K.P., Full virtual reality vs. integrated virtual reality training in welding. *Welding J.*, 92, 6, 167s–174s, 2013.
7. Kunkler, K., The role of medical simulation: An overview. *Int. J. Med. Robotics Comput. Assisted Surgery*, 2, 203–210, 2006.
8. Manca, D., Brambilla, S., Colombo, S., Bridging between virtual reality and accident simulation for training of process-industry operators. *Adv. Eng. Software*, 55, 1–9, 2013.

9. Mantovani, F., Castelnuovo, G., Gaggioli, A., Riva, G., Virtual reality training for health-care professionals. *Cyber Psychol. Behav.*, 6, 4, 389–395, 2003.

10. Rheingold, H., *Virtual reality summit*, Summit Books/Simon and Schuster, New York, 1991.

11. Iwata, K., Onosato, M., Teramoto, K., Osaki, S., Virtual manufacturing systems as advanced information infrastructure for integrated manufacturing resources and activities. *Ann. CIRP*, 46, 1, 335–338, 1997.

12. Al-Ahmari, A.M., Abidi, M.H., Ahmad, A., Darmoul, S., Development of a virtual manufacturing assembly simulation system. *Adv. Mech. Eng.*, 8, 3, 1–13, 2016.

13. Tseng, M.M., Jiao, J., Su, C.-J., Virtual prototyping for customized product development. *Integr. Manuf. Syst.*, 9, 6, 1–23, 1998.

14. Saha, S.K., Organizational visions of virtual manufacturing: Sociotechnical aspects of adopting technology computer-aided design based manufacturing process. *IEMC.*, 96, 570–575, 1996.

15. Wu, B. and Ellis, R., Manufacturing strategy analysis and system design -The complete cycle within a computer-aided design environment. *IEEE Trans. Robot. Autom.*, 16, 3, 247–258, 2000.

16. Depince, P., Chablat, D., Woelk, P.-O., Virtual manufacturing - Tools for improving design and production. 1–12, 2004. *Dans International Design Seminar - CIRP International Design Seminar.* Caire Egypt 2004.

17. Iwata, K., Onosato, M., Teramoto, K., Osaki, S., Modeling and simulation architecture for virtual manufacturing system. *Ann. CIRP*, 44, 399–402, 1995.

18. Onosato, M. and Iwata, K., Development of a virtual manufacturing system by integrating product models and factory models. *Ann. CIRP*, 42, 475–478, 1993.

19. Agoston, M.K., *Computer graphics and geometric modeling: Implementation and algorithms*, Springer-Verlag, London, 2005.

20. DeVries, W.R. and Evans, M.S., Computer graphics simulation of metal cutting. *Ann. CIRP*, 33, 15–18, 1984.

21. Lu, J., Yu, S., Wang, P., Lu, C., Research on the control of three-dimension based on the mobile internet device. *IEEE*, 10, 2, 1424–1426, 2010.

22. Hinckley, K., Pierce, J., Sinclair, M., Horvitz, E., Sensing techniques for mobile interaction. *Symposium on User Interface Software and Technology.* CHI Letters, 2, 2, 91–100, 2000.

23. Dewar, R.G., Carpenter, I.D., Ritchie, J.M., Simmons, J.E.L., Enhancing a virtual environment for manual assembly. *Proceedings of 12th International Conference on CAD/CAM Robotics and Factories of the Future*, pp. 1067–1072, 1996.

24. Nair, S.N., Gramopadhye, A.K., Vora, J., Melloy, B.J., Cognitive feedback training using 3d binocular eye tracker. *Proceedings of the Human Factors and Ergonomics Society 45th Annual Meeting*, Minneapolis, pp. 1838–1842, 2001.

25. Jo, D., Kim, Y., Yang, U., Lee, G.A., Choi, J.S., Visualization of virtual weld beads. *Proceedings of the 16th ACM Symposium on Virtual Reality Software and Technology (VRST '09)*, ACM New York, pp. 269–270, 2009.

26. Teeravarunyou, S. and Poopatb, B., Computer based welding training system. *Int. J. Ind. Eng.: Theory, Appl. Pract.*, 16, 2, 116–125, 2009.

27. Whitney, S.J. and Stephens, A.K.W., *Use of simulation to improve the effectiveness of army welding training*, pp. 1–47, Land Division, Defence Science and Technology Organization, Australia, 2014.

28. Da Dalto, L., Benus Jr., F., Balet, O., Improving the welding training by a wise integration of new technologies. *Proceedings of the IIW 2009 International Conference on Advances in Welding and Allied Technologies*, Singapore, 1–6, 2009.

29. Kreindl, J., Sandtner, H., Behmel, A., Dötsch, H., Virtual welding - A modern, innovative simulation-system for the training and education of welding personnel. *Safety and Reliability of Welded Components in Energy and Processing Industry*, 157–160, 2010.

30. Park, Y.-D. and Seo, J., The design of an intelligent augmented reality welder training system. *Int. J. Eng. Res. Technol. (IJERT)*, 6, 02, 401–404, 2017.

31. Stone, R.T., Watts, K.P., Zhong, P., Physical and cognitive effects of virtual reality integrated training. *Hum. Factors: J. Hum. Factors Ergonomics Soc.*, 53, 5, 558–572, 2011.

32. Yunus, F.A.N., Baser, J.A., Masran, S.H., Razali, N., Rahim, B., Virtual reality simulator developed welding technology skills. *J. Modern Educ. Review, U. S. A.*, 1, 1, 57–62, 2011.

33. Jo, D., Kim, Y., Yang, U., Kim, K.-H., Shin, S., Real-time graphical presentation from empirical data for virtual welding tasks. *5th ACM SIGGRAPH Conference and Exhibition on Computer Graphics and Interactive Techniques in Asia*, Singapore, 2012.

34. Jo, D., Kim, Y., Yang, U., Choi, J., Kim, K.-H., Lee, G.A., Park, Y.-D., Park, Y.W., Welding representation for training under VR environments. *Association for Computing Machinery, VRCAI 2011*, Hong Kong, China, pp. 339–342, December 11 – 12, 2011.

35. Yang, U., Lee, G.A., Kim, Y., Jo, D., Choi, J., Kim, K.-H., Virtual reality based welding training simulator with 3D multimodal interaction. *International Conference on Cyberworlds, Transactions of IEEE, Computer Society*, pp. 150–154, 2010.

36. Knoke, B. and Thoben, K.-D., Integration of simulation-based training for welders. *Simulation Notes Europe*, ARGESIM Publishers Vienna, 27, 1, 37–44, 2017.

37. Byrd, A.P., Stone, R.T., Anderson, R.G., Woltjer, K., The use of virtual welding simulators to evaluate experienced welders. *Welding J.*, 94, 389–395, 2015.

38. Engh, E., Utilizing virtual welding technology and activity based training in order to transfer skills, knowledge and competence in a life-long learning

context. *2nd Internal Technical Conference Welding Trainer, "The Future of Education"*, 94, Duisburg, Germany, 2012.

39. Quintino, L. and Fernandes, I., Education and certification in welding", welding engineering and technology, education and certification in welding, in: *Encyclopedia of Life Support Systems*, 2018.

40. Bickerstaff, G.F., *The use of welding simulators improve proficiency in entry-level welding students*, Thesis, Master of Arts Degree Concentration of Continuing, Northwestern State University, Louisiana, USA, 2015.

41. Ma, Y., Li, H., Wang, Z., Simulation and optimizing of work-station of body-inwhite welding based on RobCAD. *Proceedings of the IEEE, International Conference on Mechatronics and Automation*, pp. 2276–2281, 2007.

42. Yanping, L. and Haijiang, L., Welding multi-robot task allocation for BIW based on hill climbing genetic algorithm. *International Technology and Innovation Conference 2009 (ITIC 2009)*, 1–8, 2009.

43. Prakash, M.B. and Mahesh, N., Virtual manufacturing. *Int. J. Res. Eng., Sci. Manag.*, 2, 11, 475–482, November-2019.

44. Jerald, J., *The VR book-human centered design for virtual reality*, NextGen Interactions Copyright © 2016 by the Association for Computing Machinery and Morgan & Claypool Publishers, USA, 2016.

45. Chung, C.-C. and Tung, C.-C., Research on optimization of VR welding course development with ANP and satisfaction evaluation. *Electronics*, 9, 1673, 2020. www.mdpi.com/journal/electronics.

8

Augmented Reality in Computer-Aided Design (CAD)

Suresh Goka[1], Syed Quadir Moinuddin[2*], Ashok Kumar Dewangan[2],
Shaik Himam Saheb[2] and Barla Madhavi[2]

[1]*Department of Mechanical Engineering, National Institute of Technology,
Warangal, India*
[2]*Department of Mechatronics Engineering, ICFAI Foundation for Higher
Education, Hyderabad, India*
[3]*Department of Mechanical Engineering, National Institute of Technology,
Delhi, India*

Abstract

In many industries or fields, the metaverse presents opportunities to improve the operations and workflows supporting computer-aided design (CAD) computing projects and their maintenance for a long time. It has the advantage of developing a three-dimensional (3D) world to focus on various aspects such as creation, visualization, testing, and modeling to rework into the real world. Augmented reality (AR) is an experience where users and designers enhance the products of the physical world into computer-generated sources. It is exceptionally changing the nature of collaboration in product design. It is a cloud-based technology and is useful for changing product design. As the motivation behind digital modeling, metaverse modeling is well-suited to CAD to enhance manufacturing mechanisms. This chapter explores the potential of creating 3D parametric computer-aided models using the AR technique.

Keywords: Augmented reality, computer-aided design, metaverse, case study, applications

Corresponding author: syed@ifheindia.org

Chandrashekhar A, Shaik Himam Saheb, Sandeep Kumar Panda, S. Balamurugan and Sheng-Lung Peng (eds.)
Metaverse and Immersive Technologies: An Introduction to Industrial, Business and Social Applications, (217–234) © 2023 Scrivener Publishing LLC

8.1   Introduction

At present, computer-aided design (CAD) systems offer tremendously qualitative and perfect modeling features and functions that lead to huge production with a new way of part design even. Although 3D is the geometrical database that has been used for a long time, the user interfacing with the CAD systems is not affected significantly. Nowadays, CAD tool uses standard WIMP and desktop-based graphical user interfaces (GUI) [4]. The interactions are made employing a display unit, mouse, and keyboard [10–12]. Such interaction does not aid the designer to transform his creative ideas into useful parts or geometrical models. Hence, new interaction platforms and interfaces should be developed to help the designer in the CAD modeling of components. Therefore, the challenges are considered for many fields and their flexibility with the certain processes of AR and CAD through various applications like aerospace, academics, medical and military fields etc. The following Figure 8.1 shows the architecture of the AR interface.

There are too many attempts have done to understand the emotions of human beings and hence to develop solutions to the same. A corporation or industry's product is released into the market with a certain aim in mind, and whether it is successful or not depends on input from various public sectors. So, here the emotions of the user/consumer are mainly important to decide the status of the business of product. In this way, by knowing the emotional interaction between the product and the user, progress in the business can be assured. How specific emotions are induced and verified in

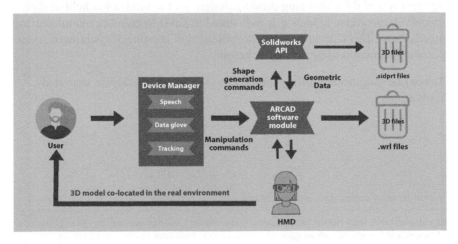

Figure 8.1 Architecture of AR interface [1].

favor of some creative activities is explored by some authors [2, 3, 13–16]. Similarly, human emotions can be elicited using many multimedia sources. A technology known as Virtual Reality (VR) is seen as promising and undoubtedly intriguing in terms of how it affects human emotions. The flexibility and complexity of VR offer plentiful possibilities for provoking these human emotions.

Thus the basic principle involved in VR could be able to engage the users in a situation where their details of any kind reflect in exciting the precise emotions using VR-based simulations completely. Emotions of any type, including even audio and video aspects corresponding to multi media are used to emphasize the emotions. Virtual Environment (VE) is another similar platform that is very interactive for both the time and user from some other media [17–20].

VR designers are the ones who work in the virtual environment following certain guidelines and methodologies. But there are no such guidelines are providing. To make a design activity, there is a need to develop a systematic, repeatable, and transferable methodology. Without a process, the risk of continually tackling an issue or problem exists. Even though there is some complexity in designing the virtual environment or the human emotions themselves, the task is not trivial. Nevertheless, there are many ways to deal with such complex issues because the space available for design is too large and one can work it out by using various process parameters. For example, the designer can able to generate genuine working conditions and combine the existing circumstances even for the known emotion also.

Nowadays, there are very highly configured computers/desktops and updated/latest software available in the market. Even though, it is necessary to have extraordinary visualization skills in developing various functional features of components with special dimensions. Hence AR can be assured the envisioning and creating complex designs, overhanging parts, and composite materials. Thus the existing AR technique can help enhance design skills and visualization skills. That results in scientific simulations and forecasting the functioning of designed tools to be served in various industries, institutes, and educational organizations. The visualization data provided by AR technology is an aid to fill the gap between the parts produced by physical methods and virtual models designed by using digital computers. In this way, the services of AR technology are useful in various sectors viz. assembly units, aerospace, manufacturing, military fields and also in medical studies, entertainment flat forms etc. [21–24].

AR technology is significantly applicable from a research point of view, especially in the aerospace industry. Boeing is one such industry and the scientists/researchers found that AR is a technology that can provide multiple configurations and various scenarios that to check the artifacts of the physical fabricated parts [4]. Simulation is the main platform here to work out the above-mentioned details. Boeing has also started to adopt the AR tool for assembly training. Hence it is possible to communicate complicated commands/instructions and able to reduce the training needs. In addition, Boeing has also extended the AR services to work with a demonstration project of NASA [5]. The project is on an International Space Station (ISS). The main aim of the project was to save the traditional training methods in space stations. Also, the astronauts can get the required information by accessing the AR library, which is updated with the space tasks that are to be performed in a critical time [25].

In addition to the aerospace applications facilitated by Boeing, AR technology is useful for car manufacturers to inculcate the interior of the model car able to conduct tests as if they were physically comfortable almost. AR technology is used by Volkswagen and BMW to visualize and modify the engine layout and car chassis etc. [6]. This technology was also incorporated into their assembly lines hence, further improving their assembly and manufacturing methods. Volkswagen uses AR technology also for comparing the actual and calculated crash test imagery, analyzing interfering edges, workshops, and planning production lines. In addition, part dimensions and variance in vehicle parts can also be compared. The functioning and effectiveness of other devices like navigation, speedo meters, and the displaying information of windshield indicators can be augmented by AR technology. AR can be employed in military training camps as the third eye for the soldier to figure out the existence of some people behind him. In addition, his location can be traced all the time without taking his eyes off the war field. In medical studies also, AR technology is employed for visualization and training aid for health education and medical diagnosis. Nevertheless, the imaging techniques like MRI, CT scans, ultrasound imaging, and sphygmomanometers are used to collect anatomical data of a patient even in 3-dimensional views using the AR technique. The collected data is further rendered and analyzed in real-time for diagnosing the patient information in detail [26–30].

8.2   AR System

In general, AR systems need some kind of clue as to where in a digital image they should place their enhancements. Usually, AR markers are used for this. The AR markers are the images that a camera might pick up and utilize with software to pinpoint the location of virtual objects placed in a scene.

The position and angle of the marker can be calculated by the computer when it detects the markers using AR software. A webcam image that is being processed by an AR platform like AR Tag, AR Google Sketch up, AR Toolkit, etc. might be added with the AR markers as simply as printing a marker design and inserting the printout in the field of the image. The software could then deduce the correct position and orientation of a virtual item using this information, as seen in Figure 8.2.

Additionally, a technique known as markerless AR allows for the creation of an AR effect without the use of markers. The same technology, called Smart AR, was created by the well-known business Sony and could produce virtual pictures of commonplace items like menus and posters on screens. The same technology implements markerless functionality via "object recognition technology." Additionally, the "3D spatial recognition technology" that Sony has developed is a proprietary system that it employs in research robots like the AIBO robot. The new markerless AR technology is not meant to be used extensively, though.

CAD applications are designers' inevitable tools for conveying innovative concepts and ideas. Even simulations are more suitable for validating innovative ideas. In earlier stages of the design process, designers were facing intangibility problems because of replacing traditional methods with CAD 3d modeling systems. Hence it was unable to interact with testing components and tools physically.

Since the 1990s, CAD modeling platform has been emerging into various fields rapidly for communicating and stimulating new ideas and revolutionary concepts. Traditional methods are replaced with three-dimensional computer-aided models resulting producing controlled sketches, hard and complex prototypes, soft study components, control volumes and replicas etc.

(a)   **(b)**   **(c)**

Figure 8.2 Three-dimensional mechanical objects are converted into an AR environment from a CAD system [7]. (a) Solid works, (b) AR Google Sketch up software (c) AR maker.

Most complex design tasks are impossible without computer-aided operations. Hence skillful operators are also required. So, CAD modeling is helped in enhancing the abilities of designers and improves the skills of the operators/programmers. Hence CAD tools are very helpful in producing and developing creative design tools. However, as the world transforms into a virtual world from the physical world, the part designers are incipient with intangible tasks. The rendering results on monitors are unable to present design models as foam reproductions or tangible replicas in a realistic and observable manner. Due to these factors, novice designers frequently estimate the outcomes of 3D CAD modeling wrong, which leads to errors. Rapid prototyping solutions were created to address such ill-defined issues [8, 31, 32].

Nevertheless, there are some restrictions on how early in the industrial design process, RP can be applied. Due to labor and cost limitations, iterative design & assessment methods are generally difficult for designers to test and improve ideas. Second, because the manufactured products are made from mock-ups made of polyurethane foam and polystyrene foam, their designs cannot be changed easily. Finally, the representation of material properties and textures and colors is not possible in some cases. Due to the mentioned reasons, the designers will understand trial and error during the process of product development.

8.3   Case Studies

The usage of contemporary rendering techniques in CAD systems aids users in seeing the designed components. However, some users and students still struggle with the specialized cognition of multi-view projections. During the first week of their academic courses, students were given a mental rotation exam to address this problem. Visualizing an object being rotated into a different orientation in space is known as mental rotation. The exam is a typical paper-based test. The students were given a set of multiple-choice questions and asked to compare 3D items that were portrayed as 2D representations on paper. The orientation of the original, the image, and the identical one is the only distinctive difference between them.

The pupils were able to engage with real, physical objects in their local vicinity as virtual models were being added to this world. They can perceive the things they see more clearly by using this method. The paper examination served as the basis for the questions that made up the AR-assisted mental rotation test, which was designed to examine the benefits of AR models in assisting students with their specialized cognitive abilities and

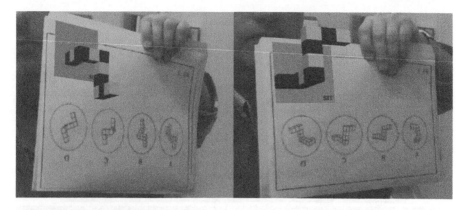

Figure 8.3 AR-assisted mental rotation test [7].

visual skills. A CAD system was used to create the 3D virtual models for the tests that used augmented reality. Then the AR software was used to turn the CAD models into AR models. In this method, as seen in Figure 8.4, 3D virtual models might be shown alongside the test paper with the questions on the computer monitor.

The AR model was located in the webcam real-time video stream using a special marker so that the AR-assisted test questions could be printed. The learner may view the virtual object that is depicted on the paper from any angle since it moves with them as they move. The results of the regular and AR-based mental rotation tests reveal potential benefits for AR in spatial cognition, as shown in Figure 8.5, despite the lack of sufficient data for statistical analysis.

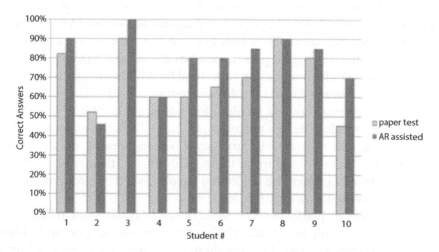

Figure 8.4 Results of the mental rotation test-comparison [7].

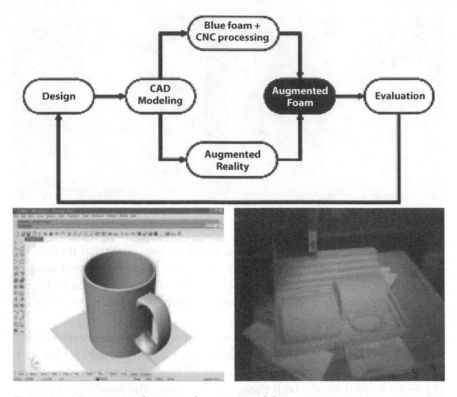

Figure 8.5 AF concept and process of construction [9].

To research the benefits of AR in the CAD process, a set of exercises utilizing AR in the system were created to boost the student's/spatial user's abilities. The augmented foam (AF) and augmented reality (AR) technology developed by authors Woohun Lee and Jun Park layer a blue foam mock-up with a 3D virtual part made from the same CAD model [9]. A cleaning robot and a mug design were tried by AF. The designers successfully inspected and evaluated the design alternatives [33–35].

Physical interactions and tactile information are helpful or even crucial in many product design processes. Up until 2205, the majority of AR design work was restricted to large-scale objects because the designers couldn't pick them up and move them. Additionally, there was no direct physical contact between the object and the observer; the information was restricted to visual data only [36, 37].

A mixed-reality platform was utilized by Lee and colleagues to build virtual products. To improve reality, the hand region was cut apart and added as a virtual augmentation. They sought to incorporate the user's hand into a virtual setting. For projector-based dioramas, Low et al are authorized for the passive haptic interface. A synergic environment made of Styrofoam blocks is lit up by projectors on its display surfaces. Physical objects were used by Hinckley and colleagues as a passive haptic interface in virtual settings (VE). The haptic interface and the visual interface, however, had a spatial difference.

By merging virtual and physical prototyping, augmented prototyping (AP) uses AR and RP technologies to enhance the product development process. The colors and textures are applied to the RP-produced pieces via AR. AF utilizes a foam mock-up made using CNC technology that is accessible throughout the first design phases and for evaluations. The visibility issue of the user's hand with the virtual products was also fixed by AF to enable active haptic interactions between the designers and the object with visibility corrections.

8.3.1   Concept of Augmented Foam (AF)

Blue foam, which is often used, reasonably priced, simple to cut, and quickly made by CNC, is combined with AR technologies by AF. The 3D virtual item is created using the same CAD model that was used to produce the blue foam mock up and is then superimposed using AF over the blue foam mock-up. The same idea of AF is depicted in the following Figure 8.6.

With the aid of 3D CAD data, AF was created to create a physical form mock-up and then superimpose a 3D model of the same data on it. Rhinoceros 3.0, for instance, was used to create a mug model, which was afterwards converted to STL format. Additionally, using blue Urethane foam, CNC was used to create foam mock-ups (Right fig). To make the hand region detection process simpler, the CNC foam mock-ups were highlighted in a dark blue color. As illustrated in Figure 8.6b1, an artificial marker was mounted on the mock-up to facilitate visual tracking. The writers, Lee and Park, put AE to the test for a potential cup design. Benefits of AF in the process of product design simulation are shown in Figure 8.3. The virtual objects (the mug and its grab) in general-purpose AR, where plan markers are employed without a mock-up, are not touchable, as shown in Figure 8.6a1-a3. The virtual object has a floating appearance, apart from the actual environment, as seen in Figure 8.6a3. Contrarily, AF improves visual presence by adding shadows and other details, as seen in Figure 8.6b3.

The visual presence of AF with hand visibility correction has been noticeably improved. The virtual overlay of the mug object, as seen in Figure 8.6b2, obscures the reviewer's hand. In contrast, the hand and the virtual object are seamlessly combined in Figure 8.6b5. As shown in Figures 8.6b4

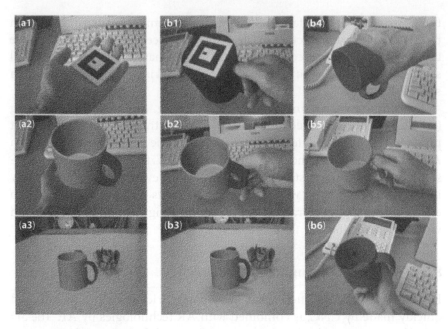

Figure 8.6 AR9 (a1-a3) and augmented foam for all purposes (b1-b6) [9].

and 8.b6, designers can mimic various aesthetic experiences by altering the product's attributes while feeling and grabbing the final design.

In summary, the design and implementation of AF, a tangible AR can speed up the process of creating very realistic prototypes for designers' design concepts. As expected, AF provided a tactile interface and a visual reality, boosting the sense of immersion by stimulating many senses and allowing designers and design outcomes to interact spatially.

8.4 Applications

8.4.1 In Academics

Engineering graphics skills are a needful characteristic for undergraduate students. The globe is currently experiencing a period of tremendous economic and information technology advancement. In light of this, engineering graphics instructors have created several methods to help freshmen engineering students develop their 3D visualization skills. The most modern solid modeling approaches use computer-aided design systems, while older techniques still use drafting tables and T-square rulers. Beginning in the late 1980s as personal computer capabilities increased, educators have been at the forefront of the movement to replace handheld instruments with CAD systems and tools for teaching engineering graphics. To create engineering drawing designs, CAD systems use graphics software and computer technology. The environment provided by computer hardware is excellent and considerably aids in the production and dissemination of both static and dynamic media. In this process, they can edit and save the design of the parts and even take printouts of the drawings. Modern CAD packages allow rotating the component in 360 degrees thus enabling viewing at any desired angle. As a result, classes in descriptive geometry and manual drawing/drafting have been removed from the academic course curriculum at practically all engineering colleges. Consequently, a reduction in engineering students' visualization was noted. Furthermore, it has been noted that the emphasis placed on using CAD platforms rather than the foundations of engineering drafting by students is a result of the content of graphics courses. Recent research indicates that 3D CAD software does not appear to enhance students' visualization skills and only provides a limited amount of real-time 3D interactions [38–40, 51].

In the education field, AR is a useful platform for generating visual models with abstract concepts. To understand chemistry, AR allows professional students to visualize the special structure of molecules. With a camera image that appeared with a pointer in the hand, they can visualize virtual models. A physics background in mechanics is an example of an augmented reality application that enables professional students to mimic real-time experiments in a variety of fields. The ability for the pupils to construct their concepts, conducts experiments, and study/examine them in multi-dimensional views on virtual world windows. There are many tools available for preprocessing, during processing, and post processing to analyze the mass and force pathways of objects. By allowing students to interact with their designs and concepts naturally, augmented reality technology can also improve the teaching and presentation abilities of engineering graphics. They may simultaneously plot the assembly process and check for component interface and interference.

8.4.2 Medical Applications

In orthopedic surgery, a crucial role has been played by computer technologies. Routinely, surgical planning was done in earlier days. Modern planning software that incorporates patient-specific multimodal and medical data has supplanted this. In addition to preoperative preparation, computers are used more frequently to assist surgeons (intra-operatively)

[41–43, 52]. For instance, CAD techniques are demonstrated to be superior to traditional implantation techniques during arthroplasty surgeries. On the other side, robotic solutions are suggested to boost accuracy while simultaneously ensuring reproducibility. They haven't yet been broadly accepted across all disciplines, though.

Fundamentally, robotic technologies are designed to assist surgeons with accurate and deliberate mechanical actions. By adding intuitive features to medical information, technologies like augmented reality (AR) improve the surgeon's abilities. When the user is entirely immersed in a virtual environment, this is referred to as augmented reality (AR). To expand the user's field of vision, one can utilize a monitor-based display system, an optical see-through system, or a video see-through system. The tracking technology that underlies AR is a key element. When putting virtual items in the right places and relationships in the actual world, tracking is crucial. Observation of a particular pattern in the world by external makers is serving as a standard [44–46, 53, 55].

There is a continuous change in surgical practice through computer-assisted solutions. AR is one such disruptive computer-integrated surgical technique. Its possible role in orthopedic surgery is not yet known even though AR has been used in several medical specialties [47–50, 54].

Although current CAD tools are powerful, they are not interactive or intuitive enough for usage by a layperson. Customers cannot use these technologies to express their design ideas, which restrict the advantages of participatory design. This paper introduces ARCADE, a quick and easy-to-use CAD environment made possible by augmented reality (AR) technologies.

8.5   Conclusions

From a scholarly perspective, improving professional students' visualization abilities is crucial for the growth of design abilities in a variety of engineering career domains. During their part of academics, the fresher students have study courses on visualization skills. Some of the students are facing troubles in dealing with projections, transformations etc. The orthogonal and isometric views are to be drawn with more caution. It is essential to be strong in geometric information and trigonometric relations even when modeling simple geometries. The lack of basic knowledge of mathematics and drawing will create troubles in CAD modeling. So, AR technology can provide a gateway for such obstacles. AR has the potential of improving the abilities of students in terms of design makings, modifications, refinements, spatial design, etc. because the design supports seeing and touching.

To provide an interactive learning experience, the authors namely Tumkor Serdar, S Aziz, Sven and Chassapis have explored the integration of AR and CAD process [7]. The many stages of the design process promote concept discovery, visualization, and evaluation. Real-time interactions between the users and designed parts could be possible through this 3D CAD modeling using a webcam view. Virtual representations and visualizations of the 3D models designed can be assured to students/users by using the AR system. In addition, Aerospace maintenance, Aerospace manufacturing, navigation, airport operations etc. also have been utilizing the services of AR.

References

1. Girbacia, F., An approach to an augmented reality interface for computer aided design. *Ann. DAAAM Proc. Int. DAAAM Symp.*, 21, 1, 791–792, 2010.
2. Isen, A.M., Daubman, K.A., Nowicki, G.P., Positive affect facilitates creative problem solving. *J. Pers. Soc. Psychol.*, 52, 6, 1122–1131, 1987.
3. Dozio, N. *et al.*, A design methodology for affective cirtual reality. *Int. J. Hum. Comput. Stud.*, 162, February, 2022.
4. Boeing Wire Bundles, An Augmented Reality Application, in: *Understanding Virtual Reality*, pp. 513–520, Elsevier, USA, 2003.
5. Hughes, D., Now see this. *Aviat. Week Sp. Technol. (New York)*, 164, 16, 46–47, 2006.
6. Firu, A.C., Tapîrdea, A., II, Feier, A., II, Drăghici, G., Virtual reality in the automotive field in industry 4.0. *Mater. Today Proc.*, 45, 4177–4182, 2021.
7. Serdar, T., Aziz, E.S.S., Esche, S.K., Chassapis, C., Integration of augmented reality into the CAD process. *ASEE Annu. Conf. Expo. Conf. Proc.*, 23, 784, 1–10, 2013.
8. Park, J., Augmented reality based re-formable mock-up for design evaluation, in: *2008 International Symposium on Ubiquitous Virtual Reality*, pp. 17–20, Jul. 2008.
9. Lee, W. and Park, J., Augmented foam: A tangible augmented reality for product design. *Proc. - Fourth IEEE ACM Int. Symp. Symp. Mix. Augment. Reality, ISMAR 2005*, vol. 2005, pp. 106–109, 2005.
10. Panda, S.K. and Satapathy, S.C., An investigation into smart contract deployment on Ethereum platform using Web3.js and solidity using blockchain, in: *Data Engineering and Intelligent Computing*, Advances in Intelligent Systems and Computing, V. Bhateja, S.C. Satapathy, C.M. Travieso-González, V.N.M. Aradhya (Eds.), vol. 1, Springer, Singapore, 2021, https://doi.org/10.1007/978-981-16-0171-2_52.

11. Panda, S.K., Rao, D.C., Satapathy, S.C., An investigation into the usability of blockchain technology in internet of things, in: *Data Engineering and Intelligent Computing*, Advances in Intelligent Systems and Computing, V. Bhateja, S.C. Satapathy, C.M. Travieso-González, V.N.M. Aradhya (Eds.), vol. 1, Springer, Singapore, 2021, https://doi.org/10.1007/978-981-16-0171-2_53.

12. Panda, S.K., Dash, S.P., Jena, A.K., Optimization of block query response using evolutionary algorithm, in: *Data Engineering and Intelligent Computing*, Advances in Intelligent Systems and Computing, V. Bhateja, S.C. Satapathy, C.M. Travieso-González, V.N.M. Aradhya (Eds.), vol. 1, Springer, Singapore, 2021, https://doi.org/10.1007/978-981-16-0171-2_54.

13. Nanda, S.K., Panda, S.K., Das, M., Satapathy, S.C., Automating vehicle insurance process using smart contract and Ethereum, in: *Advances in Micro-Electronics, Embedded Systems and IoT*, Lecture Notes in Electrical Engineering, V.V.S.S.S. Chakravarthy, W. Flores-Fuentes, V. Bhateja, B. Biswal (Eds.), vol. 838, Springer, Singapore, 2022, https://doi.org/10.1007/978-981-16-8550-7_23.

14. Varaprasada Rao, K. and Panda, S.K., Secure electronic voting (E-voting) system based on blockchain on various platforms, in: *Computer Communication, Networking and IoT*, Lecture Notes in Networks and Systems, S.C. Satapathy, J.C.W. Lin, L.K. Wee, V. Bhateja, T.M. Rajesh (Eds.), vol. 459, Springer, Singapore, 2023, https://doi.org/10.1007/978-981-19-1976-3_18.

15. Varaprasada Rao, K. and Panda, S.K., A design model of copyright protection system based on distributed ledger technology, in: *Computer Communication, Networking and IoT*, Lecture Notes in Networks and Systems, S.C. Satapathy, J.C.W. Lin, L.K. Wee, V. Bhateja, T.M. Rajesh (Eds.), vol. 459, Springer, Singapore, 2023, https://doi.org/10.1007/978-981-19-1976-3_17.

16. Panda, S.K., Elngar, A.A., Balas, V.E., Kayed, M. (Eds.), *Bitcoin and Blockchain: History and Current Applications*, 1st ed, CRC Press, 2020, https://doi.org/10.1201/9781003032588.

17. Panda, S.K., Jena, A.K., Swain, S.K., Satapathy, S.C. (Eds.), *Blockchain Technology: Applications and Challenges*, Springer, Intelligent Systems Reference Library, 1, 1-300, https://doi.org/10.1007/978-3-030-69395-4.

18. Sathya, A.R., Panda, S.K., Hanumanthakari, S., Enabling smart education system using blockchain technology, in: *Blockchain Technology: Applications and Challenges*, Intelligent Systems Reference Library, S.K. Panda, A.K. Jena, S.K. Swain, S.C. Satapathy (Eds.), vol. 203, Springer, Cham, 2021, https://doi.org/10.1007/978-3-030-69395-4_10.

19. Lokre, S.S., Naman, V., Priya, S., Panda, S.K., Gun tracking system using blockchain technology, in: *Blockchain Technology: Applications and Challenges*, Intelligent Systems Reference Library, S.K. Panda, A.K. Jena, S.K. Swain, S.C. Satapathy (Eds.), vol. 203, Springer, Cham, 2021, https://doi.org/10.1007/978-3-030-69395-4_16.

20. Panda, S.K., Daliyet, S.P., Lokre, S.S., Naman, V., Distributed ledger technology in the construction industry using corda, in: *The New Advanced Society:*

Artificial Intelligence and Industrial Internet of Things Paradigm, https://doi. org/10.1002/9781119884392.ch2.

21. Panda, S.K., Mohammad, G.B., Nandan Mohanty, S., Sahoo, S., Smart contract-based land registry system to reduce frauds and time delay, in: *Security and Privacy*, p. e172, 2021, https://doi.org/10.1002/spy2.172.

22. Panda, S.K. and Satapathy, S.C., Drug traceability and transparency in medical supply chain using blockchain for easing the process and creating trust between stakeholders and consumers. *Pers. Ubiquit. Comput.*, 2021, https:// doi.org/10.1007/s00779-021-01588-3.

23. Niveditha, V.R., Sekaran, K., Singh, K.A., Panda, S.K., Effective prediction of bitcoin price using wolf search algorithm and bidirectional LSTM on internet of things data. *Int. J. System Syst. Eng.*, 11, 3-4, 224–236, 2021.

24. Sri Arza, M. and Panda, S.K., An integration of blockchain and machine learning into the health care system, in: *Machine Learning Adoption in Blockchain-Based Intelligent Manufacturing*, vol. 1, pp. 33–58.

25. Murala, D.K., Panda, S.K., Swain, S.K., A survey on cloud computing security and privacy issues and challenges. *J. Adv. Res. Dyn. Control Syst.*, 11, 1276–1290, 2019.

26. Murala, D.K., Panda, S.K., Swain, S.K., Secure dynamic groups data sharing with modified revocable attribute-based encryption in cloud. *Int. J. Recent Technol. Eng. (IJRTE)*, 8, 4, 2019.

27. Murala, D.K., Panda, S.K., Swain, S.K., A novel hybrid approach for providing data security and privacy from malicious attacks in the cloud environment. *J. Adv. Res. Dyn. Control Syst.*, 11, 1291–1300, 2019.

28. Panda, S.K., Swain, S.K., Mall, R., An investigation into usability aspects of E-Commerce websites using users' preferences. *Adv. Comput. Sci.: An Int. J.*, 4, 1, 65–73, 2015.

29. Panda, S.K., Swain, S.K., Mall, R., Measuring web site usability quality complexity metrics for navigability, in: *Intelligent Computing, Communication and Devices*, Advances in Intelligent Systems and Computing, vol. 308, L. Jain, S. Patnaik, N. Ichalkaranje (Eds.), Springer, New Delhi, 2015, https:// doi.org/10.1007/978-81-322-2012-1_41.

30. Panda, S.K., A usability evaluation framework for B2C E-Commerce websites. *Comput. Eng. Intell. Syst.*, 5, 3, 66–85, 2014.

31. Bhalerao, V., Panda, S.K., Jena, A.K., Optimization of loss function on human faces using generative adversarial networks, in: *Machine Learning Approaches for Urban Computing*, Studies in Computational Intelligence, vol. 968, M. Bandyopadhyay, M. Rout, S. Chandra Satapathy (Eds.), Springer, Singapore, 2021, https://doi.org/10.1007/978-981-16-0935-0_9.

32. Panda, S.K. and Dwivedi, M., Minimizing food wastage using machine learning: A novel approach, in: *Smart Intelligent Computing and Applications*, Smart Innovation, Systems and Technologies, vol. 159, S. Satapathy, V. Bhateja, J. Mohanty, S. Udgata (Eds.), Springer, Singapore, 2020, https://doi. org/10.1007/978-981-13-9282-5_44.

33. Panda, S.K., A.R, S., Mishra, M., Satpathy, S., A supervised learning algorithm to forecast weather conditions for playing cricket. *Int. J. Innovative Technol. Exploring Eng. (IJITEE)*, 9 , 1, 2019.

34. Panda, S.K., Fraud-resistant crowdfunding system using Ethereum blockchain, in: *Bitcoin and Blockchain*, pp. 237–276, 2020.

35. Panda, S.K., Mishra, V., Balamurali, R., Elngar, A.A., *Artificial intelligence and machine learning in business management concepts, challenges, and case studies*, CRC Press, Boca Raton, 2021. https://doi.org/10.1201/9781003125129, pp: 1-278.

36. Joshi, S., Panda, S.K., AR, S., Optimal deep learning model to identify the development of pomegranate fruit in farms. *Int. J. Innovative Technol. Exploring Eng.*, 9, 3, 2352–2356, 2020.

37. Puranam, K.S.R., Gaddam, M.C.T., K, V.P.R., Panda, S.K., Reddy, G.S.M., Anatomy and lifecycle of a bitcoin transaction. *Proceedings of International Conference on Sustainable Computing in Science, Technology and Management (SUSCOM)*, Amity University Rajasthan, Jaipur - India, February 26-28, 2019, February 18, 2019, Available at SSRN: https://ssrn.com/abstract=3355106orhttp://dx.doi.org/10.2139/ssrn.3355106.

38. Panda, S.K. and Swain, S.K., *Quality assurance aspects of web design, design solutions for improving website quality and effectiveness*, pp. 87–129, IGI Global, 2016.

39. Panda, S.K., Bhalerao, V., AR, S., A machine learning model to identify duplicate questions in social media forums. *Int. J. Innovative Technol. Exploring Eng.*, 9, 4, 370–373, 2020.

40. Ahmareen, S., Raj, A., Potluri, S., Panda, S.K., Book shala: An android-based application design and implementation of sharing books, in: *Smart Intelligent Computing and Applications*, Smart Innovation, Systems and Technologies, vol. 159, S. Satapathy, V. Bhateja, J. Mohanty, S. Udgata (Eds.), Springer, Singapore, 2020, https://doi.org/10.1007/978-981-13-9282-5_28.

41. Panda, S.K., Das, S.S., Swain, S.K., S-model for service-oriented applications in web engineering. *Reg. Coll. Manag.*, 10, 3, 38–46, 2013.

42. Panda, S.K., An investigation into usability and productivity of ECommerce websites. https://shodhganga.inflibnet.ac.in:8443/jspui/handle/10603/123505

43. Panda, S.K., Chandrasekhar, A., Gantayat, P.K., Panda, M.R., Detecting brain tumor using image segmentation: A novel approach, in: *Data Engineering and Intelligent Computing*, Lecture Notes in Networks and Systems, vol. 446, V. Bhateja, L. Khin Wee, J.C.W. Lin, S.C. Satapathy, T.M. Rajesh (Eds.), Springer, Singapore, 2022, https://doi.org/10.1007/978-981-19-1559-8_35.

44. Sanghi, P., Panda, S.K., Pati, C., Gantayat, P.K., Learning deep features and classification for fresh or off vegetables to prevent food wastage using machine learning algorithms, in: *Intelligent Data Engineering and Analytics*, Smart Innovation, Systems and Technologies, vol. 266, S.C. Satapathy, P.

Peer, J. Tang, V. Bhateja, A. Ghosh (Eds.), Springer, Singapore, 2022, https://doi.org/10.1007/978-981-16-6624-7_44.

45. Gantayat, P.K., Mohapatra, S., Panda, S.K., Secure trust level routing in delay-tolerant network with node categorization technique, in: *Intelligent Data Engineering and Analytics,* Smart Innovation, Systems and Technologies, vol. 266, S.C. Satapathy, P. Peer, J. Tang, V. Bhateja, A. Ghosh (Eds.), Springer, Singapore, 2022, https://doi.org/10.1007/978-981-16-6624-7_45.

46. Panda, S.K., Urkude, S.V., Urkude, V.R., Vairachilai, S., An investigation into COVID 19 pandemic in India, in: *The New Advanced Society: Artificial Intelligence and Industrial Internet of Things Paradigm*, vol. 1, pp. 289–305, Wiley.

47. Panda, S.K., Das, S., Swain, S.K., Web site productivity measurement using single task size measure. *J. Inf. Sci. Comput. Technol. (JISCT)*, 4, 3, October12, 2015.

48. Hanumanthakari, S. and Panda, S.K., Detecting face mask for prevent COVID-19 using deep learning: A novel approach, in: *Smart Intelligent Computing and Applications, Volume 2,* Smart Innovation, Systems and Technologies, vol. 283, S.C. Satapathy, V. Bhateja, M.N. Favorskaya, T. Adilakshmi (Eds.), Springer, Singapore, 2022, https://doi.org/10.1007/978-981-16-9705-0_45.

49. Panda, S.K., Sathya, A.R., Das, S., Bitcoin: Beginning of the cryptocurrency era, in: *Recent Advances in Blockchain Technology,* Intelligent Systems Reference Library, vol. 237, S.K. Panda, V. Mishra, S.P. Dash, A.K. Pani (Eds.), Springer, Cham, 2023, https://doi.org/10.1007/978-3-031-22835-3_2.

50. Murala, D.K., Panda, S.K., Sahoo, S.K., Securing electronic health record system in cloud environment using blockchain technology, in: *Recent Advances in Blockchain Technology,* Intelligent Systems Reference Library, vol. 237, S.K. Panda, V. Mishra, S.P. Dash, A.K. Pani (Eds.), Springer, Cham, 2023, https://doi.org/10.1007/978-3-031-22835-3_4.

51. Rao, K.V., Murala, D.K., Panda, S.K., Blockchain: A study of new business model, in: *Recent Advances in Blockchain Technology, Intelligent Systems Reference Library*, vol. 237, S.K. Panda, V. Mishra, S.P. Dash, A.K. Pani (Eds.), Springer, Cham, 2023, https://doi.org/10.1007/978-3-031-22835-3_9.

52. Panda, S.K., Mishra, V., Dash, S.P., Pani, A.K., *Recent advances in blockchain technology real-world applications*, Intelligent Systems Reference Library (ISRL, volume 237), vol. 1, pp. 1–317, Springer, Switzerland, 2023, 978-3-031-22835-3.

53. Panda, S.K., Mohapatra, R.K., Panda, S., Balamurugan, S., *The new advanced society: Artificial intelligence and industrial internet of things paradigm*, vol. 1, pp. 1–512, John Wiley & Sons.

54. Nanda, S.K., Panda, S.K., Das, M., Satapathy, S.C., Decentralization of car insurance system using machine learning and distributed ledger technology, in: *Intelligent Data Engineering and Analytics. FICTA 2022,* Smart Innovation, Systems and Technologies, vol. 327, V. Bhateja, X.S. Yang,

J. Chun-Wei Lin, R. Das (Eds.), Springer, Singapore, 2023, https://doi. org/10.1007/978-981-19-7524-0_52.

55. Nanda, S.K., Panda, S.K., Dash, M., Medical supply chain integrated with blockchain and IoT to track the logistics of medical products. *Multimed. Tools Appl.*, 2023. https://doi.org/10.1007/s11042-023-14846-8.

9

Metaverse: Post-Pandemic Impact in Education

C.V. Suresh Babu[1]* and P. Preethi[2]

*¹Dept. of Information Technology, Hindustan Institute of Technology and Science,
Bay Range Campus, Padur, Chennai, India*
*²Department of Information Technology, Hindustan Institute of Technology and
Science, Bay Range Campus, Padur, India*

Abstract

The coronavirus disease 2019 (COVID-19) epidemic has caused a shift in education from offline learning to online learning, where most of the students are attending their classes by using video call services. This modification prevents students from actively participating in class. Video education is particularly limited in its ability to replace offline classes, which requires both experimental and theoretical expertise. Computer knowledge-related inventions have a vital role in day-to-day life as they transform and develop human commerce, communication, and societal arrangements. The fourth technological surge is indeed centered around spatial, immersive technologies like virtual reality (VR), augmented reality (AR), mixed reality (MR), and extended reality (XR) [1], which provide users with an immersive virtual experience enhanced with realistic feedback detection. This surge has the potential to transform various aspects of society, including education, business, remote work, and entertainment.

The term "metaverse" refers to a new three-dimensional virtual environment that has the potential to become the next ubiquitous computing paradigm. The term is a compound word formed from the prefix "meta", which means "beyond", and "universe", which refers to the physical universe. The metaverse is essentially a virtual space that is an extension of the physical world, where users can interact with each other and with digital objects in a three-dimensional space. It has the potential to transform the way we interact with each other and with digital content, and could have a significant impact on the future of online education,

Corresponding author: pt.cvsuresh@hindustanuniv.ac.in

Chandrashekhar A, Shaik Himam Saheb, Sandeep Kumar Panda, S. Balamurugan and Sheng-Lung Peng (eds.)
Metaverse and Immersive Technologies: An Introduction to Industrial, Business and Social
Applications, (235–258) © 2023 Scrivener Publishing LLC

business, and entertainment. The four categories listed on the metaverse roadmap are virtual fact, augmented fact, reflection, and lifelogging, which involve a virtual fact orb where the user can interact, play games, and discern effects or conditioning as they would in the literal world [24].

The online education ecosystem was taken into consideration when developing the metaverse-based platform, which suggests that holistic educational activities such as education, communication, and empathy are carried out within the metaverse in addition to online teaching and learning. On this metaverse platform, learners can feel the presence of learning, which can promote motivation and immersion in the subject matter. The independence of spatial mobility also opens the door to self-directed learning. Even when there are technical and moral constraints on using the metaverse platform, it would be preferable to place more emphasis on the interaction between students in the metaverse environment than on having high expectations.

Keywords: Augmented reality, virtual reality, online, interaction

9.1   Introduction

The COVID-19 pandemic has accelerated the adoption of online learning and other digital technologies in education, and the concept of the metaverse is gaining popularity as a tool for enhancing the educational experience. The metaverse refers to a virtual space or universe that allows for immersive, interactive experiences that can be accessed using virtual and augmented reality technologies [10]. In education, the metaverse can be used to create virtual classrooms and other learning environments, where students can interact with each other and with instructors in real time, regardless of their physical location.

The use of the metaverse in education has several potential benefits. For example, it can provide a more engaging and immersive learning experience for students, which may lead to better learning outcomes. It can also help to overcome some of the limitations of traditional online learning platforms, such as a lack of social interaction and a sense of isolation. In addition, the metaverse can enable educators to create more personalized and adaptive learning experiences, based on the individual needs and preferences of each student.

However, there are also some challenges and concerns associated with the use of the metaverse in education. One of the main challenges is the need for adequate infrastructure and technology to support the use of virtual and augmented reality. Another challenge is the potential for distraction and disengagement, as students may be more easily tempted to engage in non-academic activities in a virtual environment. In addition, there are concerns about privacy and security, as the use of the metaverse may involve the collection and storage of sensitive data about students and their activities.

Overall, while the metaverse has the potential to revolutionize the way we approach education, it is important to carefully consider the benefits and challenges before adopting it on a large scale. Education institutions should carefully evaluate the available technologies and infrastructure, as well as the needs and preferences of their students, in order to determine whether the metaverse is a viable option for enhancing the educational experience.

Neal Stephenson's 1992 science fiction novel Snow Crash is often credited with introducing the concept of the metaverse to popular culture. Since then, the idea has been explored and developed by researchers, developers, and entrepreneurs in various fields, including virtual reality, augmented reality, gaming, and social media. The Acceleration Studies Foundation, was one of the early organizations to research and define the metaverse. In 2006, the foundation published a Metaverse Roadmap report, which identified four key categories of the metaverse: virtual worlds, augmented reality, lifelogging and augmented memory, and mirror worlds. The report also highlighted the potential of the metaverse to impact various aspects of society, including education, commerce, entertainment, and social interaction.

The concept of the metaverse typically involves a 3D virtual space where users can create avatars and interact with others in a simulated environment. However, the definition of the metaverse is still evolving, and some experts argue that it could encompass a broader range of technologies and experiences beyond just 3D virtual worlds [20].

Overall, the metaverse represents a potentially transformative idea for how we interact with technology and with each other. Its development and adoption will likely continue to be shaped by advances in virtual and augmented reality technologies, as well as by changing social and cultural trends [14].

9.2 Background of the Study

Education is a vital field in today's society and economy, and although various technological inventions have emerged, the core execution styles, such as using textbooks and classrooms [18], have remained the same. The Metaverse has the potential to revolutionize the education sector by enabling users to interact with a 3D virtual world using their bodies to study in a virtual environment. However, the infrastructure, protocols, and standards that will govern the Metaverse are currently being developed by various entities, and there is intense competition to establish closed, proprietary hardware and software ecosystems as the de facto Metaverse destination. This competition has resulted in clashes between various systemic philosophies and divergent tactical approaches, with ideas like openness and privacy being at the forefront.

The winner of this race will determine the scope of user privacy rights and whether the Metaverse will be accessible to students and schoolchildren. These issues have significant educational implications since they will determine whether or not the Metaverse can be widely used in online education. Therefore, it is crucial to ensure that the Metaverse is developed in a manner that protects user privacy rights and promotes accessibility, especially for educational purposes.

9.2.1   Statement of the Problem

The metaverse basically revolves around the technologies that create a multisensory relation with the surroundings, objects, and people inside the virtual reality [17]. To make sure that people can feel everything as they do in the real world even death, a XR system is deployed by the stereoscopic displays to make it happen. This has been made possible with separate and unique displays for both the eyes which is capable of replicating the sight of the physical surroundings in the metaverse. Open education and online education are having long history than we know. The Open Education act is the one which helped in the creation of worldwide Open Universities after the 1960s. With the advancement in the field of Computer Science and Internet, the rise of Open Educational Practices, Open Educational coffers and Open Courseware was inevitable. The online literacy is slowly leaving out of the trend particularly in advanced and adult, nonstop education. Due to the outbreak of COVID-19, it caused dismembering of attendance a growing trend in all areas of education. By considering health factors where physical contact could worsen the health of an individual online tutoring was implemented world-wide. Ever since, the pandemic online education was basically relying on two main systems which are asynchronous and synchronous e-learning. Both the systems depend upon the software or web operations in 2D digital surroundings.

The operations which are executed in the 2D web environments are proved to have some limitations and even sometimes inadequacies. On a long run with the extended use of the online platforms it is leading to wonders which are similar to Zoom fatigue. Emotional insulation is most frequently agonized in the asynchronous platforms which is nothing but an impish emotion for the participation provocation. So according to a study learning courses in certain platforms faced high dropping rates. To be exact the effects are extreme in the MOOCs where the average completion rate is in and around 10.

9.3   Significance of the Study

The study's objectives include assessing the educational applicability of metaverse-based education and carefully examining its perceptions and educational requirements. Typically, the term "metaverse" conjures up images of sophisticated technology and futuristic knowledge fabrication. However, it's important to understand that the Metaverse is connected to mortal brain processes that lack any clothing. Through study, fantasy, or mind-wandering, humans can experience an alternative reality.

The concept of the Metaverse has evolved over time to include a wide range of technologies and experiences, including virtual reality (VR), augmented reality (AR), and other immersive and interactive digital environments. At its core, the Metaverse is a networked, shared, and socially connected space where users can engage with digital objects, virtual environments, and other people in real-time. Avatars, are a key part of the Metaverse experience. Avatars allow users to create digital representations of themselves that can interact with other users and digital objects within the Metaverse. Avatars can be customized to reflect a user's preferences and identity, and they can be used to navigate and explore different virtual worlds and environments. Cooperative AR environments, social VR systems, and massively multiplayer online games are all examples of the types of experiences that can be found within the Metaverse. These experiences allow users to engage with others in real-time, collaborate on tasks and projects, and explore virtual worlds and environments together. Overall, the Metaverse represents a new frontier for digital technology and social interaction. As technology continues to evolve and new applications for immersive and interactive environments emerge, the Metaverse is likely to become an increasingly important part of our digital lives.

9.3.1   Extended Reality (XR)

Extended Reality (XR) is a term used to describe the combination of virtual reality (VR), augmented reality (AR), and mixed reality (MR) [16] technologies to create immersive and interactive digital environments that blend the physical and virtual worlds. XR technologies use sensors, cameras, and other hardware to capture and interpret real-world data, which is then used to create digital overlays and interactive virtual objects that users can see and interact with.

XR technologies are being used in a wide range of applications, from gaming and entertainment to education, healthcare, and industrial design. For example, architects and engineers can use XR technologies to create virtual models of buildings and structures to test designs and identify potential issues before construction begins. In healthcare, XR technologies are being used to simulate surgical procedures and train medical professionals in a safe, controlled environment.

Overall, XR represents an exciting and rapidly evolving field that has the potential to transform how we interact with technology and with each other. As the technology continues to advance, we are likely to see even more innovative and immersive XR experiences in the years to come.

9.3.2   Multisensory Extended Reality

Multisensory extended reality (XR) has the potential to create more immersive and engaging virtual experiences by incorporating additional senses beyond just sight and sound, there are some inaccuracies in the statements made in the previous response. Firstly, the sense of taste is not currently possible to incorporate into XR technology, as it is not yet possible to replicate the experience of tasting food or drink in a digital environment. Additionally, while smell can be a powerful and evocative sense, it is currently difficult to replicate accurately in XR technology. While some companies are experimenting with scent-emitting devices, the technology is not yet widely available or reliable. Furthermore, the statement that multisensory experiences involve the "reverse engineering of the retina" is not accurate. While the retina plays a crucial role in vision, multisensory experiences involve integrating input from multiple senses, not just vision. Finally, while there is potential for XR technology to be used as a form of digital therapeutics for the limbic system, this is still an area of ongoing research and development. The field of XR is rapidly evolving, and while there are exciting possibilities for multisensory experiences, there is still much to be explored and understood in this area.

9.3.3   Virtual Reality

Virtual reality (VR) is a technology that uses computer-generated environments or simulations to create a realistic and immersive experience for the user. In a VR environment, users can interact with objects and people in a simulated world, often using specialized equipment such as headsets, controllers, and sensors.

VR technology has many potential applications in various fields, including entertainment, education, healthcare, and business. Here are some examples of how VR is being used:

Gaming and entertainment: VR can provide gamers with a more immersive gaming experience, allowing them to feel like they are inside the game world. It can also be used for virtual experiences such as concerts, sports events, and theme park rides.

Education and training: VR can simulate real-world scenarios for training purposes, such as flight simulators for pilots, surgical simulators for doctors, and military training simulations for soldiers. It can also provide immersive educational experiences in fields such as history, geography, and science.

Healthcare: VR can be used for pain management, physical therapy, and mental health treatment. For example, VR can help patients overcome phobias and anxiety disorders through exposure therapy.

Business and marketing: VR can be used for product demonstrations, virtual tours, and remote collaboration. It can also provide a unique marketing experience for businesses to showcase their products and services

While VR has many potential benefits, it also has some drawbacks. One of the main challenges is the cost of the technology, which can be prohibitively expensive for some users. Additionally, there are concerns about the potential for addiction and negative health effects from prolonged use of VR. It is important to consider these potential risks and benefits when using VR technology.

9.3.4   Augmented Reality

A real-time interactive first-person experience, augmented reality (AR), also known as mixed reality, displays computer-generated material over the user's actual environment with accurate registration (alignment) to the real world via pose tracking [19]. The user gets the idea that they are working in a mixed-reality environment as a result. Although AR primarily uses visual cues, it may also use audio, haptic, tactile, and olfactory cues [7].

In its most basic form, augmented reality may be used on a smartphone or portable gaming system. Head-mounted displays are used in more advanced AR applications. Augmented reality has frequently been employed in smartphone applications that also use GPS and Geolocation, such as well-known games like Pokémon Go. Although they are occasionally combined, GPS and AR are two different technologies.

9.4   Metaverse in Education

Some of the first application areas with outstanding results in terms of training speed, performance, and retention with AR and VR-supported instruction are laboratory simulations (such as safety training), the development of procedural skills (such as surgery), and STEM education [12, 13, 15]. This is in reference to the radical innovation that could occur in education thanks to the metaverse. Immersive journalism can accurately and impartially inform large audiences about new situations and events in distant places thanks to the metaverse. This is made possible by the ability to capture volumetric spherical video and 360-degree panoramic images. The Metaverse may also lead to the development of novel forms of distance learning that go beyond the limitations of 2D platforms. In permanent, alternative, online 3D virtual campuses where students are co-owners of the virtual environments and co-creators of fluid, customizable curriculum, meta-education can provide rich, hybrid formal and informal active learning experiences [5] (Figure 9.1).

The COVID-19 pandemic has played a significant role in driving the resurgence of interest in the Metaverse. The four types of Metaverse, including augmented reality, lifelogging, mirror worlds, and virtual reality,

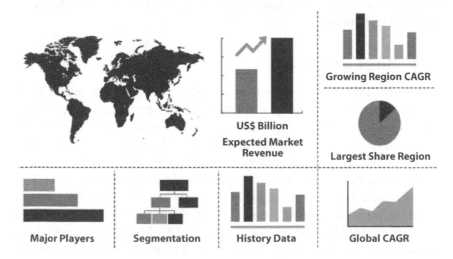

Figure 9.1 Metaverse in education.

are becoming increasingly popular as they enable people to interact in immersive virtual environments. The boundaries between these different Metaverse subtypes are also becoming increasingly blurred as they converge into new types of services.

As face-to-face interactions become more challenging due to the COVID-19 pandemic, many industries, including education, healthcare, fashion, and tourism, are turning to Metaverse technologies to provide immersive virtual experiences to their customers. For example, virtual classrooms and training sessions are becoming more popular in the education sector, while telemedicine and remote consultations are becoming more common in healthcare. Similarly, fashion brands are using Metaverse technologies to showcase their products, and the tourism industry is using them to provide virtual tours of popular destinations. The Metaverse is offering a new way for people to connect and engage with each other, and its potential applications are only limited by our imagination [2].

By using virtual avatars while wearing VR equipment and using objects in a virtual environment that is comparable to the real world, users can interact and communicate with one another. Due to the fact that all user actions are transmitted in real time to the server and other users, users can interact and meet in the same virtual environment regardless of their physical proximity [6, 28].

9.5   Research on Metaverse and Education Systems

Main technical characteristics of the metaverse and educational implications

Type	Technological characteristics	Educational implications
Augmented reality	- AR is commonly experienced through mobile devices, such as smartphones or tablets, which have built-in cameras and can display digital content on top of the camera feed. Some AR technologies also require additional hardware, such as head-mounted displays, to provide a more immersive experience.	- AR in education is often delivered through mobile devices such as smartphones and tablets. These devices use the device's camera and other sensors to overlay digital information onto the real world.

(Continued)

Type	Technological characteristics	Educational implications
	- Including elements of fantasy in virtual experiences is a common way to increase engagement and create a sense of escapism for users. Zepeto is a good example of a 3D avatar maker that incorporates elements of fantasy and allows users to create personalized avatars that can recognize their faces. This type of technology can be used to create immersive virtual experiences that allow users to interact with others in new and exciting ways.	- Learning through experience, or experiential learning, is a teaching method that involves students actively engaging in activities that allow them to apply and practice new knowledge and skills in real-world contexts. This approach can be particularly effective for helping students understand difficult-to-understand information, as it allows them to directly experience and engage with the concepts they are learning about. For example, in a science class, students might conduct experiments to learn about the properties of different materials or the laws of motion. In a history class, students might visit museums or historical sites to learn about past events and their significance. In a language class, students might engage in conversation with native speakers to practice their speaking and listening skills.
	- Effectively emphasizing information and promoting practicality. For instance, a HUD display on a car's window	- Speaking, writing, and other interactive experiences are available while participating in a learning environment.

(Continued)

Type	Technological characteristics	Educational implications
Lifelogging	- Lifelogging typically involves the use of wearable devices such as smart watches, fitness trackers, and other sensors that can collect data on various aspects of a person's life, including physical activity, sleep patterns, and heart rate [8].	- Lifelogging in education requires the use of wearable technology, such as cameras or smart watches, that can capture data about the individual's experiences. This data can include images, videos, audio recordings, and biometric data such as heart rate and activity levels.
	- Network technology has revolutionized communication and social connections, enabling individuals to connect with others all around the world through various social media platforms such as Facebook, Instagram, Twitter, and more. These platforms provide users with the ability to share their thoughts, opinions, images, and videos, and to interact with others in real-time. Furthermore, network technology allows businesses to reach a larger audience, monitor consumer behavior and trends, and make data-driven decisions. The ease and convenience of network technology have made it an integral part of our daily lives, transforming the way we communicate, learn, and do business.	- Lifelogging websites, also known as quantified self platforms, allow individuals to track and record various aspects of their daily lives, including physical activity, sleep patterns, nutrition, mood, and more. These platforms generate vast amounts of data that can be analyzed and interpreted to gain insights into one's health and well-being.

(Continued)

Type	Technological characteristics	Educational implications
	- Internet-of-things (IoT) sensors and wearable technology have become increasingly popular in recent years, and they are commonly used to track personal activity data, such as the number of steps taken, heart rate, and sleep patterns. This data can be collected and analyzed to provide insights into personal health and fitness, as well as to create additional value, such as personalized recommendations for diet and exercise. One example of a popular health tracking platform is Nike Plus, which allows users to track their running and workout data, set goals, and compete with friends. The use of IoT sensors and wearable technology for personal health tracking is a growing trend, and it is expected to continue to expand in the future as technology continues to advance.	- Learning analytics involves collecting and analyzing data from students' activities and behaviors in order to gain insights into their learning processes and outcomes. With this information, educators can identify areas where students may be struggling and make targeted interventions to improve their learning outcomes. For example, if the dashboard shows that a large number of students are not completing assignments on time, the educator can investigate the root cause of the issue, such as unclear instructions or lack of motivation. They can then make targeted interventions such as providing more detailed instructions or implementing a reward system for timely completion of assignments.

(Continued)

Type	Technological characteristics	Educational implications
		- Personalized learning is a teaching approach that focuses on tailoring instruction to meet the unique needs, interests, and learning styles of each individual student. By providing personalized learning experiences, teachers can help students to better engage with the material, build their confidence, and achieve their learning goals.
Mirror world	- The use of networking and GPS to expand the size of the real world (e.g., Google Earth, various map applications, etc.)	- Learning occurs outside of physical and geographic boundaries in the metaverse of the mirror world.
	- The act of intentionally fusing the real and virtual worlds together for a single purpose is known as augmented reality. Augmented reality involves overlaying digital information and virtual objects onto the physical world, allowing users to interact with both in real-time.	- Using collaborative and video conferencing platforms (Zoom, WebEx, Google Meet, Teams), which act as illustrative mirror worlds, conduct online lessons in real-time.

(*Continued*)

Type	Technological characteristics	Educational implications
	- Geolocation technology doesn't cover everything, and that there are certain applications of this technology that are more focused on fun, play, and social interaction. These applications use geolocation technology to expand the real world in ways that encourage exploration, creativity, and collaboration. One example of this is Minecraft, a popular video game that allows players to create and explore virtual worlds using blocks and other materials.	- The concept of "learning by doing" can be facilitated through the use of the mirror world in educational contexts. Minecraft is an example of a game that allows students to engage in this type of learning by building and renovating famous landmarks and structures from around the world. By using Minecraft to recreate historical and cultural sites such as the Eiffel Tower, Taj Mahal, Gyeongbokgung, and Bulguksa, students can gain a deeper understanding of the architecture, design, and cultural significance of these structures. This type of interactive, hands-on learning can be particularly effective for students who learn best through visual and tactile experiences.
Virtual reality	- Cutting-edge computer graphics have enabled the creation of highly immersive and visually stunning games that can be enjoyed through a flawlessly integrated interface. In particular, the use of 3D technology has opened up new possibilities for creating virtual worlds and games that allow users to explore and interact with complex environments in unprecedented ways.	- Due to high costs and risks, virtual simulation enables practice in conditions that are difficult to create (e.g., fire scenes, flight control, dangerous surgery, etc.).

(Continued)

Type	Technological characteristics	Educational implications
	- In a world with characters that are constructed differently from reality in terms of time, place, culture, and setting, they act like avatars rather than their true selves and have a variety of personalities. One example of a game that uses 3D technology to create a highly immersive virtual world is Roblox. Roblox is a massively multiplayer online game platform that allows users to create, share, and play a wide range of games and experiences in a 3D virtual world [22].	- Users can fully immerse themselves in historical or futuristic periods and locations that aren't currently accessible to them physically.
	- Virtual reality offers chat and communication features so that users can converse with other people and AI characters (e.g., multiplayer online games) [25].	- 3D virtual world-based games can provide users with opportunities to acquire skills and develop strategic and comprehensive thinking abilities that can be useful in the real world. By creating complex and dynamic virtual environments, these games can challenge users to think critically, solve problems, and collaborate with others in ways that can help to develop important cognitive and social-emotional skills.

The technical features are summarized by referring to the content and examples of J Educ Eval Health Prof [2].

9.6   Research Questions

1. What benefits does augment reality offer?

Augmented reality is the ability to overlay information on the actual world as seen through a mobile device's camera (AR). Users can now enjoy a more interesting and interactive experience. According to study, improved realism raises consumers' perceptions of an item or brand's worth. Additionally, innovative businesses that successfully use AR activity exhibit inventiveness and adaptability.

2. Is Metaverse in education a blessing or a curse?

The concept of Metaverse in education can be both a blessing and a curse, depending on how it is utilized.

Benefits of Metaverse in Education:

> Increased engagement: Metaverse can provide a more immersive and interactive learning experience, which can help students stay engaged and interested in the material.
> Enhanced collaboration: Metaverse can facilitate collaboration and teamwork among students, allowing them to work together in real-time, even if they are in different locations.
> Personalized learning: Metaverse can offer personalized learning experiences, adapting to each student's needs and pace of learning.
> Access to resources: Metaverse can provide access to a wider range of resources and experiences, including virtual field trips, simulations, and historical reenactments.
> Drawbacks of Metaverse in Education:
> Accessibility: Not all students may have access to the necessary technology or internet connection required to participate in Metaverse-based learning.
> Lack of social interaction: Metaverse-based learning may lack the social interaction and interpersonal skills development that traditional in-person learning provides.
> Potential for distraction: Students may be distracted by the virtual environment and miss important learning opportunities or objectives.
> Cost: Implementing Metaverse-based learning can be expensive, and may require significant investments in technology and infrastructure.

In conclusion, Metaverse in education can be a blessing or a curse depending on how it is implemented and utilized. It has the potential to enhance learning experiences and engage students, but it may also have drawbacks such as accessibility issues, lack of social interaction, potential for distraction, and cost. Therefore, it is important to carefully consider the benefits and drawbacks before implementing Metaverse-based learning in education.

3. Despite its many drawbacks, is VR still worthwhile?
YES. Due to existing technology, its uses are constrained, but that does not imply that it is dangerous. VR is a groundbreaking technology for the fields in which it is widely used. The future of gaming and healthcare both involves virtual reality. VR is the underdog of contemporary technology. When it decides to leave everything behind is something that cannot be fully predicted. VR's big break is only a matter of time away.

4. Is the impact of the Metaverse in education positive or negative?
The educational field benefits from metaverse. Today, the metaverse is one of the fastest growing industries on the global market. If properly used, the metaverse can play a significant role in the learning process. For instance, the escape game developed by the metaverse using a virtual reality platform can improve the likelihood of distance learning in a classroom with games [11].

9.7   Delimitations of the Study

Studies show that augmented reality poses several, previously unheard-of health issues, even though its limitations are still up for dispute. The virtual content that wearers of AR devices would be immersed in might alter their behavior and result in hearing loss, vision loss, and/or hearing impairment.

People may wrongly perceive a virtual environment to be real, according to a new Google Daydream study, which may alter how they take in and process information. Such operations would lead to PTSD and other mental health problems. In augmented reality technology, the real environment is covered with a virtual layer. It may be used in a variety of contexts, such as gaming and entertainment. There has previously been augmented reality [23].

They have only lately experienced significant technical breakthroughs that have contributed to their increased popularity, with smartphones and tablets providing users with AR experiences at an affordable price. With augmented reality, privacy or security issues might surface. This is brought on by the fact that AR makes it challenging to distinguish between actual and unreal situations, which breeds a dread of being "tricked" by an assault. Social media users, for example, may be more inclined to accept incorrect information if they feel their friends have posted it on Facebook [9].

Asynchronous e-learning allows learners to access content and interact with the learning materials at their own pace, providing greater flexibility and convenience. Learners can review and study the course materials on their own schedule, and they can communicate with instructors or peers through discussion forums, email, or messaging platforms. Asynchronous learning is often used for self-paced courses, where learners have access to pre-recorded lectures, readings, and assessments.

On the other hand, synchronous e-learning is a real-time learning environment where learners and instructors interact in real-time through live lectures, webinars, video conferencing, and chat rooms. Synchronous e-learning requires a scheduled meeting time, and learners need to be present online at the same time as the instructor and other learners. Synchronous learning is often used for interactive activities, such as group discussions, role-playing, and simulations.

Both synchronous and asynchronous e-learning have their advantages and disadvantages. Asynchronous learning provides greater flexibility, convenience, and accessibility, but it can be challenging for learners who require a structured learning environment or who need regular feedback and support. Synchronous learning provides real-time interaction, immediate feedback, and social presence, but it requires learners to be available at a scheduled time, and it may not be suitable for learners with scheduling conflicts or technical issues.

To provide an effective online learning experience, many educators combine both synchronous and asynchronous e-learning methods, leveraging the benefits of both approaches while minimizing their drawbacks. By doing so, learners can have the flexibility to learn at their own pace while also having the opportunity to interact with instructors and peers in real-time [27].

9.8   Proposed Methodology

Metaverse typically conjures up images of advanced technology and futuristic knowledge fabrication. However, it's important to understand that VR is connected to bodiless processes that take place in the mortal brain. People can experience a different reality through their imaginations when they are studying, fantasizing, or daydreaming.

For Example

Scholars detest History because they were asked to flash back those boring dates and events. What if it can be commodity Interesting? What if pupil can nearly live the moment of the history and learn. Not just history all the subjects, pupil uses imagination while learning what if scholars can interact with 3D virtual world using their incorporations to study in a virtual macrocosm.

9.9   Characteristics of the Metaverse of Virtual Reality in Education

Additionally, Book [3] offered the following six features of virtual reality: First, virtual reality ought to be a communal setting where several users can interact at once. Second, a graphical user interface enables virtual reality to be implemented and expressed visually in a 2-dimensional (2D) or 3-dimensional (3D) setting. Third, user interactions take place instantly in virtual reality. Fourthly, interactivity allows users to modify or enhance various virtual reality contents. Fifth, virtual reality must provide a sense of immersion and presence, allowing users to feel as though they are truly inside the virtual environment. This is often achieved through the use of head-mounted displays (HMDs) and other sensory input devices. Finally, virtual reality should allow for a high degree of realism, which can be achieved through the use of advanced graphics, physics simulations, and other techniques.

These six features are important for creating a fully immersive and interactive virtual reality experience. They help to ensure that users can engage with the virtual environment in a natural and intuitive way, and that they feel fully immersed in the experience. As virtual reality technology continues to evolve, we can expect to see further improvements in these areas, leading to even more realistic and engaging virtual environments.

9.10   Modern Social Interaction

It is difficult to hold private gatherings of several people or dine together at a restaurant because of the ongoing COVID-19 outbreak. In contrast, hundreds of thousands or tens of millions of people may assemble in the metaverse to host a festival or attend a concert by a beloved musician. People who were unable to leave their homes owing to COVID-19 now have a new social area to gather and unwind thanks to virtual reality metaverses like Roblox and Zepeto.

The "Classroom Map" was the most well-liked of the other 3D maps in Zepeto when schools were shut down because of COVID-19 and kids were unable to go to class. The pupils visited the Zepeto classroom as opposed to the actual classroom [21]. They interacted with their buddies after meeting them. When the idol group Black pink was unable to perform a fan signing session in person because to COVID-19, they conducted a virtual event using Zepeto. Black pink also made an avatar-based choreography music video for the song "Ice cream" [26]. Black pink hosted a virtual fan signing event where more than 46 million users could meet and snap pictures with their favorite musicians.

9.11   Using Virtualization to Produce Innovative Experiences That Are Highly Immersive

The metaverse is gaining popularity as a potential solution to the drawbacks of current 2D-based online and remote classrooms. Due to the intricate usage of numerous technologies, it may offer a unique experience value from the contemporary internet era. A unique experience that transcends space and time can also be created thanks to the metaverse. The benefit of metaverse-based education is that it allows for engagement on a par with face-to-face instruction and allows for the usage of unlimited space and data [4].

9.12   Limitation

- With others, one develops relationships based on play that are weaker than interactions in the real world, and privacy issues arise as a result of the gathering and processing of various personal data.
- Because users have such a great degree of freedom, platform managers cannot foresee every action they will take, and because of the anonymity and virtual nature of the metaverse, users are vulnerable to a variety of crimes.
- For pupils whose identities have not yet been defined, it can lead to identity uncertainty, escape from reality, and poor adaptability to the real world.

9.13   Conclusions

The potential for educational applications in the metaverse is vast. Virtual reality and the metaverse can be used to create realistic simulations that allow students to explore and learn in a hands-on way. For example, medical students can practice surgeries in a virtual environment, architecture students can design and explore buildings in a 3D space, and history students can travel back in time to explore historical events.

The convergence of different types of media in the metaverse can also lead to more complex and diverse educational experiences. For example, a virtual museum exhibit could combine text, images, videos, and interactive elements to create a more engaging and educational experience for visitors.

However, the metaverse also has its limitations for educational applications. One concern is the potential for information overload or distraction, as the immersive nature of the metaverse could make it difficult for students to focus on specific tasks or learning objectives. Additionally, there are concerns about accessibility and equity, as not all students may have equal access to the technology or resources needed to participate in the metaverse.

As the metaverse continues to develop and grow, it is important to carefully consider both the potential benefits and limitations for educational applications, and to work towards creating inclusive and accessible experiences for all learners.

The Metaverse is not a novel idea, but in the context of MR it can effectively utilize VR and AR while integrating it with social media. Additionally, it has the potential to change a number of steadfast areas of online education. If the implementation of the metaverse in the educational field is done in a creative way, it can break down the still-difficult barriers of social connection and informal literacy.

References

1. Go, S.Y., Jeong, H.G., Kim, J.I., Sin, Y.T., Concept and developmental direction of metaverse. *Korea Inf. Process Soc. Rev.*, [cited 2021 Nov 29], 28, 7–16, 2021, Available from: http://www.koreascience.kr/article/JAKO202122450520317.pdf.
2. Kye, B., Han, N., Kim, Park, Y., Jo, S., Educational applications of metaverse: Possibilities and limitations. *J. Educ. Eval. Health Prof.*, 18, 32, 2021, Published 13 December 2021, https://doi.org/10.3352/jeehp.2021.18.32.
3. Book B. In moving beyond the game: Social virtual worlds, in: *Proceedings of the Culture of Play at the Conference State of Play 2*, 2004 Oct 28-30, New York, USA. New York (NY), New York Law School, 2004.
4. Lee, S., *Log in Metaverse: Revolution of human×space×time (IS-115)*, Software Policy & Research Institute, Seongnam, 2021, [cited 2021 Nov 29], Available from: https://spri.kr/posts/view/23165?code=issue_reports.

5. Mystakidis, S., MDPI. *Metaverse,* 2, 1, 486–497. https://doi.org/10.3390/encyclopedia2010031.
6. Belei, N., Noteborn, G., De Ruyter, K., It's a brand-new world: Teaching brand management in virtual environments. *J. Brand Manag.,* 18, 8, 611–623, 2011. https://doi.org/10.1057/bm.2011.6.
7. Bermejo Fernandez, C., Lee, L.H., Nurmi, P., Hui, P., Para: Privacy management and control in emerging iot ecosystems using augmented reality, in: *ACM International Conference on Multimodal Interaction,* Association for Computing Machinery (ACM), Montreal, Canada, 2021, https://doi.org/10.1145/3462244.3479885.
8. Bruun, A. and Stentoft, M.L., Lifelogging in the wild: Participant experiences of using lifelogging as a research tool, in: *IFIP Conference on Human-Computer Interaction,* Springer, Cham, pp. 431–451, 2019, September.
9. Chayka, K., *Facebook wants us to live in the Metaverse,* 2021, Accessed from: Https://www.newyorker.com/culture/infinite-scroll/facebook-wants-us-to-live-in-the-Metaverse.
10. Cimino, C., Negri, E., Fumagalli, L., Review of digital twin applications in manufacturing. *Comput. Industry,* 113, 103130, 2019.
11. Mustafa, B., Using 3D animation and virtual reality in educations. *Technium Soc. Sci. J.,* 27, 269, 2022. A new decade for social changes.
12. Pellas, N., Dengel, A., Christopoulos, A.A., Scoping review of immersive virtual reality in stem education. *IEEE Trans. Learn. Technol.,* 13, 748–761, 2020.
13. Ibáñez, M.-B. and Delgado-Kloos, C., Augmented reality for STEM learning: A systematic review. *Comput. Educ.,* 123, 109–123, 2018.
14. Klopfer, E., *Augmented learning: Research and design of mobile educational games,* MIT Press, Cambridge, MA, USA, 2008.
15. Mystakidis, S., Christopoulos, A., Pellas, N., A systematic mapping review of augmented reality applications to support STEM learning in higher education. *Educ. Inf. Technol.,* 21, 1–45, 2021.
16. Speicher, M., Hall, B.D., Nebeling, M., What is mixed reality?, in: *Proceedings of the 2019 CHI Conference on Human Factors in Computing Systems, Glasgow, UK,* ACM: New York, NY, USA, pp. 1–15, 4–9, May 2019, 2019.
17. El Beheiry, M., Doutreligne, S., Caporal, C., Ostertag, C., Dahan, M., Masson, J.-B., Virtual reality: Beyond visualization. *J. Mol. Biol.,* 431, 1315–1321, 2019.
18. Gather, *Classroom in gather town,* p. c2021, Gather, San Bruno (CA), [cited 2021 Nov 29], 2022, Available from: Https://gather.town/.
19. Milgram, P. and Kishino, F., A taxonomy of mixed reality visual displays. *IEICE Trans. Inf Syst.,* 77, 1321–1329, 1994.
20. Han, H.W., A study on typology of virtual world and its development in metaverse. *J. Digit Contents Soc,* 9, 317–323, 2008.
21. Snow Corp, *Zepeto,* p. c2021, Snow Corp., Seongnam, 2021, [cited 2021 Nov 29], Available from: Https://zepeto.me/.

22. Long, R.U., Roblox and effect on education Drury University, Springfield, MO, 2020, http://dx.doi.org/10.13140/RG.2.2.33057.97129.

23. Lee, S. and Han, S.H., *Metaverse begins: Five issues and perspectives (IS-116)*, Software Policy & Research Institute, Seongnam, 2021, [cited 2021 Nov 29], Available from: Https://spri.kr/posts/view/23197?code=issue_reports.

24. Room key, *Room key*, p. c2021, Roomkey, London, 2012, [cited 2021 Nov 29], Available from: Https://www.facebook.com/Roomkeyapp/.

25. Book B. In moving beyond the game: Social virtual worlds, in: *Proceedings of the Culture of Play at the Conference State of Play 2*, 2004 Oct 28-30, New York Law School, New York, USA. New York (NY), 2004.

26. Black pink, *Ice-cream*, Snow Corp, Seongnam, 2021, [cited 2021 Nov 29], Available from: Https://gweb.zepeto.io/user/post/97321663.

27. Stöhr, C., Demazière, C., Adawi, T., The polarizing effect of the online flipped classroom. *Comput. Educ.*, 147, 103789, 2019.

28. Lee, H., Woo, D., Yu, S., Virtual reality metaverse system supplementing remote education methods: Based on aircraft maintenance simulation. *Appl. Sci.*, 12, 5, 2667, 2022, https://doi.org/10.3390/app12052667.

10

Inspection of Defects through Corneal Topography of a Healthy Retina

V. V. Vidyasagar

Department of Computer Science and Engineering, GITAM School of Technology,
Visakhapatnam, India

Abstract

A wide-ranging inspection is necessary to rectify flaws in materials testing, calibrations, and laboratory services to provide adequate assurance with the best quality and fit for use. Quality inspections are critical as they consider the health and safety of users, help avoid inferior goods from leaving facilities, and prevent tragedies. Bedbound residents should reposition food, automotive, manufacturing, and testing with medical devices as they are heavy sufferers; precautionary prevention is at the heart of public health protection. The government's premature measures minimized public health interventions. Different refined medical device designs affect such emerging barriers to prevent the failure of various medical devices through manufacturing. R&D plays a high-risk role. Eddy current inspection is an electromagnetic method used in nondestructive testing (NDT). The process can detect and further explore the surface and above-surface defects in every holding material to rectify existing complications. In these applications of eddy current methods, one can rectify discontinuities and magnetic permeability measures. Eddy current inspection detects surface and near-surface flaws. Eddy current testing is cost-effective and ensures the best quality control checks in medical devices. Testing ensures efficiency in quality and the integrity of materials and its components in the worst case. Joints can be replaced by endoprosthetics. Joint replacement—endoprosthesis—materials made from bio-medical alloys like conventional steel and Co-Cr alloys provide adequate mobility to countless individuals. The present study focuses on eye diseases (e.g., keratoconus) and inspection by various calculated measures through corneal topography, thus discovering eye defects.

Email: vvuna@gitam.edu

Chandrashekhar A, Shaik Himam Saheb, Sandeep Kumar Panda, S. Balamurugan and Sheng-Lung Peng (eds.)
Metaverse and Immersive Technologies: An Introduction to Industrial, Business and Social Applications, (259–294) © 2023 Scrivener Publishing LLC

Keywords: Keratoconus, epithelial profile, corneal topography, specificity, visual spacing, ray-tracing, mire, placedo, smart KC

10.1   Introduction

Corneal Topography is diagnosis through medical imaging to screen human eye. It helps in medical treatment and biomedical research on eye through non-invasive methodologies. This advanced treatment rooted ailments in the eye by applying high intercepts of computer technology and correct the refractive index of eye. This is a break to age old usages in eye-tracking. The public considered this usage as best of kind and trusted highly with present-day technologies. The awareness made them move with these pervasive techniques as needs evolve in major. Many Hospitals and Researchinstitutes are finding solutions through these observations.

10.2   Structure of the Eye

Eyes are built in a two overlapping spherically derived spheroids that create two separate segments combined together to form a prosthetic capsule. Human Eye is the distinguished sensory organ devoted to vision, hearing and stimuli that is carried to brain. The Human Eye differentiates 13 million colors and maintains a master of the suprachiasmatic nucleus of brain. This sensory organ reacts to visible light and gathers image of object. The structure and Functions of the Eye are broadly described as Internal Structures and External Structures. The anatomy of eye is shown in Figure 10.1. Eye is the best example to a camera.

10.2.1   Anatomy of Eye

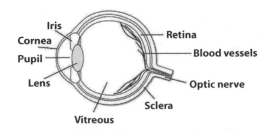

Figure 10.1 Inspection of defects through corneal topography of a healthy retina, the formation of eye.

10.2.2   Typical Eye: Nature

The typical eye regulates all the muscles and tissues to nerves and blood vessels and is responsible to visualstimuli.

The Outer Area of Eye: The front end of the eye is considered as visible optical device.

Sclera: Sclera and Cornea wraps up the outermost part of eye. The wall of the eyeball with dense connectivetissue is called sclera. The dense vitreous body - matrix of collagen is called cornea.

Cornea: Cornea focuses light rays onto the retina. The lens is transparent and can be adjusted. The lensdeteriorates the age results the need.

Conjunctiva: The conjunctiva of the eye produces the mucus glands and lipid glands.

Iris Eye: Iris is a pigmented muscular ring surrounds pupil and regulates the light that enters eyeand adjusts the size of the pupil.

Pupil: Pupil is the small aperture located in the center of the Iris that focuses light on retina.

10.2.3   The Internal Area of Eye

The internal components of an eye are:

10.2.3.1   Lens

The lens is connected to the ciliary body by ligaments. Adding the lens with cornea refracts light and focuses retina. Lens is transparent and biconvex.

10.2.3.2   Retina

Retina is sensitive film located at the innermost layer of eye. There are three neural cells in Retina; ganglion, bipolar and photoreceptor cells. Retina accepts the image and sends impulses to allthe nerves and human brain for perception.

10.2.3.3   Aqueous Humor

These are watery fluid bathes between cornea and lens nourishing the eye and keep it distended.

10.2.3.4   Vitreous Humor

The colorless gel fluid filled between the lens and the retina is called Vitreous humor. It contains water (99%), collage, proteins, etc. These safe-guard the eyes and maintain its spherical shape.

10.3   Perspective Scale Model of Eye

Glaucoma is causes accounted to reversible blindness. The model scales consider Ganglion cell axons collected visual information from retinal ganglion cell axons to brain. Experiments suggested mechanisms in bio-medical sciences are decoupling resulting in diagnosis of pathophysiology leading to ophthalmological examination. The chronic intraocular pressure (IOP) elevation results in glaucomatous neurodegeneration include loss of RBCs and optic nerve degeneration. Insertions lead to stresses of the lamina cribrosa that puts up to the axonal insult which remain unclear and its role through glaucoma. The delivery of a computational couple of two-scale analyses of large IOP induced in cribrosa at the micro scale of mess like structure. Their simulations suggest the collagen structures of the mess like structure and peripapillary sclera effectively.

10.3.1   Corneal Topography

Corneal topography is a diagnostic technique used to map the shape and curvature of the cornea, which is the clear, dome-shaped outer surface of the eye. This mapping is performed using a specialized instrument called a corneal topographer, which uses a series of computerized measurements to create a three-dimensional map of the cornea's surface. Corneal topography is a color coated map foreseen - medical imaging technique and maps the outer structure of the eye and also the fore-front surface of the cornea. If a person is affected by the corneal topography of an eye - Blue shows the flattest areas and red the steepest. The cornea represents 70% of the eye's refractive power; its topography determines the human vision.

Corneal Topography is standard to perform future treatment. The Figure 10.2 depicts the inspection of defects through corneal topography of a healthy retina.

Corneal topography is commonly used in ophthalmology to evaluate a range of conditions that affect the cornea, including astigmatism, keratoconus, and other irregularities in corneal shape. The information provided by corneal topography can help ophthalmologists make more accurate diagnoses, plan surgical procedures, and select the most appropriate contact lenses for patients. During the procedure, the patient is asked to place their chin on a support and focus on a central point while a series of rings or light patterns are projected onto their eye. The topographer then measures the reflection of these patterns from the cornea and uses this data to generate a color-coded map that displays the shape, curvature, and thickness of the cornea at different points. The resulting map provides detailed information about the cornea's surface that can help ophthalmologists diagnose and manage a variety of eye conditions.

The following defects are approved by the corneal topography:

Irregular astigmatism
Keratoconus
Corneal edema
Penetrating keratoplasty
Corneal scaring

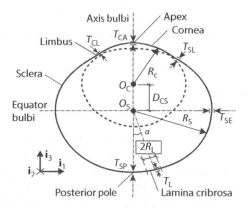

Figure 10.2 Inspection of defects through corneal topography of a healthy retina, internal parts of eye.

10.3.2   Indications of Corneal Topography

Standard of care for corneal evaluation
Corneal shape analysis
Contact lens fitting
Corneal pathology evaluation
Refractive surgery evaluation
Refractive error concerns
Monitoring changes in the cornea

10.3.3   Corneal Topography Basics

The measures go with the different standard levels while diagnosing the eye.

- Shape – Sphere vs. Cylinder
- Symmetry – Symmetrical vs. Asymmetrical
- Scaling – Standard vs. Auto-scaling
- Types of Maps – Various presentations
- Mapping Strategy – Axial, Tangential, Elevation
- Indices – CIM (Critical Illness Myopathy), SF (Substandard and falsified), TKM (Mean ToricKeratometry).

The three-dimensional map as illustrated in Figure 10.3 assists ophthalmologists in examining and diagnosing of several states and evaluating keratoconus entirely. Cornea thins and develops bulges outward into a cone shape. This causes blurry, distorted vision. Keratoconus occurs when cornea—the window of the eye - thins and bulges outward into a cone shape.

10.3.4   Keratoconus

Detection of earlier underlying eye diseases happens through Keratoconus and laser assistance. The patient gets a complete hospitality say demographic, diagnostic, and exam data. This chapter describes topography, tomography, and epithelial mapping technology to detect early Keratoconus. Confirming Keratoconus varies with topographic change and judging normal limits. Epithelial maps exclude diagnosis of Keratoconus despite suspect topography. Epithelial profiles in keratoconus screening significantly boost in avoiding iatrogenic ectasia inrefractive surgery.

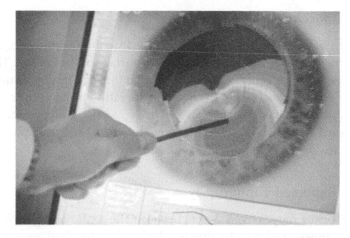

Figure 10.3 Inspection of defects through corneal topography of a healthy retina, the three-dimensional map assists ophthalmologists.

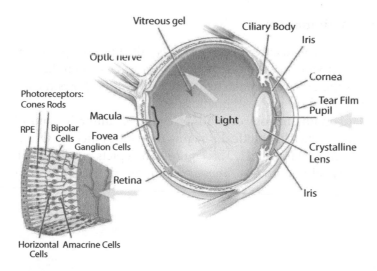

Figure 10.4 Inspection of defects through corneal topography of a healthy retina, mire diagram of eye.

10.3.5 Mire

Mire objects ophthalmometer; its image is mirrored on the corneal surface, is measured to find out the radii of curvature of the cornea. Figure 10.4 characterize the mire diagram of eye.

10.3.6   Placedo

Assessing corneal topography is carried by Placido Keratoscope. Placido Disc is a toric marker designed as elliptical surface of the cornea. Through a coil rings, reflections of cornea are recorded through the rigid support at the center of the disc. The objective of the operation protects the refractive surgery and inner surface of the eye. The light rays is a covering lens to all non-ideal refracting surfaces that reflect light. This principle valuates Purkinje images reflected of Placido discs.

10.3.7   Expected Topography

Normal Cornea ranges from 2–4 D between the center and periphery, the paranasal sinuses and the Q-value is calculated by the Pentacam. Q = -E2 and describes the corneal shape factor, or eccentricity of the cornea. The standard value is -0.26.

10.3.8   Astigmatism

Astigmatism is the disturbance in eye. It is called presbyopia an imperfection in the curvature of the eye. Astigmatism occurs when the cornea and the lens of the eye are mismatched. The Figure 10.5 shows the difference between Normal eye and Astigmatic eye.

Standard ophthalmology depends on clinical examination and advanced imaging techniques like optical imaging modalities include OCT, OCTA, PAM, SLO, AO, FAF and MI. The Figure 10.6 depicts inspection of defects through corneal topography. These operations are time- consuming and

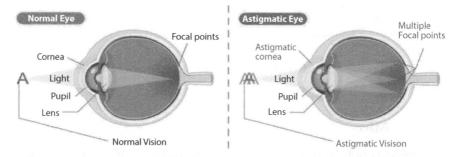

Figure 10.5 Inspection of defects through corneal topography of a healthy retina placedo disc and representative pattern of corneal shapes.

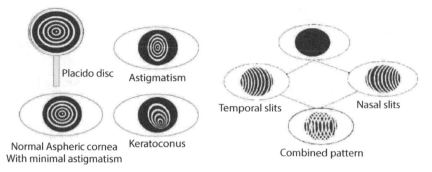

Placido disc   Astigmatism

Normal Aspheric cornea   Keratoconus
With minimal astigmatism

Temporal slits   Nasal slits

Combined pattern

Figure 10.6 Inspection of defects through corneal topography of a healthy retina overlapping scanning slits to map cornea.

carry major human errors. Even though Artificial Intelligence (AI) and Deep Learning (DL) are decouple of ophthalmology but run together in diagnostics and in predictions that yield Intraocular Pressure (IOP) regulations basically to formulate developments in diagnostics, surgical interventions and prognosis of corneal diseases.

10.4   Extended Reality Metaverse (XR)

Extended Reality (XR) makes-up the other technologies to work bycreating illusion that makes-up the reality. They comprise of physical and digital work which are real to createillusions by making the proper moments and actions. XR and metaverse are used with the sensors to identify the motions and by enhancing the resolutions of the graphic elements in the VR elements for better performance. The illusions are like magic trucks which are stimulated and get better by comprising of 3D Vision, Sound Design, Position Tracking technologies. 3D vision is the sensational of vision by creating perspective changes. Sound design makes a realistic modulation with the changes of direction. Position tracking is used to respond the positions of the various actions and sounds. Position tracking is used to track the eye in the range of activities. Metaverse work providing safe digital identity by the digital illusions that make-up the virtual access as shown in Figures 10.7 and 10.8. Cloud is used to make the better environment and better images for the operationswith better resolutions. One can share personal information in better. Metaverse is fine part of the internet, one can hang out with the fine parts of the place through Digital presence, Digital identity, and Digital assets.

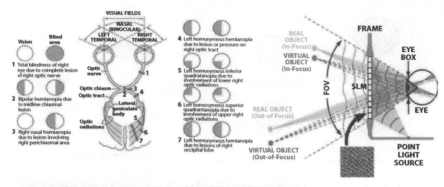

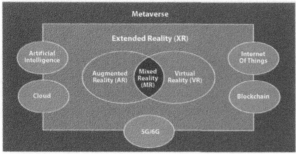

Figure 10.7 Inspection of defects through corneal topography of a healthy retina extended realty.

10.5   Computer-Aided Geometrical Design

Advent of computers saw an uneven growth in majority in technology. Observations in virtual models and real models utilize new computation tools to acquire and process the image. 3D shapes produce performance models and formulate reliability to reproduce the scalene solid structure.

CAGD tool emerge attempts to meet technological requirements that allow studies of geometrical entities, e.g. surfaces and volumes, and virtual modeling. Differences in physical models imply in constructive processes. The applications of Computers reduce service costs.

The applications of computers are diversified in biomedical engineering. The development of virtual characterization by CAGD allows the dynamic and self-organized structures to establish proof of mechanism subject to medicine. One could see in invasive and non-invasive techniques. Computers also represented in numerical methods in pathology and 3D animation.

Head–mounted camera image
(embedded in eyeglasses)
(Low resolution, Narrow angle)

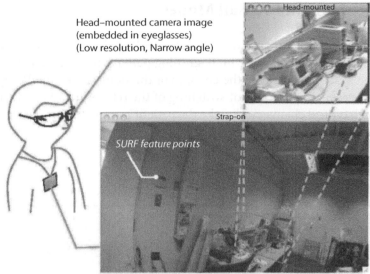

Strap–on camera image with result (High resolution, Wide angle)

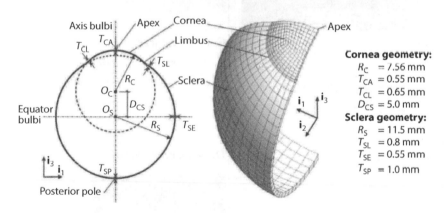

Cornea geometry:
R_C = 7.56 mm
T_{CA} = 0.55 mm
T_{CL} = 0.65 mm
D_{CS} = 5.0 mm

Sclera geometry:
R_S = 11.5 mm
T_{SL} = 0.8 mm
T_{SE} = 0.55 mm
T_{SP} = 1.0 mm

Figure 10.8 Inspection of defects through corneal topography of a healthy retina, camera image conical or biconical functions use the isolated chicken eye test method. Incomplete cornea model is reconstructed with the emergence of cloud technologies. The corneal topography was reconstructed with the CAGD and estimates the interpolations. The use of CAGD tools adopted functionalities that guarantees the data employed for geometric reconstruction and finds accuracy in detecting minor distortions formed on the corneal surface due to keratoconus.

10.6   Human Eye Ball Model

A 3B Scientific Human Eye Top shows enlarged eye by a factor of 5. It educates the treated family in diagnosing patients in the surgical and navigation system to identify the changes of the human eye. The Pedagogical activities serve in the ease of switching of the retina and adjusting the lens through typical changesand make the patient possess healthy eye free from common diseases.

Diseases and images

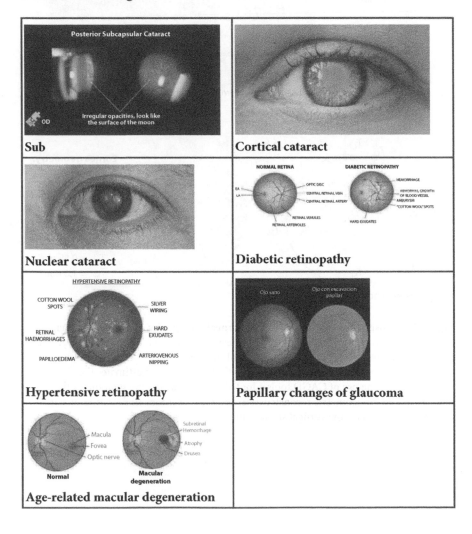

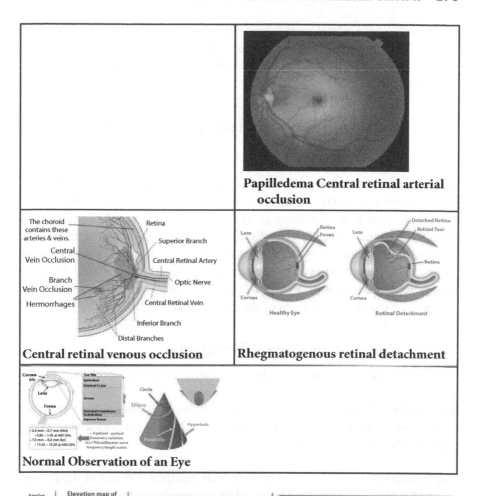

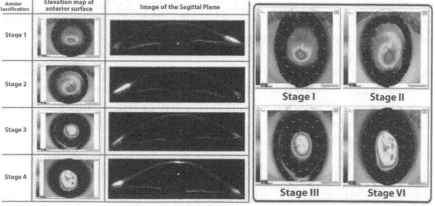

Figure 10.9 Inspection of defects through corneal topography of a healthy retina, sagittal plane.

Sagittal Plane: Sagittal plane is an anatomical plane that splits the center of the body into two halves (mid-sagittal) or away from the midline and (para-sagittal) parallel planes. Healthy retina sagittal plane is shown in Figure 10.9.

10.7   Keratoconus Characteristic Topographical Patterns

Image modules identify the Ocular diseases by studying the structure and function of cornea and anterior segment. These techniques diagnose and treat a wide variety of ocular diseases in ophthalmology and help to interpret these tests which are daunting. Beginners are trained in ophthalmology and in utilization of common diagnostic tests to provide quicker and more accurate diagnosis and management of corneal diseases. The practitioners enable the most commonly used corneal imaging techniques. An overview is shown of the design and functionality.

10.7.1   Phases of the Corneal Topography

The process of corneal topography can be divided into several phases:

Preparation: Before the topography procedure, the patient's eyes are typically numbed with anesthetic eye drops. This helps to reduce any discomfort or irritation during the procedure.

Data acquisition: The corneal topographer projects a series of light rings or patterns onto the patient's eye while a camera captures images of the reflected light. The instrument measures the corneal curvature at different points across the cornea to create a detailed map.

Analysis: The data acquired from the corneal topography is analyzed to generate a color-coded map that displays the curvature, shape, and thickness of the cornea at different points. This map provides valuable information about the cornea's topography, including any irregularities in shape or curvature that may be contributing to vision problems.

Interpretation: The ophthalmologist interprets the results of the corneal topography to diagnose any underlying eye conditions or abnormalities. This information helps the ophthalmologist determine the appropriate treatment for the patient, whether it's corrective lenses, surgery, or other interventions.

Follow-up: In some cases, corneal topography may be repeated at regular intervals to monitor changes in the cornea over time or to evaluate the effectiveness of treatment. Follow-up topography can help the ophthalmologist adjust treatment plans as needed to ensure the best possible outcome for the patient.

10.7.2   Eye-Tracking Instruments for Healthy Retina

The computer advancements enable content aware for rendering eye-tracking through MR displays and interfaces of MR users to find the intention by fine and dynamic aspects of gaze. With the integration of Computer hardware and software and applying engineering techniques generate into mixed reality (MR) technology to obtain a real-world environment. Researches on gaze input, abstract eye-tracking and human-computer interaction (HCI) practically exhibit several ways with user characteristics, intent and provide active and passive input control to MR interfaces. Eye-tracking captures a variety of eye movements using ground MR technology in the cognitive capacities. These methods include ambient interfaces, monitoring visual events across real and virtual scene elements and User Experience (UX).

Zeiss Humphrey Atlas 991: This is a CARL (Computerized Activities Results List) tool as depicted in Figures 10.10 and 10.11. one could notice the rings together through Zeiss Humphrey Atlas 991. The behavior of the epithelium in normal and suspicious eyes is the focus of Zeiss Humphrey Atlas 991. They enable those previously thought to have suspected Keratoconus to have this life-enhancing procedure.

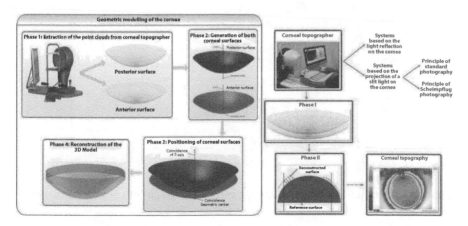

Figure 10.10 Inspection of defects through corneal topography of a healthy retina, geometric modeling of the cornea.

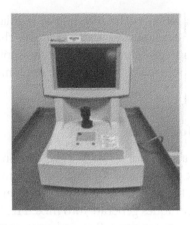
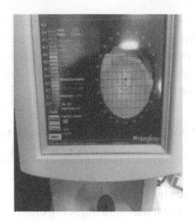

Figure 10.11 Inspection of defects through corneal topography of a healthy retina, Zeiss Humphrey Atlas 991.

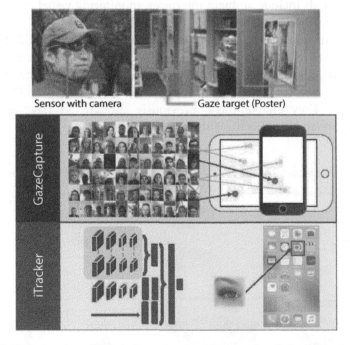

Figure 10.12 Inspection of defects through corneal topography of a healthy retina, gaze capture.

Semantic Scholar: This method is a video based eye tracking by employing gazed-index images that capture through video camera attached to the pad arms as depicted in Figure 10.12. The entire system presents through an infrared-based eye-tracking mounted on white sclera. The system possesses small phototransistors and infrared LEDs in- front of user eye and a video camera attached to the glasses. The complete feature extracts combined image processing methods and contextual information of eye direction with real-time object recognition in the visual reality. This system is applied to

(1)   Fast object recognition by using a SURF descriptor to improve IRIS description
(2)   Multiple image matching Descriptors of database.

Face recognition uses digital image feature, comprehensive recorder and apply wide-angle camera with different resolutions for regular usage. The present prototype is similar to photo transistor in the eye tracker and the development of a sensor system with high transparency. The Pentacam analysis results are depicted from Figures 10.13 to 10.19.

Pentacam Analysis:

	Normal values	Suspected values	Abnormal values
Anterior Corneal Surface			
K-Max	<49 D	>=49 D	
Important for Hyperopic Correction			
Flat K	>34 D	<=34 D	
Important for Myopic Correction			
Average K (km)	Important to selecting hinge width and flap diameter to avoid button-holeflap when km>46 D and free flap when km< 40 D.		
k-max Steep K	<1 D	>= 1D	
Difference of the K-Max between the two eyes	<2 D	>=2D	
Corneal Astigmatism (Topographic Astigmatism)	Compare with Manifest Astigmatism (MA)		
Average Q-Value	0 to -1	]0,-1[	
Thinnest Location			

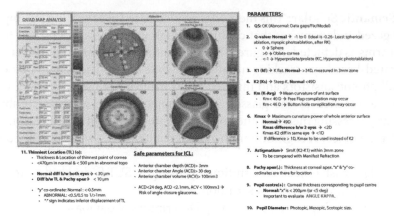

Figure 10.13 Inspection of defects through corneal topography of a healthy retina, pentacam analysis.

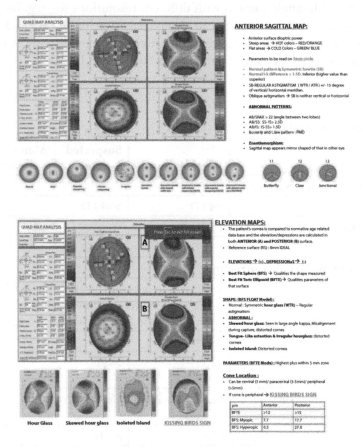

Figure 10.14 Inspection of defects through corneal topography of a healthy retina, pentacam analysis.

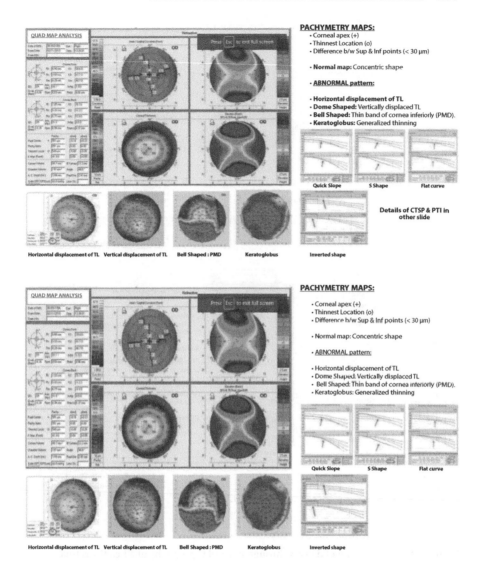

Figure 10.15 Inspections of defects through corneal topography of a healthy retina, pentacam analysis.

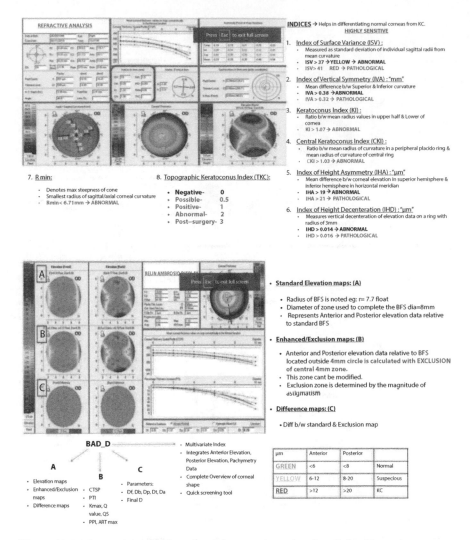

Figure 10.16 Inspection of defects through corneal topography of a healthy retina, Pentacam analysis.

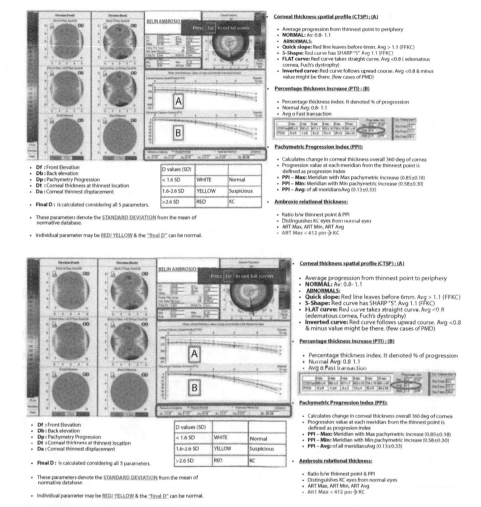

Figure 10.17 Inspection of defects through corneal topography of a healthy retina, Pentacam analysis.

13 POINT ALGORITHM :

- **Point No. 1:** The quality specification of the capture (QS);
- **Point No. 2:** The maximum keratometry (K) value;
- **Point No. 3:** The corneal thickness at the thinnest location;
- **Point No. 4:** The y (vertical) coordinate of the thinnest location;
- **Point No. 5:** The corneal asphericity at the 6-mm optical zone (Q-value);
- **Point No. 6:** The Shape and value of the anterior sagittal curvature map;
- **Point No. 7:** The shape and values of the anterior elevation map;
- **Point No. 8:** The shape and values of the posterior elevation map;
- **Point No. 9:** The shape and value of the pachymetry map;
- **Point No. 10:** The shape of the corneal thickness spatial profile (CTSP) and the average of thickness progression;
- **Point No. 11:** The amount and axis of topographic astigmatism measured by the total corneal refractive power and compared with the manifest astigmatism; and
- **Point No. 12:** A comparison between the patient's two eyes
- **Point No. 13:** BAD Display, BAD parameters, PPI, ARTmax

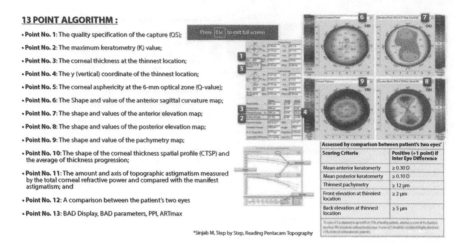

| Assessed by comparison between patient's two eyes' | |
Scoring Criteria	Positive (+1 point) if Inter Eye Difference
Mean anterior keratomerty	≥ 0.30 D
Mean posterior keratometry	≥ 0.10 D
Thinnest pachymetry	≥ 12 μm
Front elevation at thinnest location	≥ 2 μm
Back elevation at thinnest location	≥ 5 μm

*Sinjab M, Step by Step, Reading Pentacam Topography

Figure 10.18 Inspection of defects through corneal topography of a healthy retina, Pentacam analysis.

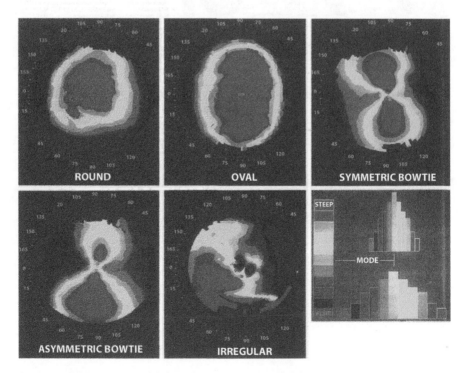

Figure 10.19 Inspection of defects through corneal topography of a healthy retina, Pentacam analysis.

CBI – Corvis Biomchanical Index

Comprehensive biomechanical screening and keratoconus detection
Deformation Parameters and Corneal Thickness Profile
Vinciguerra pioneered refractive surgery in Italy
Normal <0.45

	Normal Value (x)	Suspected Value(x)	Abnormal Value (x)
Anterior Corneal Surface			
K-Max	<49 D	>49 D	
	Important for Myopic Convention		
Flat - K	<34 D	>34 D	
	Important for Hyper-Myopic Convention		
Average K	Important for selecting hinge width and flap diameter to avoid buttonhole		
	< 1 D	>1 D	
	< 2 D	>2 D	
Corneal Astigmatism Topographic Astigmatism	Compare with Myopia astigmatism (MA)		
Average Q Value	0 to -1	30 to 41	
Thinnest Location (TL)			
Thickness	>500 µm	<400 µm <500 µm	> -1000 µm
Co-ordinates	< - 500 µm	- 500–1000 µm	> - 1000 µm
Pachy Apex -- TL	< 10 µm	> 10 µm	
Difference between the two eyes	< 30 µm	> 30 µm	

Randleman Risk Assessment Scoring System	Points				
Parameter	4	3	2	1	0
Topography	Abnormal	Irregular Corneas/SRAX		Asymmetric Bowtle	Normal
RSB	<241µm	241µm to 257µm	260µm to 279µm	280µm 295µm	to ≥300µm
Age		18 to 23	24 to 26	27 to 29	≥30
CT	<450µm	451µm to 480µm	481µm to 512µm		≥512µm
MRSE	>-140	>-121 to -140	>-102 to -121	>-82 to -102	-82 orless

Advantages:
A higher safety, as patients at risk for developing ecstasia after LASIK can be excluded.
A higher efficiency, as surgery can be performed when patients have a stiff and stable cornea.

TBI – Tomographic Biomechanincal Index

Combined parameters with tomography data from Pentacam
Tomographic and Biomechanical Index (**TBI**) for ecstasia detection
Combined tomographic and bio-mechanical data.
Developing ecstasy after refractive surgery with correlation of Confocal microscope and histology ofpatients at serious side.
Normal<0.29.

Cut off values for border line cases/KC

1. The diameter of a garden roller is 1.4 m and it is 2 m long
2. Belin-Ambrósio enhanced ectasia display total deviation value (BAD_D) >1.6

Scoring scale to proceed with LASIK Risk (Low – Moderate - High)	Recommendations
- 2	LASIK carried by the surgeon - ASA.
3	Valid informed consent; Surface ablation complications are less, No side effects and exercises refractive stability, degree of astigmatism, Symmetrical topography of eye.
4	Neither LASIK nor ASA (cannot establish)

3. Corvis Biomechanical Index >0.5
4. Tomographic Biomechanincal Index >0.29
5. CCT<480μm

Classification systems of KC

Severity: Mild, Moderate, Severe based on K-readings.
Cone: Round or nipple, Oval, Globus
Amsler Krumeich et al., Stage 1,2,3,4
Rabinowitz/Rasheed's KISA %: Central K x I-S Asymmetry x   AST (degree of regular corneal astigmatism x SRAX x 100/300.
Normal: <50 %
KC suspect: 60 – 100%
KC: >100%

Belin ABCD classification system/progression display – A, B, C are auto-generated.
A – Anterior Area of curvature in 6mm
B – Posterior Area of curvature in 6mm
C – Inferior temporal region in microns
D – Distance of predicted vision corrections in Visual Acuity

Classification of Keratoconus based on ABCD system

ABCD Criteria	ARC 3mm	PRC 3mm	BDVA
0	>7.25 mm	>5.90mm	= 20/20 (= 1.0)
1	>7.05mm	>5.70mm	< 20/20 (< 1.0)
2	>6.35mm	>5.15mm	< 20/40 (<0.5)
3	>6.15 mm	>4.95mm	< 20/100 (0.2)
4	<6.15 mm	<4.95mm	< 20/400 (< 0.05)

Explicit decision for suitability of combined refractive surgery with CXL

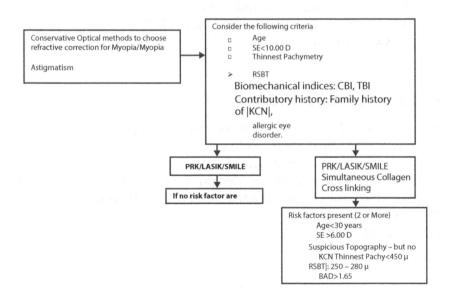

Smart KC: Software Handling the Smart KC: https://github.com/microsoft/SmartKC-A-Smartphone-based-Corneal-Topographer

LICENSE	LICENSE updated to template	10 months ago
LICENSE-CODE	LICENSE-CODE committed	10 months ago
README.md	cleaning code and repo structure	last month
SECURITY.md	SECURITY.md commited	10 months ago
arc_step_method.py	Adding analysis pipeline for open-sourcing	9 months ago
camera_size.py	Adding analysis pipeline for open-sourcing	9 months ago
crf.py	Adding analysis pipeline for open-sourcing	9 months ago
get_maps.py	Adding analysis pipeline for open-sourcing	9 months ago
main.py	Adding analysis pipeline for open-sourcing	9 months ago
metrics.py	Adding analysis pipeline for open-sourcing	9 months ago
mire_detection.py	Adding analysis pipeline for open-sourcing	9 months ago
preprocess.py	Adding analysis pipeline for open-sourcing	9 months ago
run_script.sh	Adding analysis pipeline for open-sourcing	9 months ago

preprocess.py	Adding analysis pipeline for open-sourcing	9 months ago
run_script.sh	Adding analysis pipeline for open-sourcing	9 months ago
utils.py	Adding analysis pipeline for open-sourcing	9 months ago

README.md

SmartKC: Analysis Pipeline

This directory contains the code for the image processing pipeline for *SmartKC*. The input to the system is a *mire* image and the output are the corneal topography heatmasp (*axial and tangential*), along with the quantitative metrics: *sim-k, diff, mean-k, aCLMI, PPK, KISA*.

The aim of this README is to describe in detail the setup and image processing pipeline for ease of understanding and usage by a beginner user. The readme describes in detail the analysis pipeline, example code snippets, details on the functions and parameters.

The figure below illustrates the (a) SmartKC system setup, (b) LED light arrangement, (c) 3D-printed conical photo clip-on attachment, (d) image capture of a subject's eye, and (e) captured image of the cornea with placido disc reflection (called mires).

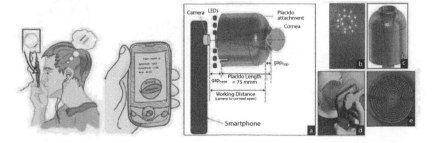

Figure 10.20 Smart KC.

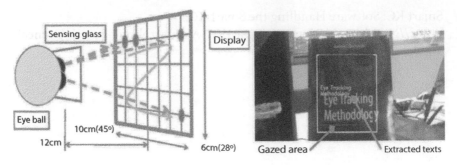

Figure 10.21 Eye tracking methodology.

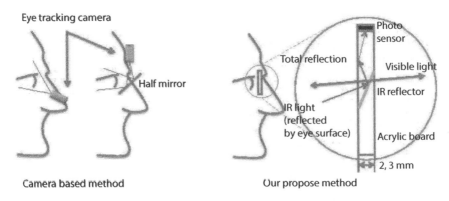

Figure 10.22 New proposed method for eye tracking.

3 Prototype Eye Gaze Recognizer with camera:

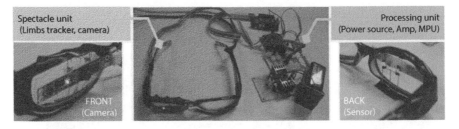

Figure 10.23 Eye gaze recognizer with camera.

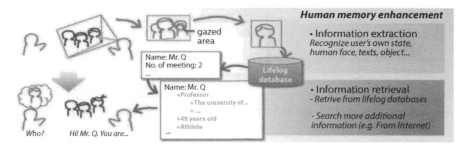

Figure 10.24 Memory enhancement.

Human Memory Enhancement:

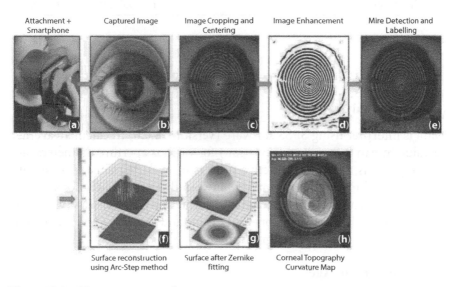

Figure 10.25 Human memory enhancement.

10.7.3 Analysis of Corneal Asphericity

An analysis is carried on 1,600 men eyes of average age of 35 and further calculations are carried of corneal Q value with the related factors with the related factors as shown from Figures 10.20 to 10.25.

Gender, age distribution of refractive index is observed on 1,600 participants eyes (considering 900 female members and 700 male members) with an average 53 years old (between 30 to 90 years). These corneal Q values of different aperture diameters are discussed.

Results:

Average Q Value	3.0mm	5.0mm	7.0mm
Anterior	0.28±0.18	-0.28±0.18	-0.29±0.18
Age was adversely linked with the anterior surface's average Q value at 5.0mm aperture diameter.			(B = negative 0.003, p< positive 0.0095) and the refractive power (B = -0.0129, p = 0.0159).
Posterior	-0.26±0.216	-0.26±0.214	-0.26±0.215
Age was favorably associated with the posterior surface's average Q value at 5.0mm aperture diameter.			(B = 0.0019, p = 0.0365) and the refractive power (B = 0.0159, p = 0.0425).

Statistical Analysis

Data is interpret using SPSS software (version 18.0.0) to calculate average Q value (mean ± Standard Deviation) for various aperture diameters, age of the persons, sex and refractive powers of eyes. Variance analysis like T-test is cited to compare Q values between different populations groups based on aperture diameters, age and refractive powers. ANOVA determines relationship between corneal Q value and primary Q-Value parameters. Value of (p- ≤0.05) is significant.

Characteristics of Age

A deep survey over 1,600 subjective of mean age of 53 ± 11 years (range 30–90) is carried. The subjective age and Values are

  30 to 39 assessed over 12%,
  40 to 49 assessed for 18%,
  50 to 59 assessed for 41.7%,
  60 to 69 assessed for 20.5%,
  70 years old and above assessed for 8% of the study population.

Age vision called - Age-related macular degeneration (AMD) - Senile cataract develops beyond 50. These characteristics are more confirmed 50 years old and above and are assessed for 70%.

Corneal Q value distribution at large aperture diameter of 7.0mm

The mean Q value of the anterior surface was -0.29 ± 0.18 (range -0.30 to -0.28, CI 95%) and for the posterior surface was -0.26 ± 0.21 (range -0.28 to -0.26, CI 95%).

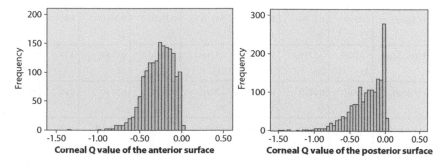

Figure 10.26 Q value of anterlor vs posterlor surface.

Corneal Q Values for Different Age Groups

Q value at different age stages are studied. The Q values of anterior surface and posterior surface are recorded with significance ($p<0.05$) at distinguished age groups. The Figures 10.26 and 10.27 shows that as people age, the corneal Q value of the front surface decreases while the Q value of the posterior surface rises.

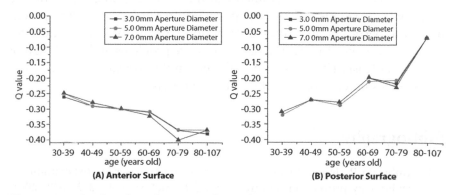

Figure 10.27 Q value of anterlor vs posterlor surface.

Group Analysis by Age for different Corneal Q Values

Aperture Diameter (mm)	30-39	40-49	50-59	60-69	70-79	80 -107	F	P
3.0 (Anterior)	0.26±0.16	0.29±0.16	0.30±0.19	0.31±0.19	0.37±0.20	0.38±0.17	1.6	0.157
3.0 (Posterior)	0.31±0.20	0.27±0.21	0.28±0.23	0.20±0.21	0.22±0.21	0.07±0.04	4.49	0
5.0 (Anterior)	0.25±0.17	0.29±0.16	0.30±0.19	0.31±0.20	0.37±0.20	0.37±0.18	1.81	0.109
5.0 (Posterior)	- 0.32±0.21	- 0.27±0.20	- 0.29±0.23	- 0.21±0.21	0.07±0.04	0.07±0.04	4.78	0
7.0 (Anterior)	0.25±0.16	0.28±0.16	0.30±0.19	0.32±0.19	0.40±0.19	0.37±0.16	2.78	0.017
7.0 (Posterior)	0.31±0.21	0.27±0.20	0.28±0.22	- 0.20±0.21	- 0.23±0.20	- 0.07±0.05	4.25	0.001

10.8 Conclusion

The corneal Q value of the anterior surface diminishes with increasing of age. With age comes an expansion in the rear surface. The age and diameter widening trend lines of the Q value are related. The Q value is a quantified indicator of spherical degree and defines radial change from Centre to peripheral of the quadric surface. The mathematical model of the cornea is obtained manually by keratometry with paired readings taken in two orthogonal meridia. The averages of 3 pairs include axes. Corneal power in dioptres (D) = 337.5/keratometry in mm, (The hypothetical refractive index of the cornea is 337.5). The optical features include refractive power, spherical aberration, aberration distribution, etc., and the Q value indicates the corneal shape. The treatment of refractive problems and the design of intraocular lenses (IOLs) both heavily rely on the corneal Q value. Only a few formal studies have gone through the process.

Bibliography

1. Ambrosio, R., Jr and Wilson, S.E., Complications of laser *in situ* keratomileusis: Etiology, prevention, and treatment. *J. Refract. Surg.*, 17, 3, 350–79, 2001.

2. Seiler, T., Koufala, K., Richter, G., Iatrogenic keratectasia after laser *in situ* keratomileusis. *J. Refract. Surg.*, 14, 3, 312–7, 1998.

3. Krachmer, J.H., Feder, R.F., Belin, M.W., Keratoconus and related noninflammatory corneal thinning disorders. *Surv. Ophthalmol.*, 28, 293–322, 1984.

4. Wilson, S.E. and Klyce, S.D., Screening for corneal topographic abnormalities before refractive surgery. *Ophthalmology*, 101, 1, 147–52, 1994.

5. Klyce, S.D., Computer-assisted corneal topography. High-resolution graphic presentation and analysis of keratoscopy. *Invest. Ophthalmol. Vis. Sci.*, 25, 12, 1426–35, 1984.

6. Rabinowitz, Y.S., Yang, H., Brickman, Y., Akkina, J., Riley, C., Rotter, J.I. *et al.*, Videokeratography database of normal human corneas. *Br. J. Ophthalmol.*, 80, 7, 610–6, 1996.

7. Rabinowitz, Y.S. and McDonnell, P.J., Computer-assisted corneal topography in keratoconus. *Refract Corneal Surg.*, 5, 6, 400–8, 1989.

8. Rabinowitz, Y.S., Videokeratographic indices to aid in screening for keratoconus. *J. Refract Surg.*, 11, 5, 371–9, 1995.

9. Rabinowitz, Y.S., Tangential vs sagittal videokeratographs in the "early" detection of keratoconus. *Am. J. Ophthalmol.*, 122, 6, 887–9, 1996.

10. Rabinowitz, Y.S. and Rasheed, K., KISA% index: A quantitative videokeratography algorithm embodying minimal topographic criteria for diagnosing keratoconus. *J. Cataract Refract Surg.*, 25, 10, 1327–35, 1999.

11. Smolek, M.K. and Klyce, S.D., Current keratoconus detection methods compared with a neural network approach. *Invest. Ophthalmol. Vis. Sci.*, 38, 11, 2290–9, 1997.

12. Maeda, N., Klyce, S.D., Smolek, M.K., Comparison of methods for detecting keratoconus using videokeratography. *Arch. Ophthalmol.*, 113, 7, 870–4, 1995.

13. Nowitz, Y.S., Maguen, E., Hofbauer, J. *et al.*, Keratoconus detected by videokeratography in candidates for photorefractive keratectomy. *J. Refract. Surg.*, 11, 3, 194–201, 1995.

14. Chastang, P.J., Borderie, V.M., Carvajal-Gonzalez, S., Rostene, W., Laroche, L., Automated keratoconus detection using the EyeSys videokeratoscope. *J. Cataract Refract Surg.*, 26, 5, 675–83, 2000.

15. Maeda, N., Klyce, S.D., Smolek, M.K., Thompson, H.W., Automated keratoconus screening with corneal topography analysis. *Invest. Ophthalmol. Vis. Sci.*, 35, 6, 2749–57, 1994.

16. Kalin, N.S., Maeda, N., Klyce, S.D., Hargrave, S., Wilson, S.E., Automated topographic screening for keratoconus in refractive surgery candidates. *CLAO J.*, 22, 3, 164–7, 1996.

17. Auffarth, G.U., Wang, L., Volcker, H.E., Keratoconus evaluation using the orbscan topography System. *J. Cataract Refract Surg.*, 26, 2, 222–8, 2000.

18. Rao, S.N., Raviv, T., Majmudar, P.A., Epstein, R.J., Role of Orbscan II in screening keratoconus suspects before refractive corneal surgery. *Ophthalmology*, 109, 9, 1642–6, 2002.

19. Tomidokoro, A., Oshika, T., Amano, S., Higaki, S., Maeda, N., Miyata, K., Changes in anterior and posterior corneal curvatures in keratoconus. *Ophthalmology*, 107, 7, 1328–32, 2000.

20. Ambrosio, R., Jr, Alonso, R.S., Luz, A., Coca Velarde, L.G., Corneal-thickness spatial profile and corneal-volume distribution: Tomographic indices to detect keratoconus. *J. Cataract Refract Surg.*, 32, 11, 1851–9, 2006.

21. De Sanctis, U., Loiacono, C., Richiardi, L., Turco, D., Mutani, B., Grignolo, F.M., Sensitivity and specificity of posterior corneal elevation measured by Pentacam in discriminating keratoconus/subclinical keratoconus. *Ophthalmology*, 115, 9, 1534–9, 2008.

22. Saad, A. and Gatinel, D., Evaluation of total and corneal wavefront high order aberrations for the detection of forme fruste keratoconus. *Invest. Ophthalmol. Vis. Sci.*, 53, 6, 2978–92, 2012.

23. Luce, D.A., Determining *in vivo* biomechanical properties of the cornea with an ocular response analyzer. *J. Cataract Refract Surg.*, 31, 1, 156–62, 2005.

24. Ambrosio, R., Jr, Caiado, A.L., Guerra, F.P., Louzada, R., Roy, A.S., Luz, A. *et al.*, Novel pachymetric parameters based on corneal tomography for diagnosing keratoconus. *J. Refract Surg.*, 27, 10, 753– 8, 2011.

25. Fontes, B.M., Ambrosio, R., Jr, Salomao, M., Velarde, G.C., Nose, W., Biomechanical and tomographic analysis of unilateral keratoconus. *J. Refract Surg.*, 26, 9, 677–81, 2010.

26. Bae, G.H., Kim, J.R., Kim, C.H., Lim, D.H., Chung, E.S., Chung, T.Y., Corneal topographic and tomographic analysis of fellow eyes in unilateral keratoconus patients using Pentacam. *Am. J. Ophthalmol.*, 157, 1, 103–9.e1, 2014.

27. Muftuoglu, O., Ayar, O., Ozulken, K., Ozyol, E., Akinci, A., Posterior corneal elevation and back difference corneal elevation in diagnosing forme fruste keratoconus in the fellow eyes of unilateral keratoconus patients. *J. Cataract Refract Surg.*, 39, 9, 1348–57, 2013.

28. Chan, C., Ang, M., Saad, A., Chua, D., Mejia, M., Lim, L. *et al.*, Validation of an objective scoring system for forme fruste keratoconus detection and post-LASIK ectasia risk assessment in Asian eyes. *Cornea*, 34, 9, 996–1004, 2015.

29. Saad, A. and Gatinel, D., Validation of a new scoring system for the detection of early forme of keratoconus. *Int. J. Kerat Ect Cor Dis.*, 1, 2, 100–8, 2012.

30. Saad, A. and Gatinel, D., Topographic and tomographic properties of forme fruste keratoconus corneas. *Invest. Ophthalmol. Vis. Sci.*, 51, 11, 5546–55, 2010.

31. Mahmoud, A.M., Nunez, M.X., Blanco, C., Koch, D.D., Wang, L., Weikert, M.P. *et al.*, Expanding the cone location and magnitude index to include corneal thickness and posterior surface information for the detection of keratoconus. *Am. J. Ophthalmol.*, 156, 6, 1102–11, 2013.

32. Randleman, J.B., Trattler, W.B., Stulting, R.D., Validation of the ectasia risk score system for preoperative laser *in situ* keratomileusis screening. *Am. J. Ophthalmol.*, 145, 5, 813–8, 2008.
33. Randleman, J.B., Woodward, M., Lynn, M.J., Stulting, R.D., Risk assessment for ectasia after corneal refractive surgery. *Ophthalmology*, 115, 1, 37–50, 2008.
34. Seiler, T. and Quurke, A.W., Iatrogenic keratectasia after LASIK in a case of forme fruste keratoconus. *J. Cataract Refract Surg.*, 24, 7, 1007–9, 1998.
35. Speicher, L. and Gottinger, W., Progressive corneal ectasia after laser *in situ* keratomileusis (LASIK). *Klin Monatsbl Augenheilkd.*, 213, 4, 247–51, 1998.
36. Geggel, H.S. and Talley, A.R., Delayed onset keratectasia following laser *in situ* keratomileusis. *J. Cataract Refract Surg.*, 25, 4, 582–6, 1999.
37. Amoils, S.P., Deist, M.B., Gous, P., Amoils, P.M., Iatrogenic keratectasia after laser *in situ* keratomileusis for less than −4.0 to −7.0 diopters of myopia. *J. Cataract Refract Surg.*, 26, 7, 967–77, 2000.
38. McLeod, S.D., Kisla, T.A., Caro, N.C., McMahon, T.T., Iatrogenic keratoconus: Corneal ectasia following laser *in situ* keratomileusis for myopia. *Arch. Ophthalmol.*, 118, 2, 282–4, 2000.
39. Holland, S.P., Srivannaboon, S., Reinstein, D.Z., Avoiding serious corneal complications of laser assisted *in situ* keratomileusis and photorefractive keratectomy. *Ophthalmology*, 107, 4, 640–52, 2000.
40. Schmitt-Bernard, C.F., Lesage, C., Arnaud, B., Keratectasia induced by laser *in situ* keratomileusis in keratoconus. *J. Refract Surg.*, 16, 3, 368–70, 2000.
41. Rao, S.N. and Epstein, R.J., Early onset ectasia following laser *in situ* keratomileusus: Case report and literature review. *J. Refract Surg.*, 18, 2, 177–84, 2002.
42. Malecaze, F., Coullet, J., Calvas, P., Fournie, P., Arne, J.L., Brodaty, C., Corneal ectasia after photorefractive keratectomy for low myopia. *Ophthalmology*, 113, 5, 742–6, 2006.
43. Randleman, J.B., Russell, B., Ward, M.A., Thompson, K.P., Stulting, R.D., Risk factors and prognosis for corneal ectasia after LASIK. *Ophthalmology*, 110, 2, 267–75, 2003.
44. Leccisotti, A., Corneal ectasia after photorefractive keratectomy. *Graefes Arch. Clin. Exp. Ophthalmol.*, 245, 6, 869–75, 2007.
45. Reinstein, D.Z. and Archer, T., Combined Artemis very high-frequency digital ultrasound-assisted transepithelial phototherapeutic keratectomy and wavefront-guided treatment following multiple corneal refractive procedures. *J. Cataract Refract. Surg.*, 32, 11, 1870–6, 2006.

11

The Metaverse in Industry and Logistics

M. Edwin[1]*, M. Saranya Nair[2] and V. A. Nagarajan[1]

[1]Department of Mechanical Engineering, University College of Engineering, Nagercoil, Anna University Constituent College, Nagercoil, India
[2]School of Electronics Engineering, Vellore Institute of Technology, Chennai Campus, Chennai, India

Abstract

Metaverse is an innovative variant of information and communication application, a sociological structure that combines a number of recent techniques (block chain, industrial IoT, artificial intelligence, deep learning, etc.) to create immersive virtual reality practices and hence establish a link between the biological and simulated worlds. The objective of the industrial metaverse is to speed up procedures such as repair and maintenance, establishing new production lines, remote monitoring, navigation system, and new consumer orientation. Metaverse technology, sometimes known as the digital twin of a workplace, provides immersive experience to the configuration layers of internet networks. Despite the fact that the framework and technologies are not yet in order to permit the widespread development of new immersive virtual environments that human avatars might traverse across platforms, academics are becoming more focused on the metaverse's potential for transformation. By integrating the enlightened narratives and multi-perspective methodology from researchers with diverse fields of knowledge on various facets of the metaverse and its revolutionary influence, this study investigates these issues in depth. The current study has been carried out to examine and pinpoint the possibilities of this developing technology in the industrial sector in perspective of the development of Metaverse technology and the significance of applying it in industry and supply chain.

Keywords: Metaverse, augmented reality, extended reality, digital twin, virtual reality

*Corresponding author: edwinme1980@gmail.com

Chandrashekhar A, Shaik Himam Saheb, Sandeep Kumar Panda, S. Balamurugan and Sheng-Lung Peng (eds.) *Metaverse and Immersive Technologies: An Introduction to Industrial, Business and Social Applications*, (295–324) © 2023 Scrivener Publishing LLC

11.1   Introduction: Metaverse – State-of-the-Art

METAVERSE – The evolution of the internet characterizes a simulated world in which people can live, work, shop, and communicate from their ease of the physical world. The phrase 'meta' is from Greek meant for beyond, and 'verse' represents the universe or the world [1]. The author calls the Metaverse as a simulated world composed of exclusive atmospheres each of them has an explicit purpose like amuse, socialize, instruct, market and so on. Apprehending the perspectives, affordances, and area of expertise and the limitations of emerging technologies is crucial to address the requirements of educators, customers, industrialists and other stakeholders. In the term Metaverse, the prefix denotes the simulated world and the suffix symbolizes the actual world. Technically, communication process is continually evolving (Figure 11.1). As a result, innovative technical advancements, the fusion of several emerging technologies, and Web - based applications have all emerged [2]. Online multimedia platforms like Second Life, Roblox and Fortnite are considered as the antecedents of the metaverse which allows customers to interact within a virtual world. Though, all such 3D interactive platforms have been available since the early 2000's with a huge record of world-wide users, in the perspective of the metaverse, they are all restricted by the application's liberty and processes. The metaverse concept defines an organized immersive bionetwork in which the obstructions amongst the virtual and real worlds are absolute to users.

There are four major transformations between the existing online platforms and the present metaverse [3]. 1) The new metaverse agreements better immersion compared to the existing platforms due to the expansion of deep learning techniques. 2) Contrast to the earlier computer-oriented

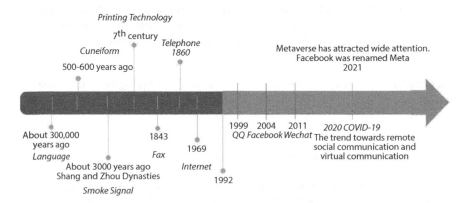

Figure 11.1 The progression of communication technologies.

metaverse, the modern one supports portable devices which upsurge approachability and stability. 3) Through the growth of security processes such as block-chain and virtual money the monetary proficiency and so the strength of metaverse facilities has been enhanced. 4) Also, owing to the restrictions of offline societal interactions especially during pandemic, attention on the computer-generated world has been developed. The main elements of the taxonomies of the metaverse are environment, interface, interaction, and security, as shown in Figure 11.2 [4].

11.1.1 Metaverse – Scope and Characteristics

The metaverse targets to link the gap among the real and imaginary worlds in every business. The expertise to empower the formation of the metaverse is progressing rapidly by the assistance of Virtual Reality headphones, haptic gauntlets, Augmented/Extended Reality processes, that facilitates consumers to abundantly relish the intense collaboration and immersive involvement [5].

The "metaverse" is a landscape of digital twins whose opportunities are exciting, where the stakeholders can build and explore their ideas in mutually simulated work-spaces without the limitations of the physical world. Industries are opening to consider the potential of the metaverse and looking for occasions to integrate it in their existing business models.

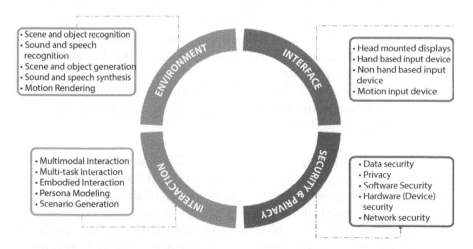

Figure 11.2 Environment, interface, communication, safety, and privacy in the metaverse [7].

11.1.2   Aspects of the Metaverse

The four aspects of the metaverse are defined as: environment, interface, communication, and societal worth.

- Environment - Metaverse comprises rational, irrational, and hybrid environments. The rational metaverse echoes physical components agreeing to the creator's requirement and imagination. However, the irrational environment has the opportunity of easy exploitation without physical restrictions and hence allows customers to practice ideas that are not possible to achieve in reality. The hybrid system contains an improved scheme that composes a new simulated world with the laws of reality.
- Interface – Metaverse includes 3D, immersive, and physical interface methods. The three dimensional system has the benefit of enhanced practicality, but it detriments in terms of facility endurance. Immersion encourages user involvement in the metaverse and preserving an uninterrupted world. Immersion can be supported by a physical tool like VR to mock the user's actual optical intelligence. Physical features (e.g., inertia) are also reflecting as a good way to enhance realism [6].
- Communication – Metaverse employs communal networking, teamwork, and personality interchange. Head-Mounted Displays (HMDs), smartphones, etc. help people to enter the virtual universe and involve irrespective of their physical whereabouts. Developments in computational discipline and communication methods are leading the Metaverse more of an actuality.
- Societal worth–Stability and reliability investigations are the significant features in providing societal morals and preserving a healthy metaverse.

Authorizing emerging technologies (5G, block-chain, AI), and moving from 2D visuals on flat screens to 3D illustrations in HMDs, the Metaverse will empower the construction of a collaborative and virtual identical of our physical biosphere (in terms of societies, locations, and objects) which users can explore through XR platforms. XR, stands for "extended reality," is a combined term for augmented, mixed, and virtual reality.

Thus, in a nutshell, the metaverse can be referred as a "3-dimensionalsimulated shared world where all activities can be agreed out with the support of AR/VR services".

11.1.3   Metaverse – Applications

- Remote Work Opportunities: Metaverse brings a new dimension to the remote work functionality by facilitating effective interaction among employees. The employer can also monitor the team's productivity and hence handle workflow time theft and goldbricks.
- Assisting Healthcare: Metaverse assists healthcare professionals to communicate with patients of remote geographic locations. They can consult with doctors in the Metaverse's virtual space and get their medications.
- Online Entertainment: Existing gaming techniques impose a huge potential challenge for both designers and producers to give their customers a live experience. However, metaverse platform provides players a close-to reality experience like they can interact with other players, trade in-game assets, and even familiarize a physical sense of touch using haptic gloves and jackets. Existing businesses employ a distributed economic model in which the designers own the in-game assets and dispense them, but the metaverse carry real-world value. It means that users can earn real money by selling their virtual assets in the Metaverse via Non-Fungible Tokens (NFTs) [7].
- Collaborative social media: The Metaverse merges virtual reality with augmented reality and hence provides consumers an immersive experience that goes beyond the competences of current social media. Online communications will become more real-life experiences.
- Education: Pandemic restricts traditional teaching-learning processes in different dimensions. Metaverse can contribute students a more engaging experience to alleviate this restriction.
- Virtual Shopping: Metaverse supports a real-life purchasing experience by enabling the customers to touch and feel the products, as well as try them out before making a purchase.

11.1.4   Metaverse in Industry and Logistics

Industries treasure a plethora of opportunities to interact with clients and other shareholders in a metaverse environment over extended reality. The digital matching has created extensive solicitations in industries like autonomous systems, economics, medical, production, and logistics. The metaverse's twin technique, is an imitation of real processes in a simulated form, facilitate industries to curtail cost of operation, mishaps, also enhanced preparation, and source sharing. End user interaction is a vital constituent in bringing up both buyer and brand justice, and metaverse has sustained the talent of transferring such communications to the virtual realm [8]. At the same time, metaverse infrastructure offers crucial evidence about consumer response to industries, thus the concept testing, prototyping, and product design could be pursued fast at a low cost.

Metaverse combines real and simulated features in production, supply chain management and logistics practices unprecedentedly. Physical manufacturing can be optimized by pretending them in a metaverse atmosphere. Virtual techniques will ease the expenses of engineering procedures, also aids in waste control, and hence supports ecological sustainability.

The Metaverse can augment delivery chain transparency by virtualizing the manufacturing, trades, dissemination procedures and exhibiting delivery information, advance and delays in the transportation processes and so expand the procuring patterns of the industry with the vendors [9]. Immerse interface with the supply chain throughout the phases of a product's lifespan, can modernize the manufacturing and logistics practices and offer well-versed resolutions for all the shareholders involved in the industrial administration. The metaverse agreements distinctive chances to convert the old-style logistics by fetching innovative deviations in the approach products are being packed and loaded in computerized trucks or drones for closing consignment to the target. Optimal design of warehouse layouts using metaverse can enhance the flow of operations among all stakeholders. Digital marketing becomes the favorite standard of advertisement as a lot of clients are interested in online shopping/purchasing of products and services. The metaverse for digital promotion has its future for more original and collaborative publicizing skills that are not likely to occur with existing social broadcasting and digital advertisements. Metaverse applications can offer products the chance to spread their practical promotion or to entirely relocate their trademarks in a new atmosphere [10].

11.1.5   Summary

This chapter provides an outline of the Metaverse, its elements, possible applications in detail by associating the well-versed chronicles from literatures with varied disciplinary backgrounds. This study recognizes the emerging nature of the metaverse, contributing a poly-perspective description on the opportunities, intricacies and challenges encountered by organizations, customers, and industries. This chapter also spotlights the insistence of creating an exhaustive cognizance of how Metaverse can influence industrial activities.

11.2   Metaverse as Creative Freedom

The Industrial Metaverse is a novel environment in which development of modern data transmission paradigms like IoT, AI, and digital twins are tightly linked with the actual economy. For the whole value chain, a new production and service system is being developed. Technology firms have long been hampered by different obstacles. One of these impediments is technologies that have failed to deliver. Similar constraints have resulted from humans being unable to be taught rapidly enough to fully utilize technologies. The Industrial Metaverse will herald a new era of artistic control for businesses, allowing them to experiment with ideas and test technology without the expenses or constraints that come with real-world deployment. The conquerors will be those who are able to create the largest goals, but also execute what they have learnt in the Industrial Metaverse in the actual world [11].

There is no doubting that the notion of the Metaverse as a 3D comprehensive domain will have an impact on many facets of our private and professional relationships, including socializing, performing, entertainment, learning, and so on. In addition to numerous potential and threats, the metaverse also raises a number of ethical concerns and questions. The majority of ethical difficulties are ones we already face in our non-digital lives, including privacy, socio-economic inequality, availability, identities controls, and freedom of artistic expression, among others [12]. They simply represent society as it is; they are not recently developed issues.

Although ethical issues have long existed, humanity has just recently begun to confront them. With this modern technology, additional issues could arise, such as the usage of many (and distinct) identities on multiple (and distinct) metaverse spaces, or the access to biometric data that could be dishonestly exploited to manipulate people's thinking and behavior.

In this current paradigm, our conception of the metaverse gives synthetic customer experiences (SCx) a crucial place in how companies engage with potential clients. Significant considerations are posed regarding the users, such as consumers, executives, and authorities, should interpret SCx in the metaverse as the emphasis of customer contact evolves toward more dependence on compounds obtained of user experience through AR, VR, and perhaps neuroenhanced reality (NeR) (Figure 11.3) [13].

11.3   Development of Industrial Metaverse

As industries begin to use Industry 4.0 technologies, the Industrial Metaverse will generate $540 billion in revenue by 2025. One of the most common applications of the Metaverse is digital twins, in which real-world things are reflected in the Metaverse. Some businesses are now utilizing the technology, but its use is anticipated to increase. The Industrial Metaverse is predicted to take the lead because to the high degree of digitalization of big industrial plants, together with gradually better infrastructure such as the Industrial IoT and 2D/3D digital twinning technologies [14].

Aside from the metaverse's application possibilities in social media and entertainment media, the industry is generally positive about the

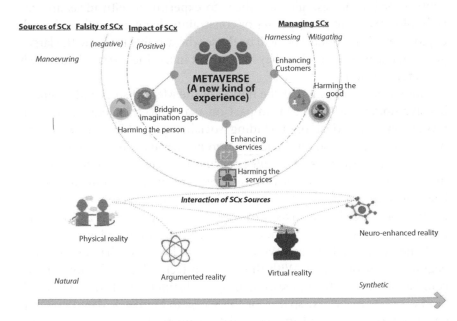

Figure 11.3 A novel form of perception that accepts deception.

"industrial metaverse" used in manufacturing. It has a more rigorous demand than the mainstream market, and the present degree of modernization of big industrial operations is typically high. Furthermore, existing infrastructure, such as the Industrial IoT and digital replicas, is being steadily upgraded, and the Industrial Metaverse is projected to lead the way in increasing its use [15].

The present metaverse is in its initial phase of development. The dominant interrogation is if there can be killer apps and business strategies; but there are numerous levels to consider: technology, platform, service content, and even rules, investment flows, data security, and so on. However, whether the manufacturing or logistics industries are utilized as the application area to investigate, the industrial application market is a closed sector, with major industrial plants typically having a high degree of digitalization. Some of the industrial metaverse's key technologies and approaches are widely employed in today's industrial systems. The metaverse is a comprehensive digital atmosphere in line to the actual physical realm, similar to the technological representations explored in recent decades. Physical individuals, processes, or systems that exist in the actual world are referred to as digital representations. It becomes an identical virtual identity on the information platform, and this avatar has all the features and characteristics of the actual world and may imitate the operation of the physical ecosphere in the simulated world. However, as the digital characterization becomes more realistic, the product must have a larger data store to increase the simulation's dependability. With the development of the notion of the metaverse, electronic simulation technology will continue to advance, and it will push the practical practice of implementing similar technologies. Included in this is the need to model more comprehensive and extensive virtual objects and places in order to increase forecast accuracy, and to develop a metaverse operating conditions on this basis, based on 5G, Wi-Fi 6, cloud technology or edge computing, smart sensing, and so on. More robust communication settings, processing platforms, and sensor devices are supported [16].

Additionally, the manufacturer has indeed advanced through the use of ERP, MES, and other control systems, or in other statements, there has been a significant amount of statistical details in the manufacturer over the last few years. As a result, all that is needed now is to open the interface to integrate this data into the electronic cloud network, and the Knowledge Terminal will then use it as the entrance to the Metaverse. The amount of information is rising in the big data age. Humans may also use AR glasses to ensure that what they see is exactly what they get. They can influence the idea of an operational war room by seeing where they go. The desire to increase work productivity will be the primary driver for AR wearables to lead the charge in the industrial arena, giving the manufacturing industry intrinsic benefits and motivation to develop a Metaverse [17].

11.4   Typical Products/Services in Metaverse

The metaverse combines the latest cutting-edge technology, including cognitive computing, natural language processing, computer vision, deep learning, artificial intelligence, etc., and has solicitations in many industries, including economics, art, and electronic games.

The representative corporations, the usual items they make, and the development planning they use change subject to the regulations of the participating countries in the Metaverse. For instance, the United States, which invented the Metaverse, has a pretty comprehensive Metaverse scheme that is castoff in diverse activities, including economics, entertainment, the culture, and societal issues. China has a substantial market, as well as a strong network of business industries and apps. Business, gaming, and art have all been gradually incorporated into the Metaverse by internet Infrastructure enterprises [2]. According to Figures 11.4 and 11.5, the uses of the metaverse may be distributed into two groups: "metaverse as a machine" and "metaverse as a target." The phrase "metaverse as a machine" refers to the application of the metaverse to address issues and challenges in the physical universe. The phrase "metaverse as a target" defines its efficient capability of achieving goals like escalating the scheme and making money [1].

Figure 11.4 Metaverse as a machine – applications.

Figure 11.5 Metaverse as a target - applications.

11.5   Role of Metaverse in Supply Chain

The metaverse has the potential to offer entirely new Supply Chain experiences in a digital environment that have never seen before. The majority of top Supply Chains are undergoing digital transformations in various aspects of their organizations. The metaverse is a cutting-edge technology that works from the bottom up. While the objective of digital operations is to digitally enhance the physical Supply Chain, the goal of the metaverse is to create a digital realm and convert it into the actual world. There are various Supply Chain issues and areas to consider.

The metaverse has the prospective to offer entirely innovative Supply Chain practices in a simulated environment that have never experienced so far. The majority of top Supply Chains are undergoing digital transformations in various aspects of their organizations. The metaverse is a front-line technology that works based on bottom to top method. Though the passion of digital processes is to globally enrich the existing physical Supply Chain techniques, the aim of the metaverse is to build a digital monarchy and convert it into the actual world. There are various Supply Chain issues and areas to consider [18].

11.5.1   Effective Cooperation Among All Supply Chain Stages

The metaverse has the potential to increase communication across all Supply Chain stages, both inside and outside. Enhanced connection possibilities allow for a direct integrated effort with suppliers to alter production costs and streamline and speedup the synchronization accompanying the supply processes. This assembly will convert the entire supply chain translucent and malleable, allowing suppliers and buyers to conduct clear and efficient cost discussions [19].

11.5.2   Chain of Custody Transparency

Even for international supply chain management experts, understanding global supply networks is complicated and difficult. At the moment, stakeholders, workers, investors, and clients want to know more about the sources of raw materials, as well as who makes the components and where they are completed. They want openness with regards to the ecological impact and other side effects on the supply chains they are working with.

The metaverse is capable of enhancing supply chain clarity by providing 3D illustrations of how businesses create, deliver, and advertise their goods. Interested parties have better access to: Lead periods; Current delivery costs; Transit duration; congestion. The Supply Chain's confidence, trust, and efficiency will increase as a result of this transparency and visibility [20].

11.5.2.1   Manufacturing

Customers will have easy access to virtual tools and 3D visualization because of the metaverse, increasing responsibility and clarity. This will boost inventiveness and accelerate the potential for mass customization (i.e. personalized items). Additionally, it will make it simpler to reproduce items digitally, enabling companies and manufacturing processes to better allocate resources among sites throughout the supply chain and to operate alternate production scenarios [21].

By decreasing downtime, promoting the acceptance of alternatives, and facilitating quick changeovers in the plant, this is expected to reduce disruption of actual manufacturing operations. Additionally, it will have a significant impact on how consumers' demands for personalized goods are met, making it possible for these things to be produced profitably in traditional facilities that are now built for mass manufacturing [10].

11.5.2.2   Product Lifecycles

The metaverse is the perfect setting for cooperation and idea sharing. It will be simple for internal and external stakeholders to collaborate on the designs of new products, present these concepts to manufacturers in the same forum, and receive prompt response. As a result, the time it takes for new products to reach the market will be shortened, and the creation of useful designs will proceed more quickly and intelligently.

11.6   Forecast of the First Application Areas

11.6.1   Smart City

Metaverse, a virtual reality that replicates reality, makes use of digital twin technology, which is a crucial tool for creating smart cities. Digital twin technology may create a visible, manageable digital twin city by digitally mapping the real environment and comprehensively capturing urban data such as individuals, cars, objects, and space. It may enhance urban management and services, increase resource use efficiency, and raise consumer quality of life [22].

11.6.2   The Entertainment and Gaming Industries

The advancement of interactive technology has significantly increased the sensation of involvement in games, which may significantly improve user experience, effectiveness, and satisfaction [23].

11.6.3   Digital Exhibit, Digital Tourist Industry

The development of a metaverse can improve digital tourist industry and digital exhibition. The advancement of digital twin technology and interactive technology enables consumers to transcend time, distance, and other constraints to easily explore picturesque locations throughout the world and have an interactive experience.

11.6.4   Education

The development of Metaverse can aid in the promotion of children's education, professional gaming, and preschool education. The following ways in which the metaverse might help education: - Immersive, replicating realistic settings to enhance the understanding of educational content; - Avoiding the harms of reality experiments [24].

11.6.5   Economy

Block chain technology, decentralization, and the growth and emergence of new sectors inside the Metaverse may all efficiently promote economic growth.

11.6.6   Social

Social platforms centered on scenarios, virtual meetups, and establishing new connections The metaverse blurs the lines between time and space, increasing the distance between humans. People in the Metaverse can interact at any time and from any location. The metaverse can facilitate numerous types of social interaction [25].

11.7   Industrial Metaverse for Remote Manufacturing

A methodical discipline called the Industrial Metaverse integrates hardware with data analytics and machine learning, time periods with network systems, consciousness with human-machine interfaces, and customization with the Metaverse. By lowering expenses associated with compliance, minimizing unexpected outages, reducing wastage of raw materials, raising productivity, and enhancing training, the Industrial Metaverse may add value to current production systems [26]. A pandemic like COVID-19 also drives businesses to use more effective practical statement to boost output. In general, implementing the Industrial Metaverse offers substantial benefits.

11.7.1   Industrial Cyber-Physical Metaverse Systems

The conceptual idea of the use of cyber-physical systems developed for mechanism/progression tracking in keen manufacturing processes using the "5C" design, which stands for connection, conversion, cyber, cognition, and configuration. The suggested "5C" design is devoid of visualization and interactivity. To increase visualization and interactivity, the Industrial Metaverse system might be constructed on top of the "5C" architecture. The cyber-physical Industrial Metaverse Systems depicted in Figure 11.6 can provide an immersive experience by acting as a virtual reality platform for human-CPS collaboration [27].

The initial connection layer in the focuses on data collecting utilizing sensor nodes and data processing chips are examples of hardware. There are four types of data collected in this selection: static property data, real-time machining operations data, real-time health monitoring data, and quality measurement data [28].

The second conversion layer is responsible for developing ways for converting raw data into meaningful data. This process includes procedures such as data processing, information extraction, data acquisition, and so on.

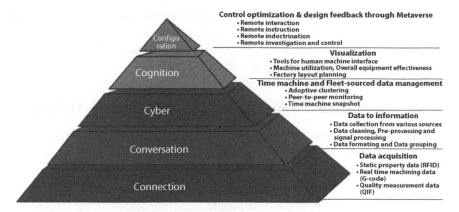

Figure 11.6 Layout of cyber-physical industrial metaverse systems.

The third cyber security layer maintains all devices' nonlinear response in order to determine the similarities of particular machine behavior in a network with previous resources. This layer focuses on peer-to-peer communication.

Through visualization tools such as risk monitors, machinery usage, enhanced power efficiency charts, and industrial topology optimization models, the fourth cognitive layer improves human-machine interaction.

The Metaverse, the fifth configuration layer, creates blueprints of what the data is displaying; the management can then make decisions and design the plan directly. The fifth configuration layer can be used for a wide range of purposes.

Improve human perception and communication with theoretical relationships, as well as between various users and CPS. This interaction can take place between humans, machines, or machines and humans. Experts can give remote guidance to address difficulties [26].

Remote programming: Provide a more user-friendly platform than physical instruction. This increases retention of knowledge.

Remote Analysis and Operate: The professional can manage the device virtually, for example, by sending command signals using Linux CNC software.

11.8   Impact of Industrial Metaverse in Manufacturing Industry

The metaverse is a collection of technologies that enable permanent, virtual models of real-world elements such as people, places, and objects. These technologies are not only restricted to digital simulations and games used for amusement, but also provide some very substantial economic potential. The following five significant impacts that AR/VR and MR will bring to manufacturing during the next few decades [29].

11.8.1   Increasing the Speed and Safety of Employee Training

Numerous companies are using Virtual reality headsets to instruct staff members on how to operate and maintain equipment rather than having them utilize actual, potentially hazardous, challenging technology. Additionally, immersive training, which blends VR's sensation of embodiment with cognitive approach, machine learning, and structural features, enhances the learning process for employees, particularly younger ones, as opposed to making them stay in a lecture whole day. In comparison to on-the-job training with heavy machinery or hazardous situations, trainees also gain from being able to commit errors in a virtualized environment without suffering real-world repercussions [30].

Due to these advantages, many businesses are trying to implement VR instruction as the initial step in on boarding new workers, particularly for situations involving major industries or other industrial environments.

11.8.2   Improvements Could be Obtained by Simulations Before Physical Implementations

Digital twins, a technology that digitally recreates every element of a physical location (or item) to create a virtual "twin," are an element of the metaverse. Digital twins can be employed in production to compare a product's design to the actual thing that is produced, checking for design flaws, for example, or virtual environments can be built up for simulation. As an illustration, many manufacturers of automated vehicles now use simulations of actual settings to improve and effectively train the automobiles how to work [31].

11.8.3   Utilizing AR/VR for Field Service Personnel to Maintain Equipment While on the Job

Frontline employees and professionals can receive help for equipment maintenance and assistance using AR, VR, and MR technologies, similar to training simulations for inexperienced employees. This picked up steam during the pandemic, as travel constraints and medical issues affected everyone support teams.

Many options for remote support don't need extra technology, such as specialist AR glasses or enormous VR headsets, which is advantageous for businesses in the sector. Many businesses are investigating the usage of augmented reality with their current technology, including mobile devices and tablets. Many businesses accelerated their use of AR/VR technology as a result of the pandemic [32].

11.8.4 Globally Integrated Product Design Collaboration

The pandemic has expedited VR-related activity in product development for manufacturers, which is another significant sector. Engineers could engage together on concepts in meeting spaces when all of them in the workplace, but when everyone started working from home, a new method was immediately required. Design engineers may work virtually from anywhere in the world using VR to develop a digital representation [33].

11.8.5 Creating Physical Assets from Digital Concepts and Incorporating Physical Objects with Digital Assets

Manufacturers will have a number of options when the real and virtual worlds merge, possibly creating new revenue sources. Simulated trading, in which a video gamer may buy digital goods with actual cash, has existed for a time. However, new ideas are emerging in which actual objects can be manufactured by designs originating in the virtual environment [34].

11.9 Six Cases of Early Industrial and Commercial Metaverse Application

11.9.1 Product Innovation and Layout

Not only is BMW utilizing augmented reality (AR) to speed up the planning and manufacturing of cutting-edge goods. As per Luis Bollinger, co-founder of Holo-Light, whose platform BMW is using to transmit and work on 3D visuals, enhanced reality (XR) streaming has now become an extremely prevalent option for companies trying to reduce expenses related to product design and shorten lead times [18].

Bollinger claims that among the greatest economic advantages derives besides not needing to construct and deliver as several complex geometries. As a result, designers may analyze designs more quickly and individually. He says, "For BMW, that implies employees can collaborate over various locations, "It saves time on travel since they can meet in this virtual area." It also emphasizes the longevity of 3D graphics as a cost-cutting factor. While real prototypes can shatter if handled excessively, their virtual equivalents can be utilized repeatedly with little deterioration.

11.9.2   Hands-On Training

Training is one of the most obvious and broadly applicable uses for metaverse technology. (See image for top results from our poll of the most compelling metaverse use cases.) In example, virtual reality (VR) may unite individuals without the cost and delay of going to a central training venue.

It's a tactic Nokia has been using since 2021, when we started to consider VR as a logical step up from connecting people via video conferencing capabilities. While teaching through video conferencing can be very one-sided, virtual reality makes learning far more useful and interactive [18].

11.9.3   Support and Preparation for Surgery

Brazilian fraternal twins Bernardo and Arthur Lima had a spectacular VR-guided treatment to separate them in August 2022, demonstrating the potential of metaverse medical advancements. Surgical intervention VR and AR solutions, like those offered by Holo-Light user Enhatch, are showing their value in the operating room even though remote treatment is still a ways off [35].

"Enhatch offers an AI software solution that takes 2D scans of bones and body components and converts them into 3D objects," says Luis Bollinger of Holo-Light. They employ augmented reality and virtual reality to see these 3D images and use them for exercise so that surgeons may better prepare for surgery. "Enhatch utilizes VR to offer a virtual training room, but according to Bollinger, when rules let it, augmented reality will be used in real-world surgeries. By placing a virtual image of the relevant body portion over the real one, surgeons may monitor the scars and actions they had intended when organizing the procedure.

11.9.4   Employee Orientation

Employee onboarding is another pandemic-inspired use case for the metaverse. With more teams functioning remotely and geographically divided, it's becoming increasingly difficult to make new workers feel accepted and involved.

Gilberto Serra of Nokia believes VR might assist in this area. "It's incredibly tough to connect individuals when the team is dispersed all around the world," he explains. "This is where additional sorts of metaverse experience, in addition to the usual Teams or Zoom experience, might be beneficial." Every Friday, Serra's team hosts a 30-minute VR-only learning session: a metaverse update on the "lunch and learn" concept that is already popular at many firms. They are currently working on broadening the concept to be used throughout the firm [18].

This will be a lot more engaging experience than desktop video conferencing software. Participants view other participants using virtual reality (VR) headsets as avatars, while the presenter is represented by a hologram with realistic facial expressions and movement. Full 3D holograms may be projected onto AR glasses when 5G-Advanced networks are deployed, according to Serra, giving participants the impression that they are all in the same room [36].

11.9.5 Virtual Assistance for Hands-On Work

One particularly effective use case for AR is the provision of virtual instruction for those performing new and technically hard hands-on labor, such as rescue workers, field technicians, or firemen. Virtual overlays can give individuals critical information about what to search for, where to focus their attention, and how to perform the activity effectively.

For example, Bosch has created an augmented reality application that instructs its aftermarket workshops on how to do specialized maintenance and repair activities on automobiles, such as readjusting driver assistance sensors after replacing the windshield. It is estimated that guided help like this can save the time required to complete some tasks by up to 15% [37].

11.9.6 Networking, Socializing, and Developing

Work means more to us than just completing the task at hand, as we learned during the epidemic. Many of us discovered that we missed the social aspects of the office, from unexpected meetings at the coffee machine to the opportunity to simply hang out with co-workers.

The internal think tank of international marketing agency Wunderman Thompson, Wunderman Thompson Intelligence, is one business that holds this opinion. Global director Emma Chiu stated on the Nokia podcast that "this feeling of social presence was overlooked during the epidemic. Microsoft and Meta are two platforms that are attempting to develop workplaces that provide this social presence [38].

11.10   Issues in Metaverse

11.10.1   Communication Issue

The Metaverse's interaction technology must adhere to the required specifications in order to serve as a bridge between the virtual and physical worlds: The wearable, accessible, inexpensive active gadget is easy to operate. Users can disregard technological evidence thanks to the interactive medium's opacity, which helps them fully become fully immersed in the virtual world [37].

11.10.2   Computational Issues

Calculation, storage, and data transfer are the three factors that make up computing power, which is the capacity to handle data. In the era of the digital economy, computing power is a crucial resource, and its structure is a crucial support for scientific advancement.

Metaverse entails a broader operator base, enhanced system capabilities, and more processing power, which is a vital component of Metaverse. The emergence of new marketing strategies and the cloud computing-based Metaverse platforms have raised the need for computational resources and opened up new opportunities for their growth. Substantial demands are placed on consumer device speed and host resilience by the cloud storage, cloud computing, cloud graphics, and other technologies employed by Metaverse. Computation intricacy, energy consumption, and speed must all be continually increased in Metaverse [39].

11.10.3   Ethical Issues

Individuals now own a new identity due to the metaverse, which has also produced a completely a fresh setting in which to exist and communicate. There, personal networks are more intricate. In order to maintain a positive and an ecosystem that is well-organized inside the Metaverse, it is necessary for the Metaverse, as a next-generation system, to govern and limit user behavior as well as create explicit ethical and moral guidelines [40].

The occurrences that emerge in the Metaverse as a result of the lack or confusion of the appropriate moral rules, which clash with the ethical norms of the actual society, are referred to as the ethical and moral dilemmas of the Metaverse.

11.10.4 Cyber-Syndrome

An excessive use of the Internet can result in the physical, societal, and rational state known as "cyber-syndrome." Electronic devices are now more compact and gotten lighter as interactive ways have continued to emerge. People are using the Internet more and more as a result of technology optimization. The Metaverse and the real world are interconnected at the same time. The problem of cyber syndrome is made even more problematic by the blending of the real and the virtual and by the extent of Metaverse involvement [41].

11.11 Challenges of Industrial Metaverse in Engineering Applications

As the Metaverse is inextricably tied to the physical realm, cyber security and data privacy must be resolved. The following are the four key challenges to establishing the Industrial Metaverse in Manufacturing:

- Cost: The cost of using Metaverse technology by SMEs must be greatly decreased.
- Standards Compliance: Statistics in a Metaverse system would be conveyed using multiple technical standards, and consistency among these specifications is one of the most difficult difficulties.
- Computational Performance: A huge amount of users in the Metaverse must communicate via coding process and connections. As a result, computational resources, i.e. data processing, retention, and transmission, is critical for its execution.

The primary aspect of the Industrial Metaverse system is that it improves direct communication with physical items, improves visibility in the cyber-physical scheme's configuration layer, and is regarded a digital twin of the workplace. It enables frontline workers by enhancing staff efficiency, quality and yield, lowering operating expenses, speeding troubleshooting, lowering the cost of professional on-site inspections, and enhancing system reliability [42].

11.12   Metaverse Accelerates Economic Development for Emerging Economies

As the market continues to falter, organizations are relying on the idea of virtual environment, often known as the "Metaverse." When a function of fragmented communities, operational mishaps, and increasing prices of centralized management, this happens just as inflationary has crested and there is an immediate need for decentralized planning. It ought to be noted that the metaverse is appealing since its central tenet is that it is a capitalistic society. Every element of the metaverse is created to improve the target appearance of the product. In general, consumers of the metaverse can establish a fantasy life and mode of living via shopping, playing online games, hanging out with friends, attending conferences, and working [43].

In the metaverse, modeling and simulation methods may be used to increase production and accessibility for users. To organize stockpiles, workforce efforts, and future forecasts, a "business metaverse system" that resembles the real context and allows for increased effectiveness of creation, growth, and execution may be employed. In addition, the upcoming decentralized financial services in the metaverse will severely undermine traditional economic models. The metaverse will allow for the shift of power from organized banks and other financial institutions to specific customers. Borrowing and lending funds will be much easier, clearer, and uncomplicated. Acquisitions, trades, commerce, and financing will all be possible in the metaverse shortly [44].

The metaverse will indeed promote overall economic growth by expanding activities and interactions as the line between the physical realm and the immersive virtual disappears. A financial market will maintain the interactions humanity has had with highly valuable virtual employment.

The metaverse has the ability to change our actual situation, though digitally, despite the current controversy and resistance. It will keep creating new opportunities to make money and contribute to the growth of the global economy.

11.13   The Metaverse in Logistics

Numerous industries, including those in the automobile, e-commerce, medical, production, and logistics, have found extensive use for the Metaverse [45]. The innovative example for showcasing cutting-edge technology in the machine-learning assisted automation architecture is the combination of production and logistical workflows for stable processes. The digital twin, a virtual representation of actual activities, has assisted businesses in reducing costs and accidents and maximizing resource allocation and planning [46]. Digital twins and other interface features are also incorporated into the metaverse. For a smooth functioning and enhanced customer experience, the academics can examine the additional demands of the digital twins and other organizational requirements that must be integrated into the metaverse stage. Using organization data from a particular industry, a service strategy paradigm based on the digital twin and an efficient allocation of resources can be investigated. This will serve as a model for other digital twin initiatives taking place in a Metaverse. Applications of the metaverse are frequently used in new methodologies developing virtual and augmented reality to improve the experience of customers and suppliers. Manufacturing, supply chain, and logistics procedures in metaverse operations incorporate physical and digital features in an unprecedented manner. Supply chain partners may now examine different products' characteristics, communicate with them, and, most significantly, acquire all the necessary current statistics from the region where their preference [47]. Immerse interface with the supply chain across all phases, from any location, may revolutionize the logistics and production workflows and give rational decisions for the producer and all the customers engaged in the operations. The metaverse presents exceptional chances to revolutionize the standard logistics process. Modern packing and loading of items into unmanned vehicles for final delivery to the location will undergo dramatic changes.

The machine learning-enabled digital twin is able to get information on anticipated and realistic delays in the completion in the manufacturer's supply of products and materials, which makes the most effective modifications in the production planning to account for the delays and disturbances. The Manufacturing Execution System (MES) is then given these suggestions by the digital twin for implementation in order to maximize on-time delivery to consumers [48]. The three functions that make up the Machine Learning-Enabled Digital Twin Framework are shown in Figure 11.7.

Instead of using offline modifications to production planning and control, the Digital Twin Learning Engine, shown in Figure 11.8, provides real-time modification of the MES and other processes based on expected modifications in the deliveries of important components to the producer. The Digital Twin receives production schedules as well as moment images of equipment performance and order data from interconnected production technologies like Metaverse [49].

The communication overload stated above can be summarized and/or reduced via augmented reality, making it easier to understand and, more significantly, accessible by a user. As seen in Figure 11.9, data from the reality can be superimposed on a computer display along with suggestions and important performance indicators. This gives users the chance to choose or circumvent a suggested scheduling conflict that would be a mistake since it goes against the digital twin's training format's cumulative

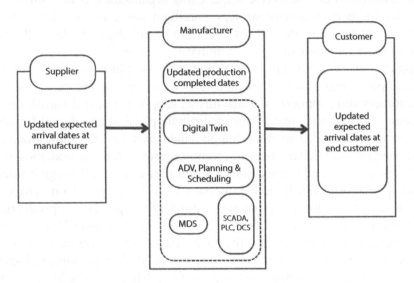

Figure 11.7 Three modules of machine learning-enabled digital twin framework.

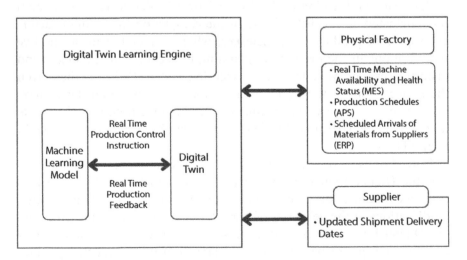

Figure 11.8 Data flow pattern of digital twin learning engine.

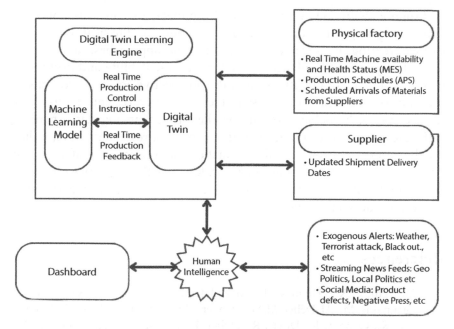

Figure 11.9 Hybrid intelligence for augmented reality combines machine and human intelligence.

memory of perception [49]. Figure 11.9 depicts three pathways of external data that could make up or endanger an established order. When these occurrences are foreseen in advance, there may be opportunity for preventive rescheduling and the deployment of preventive measures to avoid the effect from spreading throughout the production line and to speed up recovery [50].

11.14   Conclusion

For commercial processes and logistics, this research seeks to clarify the term "Industrial Metaverse." The main features of the Industrial Metaverse approach are that it enhances direct experience with tangible goods, enhances visibility in the configuration layer of the malware environment, and is viewed as a virtual environment of the workplace. It offers the Industrial Metaverse in this study to increase interaction, education, assimilation, exploration, medicine, and administration. The usage of Metaverse in numerous aspects of industrial applications is growing quickly. The use of it has expanded to include things like industrial logistics and supply chain. While the advent of the metaverse presents novel and stimulating stages of communication between the physical and virtual worlds, creating chances and future professional approaches, adoption rate presents significant challenges, moral standards, stability and protection, proper conduct, confidentiality, and the prospective emancipation of segments of society who lack access to the infrastructure required to access the metaverse. It enables frontline workers by enhancing staff efficiency, yield and improve, lowering operating expenses, resolving issues, reducing the expense of professional consultations, and enhancing safety on site. The research methodology outlines a wide range of prospective directions for additional research study of the several facets of the metaverse and its effects on industrial society.

References

1. Dwivedi, Y.K., Hughes, L., Baabdullah, A.M., Ribeiro-Navarrete, S., Giannakis, M., Al-Debei, M.M., Dennehy, D., Metri, B., Buhalis, D., Cheung, C.M.K., Conboy, K., Doyle, R., Dubey, R., Dutot, V., Felix, R., Goyal, D.P., Gustafsson, A., Hinsch, C., Jebabli, I., Janssen, M., Kim, Y.-G., Kim, J., Koos, S., Kreps, D., Kshetri, N., Kumar, V., Ooi, K.-B., Papagiannidis, S., Pappas, I.O., Polyviou, A., Park, S.-M., Pandey, N., Queiroz, M.M., Raman, R., Rauschnabel, P.A., Shirish, A., Sigala, M., Spanaki, K., Tan, G.W.-H., Tiwari, M.K., Viglia, G., Wamba, S.F., Metaverse beyond the hype: Multidisciplinary perspectives on emerging challenges, opportunities, and agenda for research, practice and policy. *Int. J. Inf. Manag.*, 66, 102542, 2022.

2. Ning, H., Wang, H., Lin, Y., Wang, W., Dhelim, S., Farha, F., Ding, J., Daneshmand, M., A survey on metaverse: The state-of-the-art, technologies, applications, and challenges. *Comput. Society.*, 1, 1–34, 2022, https://doi. org/10. 48550/arXiv.2111.09673.

3. Damar, M., Metaverse shape of your life for future: A bibliometric snapshot. *J. Metaverse.*, 1, 1, 1–8, 2021.

4. Park, S.M. and Kim, Y.G., A metaverse: Taxonomy, components, applications, and open challenges. *IEEE Access.*, 10, 4209–4251, 2022.

5. Reuters, Italy's serie a enters the metaverse to showcase new way to watch soccer, 2022, https://www.reuters.com/lifestyle/sports/.

6. Amorim, T., Tapparo, L., Marranghello, N., Silva, A.C., Pereira, A.S., A multiple intelligences theory-based 3D virtual lab environment for digital systems teaching. *Proc. Comput. Sci.*, 29, 1413–1422, 2014.

7. Fox, M., The NFT market is now worth more than $7 billion, but legal issues facing the nascent sector could hinder its growth, JPMorgan says. November 19, 2021, https://markets.businessinsider.com/news/currencies/nft-market-worth-7-billion-legal-issues-could-hinder-growth-2021–11.

8. Rauschnabel, P.A., Augmented reality is eating the real-world! The substitution of physical products by holograms. *Int. J. Inf. Manag.*, 57, 102279, 2021.

9. Ivanov, D. and Dolgui, A., A digital supply chain twin for managing the disruption risks and resilience in the era of industry 4.0. Production Planning and Control, 2020, https://doi.org/10.1080/09537287.2020.1768450.

10. Papaioannou, G., Mohammed, A.M., Despoudi, S., Saridakis, G., Papadopoulos, T., The role of adverse economic environment and human capital on collaboration within agri-food supply chains. *Int. J. Inf. Manag.*, 52, 102077, 2020, https://doi.org/10.1016/j.ijinfomgt.2020.102077.

11. Leng, J., Sha, W., Wang, B., Zheng, P., Zhuang, C., Liu, Q., Wuest, T., Mourtzis, D., Wang, L., Industry 5.0: Prospect and retrospect. *J. Manuf. Syst.*, 65, 279–295, 2022.

12. Morgan, J.P., *Opportunitiesin the metaverse*, Onyx, New York, 2022.

13. Golf-Papez, M., Heller, J., Hilken, T., Chylinski, M., de Ruyter, K., Keeling, D.I., Mahr, D., Embracing falsity through the metaverse: The case of synthetic customer experiences. *Business Horizons.*, 65, 6, 739–749, 2022.

14. Industrial metaverse' heralds a new era in automation, 2022, https://drivesn-controls.com/news/fullstory.php/aid/7081/_91Industrial_metaverse_92_heralds_a_new_era_in_automation.html.

15. The industrial metaverse will disrupt global manufacturing, 2022, https://www.market-prospects.com/articles/industrial-metaverse-will-disrupt-globalmanufacturing #:~:text=The%20Metaverse%20is%20bringing%20virtual,the%20digital%20and%20physical%20worlds.

16. What is the industrial metaverse – And why should I care?, 2022, https://new.siemens.com/global/en/company/insights/what-is-the-industrial-metaverse-and-why-should-i-care.html#:~:text=The%20Metaverse%20is%20where%20virtual, better%20and%20find%20optimal%20solutions.

17. Maddikunta, P.K.R., Pham, Q.-V., B, P., Deepa, N., Dev, K., Gadekallu, T.D., Ruby, R., Liyanage, M., Industry 5.0: A survey on enabling technologies and potential applications. *J. Ind. Inf. Integration.*, 26, 100257, 2022.

18. Six use cases from the dawn of the industrial and enterprise metaverse, 2022, https://www.nokia.com/networks/insights/metaverse/six-metaverse-use-cases-for-businesses/.

19. Holmstrom, J., Holweg, M., Lawson, B., Pil, F.K., Wagner, S.M., The digitalization of operations and supply chain management: Theoretical and methodological implications. *J. Oper. Manag.*, 65, 8, 728–734, 2019, https://doi.org/10.1002/joom.1073.

20. Rodríguez-Espíndola, O., Chowdhury, S., Beltagui, A., Albores, P., The potential of emergent disruptive technologies for humanitarian supply chains: The integration of blockchain, artificial intelligence and 3D printing. *Int. J. Prod. Res.*, 58, 15, 4610–4630, 2020.

21. Spanaki, K., Gürgüç, Z., Adams, R., Mulligan, C., Data supply chain (DSC): Research synthesis and future directions. *Int. J. Prod. Res.*, 56, 13, 4447–4466, 2018, https://doi.org/10.1080/00207543.2017.1399222.

22. Bibri, S.E. and Allam, Z., The metaverse as a virtual form of data-driven smart urbanism: On post-pandemic governance through the prism of the logic of surveillance capitalism. *Smartcities.*, 5, 2, 2022, 10.3390.

23. Brown, A., Gaming, fashion, music: The metaverse across industries. *Emerging Technol.*, 101, 1–1, 2022.

24. Mistretta, S., The metaverse—An alternative education space. *AI, Comput. Sci. Robotics Technol.*, 0, 1–23, 2022, https://doi.org/10.5772/acrt.05.

25. Oh, H.J., Kim, J., Chang, J.J.C., Park, N., Lee, S., Social benefits of living in the metaverse: The relationships among social presence, supportive interaction, social self-efficacy, and feelings of loneliness. *Comput. Hum. Behavior.*, 139, 107498, 2023.

26. Lee, J. and Kundu, P., Integrated cyber-physical systems and industrial metaverse for remotemanufacturing. *Manuf. Letters.*, 34, 12–15, 2022.

27. Lee, J., Bagheri, B., Kao, H.A., A cyber-physical systems architecture for industry 4.0-based manufacturing systems. *Manuf Letters.*, 3, 18–23, 2015.

28. Liu, C., Vengayil, H., Zhong, R.Y., Xu, X., A systematic development method forcyberphysicalmachine tools. *J. Manuf. Syst.*, 48, 13–24, 2018.

29. 5 ways the industrial metaverse will impact manufacturers, 2022, https://www. automate.org/industry-insights/5-ways-the-industrial-metaverse-will-impact-manufacturers.

30. Safi, R., Industrial metaverse: The factory of the future, 2022, https://arpost. co/2022/07/23/industrial-metaverse-factory-of-the-future/.

31. Dincelli, E. and Yayla, A., Immersive virtual reality in the age of the Metaverse: A hybrid-narrative review based on the technology affordance perspective. *J. Strateg. Inf. Syst.*, 31, 101717, 2022.

32. Neagoy, C., Using augmented and virtual reality to overcome real workforce challenges, https://www.smartindustry.com/tools-of-transformation/augmented-reality/article/11286936/using-augmented-and-virtual-reality-to-overcome-real-workforce-challenges, 2022.

33. Wang, X., Wang, J., Wu, C., Xu, S., Ma, W., Engineering brain: Metaverse for future engineering. *AI Civil Eng.*, 1, 2, 2022, https://doi.org/10.1007/s43503-022-00001-z.

34. Far, S.B. and Rad, A.I., Applying digital twins in metaverse: Userinterface, security and privacy challenges. *J. Metaverse.*, 2, 1, 8–15, 2022.

35. Garavand, A. and Aslani, N., Metaverse phenomenon and its impact on health: A scoping review. *Inf. Med. Unlocked.*, 32, 101029, 2022.

36. Chylinski, M., Heller, J., Hilken, T., Keeling, D.I., Mahr, D., de Ruyter, K., Augmented reality marketing: A technology-enabled approach to situated customer experience. *Australas. Marketing J.*, 28, 4, 374–384, 2020.

37. Hwang, G.-J. and Chien, S.-Y., Definition, roles, and potential research issues of the metaverse in education: An artificial intelligence perspective. *Comput. Educ.: Artif. Intell.*, 3, 100082, 2022.

38. Wang, B., Zheng, Yin, Y., Shih, A., Wang, L., Toward human-centric smart manufacturing: A human-cyber-physical systems (HCPS) perspective. *J. Manuf. Syst.*, 63, 471–490, 2022.

39. Bibri, S.E., Allam, Z., Krogstie, J., The metaverse as a virtual form of data-driven smart urbanism: Platformization and its underlying processes, institutional dimensions, and disruptive impacts. *Comput.Urban Sci.*, 2, 24, 2022. https://doi.org/10.1007/s43762-022-00051-0.

40. Bibri, S.E. and Allam, Z., The metaverse as a virtual form of data-driven smart cities: The ethics of the hyper-connectivity, datafication, algorithmization, and platformization of urban society. *Comput.Urban Sci.*, 2, 22, 2022. https://doi.org/10.1007/s43762-022-00050-1.

41. Tlili, A., Huang, R., Shehata, B., Liu, D., Zhao, J., Metwally, A.H.S., Wang, H., Denden, M., Bozkurt, A., Lee, L.-H., Beyoglu, D., Altinay, F., Sharma, R.C., Altinay, Z., Li, Z., Liu, J., Ahmad, F., Hu, Y., Salha, S., Abed, M., Burgos, D., Is metaverse in education a blessing or a curse: A combined content and bibliometric analysis. *Smart Learn. Environ.*, 9, 24, 2022.

42. Mystakidis, S., Metaverse. *Encyclopedia*, 2, 486–497, 2022.

43. Dubey, R., Gunasekaran, A., Childe, S.J., Bryde, D.J., Giannakis, M., Foropon, C., Hazen, B.T., Big data analytics and artificial intelligence pathway tooperational performance under the effects of entrepreneurial orientation andenvironmental dynamism: A study of manufacturing organisations. *Int. J. Prod. Econ.*, 226, 107599, 2020.

44. Thomason, J., Metaverse, token economies, and non-communicable diseases. *Global Health J.*, 6, 3, 164–167, 2022.

45. Liu, M., Fang, S., Dong, H., Xu, C., Review of digital twin about concepts, technologies, and industrial applications. *J. Manuf. Syst.*, 58, 346–361, 2021.

46. Roe, M., Spanaki, K., Ioannou, A., Zamani, E.D., Giannakis, M., Drivers and challenges of internet of things diffusion in smart stores: A field exploration. *Technol. Forecast. Soc. Change.*, 178, 121593, 2022, https://doi.org/10.1016/J.TECHFORE.2022.121593.

47. Corallo, A., Latino, M.E., Menegoli, M., Pontrandolfo, P., A systematic literature review to explore traceability and lifecycle relationship. *Int. J. Prod. Res.*, 58, 15, 4789–4807, 2020, https://doi.org/10.1080/00207543.2020.1771455.

48. Greis, N.P., Nogueira, M.L., Rohde, W., Digital Twin Framework for Machine Learning-Enabled Integrated Production and Logistics Processes. In A. Dolgui *et al.* (Eds.). *Advances in Production Management Systems,* Artificial Intelligence for Sustainable and Resilient Production Systems, APMS 2021. IFIP Adv. Inf. Commun. Technol., 630, Springer, France, 2021.

49. Greis, N.P., Nogueira, M.L., Rohde, W., Towards learning-enabled digital twin with augmented reality for resilient production scheduling. *IFAC Papers OnLine.*, 55, 10, 1912–1917, 2022.

50. Villalonga, A., Negri, E., Biscardo, G., Castano, F., Haber, R.E., Fumagalli, L., Macchi, M., A decision-making framework for dynamic scheduling of cyber-physical production systems based on digital twins. *Annu. Rev. Control.*, 51, 357–373, 2021.

12

Augmented Reality Applications in Gaming

Rohan Harish, Abhiram Vollala and Shaik Himam Saheb*

*Faculty of Science and Technology, The ICFAI Foundation for Higher Education,
Hyderabad, India*

Abstract

Creating new games is growing exponentially to satisfy the general public's demands using the game's real-world interface. To better comprehend augmented reality (AR), we first present the concept of AR technology and Unity3D's features and specialized content. Next, we use Unity3D to analyze AR using several approaches. This essay attempts to analyze Unity3D research for technology development in a systematic way, with a thorough analysis of the issue and a look at the difficulties and potential of the technology in the future. By merging Unity3D software with the Vuforia software development kit (SDK) and EasyAR SDK, AR is implemented to address the issues of low stability and constrained application conditions in traditional AR SDK. The generated results can be applied to mobile devices and the Hololens AR glasses. In parallel, the three-dimensional (3D) registration method for AR is being researched. A principle and a method for implementing AR in Unity3D and SDK are also provided. Finally, using the same image markers, the angle variation experiment was used to evaluate and examine the stability of the two SDKs. The strength of the model is increased as compared to the conventional system. Human–machine interaction and mobile apps are keenly interested in using AR based on mobile terminals. Mobile AR technology integrates intelligent display, registration tracking, virtual and real-world convergence, and human–computer interactions via portable devices or smart terminals. With the customer's actual scene fully docked, the 3D virtual object can be displayed, expanding the perceived range. Totem functions of the Vuforia engine are recognized and tracked when creating a 3D scene model using Unity3D modeling. It is possible to play both animation and video. Virtual buttons

Corresponding author: himamsaheb@ifheindia.org

Chandrashekhar A, Shaik Himam Saheb, Sandeep Kumar Panda, S. Balamurugan and Sheng-Lung Peng (eds.)
Metaverse and Immersive Technologies: An Introduction to Industrial, Business and Social Applications, (325–348) © 2023 Scrivener Publishing LLC

can also develop interactions between virtual reality and controls. The VR and AR worlds are connected using the Vuforia SDK's AR application, which acts as a central hub. 3D tracking and registration are possible because of the combination of real-world video and virtual objects on the mobile terminal's monitor. This article gives an example of developing your game and employing AR tools in a Unity3D environment.

Keywords: Game development, game interface, augmented reality technology, Unity3D, EasyAR SDK, Vuforia SDK, software development kit (SDK), Hololens, 3D registration

12.1   Introduction

In addition to the quick advancement of contemporary science and technology, the development of new technology is accelerating; one such example is augmented reality. As it is challenging to experience entity information in the real world within a specific time frame, seamless integration of real and virtual world information is described as the "seamless" integration of new technologies. By applying science and technology, for example, computer simulation, the virtual information used in the real world was perceived by the senses as a sensory experience beyond reality. In many developing technology applications, real and virtual things are concurrently overlaid onto the same image or environment [1–3, 9–11]. As people's lives get better nowadays, so do their entertainment options. People's daily life now can't function without video games. How can a reality-based scenario become a virtual feature that will become a popular trend for game producers, making the gaming interface appear more realistic? This article introduces augmented reality technology based on Unity3D development methods.

Augmented reality is a growing area in virtual reality research. The real world provides a huge amount of information that is challenging to replicate on a computer—the planets evidence this issue in video games and virtual worlds [12–14].

12.2   Augmented Reality Technology

The information from the real world and the news from the virtual world are shown in augmented reality, also known as AR, and they complement and stack on top of one another. In the visualization of augmented reality, also known as AR, the information from the actual world and the data from the virtual world appear side by side and complement one another. The augmented reality features include multimedia, three-dimensional modeling, simultaneous video display and control, multisensory fusion, real-time tracking and registration, etc. When applied broadly, augmented validity differs from the way information is perceived by individuals.

There are three key aspects of an AR system:

Integration of the real and virtual information worlds

Real-time interactive technology

To further explain, it is situated in a virtual object in three-dimensional space.

A comprehensive augmented reality system comprises several closely coupled, real-time active components, including essential hardware and software.

A sensation of illusion or virtual reality is created by superimposing digitally made visuals onto our real environment.

Due to recent advancements, this technology is now usable with a smartphone.

12.3   History of AR

The earliest instance of augmented reality as we know it now was in Sutherland's work from the 1960s, which used a see-through HMD to transmit 3D graphics. Nevertheless, over the last ten years, enough research has been done on AR to call it a research field. Virtual Fixtures, one of the earliest known AR systems, was created by Louis Rosenberg. Since then, AR has made significant growth and advancements [4, 5, 15–17]. Figure 12.1 shows the history of augmented reality.

12.4   Types of Augmented Reality

- Marker-Based Augmented Reality
- Marker-less Augmented Reality
- Projection-Based Augmented Reality
- Superimposition-Based Augmented Reality. Figure 12.2 presents the types of augmented reality used in Metaverse.

12.4.1   Marker-Based Augmented Reality

In marker-based augmented reality, also known as image recognition, a camera and some visual markers, like a QR code, are utilized to produce

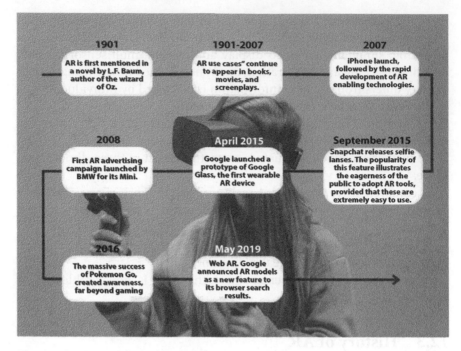

Figure 12.1 History of augmented reality.

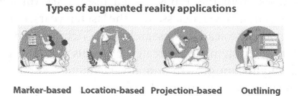

Figure 12.2 Types of augmented reality.

a result only when a reader sees the marker. Using the device's camera, applications that use markers distinguish between markers and other real-world objects; the position and orientation are then determined, and some content or information is layered on the marker [6, 18–22].

12.4.2 Marker-Less Augmented Reality

Markerless augmented reality, sometimes called location-based, position-based, or GPS augmented reality, uses an integrated GPS, digital compass, velocity meter, or accelerometer to show data based on the user's location.

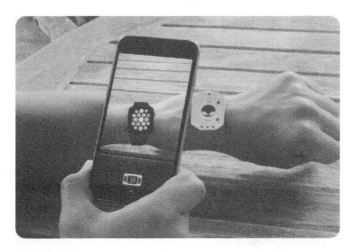

Figure 12.3 Marker-based AR.

Figure 12.3 represents the marker-based AR. The widespread use of smart-phones and their location-aware features are a major driving force behind markerless augmented reality technology. Mobile location-based mapping instructions, finding local businesses, and other apps are some of its most well-liked applications [23–26]. Figure 12.4 shows the marker-less AR.

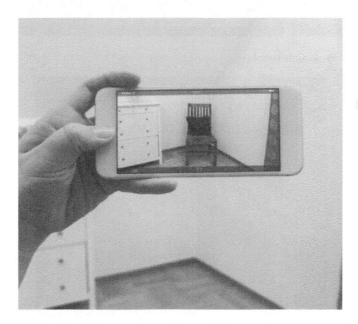

Figure 12.4 Marker-less AR.

12.4.3   Projection-Based Augmented Reality

Artificial light is projected onto actual surfaces to create projection-based augmented reality. Applications that project light onto a real-world surface and then detect when a person touches that light enables human interaction in augmented reality. Figure 12.5 presents the projection-based AR.

12.4.4   Superimposition-Based Augmented Reality

How projection-based augmented reality functions utilize artificial light to project onto actual surfaces. Applications that use projection-based augmented reality to display light on a real-world surface and detect when a person touches that light enable human interaction. Figure 12.6 represents the superimposition-based AR.

Figure 12.5 Projection-based AR.

Figure 12.6 Superimposition-based AR.

12.5   Types of AR

- Monitor-based
- Laptops
- Cell phones
- Projectors (more Ubiquitous Computing)
- Head Mounted Displays
- Video see-through
- Optical see-through

12.6   Monitor-Based

In an implementation method for augmented reality that uses a computer monitor, camera input is used to provide real-world images to the computer. The virtual scene's computer graphics system synthesizes and outputs to the screen display—enhanced user screen to display the finished scene visuals. Although deploying an augmented reality system based on monitors is straightforward, there are few immersive users [27–30].

12.6.1   Working Principle

Below is the augmented reality system work of the three components:

- The head-mounted display
- Tracking system
- Mobile computing ability

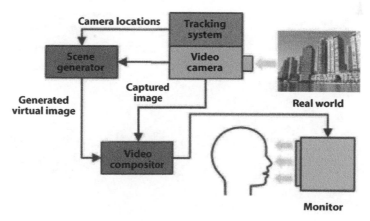

Figure 12.7 Monitor-based working principle.

According to the augmented reality developer, the three elements will be combined into one unit and bound together with a girdle of equipment. Similar to how regular glasses display information, the gadget can wirelessly transmit data [31–35]. Figure 12.7 shows the monitor-based working principle.

12.7   Virtual Reality vs. Augmented Reality

Virtual reality produces a virtual environment and immerses the user, unlike augmented reality, which mixes virtual features into the user's real-world view.

Virtual reality transfers a user into a digital environment made by a computer, unlike augmented reality, which merges the digital and physical worlds.

AR users are conscious of their location in the "real world," unlike VR, which typically has an immersive experience [7, 8, 36–38, 54]. Figure 12.8 shows the virtual vs. augmented reality.

12.7.1   Advantages of Augmented Reality

- It might broaden people's knowledge and information.
- Over great distances, people can exchange experiences.
- It makes gaming even more "real," in my opinion.
- On people's smartphones, things come to life.
- Escapism is what it is.

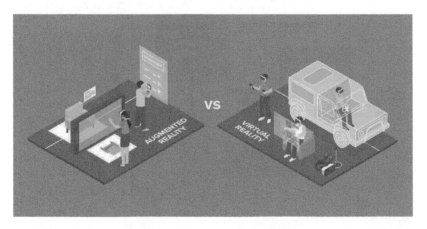

Figure 12.8 Virtual vs. augmented reality.

12.7.2   Disadvantages of Augmented Reality

- Protection from spam.
- AR use in social situations might not be appropriate, according to user experience.
- Openness: Others are free to develop and display their content tiers.

12.8   Issues in Augmented Reality

Performance Issues
Real-time picture processing can be complex and frequently causes augmented reality systems to lag.

Interaction Issues
Because of augmented reality, users find it challenging to engage normally with their surroundings in various circumstances.

Asymmetry Issues
Alignment accuracy is particularly noticeable to those working in augmented reality.

It is essential to calibrate and align properly with the global reference frame.

12.9   Applications of Augmented Reality

12.9.1   Presentation

Can now be made interesting. You can bring your entire lineup to your audience on demand with augmented reality presentations. You can focus on any element of your product lineup as necessary and give them in-depth 3D presentations of each product's features. An example of an AR presentation of a plane is below. Figure 12.9 shows the AR presentations of a plane.

12.9.2   Entertainment

Instead of just watching the show passively, it enables the audience to engage actively in the performance. The enjoyable activities we currently enjoy (movies, video games, and music) will advance in realism, immersion, and interactivity. Figure 12.10 shows the different entertainment models.

Figure 12.9 Presentations.

Figure 12.10 Entertainment.

Figure 12.11 VR/AR weather reports.

12.9.3   Weather Report

News channels and a few apps use this technology now to display weather interactively. A simulation application can simulate three types of precipitation: rain, snow, and hail. It looks at various weather phenomena and how they could be represented in a mobile augmented reality system. Figure 12.11 shows the VR/AR weather reports.

12.9.4   Virtual Studio

Uses this tech to make interactions and meetings more captivating. The Unreal Engine-compatible Swift CG editor for backgrounds allows for creating photorealistic sets, and the Swift Engine renderer comes with data-driven graphics as standard. Designers can interact with their audiences by creating 3D worlds using creative tools. In order to keep viewers interested in the events as they unfold, presenters can freely move around virtual objects like sports players or scoreboards or even through entire virtual scenarios, as seen on election news programs [39–44]. Figure 12.12 shows the virtual studio.

Figure 12.12 Virtual studio.

Figure 12.13 AR/VR clips from movies.

Figure 12.14 AR ads.

Figure 12.15 AR ads.

12.9.5 Movie Special Effects

This technology is very much shown in Sci-Fi movies. Figure 12.13 AR/VR clips from movies. The goal of using augmented reality (AR) in movies is to realistically create a world that would otherwise be impossible. Figure 12.14 shows the AR ads for different headsets. Therefore, it defeats the whole purpose if the robot or spaceship does not appear to be a real one or a component of the scene on the screen. Figure 12.15 presents the AR ads for different applications like ATM, Hotel, Parking etc.

12.10   Advertisement

The term "AR advertising" refers to a type of mobile ad that overlays virtual items, such as 3D models of products or game characters, onto the real-world setting of an AR app user using the smartphone camera [45, 46].

12.11   Simulations

12.11.1   Driving

The HARMAN Augmented Reality (AR) Platform combines the real and virtual worlds to provide real-time, intelligent overlays onto the road surface without blocking the driver's field of vision, resulting in a safer, more intuitive, and interactive driving experience [47–51]. Figures 12.16 and 12.17 shows driving simulation and AR car simulation for driver..

Figure 12.16 Driving simulation.

Figure 12.17 AR car simulation.

Figure 12.18 Airplane simulation.

Figure 12.19 Airplane simulation.

12.11.2 Flying

Used to train trainees and prep them for real-life simulated emergencies, Etc. Figures 12.18 and 12.19 presents the airplane simulation with latitude and altitude through metaverse.

12.12 Navigation

Helps in showing directions in a more interactive and fun manner. AR-based interior navigation overlays directions on a screen over real environments as seen through a smartphone or tablet's camera using this technology [52, 53].

Figure 12.20 AR car navigation.

Figure 12.21 AR CAD.

Figure 12.22 AR video games.

Figure 12.23 AR theme park.

12.13   Unity3D

By doing this, the user can easily navigate intricate buildings without needing a map or other aids. Figures 12.20, 12.21, 12.22 and 12.23 presents the AR car navigation, AR CAD, AR video games and AR theme park.

12.14   CAD

Using the EasyARTM augmented reality engine and the Unity® game engine, the CAD-to-AR for Autodesk® Inventor® technology demonstration allows users to view Inventor 3D models in augmented reality (AR). Integrate it into the Inventor UI is one of the primary aspects of CAD-to-AR for Inventor that allows the user to.

12.15   Video Fames

Physical interactions with 3D models.
You will be able to watch T.V in 3D anywhere.

12.16   Theme Park

Rides can now be even more realistic. What do augmented reality wearables represent for the community of theme parks?

Figure 12.24 Unity logo.

It entails digitally enhanced roller coaster rides that are still housed in real environments, entertaining methods to pass the time for tourists waiting in long lines, and useful ways to enlighten visitors about a particular ride. Figure 12.24 shows the unity logo.

12.17 Introduction of Unity3D

Cross-platform game engine Unity3D was created for PC and Mac OS, PS3, Xbox 360, Wii, iOS, and Android. The installation of the plug-in can be done after Unity3D game production. Unity3D can create online games for Internet Explorer, Firefox, Google Chrome, and Safari. It is not necessary to learn a difficult programming language to develop games with Unity3D because it offers simple interface operation, supports the PhysX physics engine and particle system, and offers an online multiplayer capability.

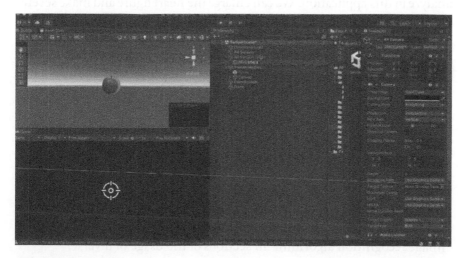

Figure 12.25 A look at unity interface.

The most recent version of Unity, 3.5.x, was released and performed the task of the Flash game. Even personal studio games are now a reality thanks to Unity3D's lowered bar for game production. Using Unity3D, game developers may speed up game creation and lower game production costs. Figure 12.25 shows the unity interface.

It uses an integrated NVIDIA PhysX physics engine to offer accurate physics calculations. Direct has been supported by graphic optimization thanks to OpenGL graphics optimization algorithms. Designers can swiftly create landscapes with natural terrain thanks to terrain processors.

12.18   About Augmented Reality Based on Unity3D

The market is currently saturated with video games and augmented reality software. A captivating technology is augmented reality, and Unity3D development software is a powerful development program. After that, we'll discuss combining augmented reality with the Unity3D game development engine. Some programs, including Anatomy, and 4D, did not previously employ Unity3D and augmented reality. Observing the complex human body structure wherever we are, allows us to learn anatomy in a new way. The application's introduction can teach developers and those curious about human organs more about the human body.

Using this program, we may investigate the human organ by using the user's photos as the research subject. Let's look at the design of the heart, for instance. In that situation, we can upload a picture of the object we like to analyze in this application. We can enlarge the heart figure and make several observations. It has a strong practical application for some individuals. With the help of this technique, we could see how the development of Unity 3D as a whole and the incorporation of augmented reality into games may be considered a specific kind of single-player, single-machine game. Utilizing this technology, which produces an augmented reality of actual events, allows us to join in on the enjoyment and improve the game's realism.

12.19   The Main Technical Problem

The most important aspect of augmented reality is image identification. The use of texture and color characteristics, broken down into global and local features, to distinguish the target from the image is referred to as an "image recognition algorithm" in sections of the usage of diverse.

A statistical classification method is used to differentiate between the targets and identify the images to compare the atlas inosculation template library and the global approach.

For target recognition with substantial obstacles such as complicated block interactions, lighting, and zooming, the global strategy is labor-intensive and has a limited range of applications. Local features of objects, such as important edges or key points, are used as the description in the local feature descriptor. When mapping an image feature to a template image collection, matching is used to assess its quality. Interior points can accurately check the feature points; exterior points, on the other hand, cannot.

Even if just part of the feature points match, the predicted, successful identification and location can still be made as long as there is a big enough interior point. Effective tactics can prevent incorrect matching. Due to the complex nature of the Augmented Reality application, the demand for a Feature descriptor is not subject to variations in visual angle and light.

The data are minimized and perfectly suited for the shading problem by the local feature descriptors' descriptions of sifting and waves. These picture recognition algorithms are now the most popular and widely utilized. Based on these two operators, there are currently numerous adjustments made to suit their various needs. Identifying and placing the angular point are corner detection procedures.

What the angular point is not evident. A common misconception is that an angular issue is a location where a 2D image's brightness changes or where a curve's edge points are where the curvature is highest. Real-time processing is made possible because these points improve calculation speed and accuracy for image matching when the image's features are kept in mind.

12.20   Conclusion

Augmented reality (AR) technology offers educators a more engaging presenting style and improves student engagement and involvement by fusing the real and virtual worlds. For students, it increases access to and appeals to knowledge and information. It's developing into a brand-new hotspot for information technology applications in education.

As a result of technical advancement, this study presented a mobile terminal-based multi-interactive and cross-platform Vuforia+Unity3D AR technology scheme. It created a "human tissue structure demonstration" AR application. The application's identification image accuracy rate achieved over 98% throughout testing. This program offers good content expansibility as well. It changes the material instantly in presentations and teaching works. The Vuforia+Unity3D augmented reality technology scheme is ideal for education and has many potential applications.

References

1. White, J., Schmidt, D., Golparvar-Fard, M., Applications of augmented reality. *Proc. IEEE.*, 102, 120–123, 2014, 10.1109/JPROC.2013.2295873.
2. Krishnamurthy, V., Nagarajan, K.K., Prasad, D.V., Kumar, G., Natarajan, A., Saravanan, S., Natarajan, A., Murugan, S., Rushitaa, D., Augmented reality and virtual reality in our daily life. *Int. J. Inf. Commun. Technol. (IJ-ICT)*, 9, 205, 2020, 10.11591/ijict.v9i3.pp205-211.
3. di, D., Julianti, M., din, J., Ramdhan, S., AK, M., Augmented reality based on android for the promotion of furniture products with geometry translation. *NeuroQuantology*, 20, 452–457, 2022, 10.14704/nq.2022.20.5.NQ22194.
4. Parekh, P., Patel, S., Patel, N. *et al.*, Systematic review and meta-analysis of augmented reality in medicine, retail, and games. *Vis. Comput. Ind. Biomed. Art*, 3, 21, 2020, https://doi.org/10.1186/s42492-020-00057-7.
5. Chowdary, A.K. and Hemasri, D., Augmented reality in gaming. *SRM Inst. Technol.*, 1–12, India 2022, 10.13140/RG.2.2.15595.21288.
6. Fan, R. and Liu, Y., Research on augmented reality interactive games. *2011 Third Pacific-Asia Conference on Circuits, Communications and System (PACCS)*, Wuhan, China, pp. 1–3, 2011.
7. Silva, R., Oliveira, J.C., Giraldi, G.A., *Introduction to augmented reality*, National Laboratory for Scientific Computation, Av Getulio Vargas, Petropolis, 2003.
8. Jani, K., Chaudhuri, M., Patel, H., Shah, M., Machine learning in films: An approach towards automation in film censoring. *J. Data, Inf Manag.*, 2, 1, 55–64, 2020.
9. Panda, S.K. and Satapathy, S.C., An investigation into smart contract deployment on ethereum platform using Web3.js and solidity using blockchain, in: *Data Engineering and Intelligent Computing*, Advances in Intelligent Systems and Computing, V. Bhateja, S.C. Satapathy, C.M. Travieso-González, V.N.M. Aradhya (Eds.), vol. 1, Springer, Singapore, 2021, https://doi.org/10.1007/978-981-16-0171-2_52.
10. Panda, S.K., Rao, D.C., Satapathy, S.C., An investigation into the usability of blockchain technology in internet of things, in: *Data Engineering and Intelligent Computing*, Advances in Intelligent Systems and Computing, V. Bhateja, S.C. Satapathy, C.M. Travieso-González, V.N.M. Aradhya (Eds.), vol. 1, Springer, Singapore, 2021, https://doi.org/10.1007/978-981-16-0171-2_53.

11. Panda, S.K., Dash, S.P., Jena, A.K., Optimization of block query response using evolutionary algorithm, in: *Data Engineering and Intelligent Computing*, Advances in Intelligent Systems and Computing, V. Bhateja, S.C. Satapathy, C.M. Travieso-González, V.N.M. Aradhya (Eds.), vol. 1, Springer, Singapore, 2021, https://doi.org/10.1007/978-981-16-0171-2_54.

12. Nanda, S.K., Panda, S.K., Das, M., Satapathy, S.C., Automating vehicle insurance process using smart contract and ethereum, in: *Advances in Micro-Electronics, Embedded Systems and IoT*, Lecture Notes in Electrical Engineering, V.V.S.S.S. Chakravarthy, W. Flores-Fuentes, V. Bhateja, B. Biswal (Eds.), vol. 838, Springer, Singapore, 2022, https://doi.org/10.1007/978-981-16-8550-7_23.

13. Varaprasada Rao, K. and Panda, S.K., Secure electronic voting (e-voting) system based on blockchain on various platforms, in: *Computer Communication, Networking and IoT*, Lecture Notes in Networks and Systems, S.C. Satapathy, J.C.W. Lin, L.K. Wee, V. Bhateja, T.M. Rajesh (Eds.), vol. 459, Springer, Singapore, 2023, https://doi.org/10.1007/978-981-19-1976-3_18.

14. Varaprasada Rao, K. and Panda, S.K., A design model of copyright protection system based on distributed ledger technology, in: *Computer Communication, Networking and IoT*, Lecture Notes in Networks and Systems, S.C. Satapathy, J.C.W. Lin, L.K. Wee, V. Bhateja, T.M. Rajesh (Eds.), vol. 459, Springer, Singapore, 2023, https://doi.org/10.1007/978-981-19-1976-3_17.

15. Panda, S.K., Elngar, A.A., Balas, V.E., Kayed, M. (Eds.), *Bitcoin and Blockchain: History and Current Applications*, 1st ed., vol. 1, pp. 1–279, CRC Press, Bona Caton, 2020, https://doi.org/10.1201/9781003032588.

16. Panda, S.K., Jena, A.K., Swain, S.K., Satapathy, S.C. (Eds.), *Blockchain Technology: Applications and Challenges*, pp. 1–300, Springer, Intelligent Systems Reference Library, Swizerland, 2021, https://doi.org/10.1007/978-3-030-69395-4.

17. Sathya, A.R., Panda, S.K., Hanumanthakari, S., Enabling smart education system using blockchain technology, in: *Blockchain Technology: Applications and Challenges*, Intelligent Systems Reference Library, S.K. Panda, A.K. Jena, S.K. Swain, S.C. Satapathy (Eds.), vol. 203, Springer, Cham, 2021, https://doi.org/10.1007/978-3-030-69395-4_10.

18. Lokre, S.S., Naman, V., Priya, S., Panda, S.K., Gun tracking system using blockchain technology, in: *Blockchain Technology: Applications and Challenges*, Intelligent Systems Reference Library, S.K. Panda, A.K. Jena, S.K. Swain, S.C. Satapathy (Eds.), vol. 203, Springer, Cham, 2021, https://doi.org/10.1007/978-3-030-69395-4_16.

19. Panda, S.K., Daliyet, S.P., Lokre, S.S., Naman, V., Distributed ledger technology in the construction industry using corda, in: *The New Advanced Society: Artificial Intelligence and Industrial Internet of Things Paradigm*, https://doi.org/10.1002/9781119884392.ch2.

20. Panda, S.K., Mohammad, G.B., Nandan Mohanty, S., Sahoo, S., Smart contract-based land registry system to reduce frauds and time delay, in: *Security and Privacy*, p. e172, 2021, https://doi.org/10.1002/spy2.172.

21. Panda, S.K. and Satapathy, S.C., Drug traceability and transparency in medical supply chain using blockchain for easing the process and creating trust between stakeholders and consumers. *Pers. Ubiquit. Comput.*, pp. 1–14, Springer, 2021, https://doi.org/10.1007/s00779-021-01588-3.

22. Niveditha, V.R., Sekaran, K., Singh, K.A., Panda, S.K., Effective prediction of bitcoin price using wolf search algorithm and bidirectional LSTM on internet of things data. *Int. J. System Syst. Eng.*, 11, 3–4, 224–236, 2021.

23. Sri Arza, M. and Panda, S.K., An integration of blockchain and machine learning into the health care system, in: *Machine Learning Adoption in Blockchain-Based Intelligent Manufacturing*, vol. 1, pp. 33–58, 2022.

24. Murala, D.K., Panda, S.K., Swain, S.K., A survey on cloud computing security and privacy issues and challenges. *J. Adv. Res. Dyn. Control Syst.*, 11, 1276–1290, 2019.

25. Murala, D.K., Panda, S.K., Swain, S.K., Secure dynamic groups data sharing with modified revocable attribute-based encryption in cloud. *Int. J. Recent Technol. Eng. (IJRTE)*, 8, 4, 9508–9512, 2019.

26. Murala, D.K., Panda, S.K., Swain, S.K., A novel hybrid approach for providing data security and privacy from malicious attacks in the cloud environment. *J. Adv. Res. Dyn. Control Syst.*, 11, 1291–1300, 2019.

27. Panda, S.K., Swain, S.K., Mall, R., An investigation into usability aspects of E-commerce websites using users' preferences. *Adv. Comput. Sci.: An Int. J.*, 4, 1, 65–73, 2015.

28. Panda, S.K., Swain, S.K., Mall, R., Measuring web site usability quality complexity metrics for navigability, in: *Intelligent Computing, Communication and Devices*, Advances in Intelligent Systems and Computing, L. Jain, S. Patnaik, N. Ichalkaranje (Eds.), vol. 308, Springer, New Delhi, 2015, https://doi.org/10.1007/978-81-322-2012-1_41.

29. Panda, S.K., A usability evaluation framework for B2C E-commerce websites. *Comput. Eng. Intell. Syst.*, 5, 3, 66–85, 2014.

30. Bhalerao, V., Panda, S.K., Jena, A.K., Optimization of loss function on human faces using generative adversarial networks, in: *Machine Learning Approaches for Urban Computing*, Studies in Computational Intelligence, M. Bandyopadhyay, M. Rout, S. Chandra Satapathy (Eds.), vol. 968, Springer, Singapore, 2021, https://doi.org/10.1007/978-981-16-0935-0_9.

31. Panda, S.K. and Dwivedi, M., Minimizing food wastage using machine learning: A novel approach, in: *Smart Intelligent Computing and Applications*, Smart Innovation, Systems and Technologies, S. Satapathy, V. Bhateja, J. Mohanty, S. Udgata (Eds.), vol. 159, Springer, Singapore, 2020, https://doi.org/10.1007/978-981-13-9282-5_44.

32. Panda, S.K., A.R, S., Mishra, M., Satpathy, S., A supervised learning algorithm to forecast weather conditions for playing cricket. *Int. J. Innovative Technol. Exploring Eng. (IJITEE)*, 9, 1, 2019.

33. Panda, S.K., Fraud-resistant crowdfunding system using ethereum blockchain, in: *Bitcoin and Blockchain*, pp. 237–276, 2020.

34. Panda, S.K., Mishra, V., Balamurali, R., Elngar, A.A., *Artificial intelligence and machine learning in business management concepts, challenges, and case studies*, 1st Edition, p. 278, Imprint CRC Press, Boca Raton, 2021. https://doi.org/10.1201/9781003125129.

35. Joshi, S., Panda, S.K., AR, S., Optimal deep learning model to identify the development of pomegranate fruit in farms. *Int. J. Innovative Technol. Exploring Eng.*, 9, 3, 2352–2356, 2020.

36. Puranam, K.S.R., Gaddam, M.C.T., K, V.P.R., Panda, S.K., Reddy, G.S.M., Anatomy and lifecycle of a bitcoin transaction (February 18, 2019). *Proceedings of International Conference on Sustainable Computing in Science, Technology and Management (SUSCOM)*, Amity University Rajasthan, Jaipur-India, February 26-28, 2019, Available at SSRN: https://ssrn.com/abstract=3355106orhttp://dx.doi.org/10.2139/ssrn.3355106.

37. Panda, S.K. and Swain, S.K., *Quality assurance aspects of web design, design solutions for improving website quality and effectiveness*, pp. 87–129, IGI Global, 2016.

38. Panda, S.K., Bhalerao, V., AR, S., A machine learning model to identify duplicate questions in social media forums. *Int. J. Innovative Technol. Exploring Eng.*, 9, 4, 370–373, 2020.

39. Ahmareen, S., Raj, A., Potluri, S., Panda, S.K., Book Shala: An android-based application design and implementation of sharing books, in: *Smart Intelligent Computing and Applications*, Smart Innovation, Systems and Technologies, S. Satapathy, V. Bhateja, J. Mohanty, S. Udgata (Eds.), vol. 159, Springer, Singapore, 2020, https://doi.org/10.1007/978-981-13-9282-5_28.

40. Panda, S.K., Das, S.S., Swain, S.K., S-model for service-oriented applications in web engineering. *Regional Coll. Manag.*, 10, 3, 38–46, 2013.

41. Panda, S.K., An investigation into usability and productivity of ecommerce websites, https://shodhganga.inflibnet.ac.in:8443/jspui/handle/10603/123505.

42. Panda, S.K., Chandrasekhar, A., Gantayat, P.K., Panda, M.R., Detecting brain tumor using image segmentation: A novel approach, in: *Data Engineering and Intelligent Computing*, Lecture Notes in Networks and Systems, V. Bhateja, L. Khin Wee, J.C.W. Lin, S.C. Satapathy, T.M. Rajesh (Eds.), vol. 446, Springer, Singapore, 2022, https://doi.org/10.1007/978-981-19-1559-8_35.

43. Sanghi, P., Panda, S.K., Pati, C., Gantayat, P.K., Learning deep features and classification for fresh or off vegetables to prevent food wastage using machine learning algorithms, in: *Intelligent Data Engineering and Analytics*, Smart Innovation, Systems and Technologies, S.C. Satapathy, P. Peer, J. Tang, V. Bhateja, A. Ghosh (Eds.), vol. 266, Springer, Singapore, 2022, https://doi.org/10.1007/978-981-16-6624-7_44.

44. Gantayat, P.K., Mohapatra, S., Panda, S.K., Secure Trust level routing in delay-tolerant network with node categorization technique, in: *Intelligent Data Engineering and Analytics*, Smart Innovation, Systems and Technologies, S.C. Satapathy, P. Peer, J. Tang, V. Bhateja, A. Ghosh (Eds.), vol. 266, Springer, Singapore, 2022, https://doi.org/10.1007/978-981-16-6624-7_45.

45. Panda, S.K., Urkude, S.V., Urkude, V.R., Vairachilai, S., An investigation into COVID 19 pandemic in India, in: *The New Advanced Society: Artificial Intelligence and Industrial Internet of Things Paradigm*, vol. 1, pp. 289–305, Wiley.

46. Panda, S.K., Das, S., Swain, S.K., Web site productivity measurement using single task size measure. *J. Inf. Sci. Computing Technol. (JISCT)*, 4, 3, October12, 2015.

47. Hanumanthakari, S. and Panda, S.K., Detecting face mask for prevent COVID-19 using deep learning: A novel approach, in: *Smart Intelligent Computing and Applications, Volume 2*, Smart Innovation, Systems and Technologies, S.C. Satapathy, V. Bhateja, M.N. Favorskaya, T. Adilakshmi (Eds.), vol. 283, Springer, Singapore, 2022, https://doi.org/10.1007/978-981-16-9705-0_45.

48. Panda, S.K., Sathya, A.R., Das, S., Bitcoin: Beginning of the cryptocurrency era, in: *Recent Advances in Blockchain Technology*, Intelligent Systems Reference Library, S.K. Panda, V. Mishra, S.P. Dash, A.K. Pani (Eds.), vol. 237, Springer, Cham, 2023, https://doi.org/10.1007/978-3-031-22835-3_2.

49. Murala, D.K., Panda, S.K., Sahoo, S.K., Securing electronic health record system in cloud environment using blockchain technology, in: *Recent Advances in Blockchain Technology*, Intelligent Systems Reference Library, S.K. Panda, V. Mishra, S.P. Dash, A.K. Pani (Eds.), vol. 237, Springer, Cham, 2023, https://doi.org/10.1007/978-3-031-22835-3_4.

50. Rao, K.V., Murala, D.K., Panda, S.K., Blockchain: A study of new business model, in: *Recent Advances in Blockchain Technology*, Intelligent Systems Reference Library, S.K. Panda, V. Mishra, S.P. Dash, A.K. Pani (Eds.), vol. 237, Springer, Cham, 2023, https://doi.org/10.1007/978-3-031-22835-3_9.

51. Panda, S.K., Mishra, V., Dash, S.P., Pani, A.K., *Recent Advances in blockchain technology real-world applications*, Intelligent Systems Reference Library (ISRL, volume 237), vol. 1, pp. 1–317, 978-3-031-22835-3.

52. Panda, S.K., Mohapatra, R.K., Panda, S., Balamurugan, S., *The new advanced society: Artificial intelligence and industrial internet of things paradigm*, vol. 1, pp. 1–512, Wiley.

53. Nanda, S.K., Panda, S.K., Das, M., Satapathy, S.C., Decentralization of car insurance system using machine learning and distributed ledger technology, in: *Intelligent Data Engineering and Analytics. FICTA 2022*, Smart Innovation, Systems and Technologies, V. Bhateja, X.S. Yang, J. Chun-Wei Lin, R. Das (Eds.), vol. 327, Springer, Singapore, 2023, https://doi.org/10.1007/978-981-19-7524-0_52.

54. Nanda, S.K., Panda, S.K., Dash, M., Medical supply chain integrated with blockchain and IoT to track the logistics of medical products. *Multimed. Tools Appl.*, 2023, https://doi.org/10.1007/s11042-023-14846-8.

13

Real-Time Applications of Virtual Reality

R. Pranith, Kavali Maruthi and Shaik Himam Saheb*

Faculty of Science and Technology, The ICFAI Foundation for Higher Education, Hyderabad, India

Abstract

Virtual reality (VR) is a powerful invention and interactive technology that significantly impacts our lives. VR, often known as immersive multimedia, replicates a physical presence for the audience in both the real and virtual worlds. It often incorporates two senses: sight and sound. VR aims to make history by allowing employees to interact with virtual objects, collaborate, and meet up without ever leaving the office. This project report provides an overview of the present state of environment-related VR, focusing on live VR experiences. VR technology, art, and business are all quickly developing. The various domains of VR are discussed in order to understand it better. This report provides brief information about VR technology in the present situation, including various types of VR; uses in different sectors; VR in business, entertainment, and games; and other interesting elements of VR.

Keywords: Virtual reality, multimedia, virtual objects, interactive technology, VR experiences, virtual worlds

13.1 Introduction

The term "virtual" is one of the most often-used words. Virtual schools, workplaces, pets, exhibitions, wind tunnels, performers, and studios are all accessible. Virtual museums and doctors are now possible thanks to virtual Reality (VR). VR makes it possible for all of this. It offers the experience of things that are not constructed or not yet available in real life, like seeing

---

Corresponding author: himamsaheb@ifheindia.org

Chandrashekhar A, Shaik Himam Saheb, Sandeep Kumar Panda, S. Balamurugan and Sheng-Lung Peng (eds.) *Metaverse and Immersive Technologies: An Introduction to Industrial, Business and Social Applications*, (349–378) © 2023 Scrivener Publishing LLC

the environment in another dimension. The world of 3-D graphics has no limits or restrictions and can be customizable by the user. A 4-D, i.e., the dimension of the user's imagination, can be added to this world. They want to interact with and experience this world, not just watch it on a monitor. *Virtual Reality* is a growing technology that became incredibly popular and stylish in the last ten years (VR).

More people are playing video games today than ever due to VR technology, and these simulations are helpful, professional tools for researchers in biology and neuroscience. The fundamental research focuses on marine research, which includes complicated tests that, with VR, might be carried out in a lab. Without VR, scientists need to conduct research directly in the field, possibly limiting their experiments due to the unpredictable outcome risk factors [1–3, 9–12].

Virtual Reality is said to have originated in the 1950s, although it was publicly recognized in the late 1990s. Jaron Lanier, a pioneering computer scientist, coined the phrase "virtual reality" in 1987. Virtual Reality's history has been chiefly one of the attempts to make an experience more lifelike. The majority of historical instances are visual, with some being audible [13–17].

13.2   History of VR

We examine the development of technology and the leading innovators who paved the way for today's "virtual reality" revolution.

1838: Stereoscopic Pictures
Charles Wheatstone's experiments in 1838 proved that the brain combines several two-dimensional images from each eye into a single three-dimensional object. "Virtual tourism" took advantage of the popular View-Master stereoscope, later developed and patented in 1939.

1950: Morton Heilig's Sensorama
The Teles-sphere Mask is the first Head-Mounted Display (HMD). The Headset offered stereo sound, broad vision, and stereoscopic 3D. Figure 13.1 describes the 1950 – VR HMD (Head-Mounted Display).

1961 Headset: First Virtual Reality HMD
In 1961, two engineers invented the prototype of HMD. Figure 13.2 describes the 1961 – VR HMD (Head-Mounted Display). It includes a magnetic attractive motion sensor device used for tracking motion connected to a closed circuit camera and a visual screen for eyes. The Headset

Figure 13.1 1950 – VR HMD.

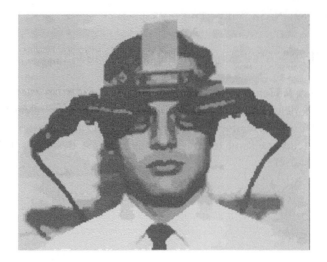

Figure 13.2 1961 – VR HMD.

was created to allow for immersive remote viewing of harsh circumstances in the military [18–21].

1989: NASA in Development of VR

NASA project "VIEW" is developed with Crystal River Engineering, an astronaut training VR simulator. View sports gloves for touch interface simulation. Figure 13.3 describes the 1989 – NASA "VIEW" Project VR simulator.

The tech used in the gloves is Nintendo.

Figure 13.3 1989 – NASA "VIEW" Project VR simulator.

Power Glove – A VR version of the human hand [4].

1993: SEGA VR Headset

The Sega VR headset for the Sega Genesis console was released in 1993. The head-mounted Headset has glasses with LCD screens in the visor and sound and head-tracking technology. Figure 13.4 describes 1993 model SEGA VR headset.

Figure 13.4 1993 SEGA VR headset.

13.3   Virtual Reality (VR)

"The application of computer modeling and simulation allows a user to connect with a virtual three-dimensional (3-D) visual or another sensory environment." Posture tracking and 3D displays are used in virtual reality (VR) to provide users with a better virtual environment experience. Companies providing Top VR Technology are the HTC Vive, PlayStation VR, and Oculus Rift.

13.3.1   Types of VR

  i.   Non-Immersive VR
 ii.   Semi-Immersive VR
iii.   Fully Immersive VR

- Non-Immersive VR: Non-immersive VR creates a virtual world on a computer, but the user is still very much aware of their physical surroundings. An example of non-immersive VR is video gaming.
- Semi-Immersive VR: When combined with extensive projection systems, such as flight simulators for aspiring pilots, this VR helps with instruction and training. It is mainly used in AirForce pilot training and military training.
- Fully Immersive VR: VR has grown in games and entertainment. Games that immerse users into a virtual world for a realistic game experience.

13.3.2   Three Types of Headsets

a.   PC-Based VR Headsets
b.   Standalone VR Headsets
c.   Mobile Headsets

- **PC-Based VR Headsets:** These headsets provide High-quality audio and video with a motion tracking system and camera tracker. PC headsets are expensive gadgets.
- **Standalone VR Headsets:** virtual reality headsets that do not need wired computers. These systems use nearby Computers to transfer System data wirelessly.

- **Mobile Headsets:** Mobile headsets are much more affordable than other VR headsets. Here lenses are used to shell devices to enclose mobiles. Mobile phones do not provide an excellent visual experience, like PC/standalone VR headset.

13.4   Uses of VR in Different Industrial Sectors

Healthcare Industry
In the Healthcare industry, VR is highly used by trainees for their medical and surgical training. Medical students and newly graduated healthcare workers learn theoretical concepts more effectively through virtual reality. With VR, students may examine 3D medical models in detail and practice speaking with AI-controlled virtual patients [22–30].

Automobile Industry
Automobile companies like BMW are using virtual reality for designing and engineering. Automobile engineers and automotive designers VR provides technology to design various models of vehicles and a virtual test run before producing costly text models and prototypes.

The first automaker to plan a production line with virtual data was Ford. Volvo lets clients use their cell phones to simulate test drives, while Audi's software allows users to personalize their automobiles [31–35].

Tourism
Virtual reality provides tours and experiences that allow users to remain at their current location while virtually leaving and traveling anywhere on Earth and beyond [36–38].

Thanks to Samsung's VR lunar experience with NASA and Samsung built, anyone may explore the lunar surface. Dubai Tour of Hamilton Island in 360-degree video within VR.

Education
Virtual reality (VR) in education helps teachers to educate, motivate, and involve students in the classroom. The benefits of virtual reality in education include student interaction and strengthening subjects.

Universities conduct virtual open days to recruit and offer classes in 4Dx Virtual classes at MIT Sloan's Executive Education big data class [39–42].

Gaming

Virtual reality has changed the gaming industry and is known for providing a more realistic user experience. VR has become a popular topic in the gaming world, grabbing the gaming market's attention and providing its users with benefits, including appealing virtual products and the capacity to immerse in the game entirely [43–47].

These benefits have improved the game experience and made the virtual world more realistic, raising players' interest. The video game industry uses hardware and software to enable coordinating body movement by wearing a VR headset.

13.5   VR in Gaming

The use of a 3D artificial world in computer games is known as VR gaming. Where software creates a virtual experience that changes the user's reality experience, it has completely transformed the way games are created and played.

Users can interact with the 3D worlds and become immersed in them rather than just watching them on a screen. Every sense, like sight, hearing, and touch, is stimulated. The head-mounted display (HMD) is a critical component of virtual reality.

13.5.1   Benefits of VR in Gaming

Computer games can be converted into VR format, resulting in a new entertaining and exciting game:

1. **Advanced user engagement:** Compared to flat-screen games, VR users are more interested as they are provided with various tools, like hand controllers and headgear.
2. **Creative capabilities:** The arrival of controllers was a game changer in the development of player engagement in the virtual world. Players have complete control over the gaming environment.
3. **Expanded content:** VR technology is now used in developing video games. Virtual reality has transformed the gameplay of shooters, adventures, and simulations.

13.5.2   Types of VR Games

People are now more interested in games since they can play various games in virtual reality.

FPS VR Games (First Person Shooter – VR)
They are the most popular VR games in which the players feel every action on the field, including the audio and visual special effects. Firearm reloading, ambient noises, flying missiles, storms, other players' dialogue, strokes, falls, and traffic all have a realistic feel.

VR Racing games (Simulation Games)
Racing and driving games are great for the VR experience. It combines the speed, intensity, and excitement of racing with an escape from reality through a wheel, pedal, and gear system.

Horror VR Games
VR horror games are the most widely played games. Because the graphics are so realistic, it is more challenging to play. Players have a more realistic experience. Everything feels extremely real with ghosts, jump scares, and dummy dolls.

Adventure VR Games
Virtual reality is perfect for exploring and solving puzzles at a slower pace through adventure games where gamers are free to explore the virtual world.

13.6   Benefits of VR in the Gaming Industry

Virtual reality transformed the gaming business by increasing user experience. VR is one of the most popular topics in gaming, and it has caught the interest of the corporate community. VR apps have numerous advantages in gaming.

- Provides engaging virtual visuals to its users.
- A capability to immerse players in the game world in real time.
- Creative capabilities that improve the gaming experience.
- Attraction n Retention among gaming players.
- Increase user engagement drastically by providing an authentic experience.

VR systems used in gaming are built with interactive software and hardware. The body's movement can be used to experience or control VR games.

13.7   VR Technology for Business and Game Development

Businesses involved in the game began developing more innovative solutions to attract more users. Through the introduction of VR game products, VR is assisting many companies in overcoming industrial problems.

The gaming business's value increased due to this new disruptive technology. Virtual reality is getting more popular among users and players. After the VR headset arrived on the market, the game industry experienced a significant change and revolution. VR headsets were launched on the market in 2016. As a result, VR games became more challenging to play. People want to view 3D creatures in a virtual environment utilizing a VR headset like the Oculus Rift [6–8, 48–51, 54].

13.8   Global Virtual Reality (VR)

"Virtual Reality Gaming Global Market is estimated to reach $90.7 billion by 2026, and with a CAGR of 31.4%."

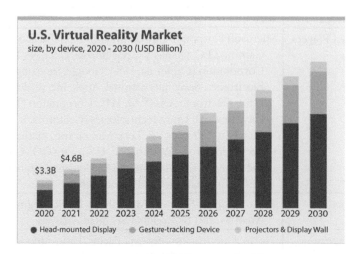

Figure 13.5 United States VR market chart from 2020-2030 [5].

According to Zion Market Research, the global Virtual Reality (VR) in the Gaming Market was worth 13.4 billion USD in 2019 and is predicted to reach 90.7 billion USD by 2026, increasing at a compound yearly growth rate (CAGR) at about 31.4% from 2020 to 2026. Microsoft, Facebook Gaming (Oculus VR), NVIDIA, Google, Samsung Electronics, Sony, Apple Inc., and other companies are important market players. Figure 13.5 describes the United States VR market chart from 2020-2030 [5].

The U.S market for VR was valued $37.0 billion in 2019 and is projected to increase to $1,274.4 billion in 2030, with a CAGR of 42.9% from 2020 to 2030.

Virtual Reality Gaming Market Size – By Component (Hardware and Software), Game Type (Desktop, Smartphone, and Gaming Console), and Region-Global Industry Perspective, Comprehensive Analysis, and Forecast, 2020–2026. Table 13.1 shows the chart for expected CAGR for VR gaming market in India from 2017-2027.

Report Scope

Table 13.1 Chart for expected CAGR for VR gaming market in India from 2017-2027.

Report attribute	Details
Market Size in 2019	USD 13.4 Billion
Projected Market Size in 2026	USD 90.7 Billion
CAGR Growth Rate	31.4% CAGR
Base Year	2019
Forecast Years	2020-2026
Key Market Players	Microsoft Corporation (Washington, U.S.), Facebook Gaming LLC, Oculus VR (California, U.S.), NVIDIA Corporation (California, U.S.), Google, Samsung Electronics, Sony International, Apple Inc. (California, U.S.), Electronic Arts (EA), HTC Corporation (Taoyuan City, Taiwan), Unity Technologies (California, U.S.), Magic Inc., Oculus VR, Leap Motion Inc., firsthand Technology Inc. (Washington, U.S.), VirZOOM, Razer Inc., Ubisoft Entertainment SA (Montreuil, France), ZEISS International, and among others.
Key Segment	By Component Segment Analysis, By Device Segment Analysis, and By Regional Segment Analysis.
Major Regions Covered	North America, Europe, Asia Pacific, Latin America, and the Middle East &, Africa.

13.9 VR in the Indian Business Market

India's gaming business has risen to the top of the global rankings, with a market value of $3.9 billion expected by 2025. Though mobile gaming now dominates the market, as improved AR and VR technology becomes more generally available, users may be attracted to more life-like gaming experiences [5].

The modern gaming industry in India is about $1.5 billion (as of 2020) and is expected to increase to $2.8 billion by 2022. The growing gaming population (from youngsters to adults) and the outstanding contribution of female players. As per Research and Markets Inc., the total AR/VR market in India will increase at a CAGR of 38.29%.

13.10 Virtual Reality Technology

Interaction with a three-dimensional virtual world. Users can actively involve themselves in the virtualized world using a head-mounted display (HMD) and controls. A powerful computer is necessary for advanced VR systems such as the HTC Vive and Oculus Rift. Some gadgets, such as Google Cardboard, take nothing more than a smartphone and apps to work. Figure 13.6 shows the AR/VR market in India.

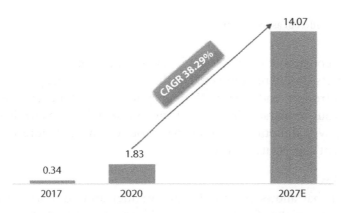

Figure 13.6 AR/VR market in India.

Figure 13.7 Different aspects using VR.

VR kit consists of eyeglasses, a headset, and a computer. More expensive headsets should be connected to the computer to run apps and games. Hand controllers and treadmills are optional attachments available to enhance your immersion in a virtual environment. Hand controllers transfer your physical motions into the game you're playing. Figure 13.7 shows the different aspects using VR.

Valve Index
A headset that allows you to virtually wander around a large area. This headset has a higher frame rate and wider view range than comparable

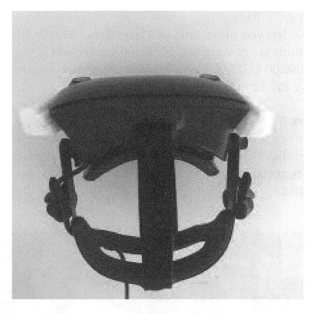

Figure 13.8 Valve index.

headsets. Price: Approximately 1000 € (Rs 195000) (available since 2019). Figure 13.8 shows the valve index of the headset.

Oculus Rift S

A headset that connects to a system and allows you to move around virtually in a small area. It is better for gaming and 3D graphics applications.

Price: $399.99 USD (₹ 49,000) on the present date. Figure 13.9 shows the Oculus Rift S.

Figure 13.9 Oculus Rift S.

HTC Vive Pro

A headset that lets you move around a large area virtually. The most common applications are gaming and 3D graphics software.

Price: $1,090.00 USD (₹ 1,69,999) in present date. Figure 13.10 shows the HTC Vive Pro head set.

Oculus Quest 2

Most of them are used for games and 3D graphics programs, but they are not as powerful as PC-connected headsets. The key advantages of Oculus Quest 2 are its portability, wireless connectivity, and wide game variety.

Price: ₹ 40,899 – ₹ 49,999. Figure 13.11 shows the Oculus Quest 2 headset.

Figure 13.10 HTC Vive Pro.

Figure 13.11 Oculus Quest 2.

Playstation VR

A virtual reality device that connects to the PlayStation 4 console. Only for PlayStation applications and gameplay. Figure 13.12 shows the Playstation VR headset.

Price: ₹39,499 Rs.

Oculus Go

A mobile headset that does not need a phone or a computer. It's ideal for watching 360-degree videos and comes with remote control. Price: ₹35,999 in India (production is suspended). Figure 13.13 shows the Oculus Go headset.

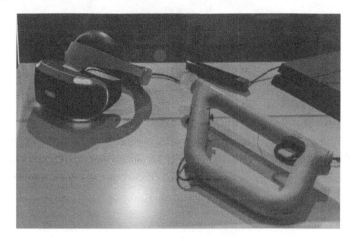

Figure 13.12 Playstation VR.

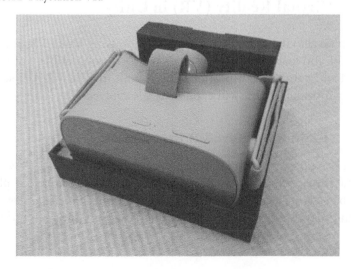

Figure 13.13 Oculus Go.

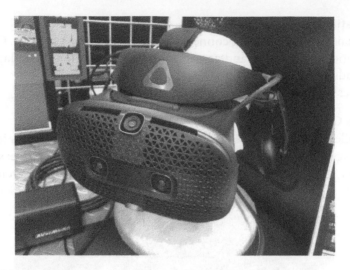

Figure 13.14 Vive Cosmos.

Vive Cosmos Series

HTC PC headset series that can be connected to a computer. Versions with base stations and inside-out tracking are available. They are commonly used for games and 3D graphics programs. Figure 13.14 shows the Vive Cosmos headset.

Price: ₹71,990.

13.11 Virtual Reality (VR) in Unity

Unity can target virtual reality devices straight using Unity VR. It provides a basic API and feature set that is cross-platform compatible. Future hardware and software compatibility has been built in. The VR API surface is purposely minimal, but it will expand as VR evolves.

13.11.1 Build Immersive VR Experiences

With Unity, you can create exciting games and virtual reality (VR) experiences that transport users to new worlds. Most headsets are cross-platform compatible. Create amazing graphics with customizable visual streams and build multiplayer experiences with cutting-edge performance and tools.

13.11.2   VR Tools in Unity

Support

They were developed for Steam VR, Meta Quest, and PlayStation VR. Graphics optimization, measurement tools, and the XR Interaction toolkit to improve development and reduce cross-platform coding needs. Figure 13.15 shows the unity VR headset and Figure 13.16 shows the unity VR graphics.

Graphics

Amazing VR games that work with a variety of hardware platforms. Unity's Universal Render (URP) enables smooth 90hz VR games.

Figure 13.15 Unity VR.

Figure 13.16 Graphics of unity VR.

Performance

The Unity real-time programming platform is simple to use and design. It lets you get started with VR templates and decrease code with visual scripting. For improved performance, advanced developers can use Unity DOTS to modify their graphics processors. Figures 13.17 and 13.18 shows the use of steam VR and View of Unity VR.

Figure 13.17 Use of steam VR.

Figure 13.18 View of Unity VR.

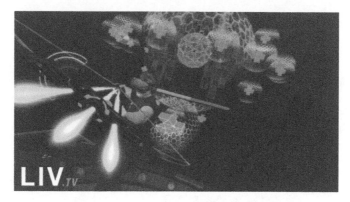

Figure 13.19 Game of unity.

13.11.3 Create with VR

Create a VR game in Unity. Unity provides a free tutorial for developing a VR game using the Unity engine, and the process interface looks like this. Figure 13.19 shows the game of unity.

13.12 VR (Virtual Reality) Games

Unity is one tool that allows us to take advantage of all the benefits of virtual reality. Unity Technologies created an engine that is used to develop immersive, high-quality 2D and 3D games and applications. Figure 13.20 to Figure 13.30 shows various real time VR games.

Fruit Ninja VR: VR Fruit Ninja Half-Brick Studios released the game, which is still one of the most popular today. Fruit Ninja is ranked ninth in the top 10 games for all downloads in both iOS and Android from 2010 to 2019 [52, 53].

Job Simulator: Convert regular workplace routines into a strange series of events in a world where robots have replaced people and taken over everything.

Beat Saber: A top VR Unity application, Beat Saber, combines your strong hand gestures, excellent music, and a rhythm experience. Use two neon sabers to crash colored blocks while moving in a specific rhythm.

Figure 13.20 Preview of unity tutorial interface for developing VR games.

Figure 13.21 Fruit ninja VR.

Figure 13.22 Job simulator VR.

Figure 13.23 Beat Saber VR game.

Figure 13.24 Superhot VR game.

Figure 13.25 Tetris effect game view.

Figure 13.26 Batman Arkham VR game.

Figure 13.27 Vader immortal game.

Figure 13.28 Resident Evil 4 VR game.

Figure 13.29 Elite: Dangerous VR game.

Figure 13.30 Half-Life VR game.

Superhot VR: Superhot VR, developed by the SUPERHOT Team in 2016, is another VR Unity app that might interest you. This game strategy is to shoot ruby people with everything available in a first-person shooter.

13.12.1 Other Famous VR Games

Tetris Effect: Tetris Effect Block Drop Puzzle video game is developed by Monstars and Resonair companies and published by Enhance Games.

Platforms: Oculus Rift, PSVR.
Batman: Arkham VR: Adventure Video Game Batman: Arkham VR is based on the comics of batman published by Warner Bros.

Platforms: Valve Index, PSVR.

Vader Immortal: There are three virtual reality adventure games in the "A Star Wars VR Series" series.

Platforms: Oculus Rift, Meta Quest 2, PSVR.
Resident Evil 4: 3rd-person survival horror game Resident Evil 4 was created by Capcom Production Studio 4 and released by Capcom in 2005.

Platforms: Meta Quest 2
Elite: Dangerous VR: One of the first big games to offer complete VR support and a superbly immersive experience in an infinite world.

Platforms: Valve Index, Meta Quest 2.
Half-Life: Alyx VR: A 2020 first-person shooter game called Half-Life: Alyx was released by Valve.

13.13 Conclusion

The Internet has bought people closer over the last couple of years. The next level of advancement can be called Virtual Reality. Technology is rapidly evolving and has excellent potential. The ability of Virtual Reality to produce realistic worlds of data, objects, and surroundings with which users can interact and manipulate realistically and naturally offers up a wide range of possibilities for work-related applications. The concept of Virtual Reality offers a unique blend of entertainment, education, and cutting-edge technology. Guests will be transported to diverse realms via virtual reality technology. Distance no longer matters when speaking with someone who is not physically present due to technological advancements. You have much freedom to explore the 3D environment and your ideas with the help of this technology. Various applications range from entertainment to industrialization. Many users are still designing their programs and setting them up specifically suited to their needs. So it is still in its early stages.

The development of technologies that handle the difficulties of 'wide scale' virtual environments is the future of Virtual Reality. As additional research is conducted, we may expect VR to become common in our homes and workplaces. As computers evolve fast, they can generate more realistic graphic pictures that better replicate reality. It will be interesting to observe how it improves artificial reality shortly. "Virtual Reality: Where reality ends, and imagination begins."

References

1. Yu, X., Research and practice on application of virtual reality technology in virtual estate exhibition. *Proc. Eng.*, 15, 1245–1250, 2011.
2. Park, J., Kang, H., Huh, C., Lee, M., Do immersive displays influence exhibition attendees' satisfaction?: A stimulus-organism-response approach. *Sustainability*, 14, 6344, 2022.
3. Taborda-Hernandez, E., Rubio-Tamayo, J.L., Fernández, M., Analysis of the narrative communication characteristics of virtual reality experiences: Meaning-making components of the immersive story. *J. Sci. Technol. Arts.*, 14, 9–31, 2022. 10.34632/jsta.2022.10055.
4. Adegoke, A.S., Oladokun, T.T., Ayodele, T.O., Agbato, S.E., Jinadu, A.D., Olaleye, S.O., Analysing the criteria for measuring the determinants of virtual reality technology adoption in real estate agency practice in Lagos: A DEMATEL method. *Prop. Manag.*, 40, 3, 285–301, 2022. https://doi.org/10.1108/PM-05-2021-0035
5. https://www.grandviewresearch.com/industry-analysis/virtual-reality-vr-market.
6. Yu, X., Research and practice on application of virtual reality technology in virtual estate exhibition. *Proc. Eng.*, 15, 1245–1250, 2011. 10.1016/j.proeng.2011.08.230.
7. Alexander, T., Westhoven, M., Conradi, J., Virtual environments for competency-oriented education and training, in: *Advances in Human Factors, Business Management, Training and Education*, pp. 23–29, Springer International Publishing, Berlin, 2017.
8. Baños, R., Botella, C., García-Palacios, A., Villa, H., Perpiñá, C., Gallardo, M., Psychological variables and reality judgment in virtual environments: The roles of absorption and dissociation. *Cyberpsychol. Behav.*, 2, 143–148, 2009.
9. Panda, S.K. and Satapathy, S.C., An investigation into smart contract deployment on ethereum platform using web3.js and solidity using blockchain, in: *Data Engineering and Intelligent Computing*, Advances in Intelligent Systems and Computing, V. Bhateja, S.C. Satapathy, C.M. Travieso-González, V.N.M. Aradhya (Eds.), vol. 1, Springer, Singapore, 2021, https://doi.org/10.1007/978-981-16-0171-2_52.
10. Panda, S.K., Rao, D.C., Satapathy, S.C., An investigation into the usability of blockchain technology in internet of things, in: *Data Engineering and Intelligent Computing*, Advances in Intelligent Systems and Computing, V. Bhateja, S.C. Satapathy, C.M. Travieso-González, V.N.M. Aradhya (Eds.), vol. 1, Springer, Singapore, 2021, https://doi.org/10.1007/978-981-16-0171-2_53.
11. Panda, S.K., Dash, S.P., Jena, A.K., Optimization of block query response using evolutionary algorithm, in: *Data Engineering and Intelligent Computing*, Advances in Intelligent Systems and Computing, V. Bhateja, S.C. Satapathy,

C.M. Travieso-González, V.N.M. Aradhya (Eds.), vol. 1, Springer, Singapore, 2021, https://doi.org/10.1007/978-981-16-0171-2_54.

12. Nanda, S.K., Panda, S.K., Das, M., Satapathy, S.C., Automating vehicle insurance process using smart contract and ethereum, in: *Advances in Micro-Electronics, Embedded Systems and IoT,* Lecture Notes in Electrical Engineering, V.V.S.S.S. Chakravarthy, W. Flores-Fuentes, V. Bhateja, B. Biswal (Eds.), vol. 838, Springer, Singapore, 2022, https://doi.org/10.1007/978-981-16-8550-7_23.

13. Varaprasada Rao, K. and Panda, S.K., Secure electronic voting (e-voting) system based on blockchain on various platforms, in: *Computer Communication, Networking and IoT,* Lecture Notes in Networks and Systems, S.C. Satapathy, J.C.W. Lin, L.K. Wee, V. Bhateja, T.M. Rajesh (Eds.), vol. 459, Springer, Singapore, 2023, https://doi.org/10.1007/978-981-19-1976-3_18.

14. Varaprasada Rao, K. and Panda, S.K., A design model of copyright protection system based on distributed ledger technology, in: *Computer Communication, Networking and IoT,* Lecture Notes in Networks and Systems, S.C. Satapathy, J.C.W. Lin, L.K. Wee, V. Bhateja, T.M. Rajesh (Eds.), vol. 459, Springer, Singapore, 2023, https://doi.org/10.1007/978-981-19-1976-3_17.

15. Panda, S.K., Elngar, A.A., Balas, V.E., Kayed, M. (Eds.), *Bitcoin and Blockchain: History and Current Applications*, 1st ed, CRC Press, Boca Raton, 2020, https://doi.org/10.1201/9781003032588.

16. Panda, S.K., Jena, A.K., Swain, S.K., Satapathy, S.C. (Eds.), *Blockchain Technology: Applications and Challenges*, Springer, Switzerland, 2021, Intelligent Systems Reference Library, https://doi.org/10.1007/978-3-030-69395-4.

17. Sathya, A.R., Panda, S.K., Hanumanthakari, S., Enabling smart education system using blockchain technology, in: *Blockchain Technology: Applications and Challenges,* Intelligent Systems Reference Library, S.K. Panda, A.K. Jena, S.K. Swain, S.C. Satapathy (Eds.), vol. 203, Springer, Cham, 2021, https://doi.org/10.1007/978-3-030-69395-4_10.

18. Lokre, S.S., Naman, V., Priya, S., Panda, S.K., Gun tracking system using blockchain technology, in: *Blockchain Technology: Applications and Challenges,* Intelligent Systems Reference Library, S.K. Panda, A.K. Jena, S.K. Swain, S.C. Satapathy (Eds.), vol. 203, Springer, Cham, 2021, https://doi.org/10.1007/978-3-030-69395-4_16.

19. Panda, S.K., Daliyet, S.P., Lokre, S.S., Naman, V., Distributed ledger technology in the construction industry using corda, in: *The New Advanced Society: Artificial Intelligence and Industrial Internet of Things Paradigm*, https://doi.org/10.1002/9781119884392.ch2.

20. Panda, S.K., Mohammad, G.B., Nandan Mohanty, S., Sahoo, S., Smart contract-based land registry system to reduce frauds and time delay, in: *Security and Privacy*, p. e172, 2021, https://doi.org/10.1002/spy2.172.

21. Panda, S.K. and Satapathy, S.C., Drug traceability and transparency in medical supply chain using blockchain for easing the process and creating trust

between stakeholders and consumers. *Pers. Ubiquit. Comput.*, 2021. https:// doi.org/10.1007/s00779-021-01588-3.

22. Niveditha, V.R., Sekaran, K., Singh, K.A., Panda, S.K., Effective prediction of bitcoin price using wolf search algorithm and bidirectional LSTM on internet of things data. *Int. J. Syst. Syst. Eng.*, 11, 3–4, 224–236, 2021.

23. Sri Arza, M. and Panda, S.K., An integration of blockchain and machine learning into the health care system, in: *Machine Learning Adoption in Blockchain-Based Intelligent Manufacturing*, vol. 1, pp. 33–58, 2022.

24. Murala, D.K., Panda, S.K., Swain, S.K., A survey on cloud computing security and privacy issues and challenges. *J. Adv. Res. Dyn. Control Syst.*, 11, 1276–1290, 2019.

25. Murala, D.K., Panda, S.K., Swain, S.K., Secure dynamic groups data sharing with modified revocable attribute-based encryption in cloud. *Int. J. Recent Technol. Eng. (IJRTE)*, 8, 4, 9508–9512, 2019.

26. Murala, D.K., Panda, S.K., Swain, S.K., A novel hybrid approach for providing data security and privacy from malicious attacks in the cloud environment. *J. Adv. Res. Dyn. Control Syst.*, 11, 1291–1300, 2019.

27. Panda, S.K., Swain, S.K., Mall, R., An investigation into usability aspects of E-commerce websites using users' preferences. *Adv. Comput. Science: An Int. J.*, 4, 1, 65–73, 2015.

28. Panda, S.K., Swain, S.K., Mall, R., Measuring web site usability quality complexity metrics for navigability, in: *Intelligent Computing, Communication and Devices*, Advances in Intelligent Systems and Computing, L. Jain, S. Patnaik, N. Ichalkaranje (Eds.), vol. 308, Springer, New Delhi, 2015, https:// doi.org/10.1007/978-81-322-2012-1_41.

29. Panda, S.K., A Usability evaluation framework for B2C E-commerce websites. *Comput. Eng. Intell. Syst.*, 5, 3, 66–85, 2014.

30. Bhalerao, V., Panda, S.K., Jena, A.K., Optimization of loss function on human faces using generative adversarial networks, in: *Machine Learning Approaches for Urban Computing*, Studies in Computational Intelligence, M. Bandyopadhyay, M. Rout, S. Chandra Satapathy (Eds.), vol. 968, Springer, Singapore, 2021, https://doi.org/10.1007/978-981-16-0935-0_9.

31. Panda, S.K. and Dwivedi, M., Minimizing food wastage using machine learning: A novel approach, in: *Smart Intelligent Computing and Applications*, Smart Innovation, Systems and Technologies, S. Satapathy, V. Bhateja, J. Mohanty, S. Udgata (Eds.), vol. 159, Springer, Singapore, 2020, https://doi. org/10.1007/978-981-13-9282-5_44.

32. Panda , S.K., Sathya, A.R., Mishra, M., Satpathy, S., A supervised learning algorithm to forecast weather conditions for playing cricket. *Int. J. Innovative Technol. Exploring Eng. (IJITEE)*, 9 , 1, 2019.

33. Panda, S.K., Fraud-resistant crowdfunding system using ethereum blockchain, in: *Bitcoin and Blockchain*, pp. 237–276, 2020.

34. Panda, S.K., Mishra, V., Balamurali, R., Elngar, A.A., *Artificial intelligence and machine learning in business management concepts, challenges,*

and case studies, pp. 1–278, CRC Press, Boca Raton, 2021. https://doi.org/10.1201/9781003125129.

35. Joshi, S., Panda, S.K., AR, S., Optimal deep learning model to identify the development of pomegranate fruit in farms. *Int. J. Innovative Technol. Exploring Eng.*, 9, 3, 2352–2356, 2020.

36. Puranam, K.S.R., Gaddam, M.C.T., K, V.P.R., Panda, S.K., Reddy, G.S.M., Anatomy and lifecycle of a bitcoin transaction. *Proceedings of International Conference on Sustainable Computing in Science, Technology and Management (SUSCOM)*, Amity University Rajasthan, Jaipur-India, February 26-28, 2019, February 18, 2019, Available at SSRN: https://ssrn.com/abstract=3355106orhttp://dx.doi.org/10.2139/ssrn.3355106.

37. Panda, S.K. and Swain, S.K., *Quality assurance aspects of web design, design solutions for improving website quality and effectiveness*, pp. 87–129, IGI Global, 2016.

38. Panda, S.K., Bhalerao, V., AR, S., A machine learning model to identify duplicate questions in social media forums. *Int. J. Innovative Technol. Exploring Eng.*, 9, 4, 370–373, 2020.

39. Ahmareen, S., Raj, A., Potluri, S., Panda, S.K., Book Shala: An android-based application design and implementation of sharing books, in: *Smart Intelligent Computing and Applications*, Smart Innovation, Systems and Technologies, S. Satapathy, V. Bhateja, J. Mohanty, S. Udgata (Eds.), vol. 159, Springer, Singapore, 2020, https://doi.org/10.1007/978-981-13-9282-5_28.

40. Panda, S.K., Das, S.S., Swain, S.K., S-model for service-oriented applications in web engineering. *Reg. Coll. Manag.*, 10, 3, 38–46, 2013.

41. Panda, S.K., An investigation into usability and productivity of ecommerce websites. https://shodhganga.inflibnet.ac.in:8443/jspui/handle/10603/123505.

42. Panda, S.K., Chandrasekhar, A., Gantayat, P.K., Panda, M.R., Detecting brain tumor using image segmentation: A novel approach, in: *Data Engineering and Intelligent Computing*, Lecture Notes in Networks and Systems, V. Bhateja, L. Khin Wee, J.C.W. Lin, S.C. Satapathy, T.M. Rajesh (Eds.), vol. 446, Springer, Singapore, 2022, https://doi.org/10.1007/978-981-19-1559-8_35.

43. Sanghi, P., Panda, S.K., Pati, C., Gantayat, P.K., Learning deep features and classification for fresh or off vegetables to prevent food wastage using machine learning algorithms, in: *Intelligent Data Engineering and Analytics*, Smart Innovation, Systems and Technologies, S.C. Satapathy, P. Peer, J. Tang, V. Bhateja, A. Ghosh (Eds.), vol. 266, Springer, Singapore, 2022, https://doi.org/10.1007/978-981-16-6624-7_44.

44. Gantayat, P.K., Mohapatra, S., Panda, S.K., Secure trust level routing in delay-tolerant network with node categorization technique, in: *Intelligent Data Engineering and Analytics*, Smart Innovation, Systems and Technologies, S.C. Satapathy, P. Peer, J. Tang, V. Bhateja, A. Ghosh (Eds.), vol. 266, Springer, Singapore, 2022, https://doi.org/10.1007/978-981-16-6624-7_45.

45. Panda, S.K., Urkude, S.V., Urkude, V.R., Vairachilai, S., An investigation into COVID 19 pandemic in India, in: *The New Advanced Society: Artificial*

Intelligence and Industrial Internet of Things Paradigm, vol. 1, pp. 289–305, Wiley.

46. Panda, S.K., Das, S., Swain, S.K., Web site productivity measurement using single task size measure. *J. Inf. Sci. Computing Technol. (JISCT)*, 4, 3, October 12, 2015.

47. Hanumanthakari, S. and Panda, S.K., Detecting face mask for prevent COVID-19 using deep learning: A novel approach, in: *Smart Intelligent Computing and Applications, Volume 2*, Smart Innovation, Systems and Technologies, S.C. Satapathy, V. Bhateja, M.N. Favorskaya, T. Adilakshmi (Eds.), vol. 283, Springer, Singapore, 2022, https://doi.org/10.1007/978-981-16-9705-0_45.

48. Panda, S.K., Sathya, A.R., Das, S., Bitcoin: Beginning of the cryptocurrency era, in: *Recent Advances in Blockchain Technology*, Intelligent Systems Reference Library, S.K. Panda, V. Mishra, S.P. Dash, A.K. Pani (Eds.), vol. 237, Springer, Cham, 2023, https://doi.org/10.1007/978-3-031-22835-3_2.

49. Murala, D.K., Panda, S.K., Sahoo, S.K., Securing electronic health record system in cloud environment using blockchain technology, in: *Recent Advances in Blockchain Technology*, Intelligent Systems Reference Library, S.K. Panda, V. Mishra, S.P. Dash, A.K. Pani (Eds.), vol. 237, Springer, Cham, 2023, https://doi.org/10.1007/978-3-031-22835-3_4.

50. Rao, K.V., Murala, D.K., Panda, S.K., Blockchain: A study of new business model, in: *Recent Advances in Blockchain Technology*, Intelligent Systems Reference Library, S.K. Panda, V. Mishra, S.P. Dash, A.K. Pani (Eds.), vol. 237, Springer, Cham, 2023, https://doi.org/10.1007/978-3-031-22835-3_9.

51. Panda, S.K., Mishra, V., Dash, S.P., Pani, A.K., *Recent advances in blockchain technology real-world applications*, Intelligent Systems Reference Library (ISRL, volume 237), vol. 1, pp. 1–317, ISBN: 978-3-031-22835-3.

52. Panda, S.K., Mohapatra, R.K., Panda, S., Balamurugan, S., *The new advanced society: Artificial intelligence and industrial internet of things paradigm*, vol. 1, pp. 1–512, Wiley, 2022.

53. Nanda, S.K., Panda, S.K., Das, M., Satapathy, S.C., Decentralization of car insurance system using machine learning and distributed ledger technology, in: *Intelligent Data Engineering and Analytics. FICTA 2022*, Smart Innovation, Systems and Technologies, V. Bhateja, X.S. Yang, J. Chun-Wei Lin, R. Das (Eds.), vol. 327, Springer, Singapore, 2023, https://doi.org/10.1007/978-981-19-7524-0_52.

54. Nanda, S.K., Panda, S.K., Dash, M., Medical supply chain integrated with blockchain and IoT to track the logistics of medical products. *Multimed. Tools Appl.*, 2023, https://doi.org/10.1007/s11042-023-14846-8.

14

Real-Time Applications of Mixed Reality

Sri Ganesh, Ram Pavan Reddy and Shaik Himam Saheb*

Faculty of Science and Technology, The ICFAI Foundation for Higher Education, Hyderabad, India

Abstract

Mixed reality is the next computing wave, following mainframes, personal computers (PCs), and smartphones. Businesses and consumers are quickly embracing mixed reality. By enabling us to engage with data inadvertently in our living environments and with our friends, it liberates us from experiences that are confined to screens. Through their devices, scores of millions of Internet users have encountered mixed reality. Hundreds of millions of online explorers around the world have experienced mixed reality via their gadgets. The most common mixed reality solutions nowadays are provided through social media and mobile augmented reality (AR). It is possible that users are unaware that the Snapchat AR filters they use create mixed-reality experiences. With stunning holographic representations of people and their surroundings, as well as amazingly detailed holographic three-dimensional (3D) models, Windows Mixed Reality enriches all of these user experiences.

Keywords: Mixed reality, mainframes, mobile augmented, AR filters, holographic 3D models, virtual reality, unity

14.1 Introduction

The idea of "Ubiquitous Computing" was made possible by the availability of powerful computers in tiny devices and their steadily falling prices. Weiser wanted computing power to be accessible to users not just at the desktop but wherever and whenever they needed it. This may happen in

---

Corresponding author: himam.mech@gmail.com

Chandrashekhar A, Shaik Himam Saheb, Sandeep Kumar Panda, S. Balamurugan and Sheng-Lung Peng (eds.) *Metaverse and Immersive Technologies: An Introduction to Industrial, Business and Social Applications*, (379–406) © 2023 Scrivener Publishing LLC

conference rooms when attendees might need to get information to better participate in discussions. In order to drive more safely and effectively, additional locations might include a doctor's operating room, an automobile, or a designer's sketchbook. How can we incorporate this new class of computing tools into the surroundings? To respond to this query and expand interaction from the confines of the computer to the real world, a variety of different paradigms have been put forth. This chapter provides an overview of the Mixed Reality (MR) paradigm, which suggests overlaying digital, computer-generated content on top of our real-world surroundings objects. It gives examples of applications and discusses problems and fixes for how to implement them technically. Virtual Reality served as a conceptual and historical foundation for MR (VR). VR systems allow users to fully immerse themselves in a virtual, computer-generated landscape [1, 7–10]. Figure 14.1 shows the mixed reality algorithm.

The initial sample was made in the 1960s. Visual, aural, and occasionally touch cues are typically used to create an immersive experience. All of these displays separate viewers from their familiar surroundings by creating the false impression that there are only computer-rendered items around them [11–14]. Users of MR systems can see both the real-world surroundings around them and digital items that are shown, such as on semitransparent displays. Imagine a system that displays virtual labels over objects in your environment to indicate the name and origin of the products, one that shows virtual arrows to direct you, or one that displays virtual badges with

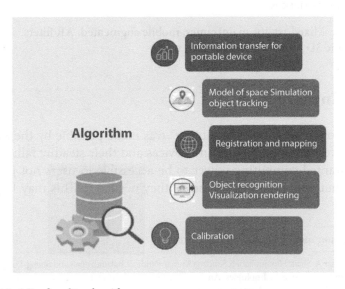

Figure 14.1 Mixed reality algorithm.

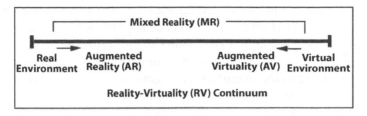

Figure 14.2 Reality–virtuality continuum.

people's names and connections. Each user's information may be displayed in their native tongue, or it could be tailored to best fit their unique profile. For instance, while a user is browsing food products, specialized information could be offered by accordance with their allergies [15–17]. Figure 14.2 shows the reality–virtuality continuum.

14.1.1 Basics

While the words Virtual Reality, Augmented Reality, and Mixed Reality all refer to a particular experience made possible by their hardware, new platforms that can combine many immersive reality technologies are beginning to emerge. The CEO of Google's AR and VR, Clay Bavor, indicated that these names are not distinct but rather labels for various spectrum points in 2017 [18–22].

14.1.2 Applications

Mixed reality (MR) is by definition an extremely multiple disciplines field that integrates digital signals, machine learning, visual effects, user interfaces, human element, wearable technologies, mobile computing, information visualization, and display and sensor design, to name just a few of the topics covered. Ideas from MR can be applied in many different situations, including as operations, the medical field, and workspaces. Other instances include installing and maintaining machinery, where guidance notes could be shown adjacent to the right area as if they were real, observable labels. Steve Feiner's research at Columbia University was among the first to present such a scenario in 1993 by developing one of the earliest MR concepts, a system to guide end-users in fundamental laser-printer maintenance operations. A monochrome, semi-transparent, head-worn display allows users to view wire-frame computer pictures highlighting specific printer components and text labels explaining how to disassemble highlight specific printer components and text labels that explain how to disassemble and replace parts. Recent presentations by Lee and

Rhee focused on a distributed, collaborative MR system for auto maintenance. Their solution comprises of client-appropriate information being
rendered by an ontology-based context identification system, as well as
mobile and desktop terminals that are connected to a server. The situation.
Another example in the manufacturing sector is a system to aid in the task
of constructing car doors and gives a tool to evaluate the placement of
new machinery or workstations in an existing production facility [2, 3].
The main advantage of MR in the latter case is that it allows the position
of new industrial machinery to be seen on actual images of an existing
environment Visual inspection can be performed to evaluate the plant's
positioning and determine the whether new tools are compatible with or
accessible from the old. However, creating a visual model of the complete
production facility is not limited to the new products. To show digital,
three-dimensional (3D) pictures on the pages of a paper book, a system
dubbed The Magic Book was developed. The book, which acts as a grasp
for the virtual objects, may be moved by the users to move the models and
view them from different angles. The technology has uses in interactive
3D children's storytelling, geological data visualization, and architectural
model visualization. Klinker and colleagues in the Fata Morgana proof-of-
concept MR system used the magic book paradigm magic book paradigm
was used by Klinker and colleagues in the Fata Morgana proof-of-con-
cept MR system to visualize upcoming automotive prototypes. Before
Fata Morgana was developed in collaboration with a vehicle production

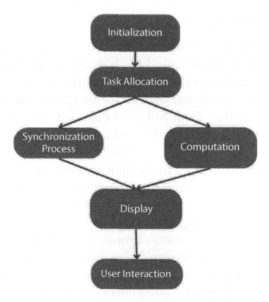

Figure 14.3 Path flow of the MR.

company, professional automotive designers assessed the technology [4, 23–26]. Figure 14.3 shows the path flow of the MR.

In the medical field, MR systems can be used to view CAT scans, MRIs, and ultrasounds directly on the patient's body, which can then be used to direct the surgeon's action. Digital versions of medical images also are accessible, and they are usually displayed on standard operating room monitors. As per a user evaluation of fine – needle aspiration on mockups, MR can be more accurate than conventional procedures.

14.2   Technical Challenges

Mixed Reality (MR) has several challenging technological limitations on how it is implemented. One challenge comes from the led displays, which need to show digital objects in to show digital things in high-resolution reso-lution contrast. A further critical is accurate position tracking. According to the type of display being used, the user's point of view (in terms of play and gaze direction) is every so often of interest, so the system should be aware of the location of pertaining accurate items in relation to the display system to create the illusion that virtual objects were also situated at fixed differ-ent places or connected to tangible things. The two subsections describe a description of the display and monitoring methods utilized to create MR sys-tems and list any known drawbacks. Its system must be aware of the positions of the items to be mingled, the location and orientation of the display, or at the very best, the location of the objects in relation to the site of the show, in order to use the majority of MR technologies. It is essential to draw attention to the display's orientation and position within its six freedom angles of free-dom. In some circumstances, the monitoring can be physically attached to the collection, enabling tracking of the wearer of such a display [5, 27–30].

14.2.1   Displays

The displays that are most frequently utilized in MR environments are described in this section. These include handheld projectors, ambient projections, head-mounted displays, and handheld displays. Figure 14.4 shows the Sony head mounted display.

14.2.2   Head-Mounted Displays

Displays that are fixed to the head. Head-mounted displays are unquestion-ably the most common type of MR display (HMDs). Initially developed for

Figure 14.4 Sony head mounted display.

Virtual Reality (VR) systems, HMDs. Even though the fact that the user's eyes are very close to the display, one or several visual display units with mechanically tuned devices enable them to provide a mental picture that is perspectively precise. See-through functionality is impossible possible with a VR headset because the user has only access to what is visible on display the display. However, to order to use MR, virtual imaging needs to be combined with images of the surrounding area. A video camera that is physically connected to the HMD can be used to achieve this. By electronically fusing the made pictures with the recorded image from the camera, an MR is produced. Utilizing semi-transparent mirrors is another technological method for combining optically real and virtual components. A video see-through HMD is the first kind, whereas an optical see-through HMD is the second kind of HMD with a camera. Two successive LC-panels are utilized in an innovative technological optical find HMD: one for image production or displaying virtual objects, and the second for either obstructing the real world (non-see-through) or displaying the outside world optical see-through the most recent generation of HMDs for sale in the marketplace has a lateral field of view of 45°, a screen of 1280 by pixel density, and a weight of roughly 750 games. It appears as though the user is rising thanks to the display 2 meters away from an 80" screen [31–37].

14.2.3   Handheld Displays

By comparing them to a higher refractive through which an improved reality can be seen, handheld screens are used for MR. Through a hologram optical element (HOE), which is illuminated with stereoscopic images from projectors run by a PC, the operator observes the large equipment.

Figure 14.5 describes the initial stages of handheld displays. The setup makes it possible for 3D annotation to appear in the workspace, adding useful information to the operator's view of the operation. Digital components using cameras mounted to the displays, a combination of actual and virtual pictures is produced (video see-through). Similar to HMDs, handheld displays need to be positioned and oriented correctly in order to produce virtual pictures. Due to the lack of optical correction, handheld screens are typically less expensive than head-mounted displays. Rekimoto first demonstrated a handheld MR device using proprietary hardware, but more recent examples use PDAs and mobile phones that are readily accessible in stores, which opens the door to widespread use of this form of display. An interactive road map application illustrates this type of mobile phone usage.

Figure 14.5 Initial stages of handheld displays.

14.2.4   Ambient Projectors

To alter a users' acceptance through a display, whether head-mounted or handheld, conventional video-projectors can be used to dynamically project browser pictures into the surroundings. The projection can fill the entire room or be limited to a particular space, like a desk, by utilizing an actuator mirror to control the video beam. To display virtual information adjacent to or onto physical objects in either scenario, the system must keep track of their positions in the mixed environment. A 3D model of the complete environment is necessary to project onto large areas of a room or specific objects. The projection is distorted because the images are typically matched to surfaces that are not horizontal to the projector. In contrast to HMDs and handheld displays, the projector positions are fixed or controlled by the system. The necessity for tracking is reduced, and the user's free movement of people is frequently limited.

14.2.5   Handheld Projectors

Because of their recent shrinking, video projectors can now be used as portable MR displays. Because of their recent shrinking projectors can now be used as mobile MR displays can be used as mobile MR displays because of their recent shrinking. These projectors could be utilized to draw users' focus to particular items. Figure 14.6 shows the Acer ambient projector. This makes it possible to project computer-generated information onto or very near an object directly project computer-generated information onto or very closely an object. The positioning of things in the environment concerning respect to the projector and the orientation of the surfaces on which the projected information should be used, and the direction of the

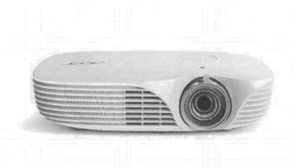

Figure 14.6 Acer ambient projector.

Figure 14.7 Handheld projectors.

characters on which the projected information should be used are both necessary for these displays. With this information, the computer-generated image may be appropriately perspective-projected onto the objects in the surrounding area. In comparison to handheld displays, these systems require more expensive and sophisticated technology, but they may provide larger display areas and make it simpler for several users to engage with the system. Figure 14.7 shows the handheld projectors.

14.2.6   Global Positioning System

Global Positioning System (GPS) receivers use radio signals sent by numerous high earth orbit satellites to identify their location. Every satellite in the system sends messages that include information on its own position, the placements of other stations, and the time the word was sent Receivers use a comparison of the times at which signals from satellites arrive to determine their location. US Department of Defense engineers first created GPS. It is still utilized for military operations and for civilian vehicle navigation, including that of cars, ships, and aeroplanes. Additionally, it is combined with other systems in outdoor transportable MR systems to provide orientation. Since the system depends on radio broadcast time, the reliability and sensitivity of the receivers can have a big impact on how precisely the positioning is determined. Satellites and local radio transmitters can also be utilized to increase accuracy. However, this calls for an expensive installation. The GPS normally won't work when the receiver doesn't have a good connection with a small number of satellites, as when it's inside or close to a tall building. Structures severely hinder the line-of-sight propagation of

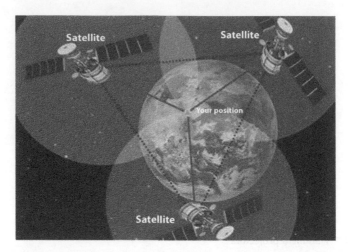

Figure 14.8 GPS satellites.

GPS signals. Figure 14.8 shows the GPS satellites. The possibility of changing radio reception close to structures depending on the time of day further complicates the problem [38–43].

14.3   Mixed Reality Research in Switzerland

In addition to other schools and institutions, Switzerland's two federal institutes of technology conduct mixed reality (MR) research. Several contributions from Switzerland are covered in this section. The initiative to enhance the Pompei archaeological site involved the Rashmi lab at the University of Geneva and the Immersive Virtual Lab at EPFL. They worked on a variety of problems, including tracking and creating virtual characters. The EPFL Computer Vision Lab has also created markerless tracking methods for MR that are based on vision. The ETH Zurich Face Recognition Lab conducted research on haptics, magnetic resonance imaging, and calibration techniques, the majority of which had a medical angle. From 1997 to 2001, four ETH Zurich departments (ARCH, MAVT, MTEC, and ANBI) worked together on the research project BUILD-IT. The resulting Design system is a computer vision-based planning tool that can tackle difficult planning and compositional problems. The system enables users to choose and manage virtual models with actual bricks while seated around a table and interacting with a virtual environment. A projection of the scene is formed onto the table. A side perspective of both the scene that is shown on the wall is possible. The storage area for originals in the plan view enables users to generate new models and activate capabilities like router and height tools. By putting a brick in the model's location, the model gets selected. Models can be fixed, rotated, even placed once they have been chosen by utilizing just regular brick manipulation. An AR system for tabletop interactivity was created at the Innovation Lab Virtual Reality (ICVR) at ETH Zurich using standard office supplies including markers, rulers, notepads, and erasers to enable collaborative work to interface with the computer. Many individuals can work with real objects at once thanks to a rear projection onto the tables. An electronic notepad, colors, and the lengths from the ruler are shown next to the objects as they are traced through to the wall by an infrared system. The research projects Blue-C, Holyport, which both centered on transforming the real world into a virtual one, were both completed by the same team. The blue-C project tracked the user's movements while they interacted with the distant 3D avatar and utilized the gadget using marker-less optical tracking [44–51].

A genuine table was made larger in the Holyport project so that team meetings could simulate sitting at the same table. An MR tool for teaching architectural design was developed at ICVR (ETH Zurich). Despite the fact that this industry now possesses a lot of 3-d (both real and virtual), it's never been able to get them in a collaborative session or from various angles.

A collaborative 3D viewer was created using the AR common Toolkit's libraries. It allowed for the simultaneous viewing of a building's model by close and distant team members, enabling them to do straightforward tasks like selecting, moving, rotating, scaling, and generating viewing planes. ETH Zurich's Experiential System Lab (SMS Lab) is also looking into how athletes learn and perfect the challenging rowing technique.

They have developed a rowing machine using MR and VR. This simulator is required to create the most effective training conditions for rowing and to provide customizable, enhanced feedback. The athlete utilizes one or two shortened oars in the computer-generated image while seated in a tiny racing boat. The oars have a Rop robot attached to them. Forces are produced based on the position and movement of the oars to simulate water resistance. The participant is surrounded by three screens that are a total of 4.44 meters and 3.33 meters in size, and on each screen, three projectors depict a river picture. The Augmented Chemistry (AC) application teaches organic chemistry using a tangible user interface (TUI).

It was first developed conjunction with IHA, ETH Zurich, and Chalmers Thin Gothenburg at Hyper Works FHNW Basel. The more traditional ball-and-stick model (BSM) and the AC are compared empirically in terms of user acceptance and learning efficacy. The results for the two learning settings were quite similar in terms of learning efficacy; the results for the two learning settings were terms of learning efficacy; results for the two learning settings were quite identical. More differences are revealed in user preference and rankings using NASATLX and SUMI, including in the platform's usability and evaluation process. It was, therefore, decided to revamp the Air conditioning with a focus primarily on improving these aspects. For better interactivity, keyboard-free system configuration, and intrinsic database (DB) access, a graphical user interface (GUI) was introduced to the TUI. Utilizing shadows and associated effects improved three-dimensional rendering as well as depth perception. The newly developed AC system was then contrasted with the old system using a quick qualitative user survey. Improvements in subjective evaluations of the system's usability and technical merits were found in this user survey. Users find it difficult to accurately manage little things on touch screens because of the size of the human finger ZHdK employees Daniel Luthi and Christian Iten demonstrated a Tangent tabletop framework using a digital tweezers tool [6, 52, 53]. Figure 14.9 shows the mixed reality and AI Zurich lab launch.

This tool allows users to select, move, and point at interactive elements as small as a few pixels. The device is a cursor with a fixed offset that can be moved with the thumb and index finger of the hand. With Emanuel Zgraggen and Simon Brauchli from IFS at HSR, Concept Map was produced utilizing the Tangent framework. An idea map, a multi-touch software, is employed to create more semantic networks and create more semantic networks, and an idea map, a multi-touch software, is used. The Real-Time Coordination and Sustainable Interaction System Group at EPF-L, the

Figure 14.9 Mixed reality and AI Zurich lab launch.

Ubiquitous Artificial Intelligence Group at the University of Canton, and the Digital Multimedia Framework Group at the Faculty of Applied Sciences of Western Switzerland, Fribourg, collaborated on the the6thSenseproject, which is also covered in this book. The study aims of the study is to improve context-aware mobile MR interactions between virtual environments and virtual augmentations. The Laboratoire d'Informatique Industrielle at the University of Applied Sciences of Western Switzerland, Geneva, and the Computer Vision and Multimedia Lab at the University of Geneva collaborated on the See Color project, which combined sound with images to create an interactive tool for people with visual impairments.

14.4   Current Challenges and Trends

The bulk of the technical systems and solutions mentioned in the aforementioned sections call for the preparation of the environment in which the VR (MR) system will work. For instance, constructing and powering IR or ultrasound lighthouses, as well as visible indicators and RFID tags, may be necessary in particular areas. For GPS to attain great location accuracy, even in outdoor settings, additional transmitters must be developed in addition to the original satellites. To place the virtual components of the interface into the real world, the systems also require a correct vector model of the outside world and an extensive mapping of the positions of the sensors. Many research paper draughts exhibit a fragile connection between the virtual and real worlds. For example, the introductions of the AR Moon Lander and AR Quake games do not make it clear how the game's elements relate to the surrounding world. In practice, it doesn't seem like there are many compelling reasons to favor a certain configuration of the real world and virtual gaming worlds. Similar to the Fata Morgana and Miracle Book projects, it is unknown what purpose the actual book object serves in the software beyond serving as a handle or controller. Instead, it appears that the MR features are just utilized to rotate the models and allow viewers to observe them from various angles. A desktop graphics workstation or possibly a virtual reality system could be used for this. In other words, it appears that certain MR prototypes adopt the VR paradigm by emphasizing just the virtual components while downplaying the significance of the actual ones and by only employing the MR features as interactive controls, such as handles. These systems continue to meet the criteria for augmented reality as defined by Azuma *et al.* since they are interactive and display virtual objects that are matched to the real world. However, it is obvious that there is just a shaky connection tying the virtual parts and the real world together. E. Costanza, A. Kunz, and M. Fjeld. Future MR research may thus focus on certain application areas, particularly medicine, where digital data generated by specialist equipment is inherently synchronized with the physical environment, as in the case of superimposing photographs onto a patient's body during surgery. Future MR studies might also consider account more extensive, inclusive applications with fewer registration requirements, making it simpler to integrate them into consumer handheld devices. Early research indicates that mobile phones may hold great promise for MR because of their widespread use and advanced computational capabilities. This could result in a looser connection between digital content and actual space in terms of resolution but a stronger one in terms of position services and applications. We observe a tendency toward more application-specific initiatives that are typically commercial and academic based on the results of Swiss MR research. Support planning responsibilities are the main emphasis of industrial applications. The fact that projects are becoming more application-focused might be a sign that MR technology is progressing. Recent applications allow for collaboration, as well as co-located and web-based use, in contrast to early MR systems, which were primarily single-user systems.

14.5   Peek into the Future

Let's take a quick glimpse at how our streets may appear if Mixed Reality technologies were implemented in head displays for cars and a wearable device for pedestrians. Figure 14.10 shows the future of GPS.

Figure 14.10 Future of GPS.

Dermot Mc Donagh provided the aforementioned statistic to illustrate how clever and practical mixed reality on the go may be. It actually meets people where their focus is going rather than just being more convenient. This straightforward program enables the operating system to quickly manage incoming alerts based on the circumstance and context and direct the user's attention and focus to the most crucial roadside occurrences.

At stoplights and other moments of waiting when the car isn't actually moving forward, notifications can then return to the display. If a child is rushing across the street or an animal is crossing the road, this focus may also be the reason someone's life may be saved. It should go without saying that employing a practical reality to our advantage is far safer for us than using a phone while driving. similar to seatbelts

However, from a purely financial perspective, replacing street signals, signs, warnings, and everything else in between can save hundreds of millions of dollars in infrastructure construction, including maintenance expenses, operational costs, and everything else in between.

While depending on mixed reality to provide drivers and pedestrians with a personalized experience that brings them the information they need to achieve their destinations, nature can be left alone with no human interference. Drilling into nature, installing street signs, and other infrastructure will become obsolete when everything else is digitized. There are countless uses for mixed reality. However, they are also fairly challenging. Every truly evolutionary step in the history of man has been accompanied by this. Let's discuss these difficulties.

14.6   Hologram Lens

You can view holograms with Holo Lens, which are made of light and sound yet behave like real objects in your environment. Holograms can react to your look, hand motions, and spoken orders. Even the surfaces around you in the real world can engage with them. Digital things called holograms exist in your environment. Figure 14.11 shows the model of hologram.

A Hologram is made of Sound and Light and Holo Lens creates holograms that are rendered in the holographic frame right in front of users' eyes. Holograms add light to your environment, so you can see both the display's light and the light of your surroundings. Figure 14.12 shows the advanced model of 3D hologram.

Figure 14.11 Model of hologram.

Figure 14.12 Advanced model of 3D hologram.

14.6.1   Light

Directly in front of users' eyes, in the holographic frame, are the holograms that the Holo Lens renders. Holograms illuminate your surroundings, so you can see both the light coming from the display and the light coming from the real world. The black color will appear translucent because HoloLens employs an additive display that adds light.

Holograms can appear differently and behave differently. Some are substantial and realistic, while others are whimsical and otherworldly.

Holograms can be used as elements in your app's user interface or to draw attention to certain aspects of your environment.

14.6.2   Sound

Holograms can also create noises that seem to emanate from a particular location in your environment. Two speakers that are placed immediately over your ears provide sound on HoloLens. The speakers work similarly to holographic displays in that they add new sounds without obstructing those from the surroundings.

A hologram interacts with you and your world. Holograms are more than just images made of light and sound; they also interact with your environment. A hologram can begin to follow you if you look at it and make a hand motion. The hologram can respond to vocal commands.

Personal contacts made possible by holograms are not possible elsewhere. A holographic character may look you in the eyes and initiate dialogue with you since the HoloLens is aware of its location in the world.

Additionally, holograms may communicate with their environment. You might suspend a hologram ball that bounces above a table as an illustration. Watch the ball bounce and make noise when it hits the table after giving it an air tap.

Real-world objects can also block the view of holograms. A holographic actor, for instance, might pass through a door and disappear behind a wall out of vie.

14.7   Pros and Cons of Mixed Reality

14.7.1   Advantages of MR

- May boost information and knowledge.
- People can communicate in real time across great distances.
- Video games that offer a more "authentic" experience.
- On people's mobile devices, things come to life.
- A method of escape.

14.7.2   Disadvantages of MR

- Security and spam.
- UX (User Experience): Using AR in social settings may not be appropriate.

- Openness: Other people are free to create and display their own layers of content

14.8   Architecture of MR Systems

The usage of appropriate software architecture is required for the creation of an MR system that will incorporate the aforementioned elements. Utilizing an appropriate architecture while integrating components makes it easier for them to communicate with one another in MR applications, which accelerates the execution of MR algorithms. The three elements that make up this architecture are the server, the client, and the network. The server manages the data and processes the execution. The network must permit communication between the server and client in order for the MR program to execute. A further element that stands between the system's core and the application and speeds up the system as a whole is the middleware, which is addressed in the following section. Therefore, the MR architecture layer is described in this section. Architecture issues, server issues, and network issues are the three components of the architecture layer. The first section explains the overall design of an MR system after giving instances of architectural structures seen in MR systems. The second part lists and describes the various server types that have been studied in the past. The third section examines new network topologies as well as the significance of the network in the MR architecture. It also discusses a number of essential traits for creating a better networking system, including privacy and network protocol. Figure 14.13 shows the 3D hologram in construction field.

Figure 14.13 3D hologram in construction field.

Depicts the general design of an MR system. A few examples of pertinent information in the MR content for MR applications are maps, virtualized models, and user context . Data like location are contained in user context. These data are gathered via social networks, wearable devices, sensors, and other databases. The system's central component, the server, handles the MR content, carries out the required operations, and transmits the finished product to the client over the network mechanism. Different analyses are carried out by servers, including image processing, user tracking, and 3D rendering, and they also determine parameters like the LOD. The server is provided with additional data through the repository as needed. Weather information, which is gleaned from web resources, is a good illustration in this regard. By utilizing methods like rendering and context management, the client replies to the user's request to see the outcome. The level of user preferences being included during rendering is increased via context management.

14.9   Unity Development for VR and Windows Mixed Reality

14.9.1   What is Unity?

Unity is a real-time 3D development platform for building 2D and 3D applications, like games and simulations, using.NET and the C# programming language.

14.9.2   Getting Started

For Windows Mixed Reality and VR development, you'll need to manually adjust a small number of Unity settings. Per-project and per-scene are the two categories into which these are divided. You'll have the resources and project settings necessary to begin developing your own apps by the conclusion of this session. Figure 14.14 shows the downloading unity.

Checkpoint	Outcome
Install the latest tools	Download and install the latest Unity package and setup your project for mixed reality
Configuring your project for VR and Windows Mixed Reality headsets	Learn how to build applications that render digital content on holographic and VR display devices

Figure 14.14 Downloading unity.

14.9.3   Core Building Blocks

You'll require some fundamental building pieces to create immersive applications after beginning a new immersive project. As with previous Unity APIs, all of the fundamental building pieces for mixed reality apps are made available. We advise doing your research early on even if you might not need all of them at once. You'll have a toolbox full of features you can incorporate into a VR project once you've delved into the fundamental building pieces listed below.

14.9.4   Advanced Features

Without the need for additional setup or installations, Unity APIs provide access to additional crucial functionalities that are important for immersive applications. You'll be able to create more intricate VR applications once you've explored Unity's more advanced features.

14.10   Future Research

This study reviews previously written studies to suggest a thorough framework that includes all of the different parts of MR applications. Current trends, problems, and potential outcomes were all taken into consideration during this process. Figure 14.15 shows the loading all the features in unity. An concept layer, an architectural layer, a connector layer, a physical layers,

Feature	Capabilities
Camera	Fully optimize visual quality and hologram stability in your Mixed Reality apps
World locking and spatial anchors	Solve stabilization issues, camera adjustment and integrate a stable coordinate system solution
Motion controllers	Add spatial actions to your Mixed Reality apps
Gestures	Use hand gestures as input in your Mixed Reality experiences
Spatial sound	Enhance your apps with immersive 3D audio
Text	Get sharp, high-quality text that has a manageable size and quality rendering
Voice input	Capture spoken keywords, phrases, and dictation from your users

Figure 14.15 Loading all the features in unity.

and a user interface layer are the five levels that make up the framework. The first tier focusses on the constituent, the second or third tiers investigate issues with architecture, the fourth layer explores how the layout is implemented, and the last layer looks at UI design for running apps with user interaction. The suggested framework considers important and practical elements. It is a very helpful introduction to the MR field and covers a wide range of issues related to MR systems, including the various development phases, analytical approaches, the simulation toolkit, system kinds, and architectures. The range of MR samples taken into consideration in this study are from the practical standpoint of many stakeholders. There are many research trends available to carry out the planned investigation. Figure 14.16 describes some of the advance capabilities.

Applications for magnetic resonance imaging (MR) need to use a technology that can handle dynamic effects such sudden environmental changes and moving objects. In order to improve MR mobile applications, more research is required to develop a brand-new computer graphic technique that can manage autonomous environment design and massive data visualization with a focus on close-to-reality simulation of a crucial scene. Due to the availability of various types of information, including

Feature	Capabilities
Tracking loss	Handle scenarios where your device can't locate itself in the applications world space
Keyboard input	Get input from real-world and Mixed Reality keyboards in your apps

Figure 14.16 Some of the advance capabilities.

Figure 14.17 Prototype of Acer head held projections.

companies, social network data, virtual objects, users, and environmental sensors, large-scale MR must include security measures. To address the complexity of MR. When enhancing MR content with IoT, new designs are required for integration within the IoT platform. Future MR systems must consider associated interface automation. This idea allows the user to adapt. All of the domains above domains must consider the application of novel tactics based on spatial analyses with methods like Delaunay triangulation and Voronoi diagrams into consideration the application of novel tactics based on spatial studies with techniques like Delaunay triangulation and Voronoi diagrams order to address memory capacity and enhance the quality of MR content reconstruction. Figure 14.17 describes the prototype of Acer head held projections.

14.11   Conclusion

This chapter reviews previously published articles in order to suggest a thorough framework that includes all of the different parts of MR applications. This was done with an emphasis on present trends, difficulties, and potential outcomes. MR can mean many different things, and one's context is always important when comprehending it. There is no one definition of MR, as we have demonstrated in this study, and anticipating the emergence of one in the future is wildly irrational.

However, as was also emphasized in the interviews with ten subject matter experts from the industry. The first tier concentrates on the component, the second and third tiers investigate issues with the architecture, the fourth layer explores how the architecture is put into practice, and the fifth layer discusses UI design for running applications that need user interaction. There are many research trends available to carry out the planned investigation. An efficient technique is needed to handle dynamic effects in MR applications, such as rapid environmental changes and object movement.

References

1. Jo, D., Kim, Y., Yang, U., Lee, G.A., Choi, J.S., Visualization of virtual weld beads. *Proceedings of the 16th ACM Symposium on Virtual Reality Software and Technology (VRST '09)*, ACM New York, pp. 269–270, 2009.
2. Teeravarunyou, S. and Poopatb, B., Computer based welding training system. *Int. J. Ind. Eng.: Theory, Appl. Pract.*, 16, 2, 116–125, 2009.

3. Whitney, S.J. and Stephens, A.K.W., *Use of simulation to improve the effectiveness of army welding training*, pp. 1–47, Land Division, Defence Science and Technology Organization, Australia, 2014.
4. Jacobs, K. and Loscos, C., Classification of illumination methods for mixed reality, in: *Computer Graphics Forum*, Wiley Online Library, Hoboken, NJ, USA, 2006.
5. Radu, I., Why should my students use AR? A comparative review of the educational impacts of augmented-reality, in: *Mixed and Augmented Reality (ISMAR), 2012 IEEE International Symposium on, (IEEE)*, pp. 313–314, 2012.
6. Rokhsaritalemi, S., Sadeghi-Niaraki, A., Choi, S.-M., A review on mixed reality: Current trends, challenges and prospects. *Appl. Sci.*, 10, 636, 2020.
7. Panda, S.K. and Satapathy, S.C., An investigation into smart contract deployment on ethereum platform using Web3.js and solidity using blockchain, in: *Data Engineering and Intelligent Computing*, Advances in Intelligent Systems and Computing, vol. 1, V. Bhateja, S.C. Satapathy, C.M. Travieso-González, V.N.M. Aradhya (Eds.), Springer, Singapore, 2021, https://doi.org/10.1007/978-981-16-0171-2_52.
8. Panda, S.K., Rao, D.C., Satapathy, S.C., An investigation into the usability of blockchain technology in internet of things, in: *Data Engineering and Intelligent Computing*, Advances in Intelligent Systems and Computing, vol. 1, V. Bhateja, S.C. Satapathy, C.M. Travieso-González, V.N.M. Aradhya (Eds.), Springer, Singapore, 2021, https://doi.org/10.1007/978-981-16-0171-2_53.
9. Panda, S.K., Dash, S.P., Jena, A.K., Optimization of block query response using evolutionary algorithm, in: *Data Engineering and Intelligent Computing*, Advances in Intelligent Systems and Computing, vol. 1, V. Bhateja, S.C. Satapathy, C.M. Travieso-González, V.N.M. Aradhya (Eds.), Springer, Singapore, 2021, https://doi.org/10.1007/978-981-16-0171-2_54.
10. Nanda, S.K., Panda, S.K., Das, M., Satapathy, S.C., Automating vehicle insurance process using smart contract and ethereum, in: *Advances in Micro-Electronics, Embedded Systems and IoT*, Lecture Notes in Electrical Engineering, vol. 838, V.V.S.S.S. Chakravarthy, W. Flores-Fuentes, V. Bhateja, B. Biswal (Eds.), Springer, Singapore, 2022, https://doi.org/10.1007/978-981-16-8550-7_23.
11. Varaprasada Rao, K. and Panda, S.K., Secure electronic voting (E-voting) system based on blockchain on various platforms, in: *Computer Communication, Networking and IoT*, Lecture Notes in Networks and Systems, vol. 459, S.C. Satapathy, J.C.W. Lin, L.K. Wee, V. Bhateja, T.M. Rajesh (Eds.), Springer, Singapore, 2023, https://doi.org/10.1007/978-981-19-1976-3_18.
12. Varaprasada Rao, K. and Panda, S.K., A design model of copyright protection system based on distributed ledger technology, in: *Computer Communication, Networking and IoT*, Lecture Notes in Networks and Systems, vol. 459, S.C. Satapathy, J.C.W. Lin, L.K. Wee, V. Bhateja, T.M. Rajesh (Eds.), Springer, Singapore, 2023, https://doi.org/10.1007/978-981-19-1976-3_17.

13. Panda, S.K., Elngar, A.A., Balas, V.E., Kayed, M. (Eds.), *Bitcoin and Blockchain: History and Current Applications*, 1st ed, CRC Press, Boca Raton, 2020, https://doi.org/10.1201/9781003032588.

14. Panda,S.K.,Jena,A.K.,Swain,S.K.,Satapathy,S.C.(Eds.),*BlockchainTechnology: Applications and Challenges*, Springer, Intelligent Systems Reference Library, Switzerland, 2021, https://doi.org/10.1007/978-3-030-69395-4.

15. Sathya, A.R., Panda, S.K., Hanumanthakari, S., Enabling smart education system using blockchain technology, in: *Blockchain Technology: Applications and Challenges*, Intelligent Systems Reference Library, vol. 203, S.K. Panda, A.K. Jena, S.K. Swain, S.C. Satapathy (Eds.), Springer, Cham, 2021, https://doi.org/10.1007/978-3-030-69395-4_10.

16. Lokre, S.S., Naman, V., Priya, S., Panda, S.K., Gun tracking system using blockchain technology, in: *Blockchain Technology: Applications and Challenges*, Intelligent Systems Reference Library, vol. 203, S.K. Panda, A.K. Jena, S.K. Swain, S.C. Satapathy (Eds.), Springer, Cham, 2021, https://doi.org/10.1007/978-3-030-69395-4_16.

17. Panda, S.K., Daliyet, S.P., Lokre, S.S., Naman, V., Distributed ledger technology in the construction industry using corda, in: *The New Advanced Society: Artificial Intelligence and Industrial Internet of Things Paradigm*, https://doi.org/10.1002/9781119884392.ch2.

18. Panda, S.K., Mohammad, G.B., Nandan Mohanty, S., Sahoo, S., Smart contract-based land registry system to reduce frauds and time delay, in: *Security and Privacy*, p. e172, 2021, https://doi.org/10.1002/spy2.172.

19. Panda, S.K. and Satapathy, S.C., Drug traceability and transparency in medical supply chain using blockchain for easing the process and creating trust between stakeholders and consumers. *Pers. Ubiquit. Comput.*, 2021. https://doi.org/10.1007/s00779-021-01588-3.

20. Niveditha, V.R., Sekaran, K., Singh, K.A., Panda, S.K., Effective prediction of bitcoin price using wolf search algorithm and bidirectional LSTM on internet of things data. *Int. J. Sys. Syst. Eng.*, 11, 3-4, 224–236, 2021.

21. Fu, Y., Li, C., Yu, F. R., Luan, T. H., Zhao, P., Liu, S. A survey of blockchain and intelligent networking for the metaverse. *IEEE Internet of Things Journal*, 10, 4, 3587–3610, 2022.

22. Sri Arza, M. and Panda, S.K., An integration of blockchain and machine learning into the health care system, in: *Machine Learning Adoption in Blockchain-Based Intelligent Manufacturing*, B.P. Jena, S. Pramanik, A.A. Elngar (eds.), vol. 1, pp. 33–58, Imprint CRC Press, Boca Raton, 2022.

23. Murala, D.K., Panda, S.K., Swain, S.K., A survey on cloud computing security and privacy issues and challenges. *J. Adv. Res. Dyn. Control Syst.*, 11, 1276–1290, 2019.

24. Murala, D.K., Panda, S.K., Swain, S.K., Secure dynamic groups data sharing with modified revocable attribute-based encryption in cloud. *Int. J. Recent Technol. Eng. (IJRTE)*, 8, 4, 9508–9512, 2019.

25. Murala, D.K., Panda, S.K., Swain, S.K., A novel hybrid approach for providing data security and privacy from malicious attacks in the cloud environment. *J. Adv. Res. Dyn. Control Syst.*, 11, 1291–1300, 2019.

26. Panda, S.K., Swain, S.K., Mall, R., An investigation into usability aspects of E-Commerce websites using users' preferences. *Adv. Comput. Sci.: An Int. J.*, 4, 1, 65–73, 2015.

27. Panda, S.K., Swain, S.K., Mall, R., Measuring web site usability quality complexity metrics for navigability, in: *Intelligent Computing, Communication and Devices*, Advances in Intelligent Systems and Computing, vol. 308, L. Jain, S. Patnaik, N. Ichalkaranje (Eds.), Springer, New Delhi, 2015, https://doi.org/10.1007/978-81-322-2012-1_41.

28. Panda, S.K., A usability evaluation framework for B2C E-Commerce websites. *Comput. Eng. Intell. Syst.*, 5, 3, 66–85, 2014.

29. Bhalerao, V., Panda, S.K., Jena, A.K., Optimization of loss function on human faces using generative adversarial networks, in: *Machine Learning Approaches for Urban Computing*, Studies in Computational Intelligence, vol. 968, M. Bandyopadhyay, M. Rout, S. Chandra Satapathy (Eds.), Springer, Singapore, 2021, https://doi.org/10.1007/978-981-16-0935-0_9.

30. Panda, S.K. and Dwivedi, M., Minimizing food wastage using machine learning: A novel approach, in: *Smart Intelligent Computing and Applications*, Smart Innovation, Systems and Technologies, vol. 159, S. Satapathy, V. Bhateja, J. Mohanty, S. Udgata (Eds.), Springer, Singapore, 2020, https://doi.org/10.1007/978-981-13-9282-5_44.

31. Panda, S.K., Sathya, A.R., Mishra, M., Satpathy, S., A supervised learning algorithm to forecast weather conditions for playing cricket. *Int. J. Innovative Technol. Exploring Eng. (IJITEE)*, 9, 1, 1560–1565 2019.

32. Panda, S.K., Fraud-Resistant crowdfunding system using ethereum blockchain, in: *Bitcoin and Blockchain*, pp. 237–276, 2020.

33. Panda, S.K., Mishra, V., Balamurali, R., Elngar, A.A., *Artificial intelligence and machine learning in business management concepts, challenges, and case studies*, pp. 1–278, https://doi.org/10.1201/9781003125129.

34. Joshi, S., Panda, S.K., AR, S., Optimal deep learning model to identify the development of pomegranate fruit in farms. *Int. J. Innovative Technol. Exploring Eng.*, 9, 3, 2352–2356, 2020.

35. Puranam, K.S.R., Gaddam, M.C.T., K, V.P.R., Panda, S.K., Reddy, G.S.M., Anatomy and lifecycle of a bitcoin transaction (February 18, 2019). *Proceedings of International Conference on Sustainable Computing in Science, Technology and Management (SUSCOM)*, Amity University Rajasthan, Jaipur - India, February 26-28, 2019, Available at SSRN: https://ssrn.com/abstract=3355106 or http://dx.doi.org/10.2139/ssrn.3355106.

36. Panda, S.K. and Swain, S.K., *Quality assurance aspects of web design, design solutions for improving website quality and effectiveness*, pp. 87–129, IGI Global, USA, 2016.

37. Panda, S.K., Bhalerao, V., AR, S., A machine learning model to identify duplicate questions in social media forums. *Int. J. Innovative Technol. Exploring Eng.*, 9, 4, 370–373, 2020.

38. Ahmareen, S., Raj, A., Potluri, S., Panda, S.K., Book shala: An android-based application design and implementation of sharing books, in: *Smart Intelligent Computing and Applications,* Smart Innovation, Systems and Technologies, vol. 159, S. Satapathy, V. Bhateja, J. Mohanty, S. Udgata (Eds.), Springer, Singapore, 2020, https://doi.org/10.1007/978-981-13-9282-5_28.

39. Panda, S.K., Das, S.S., Swain, S.K., S-model for service-oriented applications in web engineering. *Reg. Coll. Manag.,* 10, 3, 38–46, 2013.

40. Panda, S.K., An investigation into usability and productivity of ECommerce websites. https://shodhganga.inflibnet.ac.in:8443/jspui/handle/10603/123505

41. Panda, S.K., Chandrasekhar, A., Gantayat, P.K., Panda, M.R., Detecting brain tumor using image segmentation: A novel approach, in: *Data Engineering and Intelligent Computing,* Lecture Notes in Networks and Systems, vol. 446, V. Bhateja, L. Khin Wee, J.C.W. Lin, S.C. Satapathy, T.M. Rajesh (Eds.), Springer, Singapore, 2022, https://doi.org/10.1007/978-981-19-1559-8_35.

42. Sanghi, P., Panda, S.K., Pati, C., Gantayat, P.K., Learning deep features and classification for fresh or off vegetables to prevent food wastage using machine learning algorithms, in: *Intelligent Data Engineering and Analytics,* Smart Innovation, Systems and Technologies, vol. 266, S.C. Satapathy, P. Peer, J. Tang, V. Bhateja, A. Ghosh (Eds.), Springer, Singapore, 2022, https://doi.org/10.1007/978-981-16-6624-7_44.

43. Gantayat, P.K., Mohapatra, S., Panda, S.K., Secure trust level routing in delay-tolerant network with node categorization technique, in: *Intelligent Data Engineering and Analytics,* Smart Innovation, Systems and Technologies, vol. 266, S.C. Satapathy, P. Peer, J. Tang, V. Bhateja, A. Ghosh (Eds.), Springer, Singapore, 2022, https://doi.org/10.1007/978-981-16-6624-7_45.

44. Panda, S.K., Urkude, S.V., Urkude, V.R., Vairachilai, S., An investigation into COVID 19 pandemic in India, in: *The New Advanced Society: Artificial Intelligence and Industrial Internet of Things Paradigm,* vol. 1, pp. 289–305, Wiley, USA, 2022.

45. Panda, S.K., Das, S., Swain, S.K., Web site productivity measurement using single task size measure. *J. Inf. Sci. Computing Technol. (JISCT),* 4, 3, 347–353, 2015.

46. Hanumanthakari, S. and Panda, S.K., Detecting face mask for prevent COVID-19 using deep learning: A novel approach, in: *Smart Intelligent Computing and Applications, Volume 2,* Smart Innovation, Systems and Technologies, vol. 283, S.C. Satapathy, V. Bhateja, M.N. Favorskaya, T. Adilakshmi (Eds.), Springer, Singapore, 2022, https://doi.org/10.1007/978-981-16-9705-0_45.

47. Panda, S.K., Sathya, A.R., Das, S., Bitcoin: Beginning of the cryptocurrency era, in: *Recent Advances in Blockchain Technology,* Intelligent Systems

Reference Library, vol. 237, S.K. Panda, V. Mishra, S.P. Dash, A.K. Pani (Eds.), Springer, Cham, 2023, https://doi.org/10.1007/978-3-031-22835-3_2.

48. Murala, D.K., Panda, S.K., Sahoo, S.K., Securing electronic health record system in cloud environment using blockchain technology, in: *Recent Advances in Blockchain Technology,* Intelligent Systems Reference Library, vol. 237, S.K. Panda, V. Mishra, S.P. Dash, A.K. Pani (Eds.), Springer, Cham, 2023, https://doi.org/10.1007/978-3-031-22835-3_4.

49. Rao, K.V., Murala, D.K., Panda, S.K., Blockchain: A study of new business model, in: *Recent Advances in Blockchain Technology,* Intelligent Systems Reference Library, vol. 237, S.K. Panda, V. Mishra, S.P. Dash, A.K. Pani (Eds.), Springer, Cham, 2023, https://doi.org/10.1007/978-3-031-22835-3_9.

50. Panda, S.K., Mishra, V., Dash, S.P., Pani, A.K., *Recent advances in blockchain technology real-world applications,* Intelligent Systems Reference Library (ISRL, volume 237), vol. 1, pp. 1–317, 978-3-031-22835-3.

51. Panda, S.K., Mohapatra, R.K., Panda, S., Balamurugan, S., *The new advanced society: Artificial intelligence and industrial internet of things paradigm,* vol. 1, pp. 1–512, Wiley, USA, 2022.

52. Nanda, S.K., Panda, S.K., Das, M., Satapathy, S.C., Decentralization of car insurance system using machine learning and distributed ledger technology, in: *Intelligent Data Engineering and Analytics. FICTA 2022,* Smart Innovation, Systems and Technologies, vol. 327, V. Bhateja, X.S. Yang, J. Chun-Wei Lin, R. Das (Eds.), Springer, Singapore, 2023, https://doi.org/10.1007/978-981-19-7524-0_52.

53. Nanda, S.K., Panda, S.K., Dash, M., Medical supply chain integrated with blockchain and IoT to track the logistics of medical products. *Multimed. Tools Appl.,* 2023, https://doi.org/10.1007/s11042-023-14846-8.

15

Artificial Intelligence in the Development of Metaverse

Dileep Kumar Murala¹ and Sandeep Kumar Panda²*

*¹Computer Science and Engineering, Faculty of Science and Technology,
ICFAI Foundation for Higher Education, Hyderabad, Telangana, India
²Data Science and Artificial Intelligence, Faculty of Science and Technology,
ICFAI Foundation for Higher Education, Hyderabad, Telangana, India*

Abstract

The advancements that have been made in artificial intelligence (AI) have resulted in technological advancements in a wide variety of fields. AI capabilities are now being integrated into a variety of sectors, including healthcare, education, and smart-city services. Without the aid of rapid, secure, and error-tolerant communication media, these technical achievements would not have been conceivable. Traditional processing, communication, and storage technologies are incapable of maintaining high levels of user experience and scalability in immersive service environments. Users can immerse themselves in the metaverse, a three-dimensional (3D) virtual world, using cutting-edge virtual reality (VR) and augmented reality (AR) technologies. This world combines elements of fantasy and reality to create a synthetic environment. A setting like this is still in the works and will necessitate a significant amount of research to reach the highest level of completion. In this paper, we will talk about some of the most important issues that need to be addressed to realize the potential of metaverse services. This chapter provides basic information about AI, metaverse technologies, the role of AI in the metaverse, the importance of AI in the metaverse, the AI technical aspects, and the feature of the metaverse with AI technology, and finally concludes with research directions.

Keywords: Artificial Intelligence, virtual reality, augmented reality, metaverse, digital twin, Avatar, metaverse technologies

*Corresponding author: skpanda00007@gmail.com

Chandrashekhar A, Shaik Himam Saheb, Sandeep Kumar Panda, S. Balamurugan and Sheng-Lung Peng (eds.) Metaverse and Immersive Technologies: An Introduction to Industrial, Business and Social Applications, (407–436) © 2023 Scrivener Publishing LLC

15.1   Introduction

Nearly all of us are already familiar with the concept of the Metaverse. It is a topic that is receiving a lot of attention these days, and major tech companies like Microsoft and Facebook are working hard to expand the metaverse in real-time. It is thought of as the next logical step in the development of the internet. This makes perfect sense given how much more involved society is becoming with technology in today's world. We used to talk to other people via landline phones, but now we use wireless cell phones instead. Then, instead of just sending people texts and pictures, we started zooming in on them and face-timing with them. And now, with our avatars in hand, we are about to step into the metaverse and engage in real-time conversation with the avatars of other users. However, even though this new domain is currently a very popular topic, Artificial Intelligence remains the most important foundational technology of our time. The use of AI is ubiquitous [1, 21, 22]. It is impossible to overstate how important it is in our lives today. Every time it accomplishes something new, AI manages to exceed the expectations of people even further. New hardware and clever algorithms allow AI to learn new skills and penetrate inconceivable fields.

15.2   Related Works

15.2.1   Artificial Intelligence (AI)

The term AI refers to the practice of employing methods derived from computer science to generate Intelligent Agents (IA). The IA is a computer program that is capable of independent reasoning, learning, and behavior to some degree. Artificial intelligence research develops computer programs that can understand natural language, interpret data, and behave like humans. It does it by digesting the massive amounts of data we generate daily. A large amount of data can be processed by artificial intelligence systems much more quickly and effectively than by humans. The performance of machine learning systems can be improved by using data. It analyses the data to find patterns and then learns from those patterns. And as it improves itself as a result of the experience it gains, it does so while still learning from the data. To process the information for us, we are already making use of basic machine learning systems, which are a subfield of artificial intelligence. Machine learning is taking place in the background of every online activity that takes place today, such as searching for something or receiving a recommendation [2, 23, 24].

A great deal of investigation is being carried out to continue enhancing the usefulness and capabilities of AI. The number of scientific papers published in this area is also growing from year to year. Understanding the physical world and human behavior is the primary focus of the majority of AI research. The experience of computing is moving away from being static and toward becoming more contextual. Now more than ever, technology can learn from its users and improve its ability to comprehend and anticipate their needs. Additionally, artificial intelligence is very important to the Metaverse.

15.2.2 Metaverse

The exciting coming together of the real and online worlds to create a new universe called the internet is what we call the Metaverse. It is the coming together of traditional reality, augmented reality, and digital reality within a single online environment. One way to think of the Metaverse is as an internet that you are a part of, as opposed to one that you are merely observing from the outside. It is comparable to a 4D version of the internet that we use today. The Metaverse is made up of immersive worlds that have a very straightforward user interface. And while you're there, you'll have the ability to generate and interact with visual information. You will be given a first-person view of the event so that you can go through it and feel it directly. This technology is currently being brought to life by a great number of companies located all over the world. The immensely popular game Fortnite is set in a metaverse-like environment and features its economy as well as the ability to navigate between locations in the game world using an avatar [3, 25, 26].

15.2.3 Roles of AI in the Metaverse

The metaverse implements several different kinds of cutting-edge technology all at once, including AR, VR, Blockchain Technology, and AI. For example, we won't be focusing on anything other than AI. Avatars are gaining the capabilities of autonomy and self-learning as a result of developments in AI, which are elevating the concept of computer-controlled characters. The most mind-boggling and frequently debated idea associated with the metaverse is that of digital avatars. A person's graphical representation within a game or other virtual environment is referred to as their "avatar." A chatbot's digital equivalent, known as a virtual avatar, virtual avatars are used in online gaming. They can mimic human body language, making them an important component in the process of creating this immersive universe. During our travels through the metaverse, we may come across lifelike Artificial Intelligence that is capable of interacting with both us and each other. These AI entities can adapt to varied situations and interact with people naturally. They can have their own life stories, motivations, and goals that are pre-programmed into them depending on the situation and the kind of virtual world. And when and if AI reaches the level of artificial general intelligence, we might have an experience that is both incredible and surreal if we immerse ourselves in its world. It's even possible that sophisticated AI features will be incorporated into game engines. It may also analyze data to make generating virtual assets like characters, locations, buildings, character routines, avatars, and easier. Metaverse AIs construct avatars and analyze 2D and 3D photos to create hyper-realistic avatars. Developers working in the virtual realm are currently hard at work on creating an AI-based avatar similar to this one. In addition to that, it will require an AI-based system that will assist users in interacting with virtual objects. Blockchain technology will be used by the metaverse to build a digital environment in which multiple users can collaborate on projects and have fun together [4, 27, 28].

The distributed ledger technology known as blockchain is an essential part of this universe. Additionally, one of the unique characteristics of blockchain is that it enables the development of smart contracts. Transactions and agreements that are trusted can now be carried out without the need for human intervention thanks to smart contracts. The terms are automatically carried out by code running on the computer. Additionally, artificial intelligence may be utilized in the process of developing, auditing, and securing smart contracts that are stored on the blockchain. AI can also automate software development processes, making it possible to construct assets of ever-increasing complexity more quickly and with less effort. Because, as is common knowledge, the number of cyberattacks is growing, it can also be utilized to strengthen cybersecurity [5, 29].

Yahoo Finance predicts that by 2030, the artificial intelligence market would double from USD 65.48 billion to USD 1581.70 billion. AI will rise. NVIDIA is developing an AI system to let people create virtual environments. This achievement allows the metaverse to spread to create new worlds without human interference. This expands global access. Developing an artificial intelligence system for the metaverse will call for a wide variety of skills. The ability to translate between various languages is just one illustration of this. For this to take place, a model must be able to comprehend the language that is being used by one of the users and translate the text into the other language. In addition to that, it will need to be able to imitate human speech. Because the metaverse will produce a universe for users all over the world, this is a very difficult task. The fact that there are over 7,000 different languages in use across the world is the primary source of this issue [6, 30].

The diversity of vocabulary and pronunciations that make up the human language contribute to its high level of complexity. The discipline known as natural language processing (NLP) is essential for this reason. Another subfield of AI, natural language processing (NLP) seeks to model human linguistic behavior as closely as possible. Facebook's project CAIRaoke revealed an end-to-end neural model for on-device support. It makes use of the most recent advancements in conversational AI to deliver improved dialogue capabilities. The behavior of users of the Metaverse can be analyzed by these programs that make use of artificial intelligence, and the users can then be categorized according to their personalities or levels of intelligence. They are also able to ascertain the individuals' economic and intellectual standings. Metaverse AI aims to create a realistic extended reality. Once this technology is fully deployed, the virtual environment will be an extraordinary tool for humanity and its inhabitants [7, 31, 32].

15.2.4   Importance of AI in the Metaverse

Data can be produced by anything and everything in this world, including individuals and physical objects. The more real-world data provided, the more efficient machine-readable forms will be. 5 billion people use the internet and 4.65 billion utilize social media worldwide. By 2025, we will produce 463 exabytes of data, 2.5 quintillion bytes per day. We generate so much data that humans cannot comprehend it. Even if we could, the knowledge would be outdated by then. Because of this, we are increasingly using artificial intelligence to interpret our data. Artificial intelligence is benefiting the real and digital worlds [8, 33–35]. The Metaverse is a shared digital space that combines elements of the physical world to produce a heightened, augmented reality. Users of this platform will have the ability to interact with a variety of technologies, including 3D digital objects, virtual avatars, and more. The development of artificial intelligence is enabling previously unimaginable forms of immersive experiences to become a reality. The use of artificial intelligence will shape the future of the metaverse. This helps process user-generated data and create realistic avatars. The artificial intelligence will monitor the user's body movements and then interpret those movements as commands for the avatar to carry out. It can analyze user images and produce avatars that are extremely realistic and accurate.

After that, the technology will translate and audio-record texts. The technology will mimic the user's voice when completed [9, 36].

The use of digital versions of physical products will be simplified thanks to advancements in artificial intelligence. The manufacturers can see how people react to new products as well as how they are traveling, which allows them to improve the experience by modifying the features. People will be able to use virtual reality to experience products and services from a first-person perspective in the metaverse, which will usher in a new era of enormous marketing opportunities. This will coincide with the transition to design-driven manufacturing [10]. Artificial intelligence can make the future more welcome. Because the globe has many diverse norms, cultures, customs, and ethics, inclusion and diversity are crucial; however, AI has the potential to create a digital world that is either more homogenous or more exclusive. Despite the enormous potential of AI, we must proceed with caution in a digital world because of the risk of discrimination. While there are a lot of positive uses for technology, there are also a lot of ethical questions that need to be answered. Artificial intelligence, like any other form of technology, has an impact on every facet of society. To ensure that the technology is both ethical and transparent, it is necessary to have collaboration from multiple stakeholders [37–39]. The development of AI and the exploration of the Metaverse both present several difficult ethical questions. When people engage in activities within a virtual world, they are more likely to come into contact with intelligent agents of some kind. Fortunately, there are ways to use AI that do not result in the creation of a virtual world that is biased or discriminatory to increase inclusivity in the virtual world [11].

The blockchain is yet another important component of this prospective online world. AR, VR, AI, and blockchain will create a precise, multidimensional, and secure virtual environment. If it is implemented correctly, this technology will make it possible for us to experience everything that it is not currently possible for us to do in the physical world. Some people believe that the next step in making use of the natural evolution of AI is to leverage the metaverse. It is anticipated that the Metaverse will provide access to content and experiences on a scale never seen before. AI will construct immersive virtual worlds and enable low-touch operations by analyzing massive quantities of data and making judgments. People can access information, services, and communications because the internet offers a search engine that operates in two dimensions and features user-friendly interfaces. More than seven million new pieces of content, in the form of blog posts, are added to the search engine on the internet every single day. The search engine employs AI to categorize and analyze uploaded data.

To assess post quality and intent. Thus, when a user types a question or query into the search field, the search engine will comprehend what the user wants and offer the best results [12, 40]. Now, the metaverse won't simply generate a virtual world in which users can simply walk around and interact with other users, etc... Additionally, it will function as a search engine that allows users to access information within a 3D environment. Therefore, AI will also be necessary for this purpose to provide the most accurate response to user inquiries. It is also capable of translating human language into a form that can be read by machines. Likewise, AI is capable of analyzing natural languages to come up with a response. After that, these AI models may restore the language and deliver the results to its users. Learning from past data and outcomes can help them improve. In the Metaverse, the concept of an avatar is an intriguing one. The user's 2D and 3D images can be analyzed by AI, which then generates a completely new version of the user. It is also capable of reading people's voices and body language, and it can decipher the underlying meaning. There are already some digital humans using AI to create avatars for themselves. But that's not all; it can also communicate in a variety of tongues and styles with the millions of other users out there. In the end, artificial intelligence is the force that will shape the future of virtual worlds. However, given that the technology is still in its infancy, it is highly likely that there will be a great number of glitches and other issues. There is no guarantee that AI implementations will be able to identify these issues [13, 41, 42].

15.3   Artificial Intelligence

Robots can learn and perform tasks using artificial intelligence. In 1956, the concept of AI was first put forward. It has improved to the point where it is now considered the best in natural language processing, computer vision, and recommendation systems in recent years. The term "artificial intelligence" refers to a wide range of activities, such as data mining, reasoning, and representation. The field of AI has seen widespread adoption of a technique known as machine learning, which gives computers the ability to learn and improve their performance using the information that is gleaned from previous experiences. Machine learning includes supervised, unsupervised, and reinforcement. Unsupervised and reinforcement learning use unlabeled data, but supervised learning needs labeled samples. Supervised learning includes linear regression, random forest, and decision trees [43–47]. K-means, PCA, and singular value decomposition are popular unsupervised learning techniques. The Q-learning algorithm, the

Sarsa algorithm, and the policy gradient algorithm are all popular examples of reinforcement learning algorithms. The majority of the time, manual feature selection is required for machine learning [14]. Deep learning is a subfield of machine learning, which takes its cues from the biological neural networks found in the human body. Each layer of a deep neural network receives input from the layer below it, processes that data, and then outputs the results of that processing to the layer above it. Deep learning is an approach to machine learning that allows for the automatic extraction of features from large amounts of data. Deep learning, on the other hand, necessitates a larger amount of data to achieve the same level of accuracy as traditional machine learning algorithms. Two of the most popular and well-respected deep learning methods are Convolutional Neural Networks (CNNs) and Recurrent Neural Networks (RNNs) [48, 49]. The overlay of unimaginably large amounts of complicated data is, without a doubt, the defining feature of the coming metaverse. This opens the door for the use of AI to free humans from repetitive and error-prone data processing activities like monitoring, regulation, and planning. There is no question that the overlay of complex data is the primary characteristic of the emerging metaverse. This section will cover AI's involvement in metaverse development and operations. Automatic digital twin, computer agent, and avatar autonomy metaverse AI applications [15].

15.3.1 The Digital Twin that is Automatic

Automatic digital twin, computer agent, and avatar autonomy metaverse AI applications. The reproduction of the physical entity being modeled as it exists in digital form is referred to as the digital model. The metaverse and the real world are entirely distinct from one another and do not have any kind of connection or communication with one another at all. Digital shadows represent tangible entities. This entity can be a person or item. Physical changes affect the digital shadow. The metaverse and physical world can impact a digital twin. Any change made to either of them will inevitably result in a change made to the other. When we talk about digitization in the metaverse, we're referring to the third kind. Digital twins are digital clones that have a high level of integrity and consciousness, and they continue to interact with the physical world even after being modeled after a physical entity or system. These digital copies of physical things could be used to do things like classify, recognize, predict, and figure out what the physical things are. People messing with things and choosing features by hand both take a lot of time. Because of this, it is important to use software that automates the tasks of data processing, analysis, and teaching.

Deep learning makes it possible to automatically glean information from large amounts of complicated data and put that knowledge to use in a variety of contexts. This process does not require the manual engineering of features. Thus, deep learning has great promise for digital twin adoption. Cities are installing more internet-connected sensors to collect data and simplify management. In addition to this, building information models, also known as BIM, are becoming increasingly accurate [15, 50]. We could develop high-quality digital twins for smart cities if we combined the Internet of Things (IoT) with building information modeling (BIM). The creation of a digital twin of a smart city will make the process of urban planning and management simpler. For instance, we could study the effect that people's exposure to air pollution and the noise level has on the quality of their lives or investigate the role that traffic light interval plays in the flow of urban traffic.

For monitoring and predicting the energy consumption of buildings, Ruohomaki *et al.* create a digital twin for an urban area. A solution to the optimization problem posed by the placement of solar panels could also be selected with the assistance of such a system [8, 52]. Industrial systems are notoriously difficult to achieve global optimization because of their high degree of complexity and the multitude of components they contain, such as control strategies, workflows, and system parameters [16, 51]. A deep learning-driven digital twin is needed because data is heterogeneous, encompassing structured, unstructured, and semi-structured. To achieve optimal levels of production control, Min *et al.* [3] design a digital twin infrastructure for use in the petrochemical industry. The structure of the framework is developed using workflow and the knowledge of experts. After that, they use data from previous production runs to teach machine learning algorithms how to make accurate predictions and optimize the entire system.

15.3.2   Computerized Intermediary

A player does not have control over a character that is referred to as a computer agent. Non-Player Characters (NPC), have been a staple of video game culture for decades, and their roots can be traced back to arcade games. As the player proceeds through the levels of these games, the enemy characters' patterns of movement get ever more complicated. AI is being applied to non-playable characters in video games to make them behave in a manner that is intelligently similar to that of players. This is done to fulfill the players' expectations for high-quality entertainment. The intelligence of non-playable individuals is expressed in a range of areas, such as control strategy, beautiful graphics, voice acting, and so on. The Finite State Machine (FSM) model is by far the simplest and most widely used model for determining how NPCs should react to the actions of players [5]. The FSM methodology presumes that there are a limited number of states for an object throughout its lifetime. The FSM is made up of a total of four distinct components, which are the state, the condition, the action, and the subsequent state. After a predetermined condition has been satisfied, an object will perform a new action to transition from the state it is currently in into the next one. When it comes to the decision-making process of non-player characters (NPCs) in video games, FSM-based algorithms such as behavior trees and decision trees are widely used. Each node in these algorithms signifies a state, and each edge represents an action that can be taken in that state [17]. Strategies that are built on FSM are relatively easy to put into effect because of their intuitive nature. However, scalability is an issue for FSM, especially as the complexity of the game world increases. The support vector machine excels at managing non-playable characters since it is a classifier with the largest difference between the categories. State, condition, action, and state make up the FSM. After a preset condition is met, an object will take a new action to change states. Video game NPCs use FSM-based algorithms like behavior trees and decision trees to make decisions. These algorithms have nodes for states and edges for actions. FSM strategies are obvious and easy to implement. classes and can't make decisions in a lot of different ways. Classical machine learning, also known as reinforcement learning, uses an algorithm to help agents learn from their environment.

The rewards that correspond to the agent's behaviors will be given to them. A greater reward is associated with the behaviors that are desired. Reinforcement learning is utilized in a variety of video games because it provides superior results. Some examples of these games include shooter games [6] and driving games [2]. It's important to remember that the goal of making NPCs is not to make them more likely to beat human players. Instead, NPC design is focused on making the game more enjoyable overall. Therefore, the purpose of the prize can be changed to fit the game's goal. The most well-known game to use deep reinforcement learning is chess, and DeepMind's AlphaGo, which was released in 2015, is the program that uses it. A matrix is used to represent the current state of chess. The AlphaGo program, which is powered by neural networks, determines the move that offers the best chance of victory and then plays it [18].

15.3.3   The Autonomy of the Avatar

The digital version of a player in the metaverse is called their "avatar." In this setting, players use their avatars to talk to either other players or the computer agents. A user can generate a unique representation of themselves, or an avatar, for use in a variety of games and applications. For instance, the created avatar might take the form of a human, a creature from one's imagination, or an animal [8]. In distant social communication applications, face and motion characteristics must match the physical human. The majority of attention given to this topic thus far has been concentrated on two issues: avatar creation and avatar modeling. It is necessary to have a large number of different avatar representations to make more realistic virtual environments. Most video game developers use a few models or allow players to design avatars with a few optional sub-models, such as a nose, eyes, mouth, or other facial features. As a direct result of this, the players' avatars are extremely comparable. A cutting-edge deep learning model, the Generative Adversarial Network (GAN), can learn the distribution of training samples and product data with the same distribution. GAN relies on the generator-discriminator competition. To clarify, the generator network outputs fake images with the learned data distribution, and the discriminator network takes fake images as input and determines if they are real. The generator network will train until the discriminator network cannot differentiate these bogus images from real ones. After then, the discriminator network will be trained to recognize better. These networks learn from each other. At long last, we have a generator network that operates effectively. GAN has been used in several different works to automatically generate 2D avatars for use in games. Additional processing of 3D mesh and textures for the generation of 3D avatars is presented in some works [19].

15.3.4   How Can AI Make Augmented Reality and Virtual Reality More Immersive?

For augmented and virtual reality experiences to continue to advance in terms of innovation, immersion, and overall quality, the power source for these experiences will need to advance as well. Experts expect machine learning, computer vision, natural language processing, deep learning, and neural networks to define the future of virtual and augmented reality. The combination of the visual capabilities of augmented and virtual reality with the cognitive capabilities of artificial intelligence would completely improve how immersive and realistic the virtual world can be. This would be beneficial for enhancing entertainment, meetings, or even just simple hangouts with friends and family who live at a distance. Whether inside or outside of the metaverse, the incorporation of artificial intelligence is an essential component in the production of more lifelike and genuine experiences. Tools that are powered by artificial intelligence, such as Veritone Avatar and Veritone Voice, come into play at this point [18].

Veritone Avatar: Individuals and companies alike can create photorealistic digital personas with the assistance of Veritone Avatar. These personas can be used to represent a company's brand in the metaverse, and they can do so by using a stock resemblance or by capturing the likeness of a celebrity or brand ambassador. Veritone is the company that was responsible for the creation of Avatar (with permission). A few examples of probable applications include virtual meetings, natural-feeling NFT avatars, customer service, sales, interactions with social media, and patient care. If the goal is to create experiences and interactions that make it difficult to distinguish between the real world and the virtual world, then the key to successfully marketing that experience is to create avatars that look, move, and sound as realistically as possible. If the objective is to create experiences and interactions that make it difficult to distinguish between the real world and the virtual world, then this sentence contains a redundant statement [17, 65].

Veritone Voice: Veritone Voice has great potential for metaverse experiences. Despite the reality that synthetic speech works just as well in the real world. Veritone Voice ethically and cost-effectively uses stock or bespoke voices to represent companies and persons across mediums, languages, dialects, and other aspects. By using Veritone Voice, creators of immersive content can save money, customize and scale their production efforts, overcome language and visual barriers, make their content more accessible to a wider audience, add more voices to their roster, and ethically automate the voices of famous people who have passed away, such as actors, musicians, politicians, educators, and others. Use the Veriverse platform to create more immersive experiences for your target audience with the help of Veritone's selection of AI applications designed for use in metaverses. Ask for a presentation from one of our experts to see how these resources can be integrated into your brand's AR/VR/MR initiatives for enhanced user engagement [16].

15.4   Artificial Intelligence for the Metaverse: A Focus on Technical Aspects

This section discusses cutting-edge AI technologies for natural language processing, machine vision, blockchain, networking, DTs, and neural interface (Figure 15.1). Since the virtual and actual worlds are practically indistinguishable, users' metaverse experiences are greatly enhanced. "Natural language processing," often known as "computational linguistics," is an interdisciplinary field concerned with the automatic analysis and comprehension of human languages. In the metaverse, natural language processing plays an essential part in the development of intelligent virtual assistants (chatbots). NLP is the fundamental feature that enables chatbots to understand nuanced human communication in the setting of different accents and subtleties. Artificial intelligence (AI)-driven chatbots may give nuanced solutions to inquiries and enhance their overall response quality based on user interactions. Users navigating certain virtual environments, such as the metaverse, can benefit from the assistance provided by the AI chatbots that are being developed [15].

15.4.1   Natural Language Processing (NLP)

In natural language processing, language modeling is crucial. Syntactic and semantic relationships between words and basic language units are captured, allowing for word and unit predictions. Machine translation and text suggestion are two applications that could benefit from this. The Wikipedia

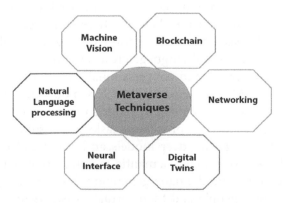

Figure 15.1 Technical aspects in the metaverse.

corpus dataset was used to train and test a large number of neural networks using key-value attention mechanisms. Research suggests that RNNs and LSTM networks equipped with attention mechanisms outperform large-scale networks with reduced memory overhead. The memory network with residual connection improved language modeling test perplexity compared to ordinary LSTM of equal size. This was accomplished by improving the performance of language modeling. Recent CNNs have tackled long-term dependencies in long phrases and small paragraphs, focusing on efficiency with specialized and complex word patterns. Gated connections and bi-directional structures were employed in language modeling deep networks [20, 53]. These features were included to improve the effectiveness of language modeling. To accommodate the wide variety of languages spoken around the world, a plethora of character-aware language models have been established by AI algorithms. CNN and LSTM architectures investigated word representation from input characters. These models were able to recognize hyphenated words, misspelled words, prefixes, and suffixes in English, German, Spanish, French, and Arabic datasets. Character- and word-aware modeling allows natural language understanding systems to extract syntactic and semantic information for metaverse tasks including part-of-speech tagging, named-entity recognition, and semantic role labeling [14, 54].

The learning limitation of traditional ML algorithms has been further exploited through DL, allowing for the efficient management of a wide range of challenging natural language processing tasks (NLP). Several sampled and highly-advanced convolutional neural networks (CNNs) were used to handle a variety of sentence-based tasks, such as sentiment prediction and inquiry classification. In addition, tasks involving sentiment analysis and recognition may involve the need to extract features of aspects and sentiment polarities [1, 55]. These enhancements may make metaverse virtual assistants more trustworthy and adaptable. Advanced chatbot features like natural language creation aims to provide text that is coherent, task-oriented, and conversational. The short text is provided by single RNN/LSTM and mixed LSTM-CNN models for image captioning, while the long text is provided by models for virtual question answering. Certain natural language processing tasks use unsupervised learning, reinforcement learning using deep models, and supervised learning. Some examples include text parsing, semantic tagging, context retrieval, language interpretation, and dialogue generation. For the best possible user experience between people and their virtual assistants in the metaverse, NLP methods need to be utilized [13, 56].

15.4.2 Machine Vision

Machine vision, which combines computer vision and XR, is needed to build the metaverse. Head-mounted gadgets, smart glasses, and smartphones display high-level data inferred from optical displays and video players. This information may also be presented to users in other ways, such as through virtual reality. Indeed, computer vision enables AR devices to analyze and comprehend the activities of users based on the visual information that is meaningful to them. Users are given the ability to freely navigate 3D maps and interact with virtual objects while inside virtual worlds, where they are given the representation of avatars [12, 60].

Extended Reality (XR): XR is defined as an umbrella term that encompasses VR, AR, and MR, as well as everything that falls between these three categories. Although VR and AR do offer some ground-breaking experiences, the innovation and development of MR are being driven by the same core technologies. VR provides immersive viewing experiences in a digital world, while AR provides real-world images, video streams, and holograms. MR can bridge AR and VR. With the help of these reality technologies, human users will be able to explore the metaverse and take advantage of a wide range of services available in both the real and the virtual worlds [20]. Even though XR and AI belong to separate industries, the two can be combined to create a fully immersive experience in the metaverse. When compared to 360-degree videos, traditional two-dimensional (2D) videos have a restricted Field of View (FoV), which makes them unsuitable for VR performance. 360-degree videos, on the other hand, offer an unlimited viewpoint in all directions. Many commercial VR headsets meet high-end user needs, including AI-driven tasks. Some of these requirements include performance and comfort. The virtual reality headgear lets users create hyperreal media in the virtual environment and use metaverse services and apps. Certain VR AI algorithms can improve human-machine interaction [11, 57, 58, 61, 64]. These algorithms are visual.

Computer Vision: In recent decades, artificial intelligence, particularly deep learning, has enabled computer vision with a variety of network designs to improve visual system accuracy at low cost thanks to high-performance graphic processing units. Fundamental computer vision technology may improve the metaverse user experience. This would allow physical users to seamlessly interact with the virtual surroundings in the digital realm. Computer vision requires object detection and semantic segmentation. Semantic segmentation assigns each pixel in an image to a pre-defined semantic class, whereas object detection draws bounding boxes with object information in the tag to localize all possible objects in an input image [13, 59, 62].

15.4.3   Blockchain

Blockchain can be thought of as a digital ledger that maintains a list of all transactions that have been carried out and all assets that have been tracked. This list is connected to a commercial network using cryptographic procedures. Blockchain can give real-time, transparent information. Only authorized network users can access this information in an immutable ledger. The typical blockchain network tracks orders, payments, accounts, and others [20, 63]. VR equipment gathers transmits, and stores a lot of data, including videos and other digital information, in the metaverse. This data presents a vulnerable target for cyberattacks because it lacks protection against unauthorized access and disclosure. In this context, blockchain, which possesses several features that are unique to itself, reveals a promising solution for security and privacy issues in the metaverse. This is particularly the case when AI technologies are used to empower blockchain. Many of the creative activities and events offered by service providers to users will produce a huge number of in-metaverse objects and goods (also known as digital assets), which should be documented and tracked using transparent blockchain smart contracts. To ensure data security and privacy, blockchain and AI technologies have been used to construct multiple unique data collection, storage, and exchange strategies during the past decade. These strategies have demonstrated a significant amount of potential for use in the metaverse. The collaborative development of blockchain and AI in the metaverse, which is characterized by the engagement of numerous parties and the provision of digital content that can assume a variety of formats and structures, can fully handle data security, privacy, and interoperability [10].

15.4.4   Networking

The metaverse serves many users with pervasive wireless network access. Over the past decade, several significant innovations have improved wireless communication and networking systems. These systems leverage AI at multiple network architecture layers. For even the most basic user experience, metaverse real-time multimedia services and applications require a reliable, high-throughput, low-latency connection. Fifth-generation (5G) networks must have 10 Gbps peak data speed and 10 ms end-to-end delay (millisecond). uRLLC allows mission-critical application development. Most 5G and 6G uRLLC optimization algorithms require a lot of processing power. ML and DL can handle complex tasks like intelligent radio resource allocation in 5G and 6G networks with minimal latency. RL solved resource slicing to improve mobile broadband [9].

15.4.5   Digital Twins (DT)

DTs can monitor, visualize, analyze, and anticipate while synchronizing operational assets, processes, and systems with the real world. DTs can conduct these acts because they represent real-world entities. DTs are where the real and virtual worlds interact through IoT connections, therefore any real-world change will not be accurately reflected in the digital depiction. These traits make DT one of the metaverse's building sectors. It replicates reality, including its structure and functions, to allow users to access and use virtual world services. Technicians can use three-dimensional models of complex systems for technical training and commercial customization. As a result, DTs let programmers and service providers create digital representations of real-world hardware and procedures [20]. AI can do any physical analysis in these virtual replications. In recent years, DT designs have successfully incorporated DL for several services and applications. DL's ability to automatically learn features from high-dimensional, unstructured data and efficiently handle spatiotemporal learning models is driving its adoption. AI analytics improve system performance, process problems, maintenance costs, company operations, and production for DT. DT lets users see the metaverse as a real-time duplicate of reality [8].

15.4.6   Neural Interface

The human experience is unquestionably being improved thanks to technological advancements, which are also completely closing the gap in the metaverse that existed between the real world and the virtual world. A virtual reality (VR) headset coupled with a controller is the most popular and immersive interface option for interacting with virtual works of art in this setting. Neural interfaces, also known as Brain-Machine Interfaces (BMIs) or Brain-Computer Interfaces (BCIs), are currently receiving a lot of attention from technology companies. These interfaces go beyond virtual reality devices [20]. The BMIs contribute to the almost complete elimination of the distinction between humans and wearable technology. Several BMIs detect neural signals using external electrodes or optical sensors that are affixed to various parts of the human body, including the skull. According to transcranial electromagnetic pulses, BMIs can alter minds. Shortly, consumer-grade mind-control devices will enable full brain-computer interfaces for the most immersive metaverse-real-world interaction [7].

15.5   Artificial Intelligence for the Metaverse: Application Aspect

Healthcare, industry, smart cities, and gaming use AI. These apps may offer metaverse services. E-commerce, HR, real estate, and decentralized finance applications are briefly discussed.

15.5.1   Healthcare

The medical field has only recently begun to implement ground-breaking technologies such as virtual reality, big data, and artificial intelligence in software and hardware to boost the efficacy of medical devices, lower the cost of medical services, enhance the efficiency of healthcare operations, and increase the number of people who have access to medical care. In a 2D or 3D metaverse, users can learn about, understand, and share patients' health issues and medical reports. By utilizing VR and XR systems, AI plays a significant part in a variety of fields of healthcare and medicine. For instance, AI can improve the speed and accuracy with which diagnoses are made, the speed with which medical decisions are made, the quality of real-time medical imaging and radiology, as well as the convenience of simulated learning environments that are used to educate interns and medical students. Artificial intelligence has been implemented in a wide variety of wearable devices [7] to automatically recognize complex patterns of sensory data. VR healthcare and medical diagnosis applications can be developed using AI-based data analytics for collaborative treatment planning and educational training. Metaverse medicine is available. Virtual assistants at virtual health centers and hospitals can help patients find healthcare, and medical students can improve their surgical abilities by completing interactive virtual medical education practice courses.

15.5.2   Manufacturing

The manufacturing industry is undergoing a digital transformation to better analyze and understand physical entities during the current industrial revolution. The metaverse creates a virtual world based on real interaction and persistence, while digital transformation improves the real world through digital operations. The manufacturing metaverse has the potential to significantly modernize its digital operations by working together to adopt cutting-edge technologies such as artificial intelligence and distributed technology amid the ongoing digital revolution. At this point, AI, comprised of ML algorithms and DL architectures, has made a sizeable contribution to the field of manufacturing through the utilization of a multitude of industrial applications. The rising expenses associated with frequent production system reconfigurations and upgrades are mostly the result of shorter product lifecycles and an increase in the number of product variants. More time and computational power are needed for fresh data gathering, preprocessing, and model learning in ML-based systems. To address the above-mentioned difficulties, a reinforcement learning technique was applied inside a human-machine learning framework [8]. This system integrated the deep learning capabilities of Q-learning models with the specialized understanding of human domain experts. This approach also considered the value of human exploration in decreasing data noise and enhancing the quality of fully automated decision-making systems. Intelligent data-driven condition supervision methods have recently drawn an increasing focus on quality assessment. Even though quality inspection plays a significant role in modern manufacturing systems, these approaches have had to contend with certain challenges brought on by a variety of operating conditions that involve a wide range of applications and tasks. Several approaches use DL with RNN and CNN architectures to simultaneously attain high accuracy and preserve real-time tracking. In manufacturing, these techniques are relied on for accurate problem diagnosis. Many factories use industrial collaborative robots to perform complex tasks. These tasks require a human with higher cognitive abilities, intelligence, and domain knowledge to react quickly and accurately to unexpected events. The ability to learn complicated patterns from multimodal data is crucial for activities associated with the manufacturing process and the production line, and this can only be accomplished with a collaborative AI model. This calls for an explanatory and rational AI model. With the help of metaverse virtual entities, AI can raise the productivity of industrial manufacturing by speeding up the design of production processes, fostering collaborative product development, lowering the risk of quality control, and increasing transparency for producers and customers [6].

15.5.3 Intelligent Cities

Intelligent cities gather useful data about the requirements of their residents by using the Internet of Things (IoT), video cameras, social media, and other sources of information. City governments must make decisions regarding which services to remove, offer, and improve based on the feedback that is automatically collected from users. Users of smart cities will be provided with more intelligent interactive services via the metaverse platform if smart cities make greater use of digital tools and pioneering technologies. The virtual world replicates air quality, weather, energy use, traffic status, and parking space for a user-friendly interface. Metaverse platforms include ITS, smart street light management, automatic parking, smart community portals, and indoor/outdoor video monitoring. These platforms and systems allow for the execution of several smart services in the virtual world, including the payment of utilities and the control of smart homes. These technologies' effects on smart cities are limited, but the metaverse could help spread smart services to inhabitants' daily lives. AI is crucial for smart cities in the real and metaverse because it automates and intelligently manages smart services. Smart green cities worry about sustainable agriculture and pollution. AI predicts productivity, quality, and pests and diseases in precision agriculture systems. Metropolitan governments struggle to create and implement the metaverse ecosystem for smart cities with all administrative functions, including environment, education, transportation, culture, and other civil services. AI data analytics can enhance metaverse administration. This will release usage rules, ethics, and security for a safe experience. Multiple authenticated sources can provide big data [5].

15.5.4   Gaming

Machine learning and deep learning are changing and revolutionizing the gaming business on console, smartphone, and PC platforms. Gaming has always been a metaverse application. This section will examine how ML and DL can revolutionize game development and construct a metaverse gaming generation. ML has shaped video game development during the past decade. Video game developers and studios are increasingly using AI to help systems and NPCs react dynamically and reasonably to player activities. This creates realistic environments with interesting problems and unique storylines. RTS AI agents were improved using Reinforcement Learning (RL) and supervised learning. To maximize tactical search time, convolutional neural networks and deep Q-learning networks inferred expensive high-level searches. CNN's outperformed Puppet search. In conclusion, artificial intelligence, along with traditional machine learning and innovative deep learning algorithms, has revolutionized gaming by improving NPC intelligence, modeling complex systems, making games more beautiful and rational, creating more realistic human-NPC inter-actions, reducing the cost of creating in-game worlds, and opening more development opportunities. They suggest metaverse integration [4].

15.5.5   Other Potential Applications

We found metaverse business applications beyond gaming, smart cities, manufacturing, and healthcare.

E-commerce: Despite mainstream consumers' distaste for VR devices, many consumer brands have entered the digital world to improve shopping experiences for E-metaverse commerce's integration. Metaverse-integrated E-commerce. Many firms have been slowly establishing digital storefronts that blend offline and online purchasing without harming customer experi-ence. Virtual shopping lets you try static products live. Avatar-represented customers can shop in 3D and talk to VR and AI-powered virtual cashiers and vendors. Retailers are beginning to realize that personalizing the shop-ping experience of their customers is essential not only to the continued existence of their companies but also to the expansion of their revenue streams. This is something that can be accomplished painlessly in the meta with the help of AI-based technologies that analyze consumer purchasing patterns [3].

The Management of People: In today's world, many large technology com-panies are getting creative to find and communicate with young job seekers who have a talent for their industry. The methods of recruitment range from sending younger workers or leaders out into the field to conducting online interviews with applicants using video calls and even holding job fairs in the metaverse. Prospective employees can log in to the metaverse using an account that has been authenticated through the use of block-chain technology. They can control their avatars and chat with business HR managers and project leaders after logging in. The applicants have the option of asking or receiving assistance from the AI-based virtual assis-tant equipped with NLP for recruitment guidance. These kinds of recruit-ment events have the purpose of creating a welcoming atmosphere for both the recruiters and the applicants, to foster free-flowing communication. The goal is to allow the applicants to actively learn more about the job positions being offered, as opposed to merely responding to the questions that are posed by the recruiters. 5G, IoT, and DL have given workers and employees numerous handy options (totally remote and hybrid offline-on-line) to traditional employment in the past decade, but the metaverse will revolutionize work and the workplace in the future decades. Horizon Workrooms, a well-designed meeting platform, was recently introduced by Facebook. This platform gives users, who are represented by avatars, the ability to work, collaborate, and communicate with others, in addition to engaging in activities such as training and coaching, in the virtual space by using VR devices [2].

Real Estate: The real estate market has seen a significant influx of capital from both individual investors and institutional investors in the form of purchases of virtual land in the metaverse. Users can access metaverses such as the Sandbox, Axie Infinity, Decentraland, and Upland. These virtual worlds and game platforms let users purchase, sell, and exchange items, including real estate. These non-fungible tokens (NFTs), which are typically associated with non-fungible real estate, have a limited supply, which ensures that their prices will increase over time due to the scarcity of the asset. The real estate in the metaverse can function as a venue for the staging of digital gatherings as well as the construction of virtual structures, such as homes and workplaces. The metaverse also provides a cost-effective distribution method for real estate companies to show potential buyers the property before they buy. Through VR tours and interactive walkthroughs, customers can get an immersive experience that is aided by virtual reality technology. This experience allows customers to learn about the property, including its interior and exterior, as well as its detailed furniture and overall structure [1].

Decentralized Finance (Defi): Cryptocurrency-based decentralized finance uses an open financial system. Smart contracts program it to build exchanges and provide major services like lending, yield farming, and insurance without centralization. Defi is also referred to as open finance. Decentralized finance (Defi) makes use of blockchain technology to enable the provision of financial services on a peer-to-peer basis, in contrast to centralized finance, which is managed or controlled by a centralized entity or person. Decentralized finance gives users complete control over their assets while maintaining their privacy and security. Real estate companies can use the metaverse to display prospective purchasers' properties at a low cost. Users can contribute liquidity to the liquidity pool of a decentralized exchange, which has an AI-based mechanism at its core, to earn incentives. Any decentralized application should prioritize token exchange first (Dapp) [19].

15.6   The Metaverse's Artificial Intelligence Future

The world in which we live is one in which AI and technology are constantly interacting with one another. Many businesses and projects are already making use of Metaverse technologies to advance their operations. The creation of supercomputers will make this future significantly easier to navigate. These enormous, parallel configurations of computers are capable of performing the most complex computations, including the analysis of enormous amounts of data. Access to the metaverse will continue to improve alongside the development of ever-more sophisticated computer systems. AI and supercomputers will be used by businesses to entice and keep customers. The importance of AI in the metaverse will only grow as it evolves. Even though the sector is still in its infancy, the market potential is enormous. Virtual universes are not only going to make new forms of computing accessible to the general public, but they are also going to revolutionize the working world. The outlook for artificial intelligence in the future is very positive. The metaverse holds the potential to make artificial intelligence easier to use and more available to more people. Blockchain, VR/AR, and AI can create scalable and accurate digital worlds. AI may analyze data from all these components concurrently. These advancements show a lot of promise, and several AI researchers think that the metaverse will be the next big thing in the field of AI research [1].

Businesses such as Microsoft and Google have already begun developing this new platform in preparation for its release. These companies are adding new products to their existing portfolios. The picture will only improve as the market grows. AI can recognize numerous languages and ways of communication at once. Lip reading can potentially reveal policy infractions. Though intriguing, the concept that artificial intelligence would bias digital environments is frightening. This technology has many uses, yet also raises ethical issues. Transparency, accountability, digital trust, and privacy will require several partners to build artificial intelligence and the metaverse. The metaverse is a mix of technologies. The future of the metaverse will be significantly impacted by the application of artificial intelligence. In addition, the gamification of the environment will increase the level of user engagement. One of the most important applications of artificial intelligence in the metaverse is computer vision, for instance. It has the potential to revolutionize how people interact online and to make the world a more welcoming and open place for all people. Additionally, the price is decreasing on an annual basis [2].

15.7　Conclusion and Future Directions

As science and technology continue to advance, AI will play an increasingly important role in streamlining users' access to various virtual environments and enhancing their ability to interact with virtual worlds. Avatars are just one example of the kinds of digital beings that people will be able to create and control in the metaverse. As this immersive realm grows, businesses must examine how AI will affect our job. Individuals will soon be able to utilize the same technology to connect with virtual people. Sell items, make digital art using non-fungible tokens, and attend virtual events. Imagine for a moment that you could go shopping in a virtual mall that featured actual clothing stores. In the virtual world, it is even possible to attend concerts by participating in a virtual concert. You might be more optimistic about the future of the metaverse than you really should be. Because technology is advancing at such a rapid rate, virtual reality glasses and headsets are becoming increasingly sophisticated, and the level of resolution in these devices is continuously improving. The metaverse will ultimately have a profound impact on our culture, and it will be up to us to determine how we wish to adapt.

It is possible that in the not-too-distant future, putting on a pair of glasses will be as easy as having a conversation in person with a friend who lives on the other side of the world. Proponents of the Metaverse contend that the idea of a virtual world that is wholly supported by virtual assets is still in its infancy. In the same way that not all forecasts came true right away when the internet was first developed, not all forecasts came true right away. Even though we do not yet know whether it is real, the idea that lies behind the concept is extremely exciting, and businesses have already begun working on it.

References

1. Chang, L., Zhang, Z. et al., 6G-enabled edge AI for metaverse: Challenges, methods, and future research directions. *J. Commun. Inf. Networks*, 7, 2, 107–121, Jun. 2022.
2. Van Huynh, D., Khosravirad, S.R. et al., Edge intelligence-based ultra-reliable and low-latency communications for digital twin-enabled metaverse. *IEEE Wireless Commun. Lett.*, 11, 8, August 2022.

3. Huang, H., Zeng, X., Zhao, L., Qui, C., Wu, H., Fand, L., Fusion of building information modeling and blockchain for metaverse: A survey, in: *IEEE Open Journal of the Computer Society,* vol. 3, pp. 195–207, 2022.

4. Lee, C.-S. *et al.,* Fuzzy ontology-based intelligent agent for high-school student learning in AI-FML Metaverse. *2022 IEEE International Conference on Fuzzy Systems (FUZZ-IEEE).*

5. Huynh-The, Thien T. *et al.,* Artificial intelligence for the metaverse: A survey." *Eng. Appl. Artif. Intell.,* 117, 105581, 2022.

6. Aloqaily, M., Bouachir, O., Karray, F., Ridhawi, I.A., Saddik, A.E., Integrating digital twin and advanced intelligent technologies to realize the metaverse, in: *IEEE Consumer Electronics Magazine,* 2022.

7. Yang, Q., Zhao, Y. *et al.,* Fusing blockchain and AI with metaverse: A survey. *Digital Object Identifier,* 3, 122–136, 2022.

8. Sun, J. *et al.,* Metaverse: Survey, applications, security, and opportunities. ArXiv abs/2210.07990, 2022.

9. Wang, Y. and Zhao, J., Mobile edge computing, metaverse, 6G wireless communications, artificial intelligence, and blockchain: Survey and their convergence, ArXiv abs/2209.14147, 2022

10. Xu, M., Ng, W.C. *et al.,* A full dive into realizing the edge-enabled metaverse: Visions, enabling technologies, and challenges, 20 Aug 2022.

11. Wang, Y. *et al.,* A survey on metaverse: Fundamentals, security, and privacy. *IEEE Commun. Surv. Tutor.,* 25, 319–352, 2022.

12. Park, S.-M. and Kim, Y.-G., A metaverse: Taxonomy, components, and open challenges. *IEEE Access,* 10, 4209–4251, 2022

13. Wang, Y. *et al.,* A survey on metaverse: Fundamentals, security, and privacy. *IEEE Commmun. Serv. Tutor.,* 25, 319–352, 2022.

14. Yu, Q., Ni, J. *et al.,* Special issue on cybertwin-driven 6G: Architectures, methods, and applications. *IEEE Internet Things J.,* 822, 16191–16194, November 15, 2021.

15. Michael, Z., Let's rename everything 'the metaverse'. *IEEE Comput. Soc.,* 55, 3, 124–29, 2022

16. Chen, S.-C., *Multimedia research toward the metaverse,* Published by the IEEE Computer Society, Digital Object, United States, 2022.

17. Faraboschi, P., Frachtenberg, E., Laplante, P. *et al., Virtual worlds (metaverse): From skepticism to fear, to immersive opportunities,* Published by the IEEE Computer Society, Digital Object Identifier, United States, 2022.

18. Kshetri, N., *Web 3.0 and the metaverse shaping organizations' brand and product strategies,* Published by the IEEE Computer Society, Digital Object Identifier, United States, 2022.

19. Cheng, R. *et al.*, Will metaverse be NextG internet? Vision, hype, and reality. *IEEE Network*, 36, 197–204, 2022

20. Thien, H.-T. *et al.*, Artificial intelligence for the metaverse: A survey. *Eng. Appl. Artif. Intell.*, 117, 105581, 2022.

21. Panda, S.K. and Satapathy, S.C., An investigation into smart contract deployment on Ethereum platform using Web3.js and solidity using blockchain, in: *Data Engineering and Intelligent Computing*, Advances in Intelligent Systems and Computing, vol. 1, V. Bhateja, S.C. Satapathy, C.M. Travieso-González, V.N.M. Aradhya (Eds.), Springer, Singapore, 2021.

22. Panda, S.K., Rao, D.C., Satapathy, S.C., An investigation into the usability of blockchain technology in Internet of Things, in: *Data Engineering and Intelligent Computing*, Advances in Intelligent Systems and Computing, vol. 1, V. Bhateja, S.C. Satapathy, C.M. Travieso-González, V.N.M. Aradhya (Eds.), Springer, Singapore, 2021.

23. Panda, S.K., Dash, S.P., Jena, A.K., Optimization of block query response using evolutionary algorithm, in: *Data Engineering and Intelligent Computing*, Advances in Intelligent Systems and Computing, vol. 1, V. Bhateja, S.C. Satapathy, C.M. Travieso-González, V.N.M. Aradhya (Eds.), Springer, Singapore, 2021.

24. Nanda, S.K., Panda, S.K., Das, M., Satapathy, S.C., Automating vehicle insurance process using smart contract and Ethereum, in: *Advances in Micro-Electronics, Embedded Systems and IoT*, Lecture Notes in Electrical Engineering, vol. 838, V.V.S.S.S. Chakravarthy, W. Flores-Fuentes, V. Bhateja, B. Biswal (Eds.), Springer, Singapore, 2022.

25. Varaprasada Rao, K. and Panda, S.K., Secure electronic voting (E-voting) system based on blockchain on various platforms, in: *Computer Communication, Networking and IoT*, Lecture Notes in Networks and Systems, vol. 459, S.C. Satapathy, J.C.W. Lin, L.K. Wee, V. Bhateja, T.M. Rajesh (Eds.), Springer, Singapore, 2023.

26. Varaprasada Rao, K. and Panda, S.K., A design model of copyright protection system based on distributed ledger technology, in: *Computer Communication, Networking and IoT*, Lecture Notes in Networks and Systems, vol. 459, S.C. Satapathy, J.C.W. Lin, L.K. Wee, V. Bhateja, T.M. Rajesh (Eds.), Springer, Singapore, 2023.

27. Panda, S.K., Elngar, A.A., Balas, V.E., Kayed, M. (Eds.), *Bitcoin and Blockchain: History and Current Applications*, 1st ed, CRC Press, Boca Raton, 2020.

28. Panda, S.K., Jena, A.K., Swain, S.K., Satapathy, S.C. (Eds.), *Blockchain Technology: Applications and Challenges*, Springer, Intelligent Systems Reference, Library, Switzerland, 2021.

29. Sathya, A.R., Panda, S.K., Hanumanthakari, S., Enabling smart education system using blockchain technology, in: *Blockchain Technology: Applications and Challenges*, Intelligent Systems Reference Library, vol. 203, S.K. Panda, A.K. Jena, S.K. Swain, S.C. Satapathy (Eds.), Springer, Cham, 2021.

30. Lokre, S.S., Naman, V., Priya, S., Panda, S.K., Gun tracking system using blockchain technology, in: *Blockchain Technology: Applications and Challenges*, Intelligent Systems Reference Library, vol. 203, S.K. Panda, A.K. Jena, S.K. Swain, S.C. Satapathy (Eds.), Springer, Cham, 2021.

31. Panda, S.K., Daliyet, S.P., Lokre, S.S., Naman, V., Distributed ledger technology in the construction industry using Corda, in: *The New Advanced Society: Artificial Intelligence and Industrial Internet of Things Paradigm*.

32. Panda, S.K., Mohammad, G.B., Nandan Mohanty, S., Sahoo, S., Smart contract-based land registry system to reduce frauds and time delay, in: *Security and Privacy*, p. e172, 2021.

33. Panda, S.K. and Satapathy, S.C., Drug traceability and transparency in medical supply chain using blockchain for easing the process and creating trust between stakeholders and consumers. *Pers. Ubiquit. Comput.*, 2021.

34. Niveditha, V.R., Sekaran, K., Singh, K.A., Panda, S.K., Effective prediction of bitcoin price using wolf search algorithm and bidirectional LSTM on internet of things data. *Int. J. of Syst. of Syst. Eng.*, 11, 3-4, 224–236, 2021.

35. Sri Arza, M. and Panda, S.K., An integration of blockchain and machine learning into the healthcare system, in: *Machine Learning Adoption in Blockchain-Based Intelligent Manufacturing*, vol. 1, pp. 33–58, 2022.

36. Murala, D.K., Panda, S.K., Swain, S.K., A survey on cloud computing security and privacy issues and challenges. *J. Adv. Res. Dyn. Control Syst.*, 11, 1276–1290, 2019.

37. Murala, D.K., Panda, S.K., Swain, S.K., Secure dynamic groups data sharing with modified revocable attribute-based encryption in cloud. *Int. J. Recent Technol. Eng. (IJRTE)*, 8, 4, 9508–9512, 2019.

38. Murala, D.K., Panda, S.K., Swain, S.K., A novel hybrid approach for providing data security and privacy from malicious attacks in the cloud environment. *J. Adv. Res. Dyn. Control Syst.*, 11, 1291–1300, 2019.

39. Panda, S.K., Swain, S.K., Mall, R., An investigation into usability aspects of E-commerce websites using users' preferences. *Adv. Comput. Sci.: An Int. J.*, 4, 1, 65–73, 2015.

40. Panda, S.K., Swain, S.K., Mall, R., Measuring web site usability quality complexity metrics for navigability, in: *Intelligent Computing, Communication and Devices*, Advances in Intelligent Systems and Computing, vol. 308, L. Jain, S. Patnaik, N. Ichalkaranje (Eds.), Springer, New Delhi, 2015.

41. Panda, S.K., A usability evaluation framework for B2C E-commerce websites. *Comput. Eng. Intell. Syst.*, 5, 3, 66–85, 2014.

42. Bhalerao, V., Panda, S.K., Jena, A.K., Optimization of loss function on human faces using generative adversarial networks, in: *Machine Learning Approaches for Urban Computing*, Studies in Computational Intelligence, vol. 968, M. Bandyopadhyay, M. Rout, S. Chandra Satapathy (Eds.), Springer, Singapore, 2021.

43. Panda, S.K. and Dwivedi, M., Minimizing food wastage using machine learning: A novel approach, in: *Smart Intelligent Computing and Applications*, Smart Innovation, Systems and Technologies, S. Satapathy, V. Bhateja, J. Mohanty, S. Udgata (Eds.), vol. 159, pp. 465–473, Springer, Singapore, 2020.

44. Panda, S.K., A.R, S., Mishra, M., Satpathy, S., A supervised learning algorithm to forecast weather conditions for playing cricket. *Int. J. Innovative Technol. Exploring Eng. (IJITEE)*, 9, 1, 2019.

45. Panda, S.K., Fraud-resistant crowdfunding system using Ethereum blockchain, in: *Bitcoin and Blockchain*, pp. 237–276, 2020.

46. Panda, S.K., Mishra, V., Balamurali, R., Elngar, A.A., *Artificial intelligence and machine learning in business management concepts, challenges, and case studies*, pp. 1–278, Boca Raton, CRC Press, 2021.

47. Joshi, S., Panda, S.K., AR, S., Optimal deep learning model to identify the development of pomegranate fruit in farms. *Int. J. Innovative Technol. Exploring Eng.*, 9, 3, 2352–2356, 2020.

48. Puranam, K.S.R., Gaddam, M.C.T., K, V.P.R., Panda, S.K., Reddy, G.S.M., Anatomy and lifecycle of a bitcoin transaction. *Proceedings of International Conference on Sustainable Computing in Science, Technology and Management (SUSCOM)*, Amity University Rajasthan, Jaipur - India, February 26-28, 2019, February 18, 2019, Available at SSRN: https://ssrn.com/abstract=3355106 or http://dx.doi.org/10.2139/ssrn.3355106.

49. Panda, S.K. and Swain, S.K., *Quality assurance aspects of web design, design solutions for improving website quality and effectiveness*, pp. 87–129, IGI Global, United States, 2016.

50. Panda, S.K., Bhalerao, V., AR, S., A machine learning model to identify duplicate questions in social media forums. *Int. J. Innovative Technol. Exploring Eng.*, 9, 4, 370–373, 2020.

51. Ahmareen, S., Raj, A., Potluri, S., Panda, S.K., Book Shala: An android-based application design and implementation of sharing books, in: *Smart Intelligent Computing and Applications*, Smart Innovation, Systems and Technologies, vol. 159, S. Satapathy, V. Bhateja, J. Mohanty, S. Udgata (Eds.), Springer, Singapore, 2020.

52. Panda, S.K., Das, S.S., Swain, S.K., S-model for service-oriented applications in web engineering. *Reg. Coll. Of Manag.*, 10, 3, 38–46, 2013.

53. Panda, S.K., An investigation into usability and productivity of ECommerce websites. https://shodhganga.inflibnet.ac.in:8443/jspui/handle/10603/123505

54. Panda, S.K., Chandrasekhar, A., Gantayat, P.K., Panda, M.R., Detecting brain tumor using image segmentation: A novel approach, in: *Data Engineering and Intelligent Computing,* Lecture Notes in Networks and Systems, vol. 446, V. Bhateja, L. Khin Wee, J.C.W. Lin, S.C. Satapathy, T.M. Rajesh (Eds.), Springer, Singapore, 2022.

55. Sanghi, P., Panda, S.K., Pati, C., Gantayat, P.K., Learning deep features and classification for fresh or off vegetables to prevent food wastage using machine learning algorithms, in: *Intelligent Data Engineering and Analytics,* Smart Innovation, Systems and Technologies, vol. 266, S.C. Satapathy, P. Peer, J. Tang, V. Bhateja, A. Ghosh (Eds.), Springer, Singapore, 2022.

56. Gantayat, P.K., Mohapatra, S., Panda, S.K., Secure trust level routing in delay-tolerant network with node categorization technique, in: *Intelligent Data Engineering and Analytics,* Smart Innovation, Systems and Technologies, vol. 266, S.C. Satapathy, P. Peer, J. Tang, V. Bhateja, A. Ghosh (Eds.), Springer, Singapore, 2022.

57. Panda, S.K., Urkude, S.V., Urkude, V.R., Vairachilai, S., An investigation into COVID 19 pandemic in India, in: *The New Advanced Society: Artificial Intelligence and Industrial Internet of Things Paradigm,* vol. 1, Wiley, USA, 2022.

58. Panda, S., Das, S., & Swain, S., Web site productivity measurement using single task size measure. *J. Inf. Sci. Comput. Technol.,* 4, 3, 347–353, 2015.

59. Hanumanthakari, S. and Panda, S.K., Detecting face mask for prevent COVID-19 using deep learning: A novel approach, in: *Smart Intelligent Computing and Applications, Volume 2,* Smart Innovation, Systems and Technologies, vol. 283, S.C. Satapathy, V. Bhateja, M.N. Favorskaya, T. Adilakshmi (Eds.), Springer, Singapore, 2022.

60. Panda, S.K., Sathya, A.R., Das, S., Panda, S.K., Bitcoin: Beginning of the cryptocurrency era, in: *Recent Advances in Blockchain Technology,* Intelligent Systems Reference Library, vol. 237, V. Mishra, S.P. Dash, A.K. Pani (Eds.), Springer, Cham, 2023.

61. Murala, D.K., Panda, S.K., Sahoo, S.K., Securing electronic health record system in cloud environment using blockchain technology, in: *Recent Advances in Blockchain Technology,* Intelligent Systems Reference Library, vol. 237, S.K. Panda, V. Mishra, S.P. Dash, A.K. Pani (Eds.), Springer, Cham, 2023.

62. Rao, K.V., Murala, D.K., Panda, S.K., Blockchain: A study of new business model, in: *Recent Advances in Blockchain Technology,* Intelligent Systems Reference Library, vol. 237, S.K. Panda, V. Mishra, S.P. Dash, A.K. Pani (Eds.), Springer, Cham, 2023.

63. Panda, S.K., Mishra, V., Dash, S.P., Pani, A.K., *Recent advances in block-chain technology real-world applications*, Intelligent Systems Reference Library (ISRL, volume 237), vol. 1, pp. 1–317, 978-3-031-22835-3.

64. Panda, S.K., Mohapatra, R.K., Panda, S., Balamurugan, S., *The new advanced society: Artificial intelligence and industrial internet of things paradigm*, vol. 1, pp. 1–512, Wiley, USA, 2022.

65. Nanda, S.K., Panda, S.K., Das, M., Satapathy, S.C., Decentralization of car insurance system using machine learning and distributed ledger technology, in: *Intelligent Data Engineering and Analytics. FICTA 2022*, Smart Innovation, Systems and Technologies, vol. 327, V. Bhateja, X.S. Yang, J. Chun-Wei Lin, R. Das (Eds.), Springer, Singapore, 2023.

16

The Internet of Things in Developing Metaverse

Dileep Kumar Murala[1] and Sandeep Kumar Panda[2*]

*[1]Computer Science and Engineering, Faculty of Science and Technology,
ICFAI Foundation for Higher Education, Hyderabad, Telangana, India
[2]Data Science and Artificial Intelligence, Faculty of Science and Technology,
ICFAI Foundation for Higher Education, Hyderabad, Telangana, India*

Abstract

The term "metaverse" refers to a collection of technological devices including those related to the Internet of Things (IoT), blockchain, artificial intelligence, and any other technical businesses, including the medical sector. The IoT and metaverse are each other's digital twins; in their virtual workstations, the metaverse makes extensive use of IoT gadgets. The blockchain-based metaverse makes use of these data, which carry an identifying tag that is unique to it, as traceable data. The use of such data as a resource for artificial intelligence is becoming increasingly important in the metaverse. You will be able to engage in social and economic activities not constrained by the limitations of the real world in a secure and unrestricted manner in the digital virtual world being built by the metaverse with the help of artificial intelligence and blockchain technologies. The deployment of these cutting-edge technologies will be accelerated. In this chapter, we will explore basic information about IoT; the metaverse; the relationship between IoT and the metaverse; the importance of the metaverse in IoT; the contribution of IoT for creating the metaverse; and the applications, advantages, and challenges of the IoT-based metaverse. We will conclude with future research directions.

Keywords: Internet of Things, metaverse, digital twins, IoT plus metaverse, artificial intelligence, machine learning, blockchain, IoT gadgets

*Corresponding author: skpanda00007@gmail.com

Chandrashekhar A, Shaik Himam Saheb, Sandeep Kumar Panda, S. Balamurugan and Sheng-Lung Peng (eds.)
Metaverse and Immersive Technologies: An Introduction to Industrial, Business and Social
Applications, (437–466) © 2023 Scrivener Publishing LLC

16.1 Introduction

The science fiction metaverse we saw had endless possibilities. Avatar and Ready Player One are great examples. Selina Yuan, general manager of Alibaba Cloud Intelligence's international business section, describes the metaverse as a three-dimensional digital realm in movies where users can interact as avatars and experience everything they desire. In this universe, players can also escape the physical reality of their own lives. The true potential of the metaverse lies in its capability to make more effective use of the digital intelligence we already possess and to visualize that intelligence in a way that reveals novel insights that could have otherwise stayed hidden. This is where the metaverse promise lies. If we use this technology, it may be possible for us to solve problems that exist in the real world and build a society that is more inclusive, environmentally conscious, and technologically advanced. The fact that the IoT is currently driving this trend comes as no surprise to anyone. The proliferation of low-cost, pervasive sensors has sped up the development of a concept called "Ambient Intelligence." This concept describes a system's ability to monitor its surroundings and respond appropriately to the presence of humans as well as specific events or conditions. Because of this, there has been a rise in interest in the IoT, which has been fueled by the proliferation of mobile information technology [2].

16.1.1 Internet of Things (IoT)

Over the past few years, a whole new study subfield known as the Internet of Things has emerged. As part of the transformation brought on by the IoT, technological and social elements are being incorporated into the existing healthcare systems [1]. It is anticipated that both the economic and social climate will improve in the not-too-distant future. It is moving away from the traditional method of carrying out these tasks and changing the way healthcare systems are managed. A primary focus should be placed on the development of healthcare systems that are more focused on the needs of the patients, make it simpler for patients to receive treatment, and monitor them more carefully. The IoT is becoming an increasingly important component of healthcare delivery systems because it enables providers to offer higher-quality care at reduced costs to patients while also enhancing the user experience. The applications of this technology are quite varied and extensive [3].

The terrible respiratory outbreak that takes place in the book is currently putting the health of people all around the world in jeopardy. Since then, the pandemic that began in 1918 and was caused by the introduction of the syncytial coronavirus has been regarded as the worst emergency affecting public health on a global scale. This illness has symptoms similar to those of the flu, such as a temperature. Both a cough and a feeling of weariness are indicators that should be picked up on as early as possible in the diagnostic process. Incubation times for COVID-19 have been shown to range anywhere from one to fourteen days [4]. The doctors were taken aback by a patient who hadn't been participating in any kind of treatment. There is a wide variety of symptoms that could indicate that someone has been exposed to the COVID-19 virus. Putting these individuals in isolation is very necessary at this time. As a direct consequence of this, the duration of the healing process has significantly increased. It is not possible to make an accurate prognosis on the severity of this illness based on the age of the patient or any other signs [5].

16.1.2   Characteristics of the Internet of Things

Connection: IoT connectivity is the most significant characteristic. Any business use case requires smooth communication between IoT ecosystem components including sensors, computation engines, data hubs, etc. Radio waves, Bluetooth, Wi-Fi, Li-Fi, etc. connect IoT devices. We can maximize efficiency and develop generic communication across IoT ecosystems and Industries by using internet connectivity layer protocols. An intranet or on-premises IoT ecosystem may be possible.

Detecting: Based on past experiences, humans can easily understand and analyze their conditions. In IoT, we must read the analog signal and transform it to gain relevant insights. Based on an issue, we collect data using electrochemical, gyroscope, pressure, light sensors, GPS, RFID, and more. Light, pressure, velocity, and imaging sensors are used in automotive applications. A use case needs the right sensing paradigm [6, 23].

Active Engagements: IoT devices actively engage products, cross-platform technology, and services. We employ blockchain cloud computing to engage IoT components. Industry-grade IoT solutions require raw analog data to be gathered, preprocessed, and scaled to business capacity. Google says only 50% of organized and 1% of unstructured data is used for business decisions. Carriers must anticipate future data manipulation needs while creating IoT ecosystems. Active engagements require your systems to handle massive data spanning technologies, platforms, products, and sectors [7, 24].

Scale: The design of scaled Internet of Things devices ought to be such that they can be easily scaled up or down in response to changes in demand. The Internet of Things is being used for a wide variety of purposes, ranging from the automation of workstations in huge factories to the smart home automation of individual homes. A carrier's IoT infrastructure should be designed with consideration for both their existing and future levels of customer engagement [8].

The Nature of Change: Any use case for the Internet of Things must begin by gathering and transforming data in such a way that it may be utilized to inform business choices as the very first and most important stage. Throughout this entire procedure, several different Internet of Things components will need to dynamically modify their states. For instance, the input of a temperature sensor will change continuously depending on a variety of factors such as the weather, location, and so on. The Internet of Things (IoT) devices ought to be developed with this consideration in mind [25–27].

Intelligence: In almost every IoT use case today, data is used to get valuable business insights and make crucial business decisions. We employ machine learning and deep learning to get insights from this massive data set. Preprocessed analog signals are utilized to train machine-learning models. We must consider business-appropriate data infrastructure [28–30].

Energy: The overall ecosystems require a significant amount of energy, from the end components up to the connectivity and analytics layers. When developing an ecosystem for the Internet of Things, we need to consider design methodology to ensure that energy usage is kept to a minimum.

Safety: Internet of Things ecosystems requires security. Connectivity components send sensitive data from endpoints to the analytics layer of an IoT ecosystem. This happens throughout an IoT ecosystem. We must utilize safety, security, and firewalls while creating an Internet of Things system to prevent data abuse. If even one part of an Internet of Things ecosystem is compromised, the system as a whole may eventually be rendered inoperable [31–34].

Integration: The Internet of Things combines a variety of models that span many domains to enhance the user experience. In addition to this, it guarantees an appropriate balance between the costs of infrastructure and operations [35–38, 67].

16.1.3   Metaverse

Virtually augmented physical reality and physically persistent virtual space created the "metaverse," a shared virtual environment. This space includes all virtual worlds, AR, and the internet. Virtually upgraded physical reality and physically persistent virtual space created a shared virtual space. All virtual worlds, AR, and the internet are included. It allows real-time user interaction with virtual objects and environments. In recent years, the idea of the metaverse has come to garner a greater amount of interest as a potential future application of technologies involving virtual and augmented reality [9].

16.1.4   Applications of Metaverse

The Metaverse can be utilized in a diverse assortment of contexts. It has applications in many different fields, ranging from the commercial world to the entertainment industry. The most prevalent application for it is communicating via various social media sites [10]. Before we go into the specifics, let's look at a few samples, which are as follows:

Commercial Purpose: Additionally beneficial to organizations could be emerging technical possibilities. The use of social media has altered the practices of digital marketing and advertising by making it possible for businesses to promote their goods and services in a more immersive manner. This can be accomplished through the use of similar marketing materials and advertisements, virtual shops, and highly interactive engagement and customer care.

The Education Industry: When compared to other methods of education delivery, online learning through video conferencing and asynchronous courses is typically characterized by a greater emphasis on passivity and indirectness.

Entertainment: To put it another way, virtual reality (VR) may be integrated into theme parks and amusement parks, making these establishments' prime locations for VR applications.

Simulation aimed at Saving Lives: It's possible that those who aren't familiar with computers won't be able to access the new social economy or experience it, yet simulations like this could end up saving people's lives. A primary focus should be placed on widening participation in the Metaverse to accommodate more people.

Interactions with Other People: Facebook and Twitter are two-dimensional since users can only communicate screen-to-screen. Real-time face-to-face conversation and realistic use of virtual content are now conceivable.

16.2   Related Works

IoT and metaverse research are growing. Users can interact with each other and virtual items and surroundings in the metaverse [11]. This connection has several possible applications, one of which is the usage of IoT devices to improve the immersive experience of the metaverse by delivering real-time data and interactions with the actual world. For instance, a metaverse that is driven by the Internet of Things might give users the ability to interact with virtual representations of real-world things or surroundings, as well as the ability to manage and monitor equipment in the real world from within the virtual realm. Another possible use for the combination of the Internet of Things with the metaverse is in the creation of apps for virtual and augmented reality that can be used in a variety of fields, including education, entertainment, and healthcare. Users might be able to learn and practice complicated operations in an environment that is both safe and under control if, for instance, virtual reality training simulations are driven by the IoT [12]. There is also the possibility of applications in the field of smart cities, where the combination of IoT and metaverse could make it possible to create virtual city models and simulations that can be used for planning and decision-making. In general, the combination of the IoT and the metaverse has the potential to transform how we interact with both the real world and the digital world. It is an interesting area of study and development that will likely continue to advance in the years to come [13].

16.2.1   Metaverse and its Architecture

The COVID-19 pandemic limits and marketing by Facebook and Microsoft have highlighted the usefulness and ease of the virtual world (Metaverse). [3] Builds a university campus prototype to explore social good in the Metaverse, whereas [5] proposes a Blockchain-based platform for Metaverse applications. Despite early consideration of virtual service user experience benefits and problems [4]. [6] Investigates incentive mechanisms for Metaverse services using programmed distributed computing. The authors of [8] address an attempt to overcome this issue, although they focus on the VSP selection problem of unmanned aerial vehicles (UAVs) and ignore synchronization intensity control and DT temporal values. Several Metaverse architectures have been proposed, including a seven-layer system [5] and a three-layer design [1]. However, considering the Metaverse's overall functionality, its architecture should include the following four components, interface (immersive technologies like AR, VR, [7], [9], and XR [10] and next-generation human-brain interconnection to enrich a user's subjective sense in the virtual life), infrastructure (the fundamental resources to support the platform, such as communication [7], computation, blockchain [8], a see [3] for more on Metaverse architecture and difficulties. This presentation will focus on the Metaverse cross-world system, which attempts to unite the two realms.

16.2.2   Digital Twins (DTs) in the Age of the Metaverse

The idea of digital twins is not brand new. Grieves initially mentioned them in 2003 [6] during a lecture on "product life cycle management," which describes DTs in terms of the physical product, the virtual product, and their relationships. NASA defined DTs as "integrated multi-physical, multiscale, probabilistic simulations of an as-built vehicle or system using the best available physical models, sensor updates, and historical data" in the second part of 2012 [7]. These early definitions show that DTs mirror physical objects. Since a physical object's state changes over time, physical & Virtual updates are needed. There is no consensus on DT updates to physical objects. On the other hand, [17] and [9] believe that virtual and real DTs are updated in both directions. Digital models are used by [8] to describe the case of no updating between spaces. Digital shadows relate to one-way updates from physical space to cyberspace. The digital object changes when the physical object changes, but not vice versa. This is done so that the authors can emphasize that there are updates in both directions. On the other hand, some other works, such as [6], [4], and [1], use DTs exclusively in simulation-based contexts. They only see DTs as physical virtual digital shadows. Cyber-physical systems (CPS) [14] are being studied to control physical assets via their DTs (physical virtual). CPS supports large-scale distributed control applications including automated traffic control and omnipresent healthcare monitoring and delivery. DTs, digital shadows, and CPS distinctions have been advocated for in several works

[15, 18]. DT definitions are ambiguous. This article's DTs pertain to the Metaverse's digital presence, unlike other DT research. The physical object is replicated digitally. DTs should be looser for these reasons. First, unlike smart manufacturing or Industry 4.0, where DTs are designed and explored only for a company's application [9], the Metaverse's platform feature may support numerous virtual enterprises [3]. Thus, many VSPs can share DTs. If all VSPs have bi-directional communication between physical and cyberspace and each VSP changes its DTs, it may be unclear which VSP's DT state change should be synchronized with the physical counterpart. We ignore the complex case of bi-directional communication and uncertain DT ownership in an interoperable Metaverse. Second, the Metaverse will create many new applications. Interoperability [8] (for example, VSPs sharing DTs), human experience [3], and blockchain technology and artificial intelligence [2] contribute to this. The next step in NFT development is combining NFTs and DTs [3]. In this case, a physical asset's status affects the value of an NFT. Because of this, our definition of DT may be extended to work with a larger range of Metaverse applications by using the Internet of Things (IoT) to sense real entity states.

16.3   The Connection Between the Metaverse and the Internet of Things

Many industry professionals and analysts believe that the Metaverse will soon become extremely popular. It will have a profound and long-lasting impact on the internet. This virtual environment will revolutionize how we view and interact with the internet, and it will have an impact on all areas, including e-commerce, social media, real estate, and education, among others.

Because the greatest hurdle for Metaverse is its ability to map data from real-life and convert it into virtual reality, the connection between the IoT and Metaverse may now be obvious. These data must be precise, well-organized, understandable, and protected, and they ought to be current. While the Internet of Things has been operational for several years now, the Metaverse is getting ready to accept hundreds of sensors, cameras, wearable devices, and other kinds of electronic gadgets [16, 39, 40].

The Metaverse and the Internet of Things will mutually strengthen one another. Already being referred to as a "technological twin" by certain professionals. While the Internet of Things will make it possible for Metaverse to analyze and interact with the actual world, Metaverse will also operate as a 3D user interface to the Internet of Things devices, paving the way for a new type of user experience that is specifically customized to the Internet of Things. Both the Metaverse and the Internet of Things will assist people all over the world in making data-driven judgments with minimal effort and mental preparation [17].

16.3.1   What Does "IoT plus Metaverse" Stand For?

Examining the points at which the Internet of Things and the Metaverse converge is a necessary step if we are going to comprehend either concept. The digital twin can be thought of as existing at this point of intersection. Several fascinating ramifications might be discussed regarding this situation, even though this would be an unusual application of digital twins.

NASA and Product Lifecycle Management are behind the new buzzword "digital twin" (PLM). Digital avatars are more like fantasy massively multiplayer online role-playing game characters than digital twins (Massively Multiplayer Online Role-Playing Game). In most cases, rather than appearing to be your actual physical self, you take on the appearance of a Silvan elf, such as Legolas [18].

Then, can you explain what a digital twin is? A digital twin is, to put it plainly, a digital mirror of the physical state and condition of a one-of-a-kind physical entity. In an ideal scenario, the reflection would be as near to real-time as possible and would be applicable in everyday situations. Digital twinning is utilized in the Internet of Things application known as condition monitoring, which has been around for quite some time. The data that you are monitoring, which reflects the dynamic properties of an object, can be given digital significance through the deployment of something called a digital twin. Consider something like your temperature, your blood pressure, or your heart rate as an example. These aspects of yourself are not fixed characteristics. They are not static like the color of your eyes; rather, they are constantly shifting. Water pumps have dynamic features including vibration, impeller speed, and motor temperature [19, 41].

Two camps debate digital twin borders. Digital twins include data input, management, modeling, and simulation. This technique has made the concept of a digital twin more complicated and burdensome. I think digital twins should focus on their main function, which is to mirror a single real object and its digital replica. Why? Mirror-making is complicated. Modeling and simulation can be built on top of a digital twin using its data exhaust or historical data [20, 42, 43].

What is a metaverse "digital twin"? The fitness tracker or smartwatch that can measure your heart rate and submit the data to a social fitness app is the closest device to a metaverse digital twin application. Sony's Playstation Eye and Microsoft's Kinect motion controller, both discontinued, are early examples. Motion controllers used gesture and bone detection to control games. A digital twin was needed to link gesture control signals to a game avatar's limbs [21].

16.3.2   Why Will the Convergence of the Internet of Things and the Metaverse be Important?

It would appear that there are two distinct types of metaverses, or at the very least, two distinct lines of thought regarding metaverses. The first is the virtual reality metaverse, which is being promoted by Meta (which was once known as Facebook). The other type is known as augmented reality, or AR for short. This type focuses on cyber-physical meta environments, which are expected to serve as AR's primary foundation in the years to come. These archetypes, which belong to the "metaverse," are already in use [22, 44, 62]. The maps application that comes preinstalled on your phone is a great illustration of a core application. This is almost certainly the most important augmented reality application that we utilize at the moment. Simply put, we do not consider it to be such at this time because it is only informative and requires you to either glance at the screen of your smartphone or listen carefully for directional or contextual clues. We don't call it augmented reality because we've been taught to believe that AR can only happen with stylish glasses, which people who don't need glasses would wear regardless [1].

Your experiential interface into a virtual world, also known as a metaverse, will be augmented by IoT for the VR Metaverse. Like current gaming interfaces that record and control movements. Internet of Things devices or a sensor-laden body suit will measure your health and condition to trigger a virtual response. Wear a sensor-equipped body suit [22, 46, 63]. A higher heart rate and breathing rate could lead your avatar, which may not look like you, to perspire. Your avatar's virtual constitution may decrease, making it weaker and more fatigued. A Dungeons & Dragons metaverse or sports simulation may use this strategy. The Internet of Things acts as a sensory network for the augmented reality metaverse, bringing real-world objects into the digital world. It enables augmented reality applications context and situational awareness and causes digital and virtual objects to interact with you in the real world. The Internet of Things (IoT) bridges the physical and cyber worlds by placing digital objects in your field of view, reacting to your finger motions, or initiating a cyber-physical application or function based on a physical occurrence [21, 45].

16.3.3   What Do You Think the Internet of Things Will be Responsible for in the Metaverse?

The Internet of Things will make it possible for us to solve one of the most difficult problems we are now facing in the metaverse, which is figuring out how to map data from real life, in real-time, into a digital reality. The Internet of Things' primary function will be to integrate the real world with the digital sphere. To support the metaverse and its immersive virtual environment, there is no question that more sophisticated Internet of Things infrastructures will be required. But augmented reality (AR), not virtual reality, is where all the excitement is happening in the metaverse right now (VR). The Internet of Things will create a metaverse digital duplicate of each user, comparable to an "avatar."

16.3.4   How Important is Metaverse Data Collection and Data?

Data is now valuable. Digital information unlocks value. Without data, the metaverse is an online forum depicting the universe. Capturing data from the "real" world, especially from IoT devices, may determine the metaverse's success. This metaverse data must be responsive, secure, and meaningful. 84% of IT, telecom, and technology leaders want to investigate virtual world data intelligence solutions within two years to support their metaverse strategy.

16.3.5   How Can the Internet of Things Connect the Metaverse to Devices that Exist in the Actual World? Why Should We Care About This?

Cloud technology is essential to establishing a genuine connection between the Internet of Things and the metaverse. Access to the cloud and the data collection and processing capability it offers organizations has been made infinitely scalable thanks to pioneering cloud providers such as Amazon Web Services and Microsoft. In the coming years, cloud-native platforms will be the driving force behind innovation. These platforms will allow developers to build change-resistant and nimble application architectures to quickly incorporate the metaverse [20]. Cloud technology provides the processing capability and speed to send IoT data to the metaverse in real-time. This is because cloud technology is hosted in the cloud. The foundational infrastructure consisting of Internet of Things devices, data analytics, and services, which will be developed on top of cloud technology, is what will make it possible for us to have a real-time avatar in the metaverse. The smooth interoperability of AR and IoT data, supported by the cloud, will be essential to the success of the metaverse because it will enable the creation of new, advanced applications that will assist in the resolution of problems that occur in the real world [19, 47, 48, 64].

16.3.6   The Internet of Things and the Metaverse: How Will They Complement One Another?

The Internet can be compared to an older version of what is now known as the Metaverse. The Metaverse does not require the use of a computer monitor; rather, it functions as the optimal medium for humans to engage in extensive social interactions with one another.

People are now able to communicate with one another while engaging in activities like viewing movies, playing video games, or virtually traveling to well-known tourist destinations thanks to advancements in technology. Metaverse can successfully broaden the potential of the internet by utilizing 3D technology, virtual reality, augmented reality, and artificial intelligence. Even though the IoT has previously been utilized to successfully connect real-world things to the internet. Incorporating Metaverse, on the other hand, can unquestionably provide customers with new opportunities. These technologies, when combined, would make it possible to transport data in real-time from the physical world into the digital realm [3, 49, 50].

As a direct consequence of this, the gulf that exists between the real world and the virtual world will be significantly narrowed. IoT devices will have a greater degree of connectivity both online and offline with the assistance of the Metaverse. Consumers might also easily create their digital avatars with the help of devices connected to the IoT. It is anticipated that the Metaverse will have a substantial impact on the IoT, in part thanks to the deployment of Digital Twins. In point of fact, because of the continual installation of Metaverse, Internet of Things technology will advance considerably more swiftly [4, 51, 65].

The IoT will be impacted in a variety of ways, some of which are listed below:

> ➤ *Improving Preparedness for Real-World Situations:* Artificial intelligence and practical expertise is vital to Metaverse's primary assumption. The utilization of

Metaverse in the Internet of Things to conduct virtual simulations will prove to be extremely beneficial to companies, as it will expand the breadth and depth of training. The Internet of Things can be used to help collect data from the more accurate real world and up to date, which will make the process of studying for exams more effective. Participants in the Metaverse can develop more complex software or AI algorithms, which can be used to discover problems and explain their impact on real life. As a consequence of this, the virtual world of the Metaverse is capable of properly representing reality when the Internet of Things is taken into consideration [5, 66].

➢ *An Environment with a Customizable and Personalized User Interface:* IoT devices typically have an easy-to-use user interface and can communicate with other devices in the physical environment. However, typical Internet of Things devices that have screens may use Metaverse to provide users with a 3D digital experience. As a consequence of this, consumers of IoT devices will have a more immersive experience. It will be possible to maintain a presence in both the actual and virtual worlds at the same time. As a consequence of this, businesses now have the opportunity to employ IoT app developers, who can significantly alter both the user interface and the user experience. When Internet of Things technology is implemented, the Metaverse will have a sense that is more comparable to the real world. It will be feasible for individuals and Internet of Things devices, as well as the complex environment and operations of the Metaverse, to engage with one another more [6]. The immersive quality of the Metaverse combined with the real-world use cases will allow us to improve our decision-making abilities while simultaneously reducing the amount of time spent studying and being trained [7].

➢ *Useful for Making Decisions in the Long Term:* The amount of digital material that is drawn from real-world objects, such as buildings, people, automobiles, clothing, and so on, is continually growing in the Metaverse. This includes things like structures and people. As a direct consequence of this, companies strive to create an identical digital reproduction of the real world. With the help of IoT and Metaverse, businesses can better prepare for a variety of scenarios and advance their long-term objectives. For the sake of accurately simulating a variety of situations and engaging in fruitful long-term planning, having access to data in real-time is essential. This might be very beneficial to many other industries, like the ones dealing with energy, transportation, healthcare, fashion, and so on. First and foremost, it's possible that AI and machine learning will play a significant part in long-term planning [8].

➤ *A Substantial Influence on The Development of Cloud Technology:* Both the Internet of Things and the Metaverse rely heavily on cloud technologies. However, the combination of these two factors might surely alter the potential of cloud technology. The incorporation of the Metaverse into the Internet of Things devices may cause cloud platforms such as Amazon Web Services and Microsoft Azure to appear and function very differently. Cloud service providers may be able to fulfill the full potential of cloud computing with the assistance of the Internet of Things Metaverse. It will be possible for developers of cloud technologies to achieve better scalability, robustness, and seamless functionality with their structural infrastructures. Users of cloud computing will have access to an increased amount of processing power as a result of the Metaverse [9].

➤ *IBC or Computing Based on Interaction:* The vast majority of digital interactions with computers are performed through the use of an input device or screen on a computer. People are required to enter data into IoT devices by utilizing a console or pressing a few buttons. The utilization of AR and VR technology in the Metaverse will change how we interact with devices connected to the IoT. Users won't even be able to distinguish whether they are communicating in a real or virtual setting because there will be no discernible difference. Because of this, the experience will be incredibly realistic and well-contextualized [10]. IoT devices that are equipped to handle augmented and virtual realities will make this a reality. With the help of the IoT, motion detection, AI-enabled edges, and customized data-gathering sensors, it will be feasible for computing to become more immersive and interaction-based.

16.4   The Importance of Metaverse in the IoT

Although IoT is already an extremely successful technology that connects physical things to the internet, the importance of Metaverse cannot be overstated. However, integrating Metaverse can most definitely provide consumers with access to previously unavailable opportunities. When combined, these technologies would make it possible for humans to collect data in real-time from the physical world and place it in the digital realm. As a result, it would make the gap between the real world and the virtual world substantially less [11, 52]. With the assistance of the Metaverse, Internet of Things devices will have a greater degree of connectivity in both the digital and the physical worlds. In addition, with the assistance of Internet of Things devices, individuals will have a much simpler time developing their digital avatars. The implementation of Digital Twins and other innovations inside the Metaverse is going to have a significant effect on the Internet of Things. The continued adoption of the Metaverse will lead to a significant acceleration in the development of the Internet of Things technology. Figure 16.1 describes the importance of IoT in Metaverse [12].

Enhancement of Training for Real-World Situations: The concept of the Metaverse as a whole is dependent on Artificial Intelligence (AI) as well as training in the actual world. The incorporation of Metaverse into IoT will be of tremendous assistance to businesses in the operation of virtual simulations, which will increase both the breadth and the authenticity of

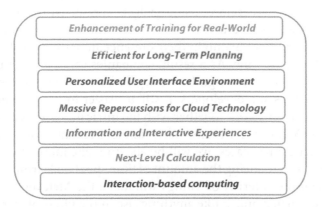

Figure 16.1 Importance of metaverse in the IoT.

training. Using IoT, we will be able to improve the process of test preparation by collecting data from the actual world that is both more accurate and updated in real-time. When we include IoT in the Metaverse's virtual environment, we give it the ability to accurately represent the real world. People working on Metaverse can design more refined software or AI algorithms that can detect issues and indicate what the ramifications are for real life [13, 53].

Efficient for Long-Term Planning: Because the Metaverse is constantly gaining digital content from real-world entities such as buildings, people, automobiles, clothing, and so on, it is an excellent tool for long-term planning. Therefore, companies aim to produce an exact reflection of our real world but in the virtual environment where they operate. The Internet of Things (IoT) and Metaverse can assist organizations in planning various scenarios and optimizing their long-term strategies. This might be of tremendous use in a variety of fields, including the fashion industry, healthcare, transportation, and others. Consequently, utilizing real-time data is essential for efficient long-term planning in addition to the accurate simulation of a variety of different scenarios. First and foremost, AI and Machine Learning (ML) have the potential to develop into substantial contributors to long-term planning [14, 54].

Personalized User Interface Environment: Internet of Things (IoT) devices often have a rudimentary user interface and are designed to work with other real-world devices. On the other hand, Metaverse has the potential to add a 3D digital user interface to conventional Internet of Things devices that have screens. Therefore, using gadgets connected to the internet of things will also provide users with a more immersive experience. They will have the ability to maintain their presence in both the real and virtual worlds at the same time. As a result, companies can tailor the user interface and experience to a significant degree by employing the services of internet of things app developers. It will be easier for people and Internet of Things devices to work together with the intricate systems and environments of the Metaverse. Because of the immersive nature of the Metaverse and the practical use cases, we will be able to make more informed judgments while also reducing the amount of time spent on learning new skills. Above, using the Internet of Things will make the Metaverse seem more natural and normal, much like anything else in the physical world [15].

Massive Repercussions for Cloud Technology: The Internet of Things and the Metaverse are both highly reliant on cloud technologies. However, the combination of these two technologies has the potential to completely transform the possibilities of cloud computing. With the assistance of Metaverse in IoT, cloud service providers may be able to realize the full potential of cloud computing. The incorporation of the Metaverse into IoT devices may cause cloud platforms such as Amazon AWS and Microsoft Azure to appear and operate in an entirely different manner. Cloud technology developers will have the capacity to ensure improved scalability possibilities, increased robustness, and seamless functionality from their structural infrastructures. Users of cloud computing will have access to increased processing power as a result of the world of Metaverse. As a result, they will have the ability to effectively send information that has been gathered by the Internet of Things devices to the Metaverse in real-time. In addition, the technology of the Metaverse will unquestionably improve the compatibility between VR-AR devices and the digital data of the IoT. This would give SaaS developers the ability to produce solutions of the highest caliber [16].

Information and Interactive Experiences: The incorporation of the Metaverse into conventional technologies would result in an increasing emphasis on the development of more refined designs to produce interactive experiences for clients and businesses. As a result, it will significantly fuel the rising and shifting demands of the information processing technology business and the internet of things industry [17, 55].

Next-Level Calculation: The incorporation of edge computing and the Metaverse are bringing speeds of computation to the IoT world that are next level. Technologies such as the Metaverse augmented reality, artificial intelligence, 3D digital twins, and the internet of things will make it a lot simpler for regular computers to analyze large amounts of data.

Interaction-based computing: The bulk of digital interactions with computers takes place with an input device or the screen of the computer. This type of computing is known as interaction-based computing. For their inputs to be registered by IoT devices, users are required to either make use of a console or press a few buttons. The AR and VR that are employed in the Metaverse are intended to transform how we interact with the Internet of Things (IoT) devices. Because of this, the experience will be much more contextualized, and it will feel quite realistic. The users won't even be aware of whether they are interacting with something in the real world or the virtual one. This will be made possible by devices that support extended reality, which will in turn empower a large number of Internet of

Things devices. IoT technology that includes motion sensing, AI-enabled edge computing, and tailored data-gathering sensors will be of assistance in the process of developing computing that is more immersive and interaction-based [18, 56].

16.5   IoT's Contribution to the Creation of the Metaverse

Here are five ways in which the Internet of Things could play an important role in the development of the Metaverse:

The use of connected devices could provide the impression that one is in the real world: It is essential to recreate situations and scenarios from the real world if one wants the Metaverse to converge more and more closely with reality. The fundamental yet hard problem of integrating hybrid data with the cloud or digital infrastructure will be solved by connected devices shortly. The successful construction of complex systems, such as virtual simulations, depends on the integration of these components [19, 57].

The Internet of Things will make it easier to incorporate digital content into a physical setting: The Internet of Things is required for the Metaverse to be able to build a fully integrated collaboration with the physical world. The Internet of Things will play an essential part in the construction of a variety of building blocks for the metaverse. An interoperable and seamless system of technologies will merge digital material into physical space. This may be as important as using digital twins and immersive experiences to provide real-time feedback control to real-world machinery and equipment [20].

The gathering of data will be the most important aspect of the metaverse: The Metaverse requires data from the real world to enable digital twins and virtual simulations; this data must have responsiveness while also being appropriately safeguarded through mass ingestion. In its most basic form, the Metaverse calls for the incorporation of scanned artifacts alongside authentic information and live data collected from the surrounding physical world [21, 58].

The Internet of Things will serve as a connection point between the metaverse and other gadgets: The Internet of Things is all about bringing together the various digital senses that are present in a given setting. The norm will soon be that raw data from the Internet of Things needs to be processed before it can be ingested in real-time by the Metaverse, and this transition is presently taking place. To derive decentralized value generation within the system, it is needed to connect metadata to actual devices in the world [22, 59].

The combination of Internet of Things technology and digital twin technologies will give meaning to the Metaverse: We will be able to access, visualize, and analyze equipment performance data with the help of the Internet of Things (IoT). This will also make it possible for us to group sensors and the data they produce in near real-time, which will allow for a more meaningful connection between the "real" world and the "virtual" world. Scanned items that can interact with the physical world are what make up the Metaverse. The connection of a physical thing with real metadata and live data stream from sensors and other sources is what gives meaning to the Metaverse, and the combination of IoT and Digital Twin technology will make it possible for this to happen [1, 60, 61].

16.6   Applications, Advantages and Challenges of IoT-Based Metaverse

16.6.1   IoT-Based Metaverse Applications

The Internet of Things could be put to use in a wide variety of ways in the metaverse, including the following examples:

Virtual Reality (VR) and Augmented Reality (AR) Applications: In the metaverse, VR and AR experiences can be enhanced with the help of devices connected to the IoT. For instance, users could interact with virtual items or settings in a way that feels more natural and intuitive by employing IoT devices like sensors or controllers [3].

Smart cities: Internet of Things devices might be used to generate virtual representations of real-world cities in the metaverse. This would let users explore and interact with virtual replicas of buildings, streets, and other features inside the smart city. This might be used to visualize and try out new urban ideas, or it could be used to develop and explore virtual cityscapes for amusement [5].

Education and training: The metaverse has the potential to serve as a platform for the delivery of interactive and immersive educational and training experiences made possible by the Internet of Things (IoT). Students, for instance, may use the Internet of Things devices to take part in virtual field trips or to carry out experiments in a virtual laboratory [7].

Healthcare: Internet of Things devices could be used to construct virtual healthcare environments in the metaverse. This would make it possible for patients to get treatment and consultations from a distance. This might be especially helpful in situations in which patients are unable to travel or in which there is a shortage of medical experts [9].

Gaming: The incorporation of Internet of Things devices into the metaverse may make it possible to create new categories of games and experiences for gamers to enjoy that are both more immersive and participatory. Users could, for instance, use gadgets connected to the internet of things (IoT) to take control of virtual characters or vehicles, or to interact with virtual items and environments [11].

E-commerce: The metaverse has the potential to serve as a marketplace on which people may purchase and sell a variety of goods and services by leveraging IoT devices. For instance, consumers could utilize IoT devices to browse and purchase virtual goods or to access virtual markets to do these tasks [13].

Work done remotely and in collaboration: Internet of Things devices might be utilized to enable work done remotely and in collaboration in the metaverse. This would make it possible for individuals and teams to cooperate on projects and tasks while working in a digital setting. This could be of particular benefit in situations in which teams are located in different parts of the world or in which face-to-face meetings are not feasible.

16.6.2   Advantages of Using IoT in Metaverse

IoT is a network of physical objects, vehicles, buildings, and other items with sensors, software, and network connectivity that collect and share data. "Internet of Vehicles" and "Internet of Buildings" are examples. All virtual worlds are augmented realities, and the internet comprises the metaverse. Virtually upgraded physical reality and physically persistent virtual space created a shared virtual cosmos [15]. Utilizing IoT in the metaverse can provide several benefits, including the following:

Improved data collection and analysis: IoT devices can collect data from the physical world and communicate it to the metaverse, where it can be analyzed. This results in improved data collecting and analysis. This can assist companies and organizations in better understanding and optimizing their operations, as well as locating new prospects for growth and innovation in their fields [17].

Enhanced security and privacy: IoT devices can be used to increase security and privacy in the metaverse by enabling real-time monitoring and alerting of potential security concerns. This can be accomplished by the devices monitoring and alerting users in real-time.

Greater immersion and interactivity: The integration of Internet of Things devices into the metaverse enables users to experience a virtual environment that is both more immersive and engaging than before. For instance, users could interact with virtual objects in the metaverse by using their physical body movements or gestures, or they could control virtual devices and machines by using physical devices such as smartphones or controllers. Additionally, users could interact with virtual objects in the metaverse by using their physical body movements or gestures [19].

Increased levels of efficiency and productivity: It can be attained by utilizing IoT devices, which can assist in the automation of processes and tasks inside the metaverse. This enables users to perform their work in a more timely and effective manner. For instance, users could utilize the Internet of Things devices to remotely monitor and manage machines or equipment in the metaverse, or to automate operations like data entry or analysis. These are just two examples of what IoT devices are capable of [21].

New business opportunities: The integration of the Internet of Things and the metaverse can produce new business opportunities, such as the creation of new virtual products and services or the establishment of virtual marketplaces for the purchase and sale of goods and services. Other examples of potential new business opportunities include.

16.6.3   Challenges of Using IoT in the Metaverse

Utilizing IoT in the metaverse presents several issues, including the following:

Security and privacy concerns: The usage of IoT devices in the metaverse poses security and privacy problems, just as does the use of any networked system. These concerns are similar to those raised by other networked systems. Hackers and other bad actors can seek to obtain unauthorized access to the data that is transmitted by IoT devices, or they may attempt to control the devices themselves.

Complexity and interoperability: The process of integrating Internet of Things devices into the metaverse can be difficult and time-consuming, particularly if the devices were not built to be interoperable with the metaverse platform. Complexity and interoperability are also factors in this process [20].

Limited battery life and connectivity: The fact that many devices connected to the internet of things are powered by batteries also presents a challenge when it comes to the metaverse's potential applications for these devices. Connectivity issues can also arise with IoT devices, which is especially problematic in locations with spotty or nonexistent network coverage [18].

Cost: Putting in place an Internet of Things (IoT) system in the metaverse can be expensive, particularly if it requires the installation of a significant number of different devices.

Lack of standards and regulations: Because there are currently no widely accepted standards or regulations for the use of IoT in the metaverse, it can be difficult for businesses and organizations to ensure the security and privacy of their data. Because of this, there is currently a lack of standards and regulations for the use of IoT in the metaverse [22].

Acceptance by Users: There is a possibility that some users will be reluctant to make use of IoT devices in the metaverse. This is especially likely if the users are concerned about their privacy or other security concerns. It's possible that to boost adoption, it will be required to educate people about the benefits and risks of using Internet of Things devices in the metaverse [16].

16.7   Conclusion

The convergence of the Internet of Things and the Metaverse will make it possible for tech professionals to express their innovative ideas in a manner that is not constrained by the conventional organizational structure. Since the Metaverse is still in the process of development, it is currently impossible for us to precisely define its potential or assign particular labels to it. The Internet of Things, on the other hand, has been around for some time now; consequently, a collaboration between the two will be of great benefit to both of the concepts. IoT has the potential to uncover new working capacities as a result of collaboration, whereas the metaverse can seek deeper penetration from it. Nevertheless, despite everything, we must continue to be alarmed about the cyber threats that have the potential to exacerbate the vulnerabilities that are present within the metaverse ecosystem. The users ought to make the most of the growth and investigate Metaverse-IoT to open up new doors of opportunity for themselves within the industry.

The convergence of the Internet of Things and the Metaverse will make it possible for technology experts to release their unrealized potential, which is currently constrained by conventional configurations. However, given that the Metaverse is still in the process of development, it is too soon to speculate on what it is capable of providing or to label it. The Internet of Things, on the other hand, has been around for some time now; consequently, a collaboration between the two should help both ideas develop further. If deeper penetration can be achieved by either the Metaverse or the IoT thanks to a partnership between the two, then it will be to the great benefit of both. Despite this, every participant in the ecosystem needs to continue to exercise caution regarding cyber risks and vulnerabilities. Users shouldn't hesitate to take advantage of this growth and investigate the uncharted territory that lies ahead of them in terms of the opportunities that lie within these two industries.

Improvements to the Features

If we take into account the expert speculations and rumors that are currently circulating in the market, we can deduce that the Metaverse and the Internet of Things will fundamentally transform the technological landscape. When combined, the Metaverse and the Internet of Things will make new opportunities available for the industrial sector, as well as for individual needs and social requirements. The scope of this partnership will assist Metaverse in overcoming its limitations and expanding its usability to more diverse realms, which will be possible as a result of this collaboration. The Internet of Things will make it possible for virtual spaces to interact with and gain seamless access to the real world, while the Metaverse technology will provide the required 3D user interface for the IoT device cluster. Users will have an Internet of Things and metaverse experience that is centered around them as a result of this. The combination will enable streamlined data flow and support data-based decisions while requiring minimal effort and training on the user's part.

References

1. El Saddik, A., Digital twins: The convergence of multimedia technologies. *IEEE MultiMed.*, 25, 2, 87–92, Apr. 2018.
2. Lin, H., Wan, S., Gan, W., Chen, J., Chao, C., Vision, opportunities, and challenges, in: *2022 IEEE International Conference on Big Data (Big Data)*, pp. 2857-2866, Osaka, Japan, 2022.
3. Sangeeta, Guila, P., Gill, N.S., Chatterjee, J.M., Metaverse and its impact on climate change, in: *The Future of Metaverse in the Virtual Era and Physical World. Studies in Big Data.* A.E., Hassanien, A. Darwish, M. Torky, (eds), vol. 123, pp. 211–222. Springer, Cham, 2023.
4. Lee, C.-S. *et al.*, Fuzzy ontology-based intelligent agent for high-school student learning in AI-FML metaverse. *2022 IEEE International Conference on Fuzzy Systems (FUZZ-IEEE)*, 2022.
5. Petrova-Antonova, D. and Ilieva, S., Digital twin modeling of smart cities, in: *Proc. Int. Conf. Human Interact. Emerg. Technol,* pp. 384–390, 2020.
6. Van Huynh, D., Khosravirad, S.R. *et al.*, Edge intelligence-based ultra-reliable and low-latency communications for digital twin-enabled Metaverse. *IEEE Wireless Commun. Lett.*, 11, 8, 1–16, August 2022.
7. Fuller, Fan, Z., Day, C., Barlow, C., Digital twin: Enabling technologies, challenges, and open research. *IEEE Access*, 8, 952–971, 2020.
8. Duan, H., Li, J., Fan, S., Lin, Z., Wu, X., Cai, W., Metaverse for social good: A university campus prototype. *Proc. ACM Multimed.*, 1, 153–161, 2021.
9. Huang, H., Zeng, X. *et al.*, Fusion of building information modeling and blockchain for metaverse: A survey. *Digital Object Identifier*, 3, 195–207, 2022.
10. Radoff, J., *The Metaverse value-chain,* https://medium.com/building-the-metaverse/the-metaverse-value-chainafcf9e09e3a7, Jun. 2021 (accessed 2021-09-08).
11. Li, K. *et al.*, When Internet of Things meets metaverse: Convergence of physical and cyber worlds, in: *IEEE Internet of Things Journal*, vol. 10, no. 5, pp. 4148-4173, 2023.
12. Yan, H. *et al.*, A dynamic hierarchical framework for IoT-assisted digital twin synchronization in the metaverse, in: *IEEE Internet of Things Journal*, vol. 10, no. 1, pp. 268-284,

13. Chang, L., Zhang, Z. *et al.*, 6G-enabled edge AI for metaverse: Challenges, methods, and future research directions. *J. Commun. Inf. Networks*, 7, 2, 107–121, Jun. 2022.
14. Mozumder, M.A.I., Sheeraz, M.M., Athar, A., Aich, S., Kim, H.-C., Overview: Technology roadmap of the future trend of metaverse based on IoT, blockchain, AI technique, and medical domain metaverse activity, in: *2022 24th International Conference on Advanced Communication Technology (ICACT)*, pp. 256-261, PyeongChang Kwangwoon_Do, Korea, Republic of, 2022.
15. Wu, D., Yang, Z., Zhang, P., Wang, R., Yang, B., Ma, X., Virtual-reality inter-promotion technology for metaverse: A survey, in: *IEEE Internet of Things Journal*, 2023.
16. Veeraiah, V., Ahamad, G.P.S., Talukdar, S.B., Gupta, A., Talukdar, V., Enhancement of meta verse capabilities by IoT integration, in: *2022 2nd International Conference on Advance Computing and Innovative Technologies in Engineering (ICACITE)*, pp. 1493-1498, Greater Noida, India, 2022.
17. Kusuma, P.S.D., Children virtual concert in the Covid-19 pandemic. *J. Music Sci. Technol. Industry*, 3, 2, 247–260, Oct. 2020.
18. Schroeder, R., Social interaction in virtual environments: Key issues, common themes, and a framework for research, in: *The Social Life of Avatars*, pp. 1–18, Springer, London, 2002.
19. D. Maheswari, F. B. F. Ndruru, D. S. Rejeki, J. V. Moniaga and B. A. Jabar, systematic literature review on the usage of IoT in the metaverse to support the education system, in: *2022 5th International Conference on Information and Communications Technology (ICOIACT)*, pp. 307-310, Yogyakarta, Indonesia, 2022
20. Taheri, S.M., Matsushita, K., Sasaki, M., Virtual reality driving simulation for measuring driver behavior and characteristics. *J. Transp. Technol.*, 7, 02, 123–132, 2017.
21. Elawady, M., Sarhan, A., Alshewimy, M.A.M., Toward a mixed reality domain model for time-Sensitive applications using IoE infrastructure and edge computing (MRIoEF). *J. Supercomput.*, 78, 10656–10689, 2022.
22. Han, Y., Leung, D.N.C., Miao, C., Kim, D.I., A dynamic hierarchical framework for IoT-assisted digital twin synchronization in the Metaverse. *Journal of Latex Class Files*, 14, 8, August 2021.
23. Panda, S.K. and Satapathy, S.C., An investigation into smart contract deployment on Ethereum platform using Web3.js and solidity using blockchain, in: *Data Engineering and Intelligent Computing*, Advances in Intelligent Systems and Computing, vol. 1, V. Bhateja, S.C. Satapathy, C.M. Travieso-González, V.N.M. Aradhya (Eds.), Springer, Singapore, 2021.
24. Panda, S.K., Rao, D.C., Satapathy, S.C., An investigation into the usability of blockchain technology in Internet of Things, in: *Data Engineering and Intelligent Computing*, Advances in Intelligent Systems and Computing, vol. 1, V. Bhateja, S.C. Satapathy, C.M. Travieso-González, V.N.M. Aradhya (Eds.), Springer, Singapore, 2021.

25. Panda, S.K., Dash, S.P., Jena, A.K., Optimization of block query response using evolutionary algorithm, in: *Data Engineering and Intelligent Computing*, Advances in Intelligent Systems and Computing, vol. 1, V. Bhateja, S.C. Satapathy, C.M. Travieso-González, V.N.M. Aradhya (Eds.), Springer, Singapore, 2021.

26. Nanda, S.K., Panda, S.K., Das, M., Satapathy, S.C., Automating vehicle insurance process using smart contract and ethereum, in: *Advances in Micro-Electronics, Embedded Systems and IoT*, Lecture Notes in Electrical Engineering, vol. 838, V.V.S.S.S. Chakravarthy, W. Flores-Fuentes, V. Bhateja, B. Biswal (Eds.), Springer, Singapore, 2022.

27. Varaprasada Rao, K. and Panda, S.K., Secure electronic voting (E-voting) system based on blockchain on various platforms, in: *Computer Communication, Networking and IoT*, Lecture Notes in Networks and Systems, vol. 459, S.C. Satapathy, J.C.W. Lin, L.K. Wee, V. Bhateja, T.M. Rajesh (Eds.), Springer, Singapore, 2023.

28. Varaprasada Rao, K. and Panda, S.K., A design model of copyright protection system based on distributed ledger technology, in: *Computer Communication, Networking and IoT*, Lecture Notes in Networks and Systems, vol. 459, S.C. Satapathy, J.C.W. Lin, L.K. Wee, V. Bhateja, T.M. Rajesh (Eds.), Springer, Singapore, 2023.

29. Panda, S.K., Elngar, A.A., Balas, V.E., Kayed, M. (Eds.), *Bitcoin and Blockchain: History and Current Applications*, 1st ed, CRC Press, Boca Raton, 2020.

30. Panda, S.K., Jena, A.K., Swain, S.K., Satapathy, S.C. (Eds.), *Blockchain Technology: Applications and Challenges*, Springer, Intelligent Systems Reference Library, Switzerland, 2021.

31. Sathya, A.R., Panda, S.K., Hanumanthakari, S., Enabling smart education system using blockchain technology, in: *Blockchain Technology: Applications and Challenges*, Intelligent Systems Reference Library, vol. 203, S.K. Panda, A.K. Jena, S.K. Swain, S.C. Satapathy (Eds.), Springer, Cham, 2021.

32. Lokre, S.S., Naman, V., Priya, S., Panda, S.K., Gun tracking system using blockchain technology, in: *Blockchain Technology: Applications and Challenges*, Intelligent Systems Reference Library, vol. 203, S.K. Panda, A.K. Jena, S.K. Swain, S.C. Satapathy (Eds.), Springer, Cham, 2021.

33. Panda, S.K., Daliyet, S.P., Lokre, S.S., Naman, V., Distributed ledger technology in the construction industry using Corda, in: *The New Advanced Society: Artificial Intelligence and Industrial Internet of Things Paradigm*.

34. Panda, S.K., Mohammad, G.B., Nandan Mohanty, S., Sahoo, S., Smart contract-based land registry system to reduce frauds and time delay, in: *Security and Privacy*, p. e172, 2021.

35. Panda, S.K. and Satapathy, S.C., Drug traceability and transparency in medical supply chain using blockchain for easing the process and creating trust between stakeholders and consumers. *Pers. Ubiquit. Comput.*, 1–14, 2021.

36. Niveditha, V.R., Sekaran, K., Singh, K.A., Panda, S.K., Effective prediction of bitcoin price using wolf search algorithm and bidirectional LSTM on internet of things data. *Int. J. Syst. Syst. Eng.*, 11, 3-4, 224–236, 2021.
37. Sri Arza, M. and Panda, S.K., An integration of blockchain and machine learning into the health care system, in: *Machine Learning Adoption in Blockchain-Based Intelligent Manufacturing*, vol. 1, pp. 33–58.
38. Murala, D.K., Panda, S.K., Swain, S.K., A survey on cloud computing security and privacy issues and challenges. *J. Adv. Res. Dyn. Control Syst.*, 11, 1276–1290, 2019.
39. Murala, D.K., Panda, S.K., Swain, S.K., Secure dynamic groups data sharing with modified revocable attribute-based encryption in cloud. *Int. J. Recent Technol. Eng. (IJRTE)*, 8, 4, 9508–9512, 2019.
40. Murala, D.K., Panda, S.K., Swain, S.K., A novel hybrid approach for providing data security and privacy from malicious attacks in the cloud environment. *J. Adv. Res. Dyn. Control Syst.*, 11, 1291–1300, 2019.
41. Panda, S.K., Swain, S.K., Mall, R., An investigation into usability aspects of E-commerce websites using users' preferences. *Adv. Comput. Sci.: An Int. J.*, 4, 1, 65–73, 2015.
42. Panda, S.K., Swain, S.K., Mall, R., Measuring web site usability quality complexity metrics for navigability, in: *Intelligent Computing, Communication and Devices*, Advances in Intelligent Systems and Computing, vol. 308, L. Jain, S. Patnaik, N. Ichalkaranje (Eds.), Springer, New Delhi, 2015.
43. Panda, S.K., A usability evaluation framework for B2C E-commerce websites. *Comput. Eng. Intell. Syst.*, 5, 3, 66–85, 2014.
44. Bhalerao, V., Panda, S.K., Jena, A.K., Optimization of loss function on human faces using generative adversarial networks, in: *Machine Learning Approaches for Urban Computing*, Studies in Computational Intelligence, vol. 968, M. Bandyopadhyay, M. Rout, S. Chandra Satapathy (Eds.), Springer, Singapore, 2021.
45. Panda, S.K. and Dwivedi, M., Minimizing food wastage using machine learning: A novel approach, in: *Smart Intelligent Computing and Applications*, Smart Innovation, Systems and Technologies, vol. 159, S. Satapathy, V. Bhateja, J. Mohanty, S. Udgata (Eds.), Springer, Singapore, 2020.
46. Panda, S.K., Sathya, A.R., Mishra, M., Satpathy, S., A supervised learning algorithm to forecast weather conditions for playing cricket. *Int. J. Innovative Technol. Exploring Eng. (IJITEE)*, 9, 1, 1560–1565, 2019.
47. Panda, S.K., Fraud-resistant crowdfunding system using Ethereum blockchain, in: *Bitcoin and Blockchain*, pp. 237–276, 2020.
48. Panda, S.K., Mishra, V., Balamurali, R., Elngar, A.A., *Artificial Intelligence and Machine Learning in Business Management Concepts, Challenges, and Case Studies*, pp. 1–278, CRC Press, Boca Raton, 2021.
49. Joshi, S., Panda, S.K., AR, S., Optimal deep learning model to identify the development of pomegranate fruit in farms. *Int. J. Innovative Technol. Exploring Eng.*, 9, 3, 2352–2356, 2020.

50. Puranam, K.S.R., Gaddam, M.C.T., K, V.P.R., Panda, S.K., Reddy, G.S.M., Anatomy and lifecycle of a bitcoin transaction. *Proceedings of International Conference on Sustainable Computing in Science, Technology and Management (SUSCOM)*, Amity University Rajasthan, Jaipur - India, February 26-28, 2019, February 18, 2019, Available at SSRN: https://ssrn.com/abstract=3355106 or http://dx.doi.org/10.2139/ssrn.3355106.

51. Panda, S.K. and Swain, S.K., *Quality assurance aspects of web design, design solutions for improving website quality and effectiveness*, pp. 87–129, IGI Global, USA, 2016.

52. Panda, S.K., Bhalerao, V., AR, S., A machine learning model to identify duplicate questions in social media forums. *Int. J. Innovative Technol. Exploring Eng.*, 9, 4, 370–373, 2020.

53. Ahmareen, S., Raj, A., Potluri, S., Panda, S.K., Book shala: An android-based application design and implementation of sharing books, in: *Smart Intelligent Computing and Applications*, Smart Innovation, Systems and Technologies, vol. 159, S. Satapathy, V. Bhateja, J. Mohanty, S. Udgata (Eds.), Springer, Singapore, 2020.

54. Panda, S.K., Das, S.S., Swain, S.K., S-model for service-oriented applications in web engineering. *Reg. Coll. Manag.*, 10, 3, 38–46, 2013.

55. Panda, S.K., An investigation into usability and productivity of ecommerce websites. https://shodhganga.inflibnet.ac.in:8443/jspui/handle/10603/123505

56. Panda, S.K., Chandrasekhar, A., Gantayat, P.K., Panda, M.R., Detecting brain tumor using image segmentation: A novel approach, in: *Data Engineering and Intelligent Computing, Lecture Notes in Networks and Systems*, vol. 446, V. Bhateja, L. Khin Wee, J.C.W. Lin, S.C. Satapathy, T.M. Rajesh (Eds.), Springer, Singapore, 2022.

57. Sanghi, P., Panda, S.K., Pati, C., Gantayat, P.K., Learning deep features and classification for fresh or off vegetables to prevent food wastage using machine learning algorithms, in: *Intelligent Data Engineering and Analytics, Smart Innovation*, Systems and Technologies, vol. 266, S.C. Satapathy, P. Peer, J. Tang, V. Bhateja, A. Ghosh (Eds.), Springer, Singapore, 2022.

58. Gantayat, P.K., Mohapatra, S., Panda, S.K., Secure trust level routing in delay-tolerant network with node categorization technique, in: *Intelligent Data Engineering and Analytics, Smart Innovation, Systems and Technologies*, vol. 266, S.C. Satapathy, P. Peer, J. Tang, V. Bhateja, A. Ghosh (Eds.), Springer, Singapore, 2022.

59. Panda, S.K., Urkude, S.V., Urkude, V.R., Vairachilai, S., An investigation into COVID 19 pandemic in India, in: *The New Advanced Society: Artificial Intelligence and Industrial Internet of Things Paradigm*, vol. 1, Wiley, USA, 2022.

60. Panda, S., Das, S., & Swain, S., Website productivity measurement using single task size, measure. *J. Inf. Sci. Comput. Technol.*, 4, 3, 347–353, 2015.

61. Hanumanthakari, S. and Panda, S.K., Detecting face mask for prevent COVID-19 using deep learning: A novel approach, in: *Smart Intelligent*

Computing and Applications, Volume 2, Smart Innovation, Systems and Technologies, vol. 283, S.C. Satapathy, V. Bhateja, M.N. Favorskaya, T. Adilakshmi (Eds.), Springer, Singapore, 2022.

62. Panda, S.K., Sathya, A.R., Das, S., Bitcoin: Beginning of the cryptocurrency era, in: *Recent Advances in Blockchain Technology,* Intelligent Systems Reference Library, vol. 237, S.K. Panda, V. Mishra, S.P. Dash, A.K. Pani (Eds.), Springer, Cham, 2023.

63. Murala, D.K., Panda, S.K., Sahoo, S.K., Securing electronic health record system in cloud environment using blockchain technology, in: *Recent Advances in Blockchain Technology,* Intelligent Systems Reference Library, vol. 237, S.K. Panda, V. Mishra, S.P. Dash, A.K. Pani (Eds.), Springer, Cham, 2023.

64. Rao, K.V., Murala, D.K., Panda, S.K., Blockchain: A study of new business model, in: *Recent Advances in Blockchain Technology,* Intelligent Systems Reference Library, vol. 237, S.K. Panda, V. Mishra, S.P. Dash, A.K. Pani (Eds.), Springer, Cham, 2023.

65. Panda, S.K., Mishra, V., Dash, S.P., Pani, A.K., *Recent advances in blockchain technology real-world applications,* Intelligent Systems Reference Library (ISRL, volume 237), vol. 1, pp. 1–317, Springer, Switzerland, 2023.

66. Panda, S.K., Mohapatra, R.K., Panda, S., Balamurugan, S., *The New Advanced Society: Artificial Intelligence and Industrial Internet of Things Paradigm,* vol. 1, pp. 1–512, Wiley, USA, 2022.

67. Nanda, S.K., Panda, S.K., Das, M., Satapathy, S.C., Decentralization of car insurance system using machine learning and distributed ledger technology, in: *Intelligent Data Engineering and Analytics. FICTA 2022. Smart Innovation, Systems and Technologies,* vol. 327, V. Bhateja, X.S. Yang, J. Chun-Wei Lin, R. Das (Eds.), Springer, Singapore, 2023.

Index

Printed and bound by CPI Group (UK) Ltd, Croydon, CR0 4YY

27/10/2024

14580470-0005